MW01106587

The Politics
of Cultural Nationalism
in South India

The Politics of
Cultural Nationalism
in South India

MARGUERITE ROSS BARNETT

Princeton University Press, Princeton, New Jersey

Library of Congress Cataloging In Publication date
will be found on the last printed page of this book

PRINTED IN THE UNITED STATES OF AMERICA
by Princeton University Press, Princeton, New Jersey

ISBN 978-0-691-64407-3

TO MY MOTHER

Mary Ross Eubanks

Note on Transliteration

Generally I have tried to spell Tamil words as they would appear in English texts in Tamil Nadu. When referring to authors and titles of Tamil articles and books I have used a modified version of the Tamil lexicon system of transliteration. Newspaper names, publishers, and places of publication, however, have been translated as they normally appear in English.

Contents

List of Tables, Figures, and Map

TABLES

FIGURES

MAP

x

Preface

THE development of a nationalist movement into a political party and eventually a state administration is too complex to comprehend using a single methodology. As I probed deeper into history and institutionalization, I employed distinct research strategies: archival research, interviews, analysis of pamphlets and other propaganda material, surveys, and direct observation. The success of these strategies required the cooperation and assistance of many people.

Research from 1967 to 1969 and during two months in 1973 was supported by funds from the Committee on Southern Asian Studies of the University of Chicago; the Committee on Comparative Politics at the University of Chicago; and the Princeton University Fund for Research in the Humanities and Social Sciences. Funds from the Woodrow Wilson School of Public and International Affairs at Princeton University provided time for additional research and writing. None of these sponsors is responsible for the views expressed in this work.

While I was in India, numerous people were enthusiastic supporters of this project and extremely helpful in its execution. I would like to thank the late C. N. Annadurai, leader of the DMK and chief minister of Tamil Nadu from 1967 to 1969, as well as his successor Mu. Karunanidhi. Also, A. P. Janarthanam; K. Anbazhagan; Mrs. Anandanayaki; and T. K. Ponnuvelu were other political leaders who gave consistent help, advice, and support. Many people allowed me to use their private libraries and often lent or gave me pamphlets otherwise difficult to get. Among the most generous were N. R. Sadagopan Mudaliar, N. S. Rajagopal, and K. Veeramani. I would also like to thank the staff of the DMK ₁nd Congress headquarters for their cooperation in providing the materials necessary to conduct the leadership survey reported in Chapter 8. C. Subramaniam of the Congress party and C. N. Annadurai generously gave permission for these surveys to be done.

Access to contemporary government documents up to 1962 in the Tamil Nadu State Archives was provided by S. Singarajan, director of the Tamil Nadu Archives, where my opportunity for research was invaluable. His probing questions and experienced suggestions were also enormously helpful.

I am grateful to my Tamil tutor, R. Manian; to the more than two hundred political leaders interviewed, and the more than one thousand leaders and ordinary citizens who participated in the survey research.

Insightful suggestions and comments on earlier versions of this manuscript were made by Leonard Binder, Lloyd Rudolph, and Duncan MacCrae.

In addition to reading and commenting on this manuscript, Steve Barnett provided crucial insights into the theoretical and methodological issues of Indian anthropology generally, and Tamil Nadu specifically. His assistance and understanding have been enormously important in completion of this work.

Finally, my mother, to whom this book is dedicated, has been a source of constant inspiration and support.

The Politics
of Cultural Nationalism
in South India

CHAPTER ONE

Introduction

THE founding of the Dravida Munnetra Kazhagam (henceforth DMK) political party in 1949 was a turning point in the political history of Tamil Nadu,[1] south India, because it ushered in the era of Tamil cultural nationalism. Nationalism existed before 1949, but in nascent form, encompassed and overshadowed by other political themes. In the hands of the DMK, Tamil nationalism became an ideology of mass mobilization, and has shaped the articulation of political demands for a generation. In fact, to analyze Tamil nationalism is to probe the very dynamics of Tamil Nadu political development.

More broadly, Tamil nationalism encapsulates the complexities, contradictions, and conundrums of all nationalisms. Hans Kohn captured the Janus-headed quality of nationalism when he stated, "The garb of nationalism clothes on the one hand the human aspirations for equality and dignity and on the other hand the passion for power over others."[2] In its most progressive form, Tamil nationalism has been a vehicle for one of the most significant social reform movements in Indian history; as a reactionary force, it is narrow, parochial, and chauvinistic.

Describing the circumstances in which Tamil nationalism becomes a progressive political force and the circumstances in which, conversely, its impact is reactionary is complex but possible when nationalism and nationalist politics are viewed diachronically. Similarly, many of the baffling issues in the vast literature on nationalism are elucidated or reconciled (at least in the case of Tamil nationalism) by diachronic analysis. The central questions of this study involve political identity—its emergence, development, and transformation. Specifically: Why do certain forms of identity emerge and win mass adherence? Under what circumstances do ideologies of nationalism arise? Why (and under what circumstances) are nationalist ideologies successful tools of political mobilization? What kinds of interests and demands are articulated by nationalist movements? What is the relationship between class and nationalism? What is the political significance of economic cleavage in an arena dominated

by nationalism? Do economic issues, in fact, give rise to nationalism? And, in general, what is the impact of modernization on
perceptions of political identity? These questions emerge from
a framework that challenges the notion that political identity
is a direct reflection of cultural "givens," or atavistic, nonrational,
primordial sentiments.

CULTURAL NATIONALISM AND THE QUEST FOR POLITICAL IDENTITY

Political identity refers to the subjective basis of individual
attachment to a political community.[3] What has become known
as the political identity crisis "arises, in part, from the insistence
that subjective identity and objective political identity coincide."[4]
Typically, the stress on developing attachments to a territorially
defined nation-state is accompanied by attempts to undermine
or destroy tribal, ethnic, religious, and linguistic identities and
loyalties. This approach to "national integration" stems from
the conceptualization of political identity as a zero-sum game.
As such, ethnic, tribal, and linguistic loyalties ipso facto detract
from, weaken, dilute, or blur territorial nationalism. Nehru
forcefully articulated this point of view in a letter to the Chief
Ministers of the Indian States in 1961: "Communalism is one
of the obvious examples of backward-looking people trying
to hold on to something that is wholly out-of-place in the modern
world and is essentially opposed to the concept of nationalism.
In fact it splits up nationalism into a number of narrower
nationalisms."[5]

The basis of this conceptualization rests on a dichotomous
view of political identity; specifically, the postulation of two
kinds of attachments or ties to the nation: the primordial and
the civil. A primordial tie stems from the "givens" of social
existence. According to Clifford Geertz, "the congruities of
blood, speech, custom, and so on, are seen to have an ineffable,
and at times overpowering, coerciveness in and of themselves."[6]
In contrast,

> in modern societies the lifting of such [primordial] ties to
> the level of political supremacy—though it has, of course,
> occurred and may again occur—has more and more come
> to be deplored as pathological. To an increasing degree national
> unity is maintained not by calls to blood and land but by

vague, intermittent, and routine allegiance to a civil state [civil ties], supplemented to a greater or lesser extent by governmental use of police power and ideological exhortation.[7]

At best, this view relegates important segments of recent and contemporary world history (Nazi Germany and recent developments in Ireland, Belgium, and so on) to a recidivist limbo, explaining them away rather than explaining them. Geertz does say, of course, that granting supremacy to primordial ties is increasingly deplored as pathological. But deplored by whom? the masses? the social scientists? the political elite? Did not De Gaulle adroitely manipulate the symbols of Frenchness when convenient? Enoch Powell and "British Blood" are not anachronisms or genetic "sports." The unstated premise of Geertz is that he, the social scientist, knows what is rational; but Hans Kohn and others have shown what he calls natural developments to be historical phenomena. Geertz thus mistakes what is historically derived for what is intrinsically natural.

In the United States, an ideology of white supremacy ("blood," again) exists, and has been used to foster political unity in both North and South. In *Hirabayashi* v. *United States* the Supreme Court was candid in revealing the relationship between "white" blood and loyalty. The case involved the program undertaken by the United States government during World War II to exclude Japanese Americans (many of whom were American citizens) from the West coast. There were many aspects of the program, ranging from curfew regulations to prison-camp detention. *Hirabayashi* v. *United States* upheld the curfew features of the program. In that case the Supreme Court stated:

There is support for the view that social, economic and political conditions which have prevailed since the close of the last century, when the Japanese began to come to this country in substantial numbers have intensified their solidarity and have in large measure prevented *their assimilation as an integral part of the white population.* . . .

Whatever views we may entertain regarding the loyalty to this country of the citizens of Japanese ancestry, we cannot reject as unfounded the judgment of the military authorities and of Congress *that there were disloyal members of that*

*population, whose number and strength could not be precisely
and quickly ascertained* (emphasis added).[8]

The ideas of individual, personal guilt before the law and civil
rather than blood ties as the basis of national unity are directly
challenged in the Japanese exclusion cases. While the Japanese
exclusion cases do not represent the court's final or only view
on these matters, the easy identification of the American nation
with the white population and the blithe equation of loyalty
with "white blood" can not be ignored. While they existed,
Jim Crow laws were an even more blatant example of the role
of "blood" in defining the relevant political community in the
United States.[9] It would seem closer to the truth of historical
events to say, in fact, that nationalism finds its most comfortable
manifestation when territorial and ethnic boundaries coincide.

One explanation of the persistence of "primordial sentiments"
is that they are "rooted in the non-rational foundations of
personality."[10] But again, how do we know? Are primordial
sentiments also nonrational? If all national ties are infused with
beliefs about blood and land, what exactly is the utility of the
"primordial" concept?

Having postulated a conflict between primordial and civil
sentiments, it is an easy step for politicians and social scientists
to argue in favor of the substitution of one (civil ties) for the
other (primordial ties).[11] Even when theorists are careful not
to postulate a dichotomy, primordial ties are believed, to be
traditional (their modern recrudescence notwithstanding) and civil
ties are believed to be modern. If all nationalisms (ideologies
of national unity) are infused with notions of blood and soil,
however, and specifically evoke these emotional "primordial
sentiments" at the first sign of the "nation in danger," the
dichotomy of the civil and the primordial falls apart.[12] But the
problem goes beyond the false dichotomy between (modern)
civil ties and (traditional) primordial ties. We have seen that notions
of "blood" are present and important in both modern and
traditional contexts; but are they the result of biological givens,
atavistic urges, and primordial sentiments? Or are these notions
themselves subject to creation, change, and transformation? The
fact that concepts of "blood" are central to political identity
does not necessitate their being primordial, nonrational, or
atavistic. We must ask under what circumstances some forms

of identity attain political significance and become defined as natural, primary, or ineffable.

NATIONALISM AS A FORM OF IDENTITY

Nationalism (used here to mean a state of mind, in which the supreme loyalty of the individual is to the nation-state)[13] is a recent phenomenon in world history. As Hans Kohn emphasizes, "it was not until the end of the eighteenth century that nationalism in the modern sense of the word became a generally recognized sentiment increasingly molding all public and private life."[14] When the nation-state emerged with the gradual dissolution of the medieval unity of empire and church, the state was identified with the sovereign or the ruling classes.[15] Luther regarded the "German nation" as constituted by "the bishops and princes,"[16] and Louis XIV's identification of the French nation with the king is well known. While for most of Europe this period ended with the Napoleonic Wars, in Eastern Europe this notion of the state carried over into the nineteenth century. "It was said of a Croat landowner of the 19th century that he would sooner have regarded his horse than his peasant as a member of the Croat nation. In the middle of the 19th century, and even later, the distance which separated the Polish gentry from the Polish speaking peasantry was still so great that the latter did not as a rule look on themselves as part of the Polish nation."[17]

Rousseau was the founder of modern nationalism. "Rejecting the embodiment of the nation in the personal sovereign or the ruling class, [Rousseau] boldly identified 'nation' and 'people.' "[18] In general, as the nation-state idea was evolving, European philosophical development was moving in the direction of individualism, and toward the idea of a "social contract" as the link between antecedently autonomous selves and the state. The concepts of natural law, the social contract, and individualism provide the ideological basis for granting sovereignty to the nation-state. At the heart of this is the concept of the individual as the basic unit of society:

The societies of the past, most societies, have believed themselves to be based in the order of things, natural as well as social: they thought they were copying or designing their very conventions after the principles of life and the world.

Modern society wants to be "rational," to break away from nature in order to set up an autonomous human order. To that end, it is enough to take the true measure of man and from it to deduce the human order. No gap between the ideal and the real: like an engineer's blue print, the representation will create the actuality. At this point the society, the old mediator between man in his particularity and nature disappears. There are but human individuals, and the problem is how to make them all fit together. . . .

The individual becomes the measure of all things, the source of all "rationality."[19]

As the measure of all things, it was the individual who became the relevant political and legal unit. Nationalism was a way of democratically linking autonomous individuals to the nation-state. As E. H. Carr has noted, "The 19th century was passionately devoted to individualism and to democracy as it was then understood; and nationalism seemed a natural corollary of both."[20]

Territorial nationalism, the idea that loyalty and commitment of the individual should be to the territorially defined nation-state, emerged, therefore, out of a particular set of economic and social conditions and developed in a particular intellectual and political climate. What now seems a natural—almost primordial—loyalty is in fact a concommitant of post-Napoleonic European social change.

Tamil nationalism is not territorial but cultural nationalism. The cultural nationalist sees the nation as inherent in the group of people who possess certain cultural characteristics; And so, while the territorial nationalist gives priority to the direct relationship of the individual to the territorially defined nation state, the cultural nationalist gives priority to collective cultural realization through nationalism. Cultural nationalists within a culturally heterogenous territorial state are likely to stress equality of culturally defined "nations" or groups; the territorial nationalist, in contrast, would stress the equality of individuals.

For cultural nationalists, concentrated group settlement on contiguous land is not a necessary or sufficient condition of nationalism. Thus a cultural nationalist can speak of a nation made up of groups of people that span existing states, or people who are widely scattered within a larger territorial unit. Poland is an example. Sociologist Florian Znaniecki states:

> I was born and brought up in Poland at a time when that country was divided into three territories. The territory in which I lived, although inhabited by Poles, was included in the Russian Empire and subjected to complete control of the Tsarist government; while the other two territories, also inhabited by Poles, were parts of Prussia and Austria. For more than a century there was no united Polish state and no common Polish government. Yet this division did not prevent the Poles from maintaining and developing cooperatively a common Polish culture and an active solidarity which cut across the political boundaries. . . .
>
> Thus, the history of the Poles from the partition of Poland in 1795 up to 1919 not only seemed to disprove the doctrine that a common state is indispensable for social unity, but also suggested that the idea of those social philosophers who considered a common national culture as a more lasting and influential bond of social solidarity than a common government might prove to be a scientifically valid theory.[21]

For the territorial nationalist the role of land is crucial. Occupation of land by a group can be a sufficient condition for the existence of a nation. However, cultural nationalists can also have territorial aspirations and, as we have seen, consanguinity is often assumed or desired by territorial nationalists.

Cultural nationalism and territorial nationalism are not dichotomous; one is not traditional and the other modern, and cultural nationalism is not a stage in transition to territorial nationalism. Rather, both are forms of nationalism stressing different themes and emerging out of different socio-political and economic contexts. Rather than seeing cultural nationalism as atavistic and primordial, an inherent threat to the integrity of territorially defined nation-states, and an irrational destabilizing force, we shall analyze the social, political, and economic factors that give rise to cultural nationalism, examine the interplay between cultural nationalist and territorial nationalist political leaders, and discuss the role of cultural nationalism in a heterogeneous nation-state.

Although this study is not directly concerned with the epistemological foundations of social inquiry, the very choice of topic and its treatment in terms of actors' orientations implies a critique of scientistic methods that bracket their own assumptions. Detailed analysis of cultural nationalism is, perhaps, rare because of the ideas that are taken for granted about the autonomous self. The personally comfortable civil identity (territorial nationalism) of many social scientists is based on an "abstract individualism," [22] in which the individual is theoretically prior to society, and each autonomous person is equivalent to each other person. The contradiction between autonomy (and free choice) and equivalence (in which choice does not really matter) is not clearly recognized. Cultural nationalism, on the other hand, posits selves that are not denatured abstract individuals but include, as part of the very construction of the self, a commitment to a tradition. Such persons are, therefore, not abstractly equivalent units forming a polity.

Analysis of Tamil nationalism inevitably entails analysis of the DMK political party and the Dravidian movement. Tamil nationalism has been a central part of DMK ideology for more than two decades, but it is linked to themes of identity that can be traced back in Tamil political history to the turn of the century. Tamil nationalism—Tamil political identity—is itself a redefinition of older political identities, and the end product of transformations in identity that go back to the emergence of the Dravidian movement. And it was the Dravidian movement that first made political identity an ideological and public policy issue in South India.

[1] Tamil Nadu was formerly Madras State. The name was changed in 1968 by the DMK state government.

[2] Hans Kohn, *The Age of Nationalism* (New York: Harper and Row, 1962), p. xvi.

[3] Leonard Binder, et al., *Crises and Sequences in Political Development* (Princeton: Princeton University Press, 1972), p. 72.

[4] *Ibid.*, p. 54.

[5] Letter from Prime Minister Nehru to Chief Minister of Madras State Kamaraj Nadar. Tamil Nadu Archives, Madras. Government Order 2089, December 16, 1961.

[6] Clifford Geertz, "The Integrative Revolution: Primordial Sentiments and Civil Politics in the New States," in Clifford Geertz, ed., *Old Societies and New States: the Quest for Modernity in Asia and Africa* (New York: Free Press, 1963), p. 109.

[7] *Ibid.*, p. 110.

[8] *Hirabayashi v. United States*, 320 U.S. 81 (1943).

[9] See Marguerite Ross Barnett, "A Theoretical Perspective on Racial Public Policy," in Marguerite Ross Barnett and James A. Hefner, eds., *Blacks and Public Policy: Strategies and Perspectives* (Port Washington, N.Y.: Alfred Press, forthcoming).

[10] Geertz, *Old Societies and New States*, p. 128.

[11] Also see Lloyd I. Rudolph and Susanne Hoeber Rudolph, *The Modernity of Tradition* (Chicago: University of Chicago Press, 1967), who suggest that communalism or cultural naturalism may be, in fact, a persistant feature of social change, and that dichotomous modernity-tradition models have obscured this.

[12] This is not to say that ties of blood and land are one-dimensional in Western society. In and out-group definitions of ethnicity, race, and citizenship have hardly been explored.

[13] Hans Kohn, *Nationalism: Its Meaning and History* (Princeton: D. Van Nostrand, 1955), p. 9.

[14] *Ibid.*, p. 12.

[15] Edward Hallett Carr, *Nationalism and After* (New York: Macmillan, 1945), pp. 2-6.

[16] *Ibid.*, p. 2.

[17] *Nationalism, a Report by a Study Group of the Royal Institute of International Affairs*, p. 96; quoted *ibid.*, p. 3, n.1.

[18] *Ibid.*, p. 7.

[19] Louis Dumont, *Homo Hierarchicus: an Essay on the Caste System* (Chicago: University of Chicago Press, 1970), p. 253.

[20] Carr, *Nationalism and After*, p. 9.

[21] Florian Znaniecki, *Modern Nationalities: a Sociological Study* (Urbana: University of Illinois Press, 1952), p. ix-x. Zionism is another example. As pointed out by Karl W. Deutsch (*Nationalism and Social Communication*, Cambridge: M.I.T. Press, 1953, p. 18), "the nationalist movement of Zionism which culminated in 1948 in the erection of the sovereign state of Israel had been carried on actively for two generations by members of a people which had not had a common territory for many centuries."

[22] For a discussion of this concept see C. B. MacPherson, *The Real World of Democracy* (Oxford: Clarendon Press, 1965).

PART ONE

Origins of Tamil Nationalism

CHAPTER TWO

The Justice Party, the Non-Brahmin Movement, and Early Conceptions of Dravidian-ness

MANY symbols associated with Tamil political identity reach deep into Tamil history and culture. Paradoxically, politicization of these ancient cultural symbols was a concommitant of social change associated with modernization. It is not my intention to recount here the complex history of this period, only to trace the origins of the particular ideology associated with the Dravidian movement.

Madras Presidency politics in the early part of the twentieth century were dominated by the "Brahmin-non-Brahmin" conflict. During this early period, the caste identity of certain groups of elite non-Brahmins was challenged in the process of South Indian social change. Also, social and cultural differences were politicized in ways that prefigured the emergence of Tamil political identity in the 1950s. The basic political entity was the "non-Brahmin community" as propagated by what was termed the non-Brahmin movement.[1] Since Dravidian and Tamil identity meld at a still later stage, examination of the emergence of Dravidian political identity in the context of the non-Brahmin movement is the first and a key step in understanding the creation of the "Tamil people."

Fundamental to any analysis of politics during the period of the non-Brahmin movement is an understanding of south Indian society. The Vedic theory of the Hindu caste system designates four divisions or varnas: Brahmin, Kshatriya, Vaisya, and Suddhra. These varnas are differentiated hierarchically according to occupation and ritual status. Brahmins, said to have originated in the mouth of Purusha (God), are the highest, and are priests and scholars. Kshatriyas originate in Purusha's arms and are rulers and soldiers; Vaisyas are born from his thighs and are merchants and landowners; and Suddhras, originating from the feet of Purusha, are peasants, laborers, and servants. Below the Suddhras and outside the varna system are the outcastes or Untouchables.[2]

15

In north India the Vedic theory of varna is realized at least
to the extent that we find castes claiming Brahmin, Kshatriya,
Vaisya, and Suddhra status. In south India, there are no Kshatriyas or Vaisyas, so all castes are either Brahmin, Suddhra,
or Untouchable. This potential for the cultural isolation of
Brahmins, although not salient in premodern history, became
significant in the late nineteenth and twentieth centuries.

CASTE IN PRE-TWENTIETH-CENTURY SOUTH INDIA

Prior to the twentieth century, intercaste relations in south India
involved competition, conflict, and cooperation between or
among jatis (endagomous caste units) in localized village or district
areas. As early as the fourteenth century, Burton Stein reports,
there were alliances and close cooperation between Brahmins
and "respectable cultivating groups."[3] Brahmins and these cultivating groups shared local control. Stein describes these alliances
as "the distinctive social and political elements up to the fourteenth century."[4]

Stein also reports that the most important landowning castes,
the Vellalas, Reddiars, and Kammas, sought to remain above
and apart from other non-Brahmin groups. These groups, among
others, later became known as "forward non-Brahmins."[5] Re-
maining above other non-Brahmin groups "required a special
relationship with Brahmins based upon ritual opportunities not
shared by other non-Brahmins. In later medieval times, especially
among Srivaisnavas, such people often achieved considerable,
if insecure, prominence in temples, and there were some castes
of Saivite Vellalas about whom little has been written, that
enjoyed a special relationship with Brahmins for substantial
periods."[6] During the eighteenth and nineteenth centuries, however, Brahmins entrenched their position vis-à-vis these non-
Brahmins. T. V. Subramaniam attributes increasing Brahmin
dominance in the nineteenth century to British rule.[7] Brahmins
entered the British administration and newly created urban
professions in disproportionately large numbers. As these positions increased in importance with consolidation of British rule,
the Brahmin position improved.[8] Non-Brahmin landowning
groups, however, maintained their dominance in many rural
districts. Urbanization and Brahmin dominance were interrelated
features of ninteenth-century social change resulting in the

dichotomization of socio-economic elites into non-Brahmin and Brahmin segments.[9]

Although the non-Brahmin–Brahmin conflict was styled by non-Brahmins as a conflict between the "forward" Brahmins and the "backward" non-Brahmins, this is an emotional metaphor that masks more than it illuminates. It might more accurately be defined as a conflict between a landowning non-Brahmin elite with a history of rural dominance, and a nascent urban Brahmin elite that had used the opportunities presented by British rule. Not all non-Brahmins were initially involved in this conflict, but only a small segment of Sat ("clean") Suddhras.

Before the non-Brahmin movement, "non-Brahmin" was not a relevant social, cultural, or political category. Groups that later became known as "non-Brahmin" first identified themselves only as specific jatis. Put another way, prior to politicization there were no "non-Brahmins" in south India, only the Vellalas, Nairs, Reddiars, Chettiars, and so on. Therefore the very idea of a "non-Brahmin" movement represents a significant reorientation of perceptions about castes and communities.

CULTURAL UNITY AND THE DRAVIDIAN PAST

The roots of the concept "non-Brahmin" are intrinsically tied to the idea of the cultural unity and integrity of south India based on a Dravidian past. Paradoxically, this Dravidian-ness was first postulated by Europeans. Eugene Irschick suggests that Christian missionaries were the first westerners to show an interest in Tamil culture, and to study the Tamil language.[10] Roberto di Nobili (1577–1656), Constantius Beschi (1680–1743), Rev. Robert Caldwell (1819–1891), and G. U. Pope (1820–1907) were all outstanding Tamil scholars. Caldwell developed the theory that "Sanskrit has been brought to south India originally by Aryan Brahman colonists, and with it a peculiar type of Hinduism, which embodied the worship of idols."[11] According to him, Tamil had been "cultivated by 'native Tamilians' called Sudras by the Brahmans, even though they had been Dravidian chieftains, soldiers, and cultivators, never conquered by the Brahmans."[12] Indeed, adds Caldwell, "the term Sudra should be dropped because its usage was associated with Brahmans and 'those Europeans who take their nomenclature from Brahmans'," and instead the name of each "Dravidian caste," according to the locality, should be used." [13]

Some British officials echoed the sentiments of these mission-aries. For example, J. H. Nelson agreed with Caldwell that neither Vellalas nor other non-Brahmins of south India should be called Suddras because this was a term forced upon them by Brahmins from the north. [14] In 1886 the governor of Madras, Mountstuart Elphinstone Grant-Duff, said in an address to the graduates of the University of Madras: "It was these Sanskrit speakers, not Europeans, who lumped up the Southern races as Rakshusas-demons. It was they who deliberately grounded all social distinc-tions on Varna, Colour." [15] The ideological category "non-Brah-min," therefore, was preceded by the development of a sense of a Dravidian cultural history separate, distinct, and perhaps superior to that of the south Indian Brahmins.

THE JUSTICE PARTY AND THE RISE OF POLITICAL CONSCIOUSNESS

Prior to 1916 and the founding of the South Indian Liberal Federation (Justice party), political activity in Madras Presidency was dominated by Brahmins oriented toward achieving Home Rule for India. The Justice party came into existence during the period when Madras Congress politics, under the leadership of Mrs. Annie Besant, were recovering from prolonged disorgani-zation and inactivity.

Political activity had declined especially after the ejection of the extremists from Congress in 1907 and the imprisonment of Tilak and the transportation of such active South Indian workers as Chidambaram Pillai and Subrahmania Siva in 1908. In the latter year V. S. Srinivasa Sastri and other moderates set up a number of District Congress Committees for continuing work in the Tamil and Telegu areas, but these 'collapsed after a time,' and in 1911 the Madras moderates were deprived of their major leader by the death of V. Krishnaswami Iyer. By 1914, then, national politics in Madras, both moderates and extremists, were in considerable disarray. [16]

Annie Besant had come to India in 1893 as a member of the Theosophical Society. In 1907 she was elected its World President and established her headquarters in Madras. From the beginning, she was a vigorous supporter of Indian religion and culture, and extolled the greatness of Indian civilization to English audiences inside and outside of the Theosophical Society. In 1914, during a visit to England, she argued that India was ready for self-government.[17]

In 1916 she founded the Home Rule League. By 1917 it had 132 branches in Madras Presidency.[18] The Home Rule League and the Congress party drew support from the same strata of society as the Theosophical Society—Western-educated Indians of professional and, to a lesser extent, business and landowning groups.[19] More importantantly, in terms of the relationship between caste rank and politics, they were mostly Brahmins.[20]

Brahmin dominance in the political arena was paralleled by Brahmin dominance in the administrative arena and university admissions. For example, Government Order 22 (January 27, 1919) reported that

> In the year 1911, statistics were obtained from heads of departments as to the distribution of appointments in the several offices under their control. . . . The figures obtained showed the preponderance of Brahmins which was specially marked in some departments; and instructions were thereupon issued to heads of departments in order to secure a proper distribution of appointments among the various castes. . . .
>
> The instructions issued by government in 1912 had had no effect.[21]

The figures of Bachelor of Arts degrees awarded from 1870 to 1918 (table 2-1) show Brahmin predominance in that area. A major reason, therefore, for the development of the non-Brahmin movement generally and the Justice party specifically was the self-interest of those members of forward non-Brahmin jatis who were well educated, had left traditional, rural occupations, and hoped to enter administrative service or other urban pursuits.

However, self-interest or the view of the non-Brahmin ideology as merely a weapon in the struggle for economic and political advantage cannot explain the specific form of the movement or its ideological development. The Justice party need not have

TABLE 2-1
Bachelors of Arts of Madras University[a]

(1911)	Brahmins[b]		Non-Brahmin Hindus		Indian Christians		Mohammadans		Europ. Euras.		Total
	Number	%	Number	%	Number	%	Number	%	Number	%	
1870-71	110	67.0	86	22.0	10	6.0	—		8	5.0	164
1880-81	492	64.0	171	22.0	47	6.0	2	.25	58	7.5	770
1890-01	1,461	67.0	445	20.5	168	8.0	20	1.00	75	3.5	2,169
1901-11	4,074	71.3	1,033	18.0	306	5.3	69	1.25	225	4.0	5,707
1918	10,262	67.5	3,213	21.1	1,343	8.8	186	1.20	205	3.0	15,209

[a]Table found in Government Order No. 22, January 27, 1919. Statistics taken from Madras University Calendar, Vol. I, 1918, pp. 367-377.

[b]Brahmins were approximately 3 percent of the Presidency population.

challenged *varnashrama dharma* (duty according to caste) to claim seats in universities or more posts in the administrative service. [22] Furthermore, although Brahmin–non-Brahmin antipathy is an important aspect of the early "non-Brahmin movement," it is not the only or even the most important consequence. The most interesting problem is not why these two rival elite groups found themselves at loggerheads, but how the contest led to development of a radical political ideology and a Dravidian political identity. For this, we must look beyond the role of ideology as a weapon in elite political competition to the symbolic structure of the ideology and ask: What did these political symbols symbolize? And why did they arise? [23]

The Dravidian ideology, like many other ideologies, is difficult to analyze because of its descriptive pretensions and its metaphoric content. "Non-Brahmin" is a case in point. Non-Brahmins, taken literally, include Muslims, Christians, Anglo-Indians, and Untouchables. But Muslim and Untouchable support for the Justice party was shortlived, and Christian and Anglo-Indian support hardly perceptible. "Backward non-Brahmins" (a term coined in the 1940s) were essentially unmobilized during this early twentieth-century period. Legally limited adult franchise meant that the exercise of the vote was restricted to the property-owning and educated segments of the population (forward non-Brahmins). The fact that English, not Tamil, was the language of political discourse illustrates the elite nature of the politics of this period.

Not only was the political arena between the 1900s and 1920s an elite arena, but the style of politics largely consisted of petitioning the British government. There were, of course also other activities, including labor organization, and even scattered acts of terrorism. The dominant political style was, however, petitional and peaceful. For example, the Justice party continually submitted petitions to the government seeking increased non-Brahmin representation in the administration. Various castes also submitted petitions to the government seeking changes in their identification in the census or an increase in their representation in the Legislative Council or in the administration. Newspapers attempted to influence both the government and educated public opinion. For example, the South Indian Liberal Federation (Justice party) began *Justice* in 1917 as an English weekly, and *Dravidan* as a Tamil weekly.

SUDDHRA-HOOD AS AN ORGANIZING CONCEPT

In examining the origin of the Dravidian ideology, we must look primarily at the expectations and circumstances of wealthy, educated non-Brahmin elites and their characterization as "Suddhras." In interviews with Justice party members, I was particularly struck by the consistent pattern of response about the formation of the Justice party. Usually the first reason mentioned was the backward state of non-Brahmins, the need for their uplift, and Brahman dominance of administrative posts and politics. But then the tone of the respondent would change, and with emotion he would recount some personal incident, insult to his dignity, or psychic injury suffered at the hands of the Brahmins, and would relate this to being designated a Suddhra.

For example, Sir P. T. Rajan, a prominent Justice party leader and ex-cabinet member, recounted two incidents to me that he considered examples of Brahmin "snobbishness."[24] In one, Sir P. T. Rajan (a Kondaikkati Vellala, that is, a wealthy member of a highly orthodox, highly orthoprax dominant landowning caste) recalled how his transition from a village to a town school meant a change from taking drinking water from the same pot as Brahmins (in the village) to taking drinking water from a separate pot—a pot used by all other non-Brahmin castes (in the town). This was a behaviorial manifestation of the culturally undifferentiated status of non-Brahmins (i.e., Suddhrahood) in urban areas. The second incident had to do with visiting Brahmin houses. If he was given water, his empty cup would subsequently be set before the fire to be purified.

Not only did Suddhrahood become a highly emotional issue, but the frustration, disgrace, and emotive content attached to Suddhra status became linked to the concepts "Dravidian" and "non-Brahmin," all becoming symbolically synonymous. That is, a member of the Justice party would at the same time be a Suddhra (since there were no Vaisyas or Kshatriyas), a Dravidian (meaning a speaker of a Dravidian language and a member of the Dravidian "race"), and a non-Brahmin. Attacks on *varnashrama dharma* (duty according to varna, caste) were directed against its justification of Suddhra status. Opposition to *varnashrama dhrama* and to Gandhi's early endorsement of it was intense and frequently articulated. In 1927 the *Justice* wrote:

We are told that Mahatama Gandhi held up as a lofty institution *varnashrama dharma* and extolled Brahminism. No doubt he referred to a few incidents like untouchability, and child marriage and the spoilation of young children of twelve years of age and stated that they were a parody of Brahminism. But if these did not exist he "adored Brahminism and varnashrama dharma."

We must confess to considerable mystification at the attitude of the Mahatma. Is it suggested that untouchability is removed by merely treating the depressed classes as touchables and giving them the same privileges—if they can be called such— which the touchable classes enjoy at the hands of the Brahmans?

Does the Mahatma think that if the Adi-Dravida is made to have the rights of a Vellala, Vannia, or an Agambadia, or to use a more compendious term which the Mahatma may understand though it is objected to as connoting to a vulgar meaning—a Suddhra—he could adore *varnashrama dharma?*

Also, "*Varnashrama dharma* as in practice Mahatma Gandhi ought to have found out, is the quintessence of the idea of privilege, of superiority and snobbishness."[25]

Criticisms of *varnashrama dharma* such as these constituted the basis for development at a later stage of the radical tenets of the Dravidian ideology.

URBANIZATION AND RELATIVE DEPRIVATION

So far, several variables that explain the rise of the early Dravidian ideology have been examined as well as some of the initial focal points of that ideology. But what factors triggered establishment of the emotional link between Suddhra status, *varnashrama dharma*, and Dravidian identity? What forces produced the emotive content attached to the term "Suddhra"? How was the connection between ideology and political action defined? The key explanatory factor is urbanization and urban contact, as it affected those upper non-Brahmin caste Hindus (principally Sat Suddhras) that historically occupied a structural position close to Brahmins, above and apart from other upper (or forward) non-Brahmins.

Urbanization entailed the discovery of a new Vedic, theological, moral definition of forward non-Brahmin identity that conflicted with previous rural experience.[26] Theological definitions of "Suddhra" conflicted with cultural assumptions underlying their religious orthopraxy (including vegetarianism, no animal sacrifice, and a general concern with purity). Secondly, the increasing importance of urban occupations such as law, positions in the British administration, and places in universities became a concrete behavioral manifestation of the realignment of the position of elite, forward non-Brahmins vis-à-vis Brahmins. Brahmin domination of politics despite their numerical minority was the third element in a triangle of seeming Brahmin control.

The concept of relative deprivation, as developed by Samuel Stouffer and elaborated in the work of T. Gurr and others, provides the best explanatory framework for analysis of this phenomenon.[27] Relative deprivation describes a sense of disjunction between expectations and reality. T. Gurr defines it as: "actors' perception of discrepancy between their value expectations and their value capabilities. Value expectations are the goods and conditions of life to which people believe they are rightfully entitled. Value capabilities are the goods and conditions they think they are capable of getting and keeping."[28] Merton places the concept of relative deprivation in the theoretical framework of reference-group theory. Relative deprivation is seen as a tendency to define and evaluate one's own position in comparison with a relevant reference group.[29] However, an actor's referent may also be the past, an ideal articulated by political leaders or by philosophy, or locational differences, such as a rural-urban contrast.

VILLAGE SOCIAL ORGANIZATION

At the village level in Tamil Nadu, jati relationships are of primary significance. The villager's social universe is largely defined in terms of transactions among the various endogamous Hindu jatis in one village or in a localized village cluster.[30] Brahmins are only three percent of the population in south India, and their percentage in villages is even less. In these villages, Brahmin relations with caste Hindus are by no means those of exalted superiority and abject inferiority. Rather, where there are lower-caste Hindus of sufficiently high economic status, Brahmins, particularly poor Brahmins, must show concomitant respect and deference.

While adjustment for Brahmins in urban areas was relatively easy, and urbanization enhanced their status, for many non-Brahmins city life challenged their caste identity and rank. Their position, unlike Brahmins, was dependent upon very specific localized transactional relationships and deference patterns. The lack of generalized ranking (that is, throughout Madras Presidency), and even of general knowledge of the position of various non-Brahmin castes, meant that some castes previously ranked above and apart from other non-Brahmins were now lumped with non-Brahmin masses in cities and towns.[31]

RELATIVE DEPRIVATION AND ELITE NON-BRAHMINS IN URBAN AREAS

In urban areas non-Brahmins from highly orthodox and orthoprax castes were treated as part of the undifferentiated category—Suddhra. The contrast with Brahmins can be neatly stated: for Brahmins their position and status was independent of their residence in any given local area; for non-Brahmins (especially the highest castes) rank was directly dependent on village economic and ritual dominance, transactionally corroborated. For non-Brahmins, rural-to-urban movement meant a transition from a secure transactional system to a system in flux, a system where deference patterns below Brahmin and above Untouchable were being renegotiated.[32]

Educated, wealthy members of orthodox and orthoprax castes found social strain to be an attendant feature of urbanization and urban contact. This strain took the form of a sense of relative deprivation. Many elite non-Brahmins developed a sense of (comparative) loss of status in the urban context. Comparison of urban to rural status was unfavorable. Men who were identified as proud, orthodox landlords in villages were "just" Suddhras in cities. *Varnashrama dharma,* not specific transactions, normatively defined the negative connotation of Suddhra. Following the same theory, Brahmins were culturally separated from all others as the only twice-born caste in Tamil Nadu. Rejection of Suddhra status was therefore linked to rejection of *varnashrama dharma,* a construction not pertinent in villages. Rejection of *varnashrama dhrama* meant rejection of the religious justification of Brahmin superiority. Redefinition of Brahmin as a negative symbol led to the elaboration of non-Brahmin as a positive symbol. From the theories of Caldwell and others, extolling past Dravidian greatness, and from a belief in Aryan-Dravidian racial distinctness, emerged outlines for situating non-Brahmin social strain. It should be recalled that while the *varnashrama dharma* view ranked Brahmins first, a pre-Aryan, Dravidian hierarchy would have been headed by forward non-Brahmins. This ideological framework also defined a new Dravidian identity for non-Brahmins.

To summarize the argument:

1. A potential existed in south Indian culture and society for the separation of Brahmins. This potential was the lack of Kshatriya and Vaisya varnas, as well as the putative coexistence of a distinct Dravidian cultural tradition. However, this potential was not realized prior to the late nineteenth and early twentieth centuries, since the all-India varna scheme was irrelevant to village transactions in which some so-called "Suddhras" were, in fact, allied with local Brahmins.

2. Realization of the cultural separation of Brahmins resulted from the breakdown of some integrative features of pre-eighteenth-century south Indian life.

3. British rule led to the enhancement of Brahmin status vis-à-vis forward non-Brahmins. Brahmins were prominent in urban occupations and in the British administration. They were also the first to develop political consciousness, and hence dominated early Madras Presidency political parties and politics.

4. This increasing political, social, and cultural isolation became significant (that is, necessitated action) as increasing urbanization and mobility challenged forward non-Brahmin status, rendered the symbol "Suddhra" exceptionally meaningful, and led to development of a sense of relative deprivation. Politically, Home Rule was identified with Brahmin rule. The first Justice party demands were, therefore, political and administrative, attempting to counteract Brahmin dominance in those areas. However, Justice party ideology and demands did not long remain so limited.

5. Elite Suddhras focused their ire on Brahmins and, utilizing the research on Dravidians by European scholars, began elaborating a counter-cultural tradition. To give some examples from newspapers of the period (all exerpts are from the Madras Native Newspaper Report):[33]

Brahmins and Swaraj

Dravidan October 11, 1921 details categorically selfishness, trickery, mischief, partiality for their own class, hatred and avarice as the traits of Brahmins and remarks "their selfishness is exhibited in their demanding immediate swaraj with the idea that they may thereby advance the cause of their class and making other classes their servitors, retard the progress of the world."

Dravidan January 22, 1923 "From the very beginning of the English rule, the cunning Brahmans in Madras have occupied all posts in the government from the lowest to the highest and have been successfully keeping out the other communities by filling up the vacancies with men of their own community."

Brahmins as Foreigners

Nyaya Dipika January 25, 1923 "The Brahmans are also foreigners to India as are the British. The English have been ruling India for the last one century and a half. The Brahmans, coming into India from Central Asia three thousand years ago, put down the ancient inhabitants of the country, have created disaffection among them by bringing into being racial, religious, and caste differences, and have been commanding the Indians ever since."

Importance of Tamil

Dravidan September 29, 1920, an article appeared which ". . . expresses satisfaction at the Trichinopoly non-Brahmin conference resolution that a Tamil university should be established, complains that Tamil is not properly encouraged now in the present universities and that many foreign Aryans, who wielded an influence in the University, brought the language to its present low condition and observes that the Tamilians will attain progress and acquire political influence . . . only if the Tamil language is improved."[34]

CONCLUSION

A number of linked factors are related in the emergence of Dravidian identity. Crucial to understanding this process is the

interplay of caste and class in shaping political alternatives in
the Madras Presidency arena. The non-Brahmin elite, for whom
caste identity melded into non-Brahmin identity during this period,
largely consisted of wealthy, orthodox, orthoprax members of
Tamil Nadu society. Many combined two normative models of
caste dominance—a "Brahmanic" and a "kingly" model. The
Brahmanic model emphasizes those variables related to ritual
status—that is, orthodoxy and orthopraxy. The kingly model,
based on land ownership and economic dominance, stresses
command over village labor.[35]

While Brahmins generally approach the Brahmanic model,
major forward non-Brahmins can be placed on a continuum
defined by the extent to which their conduct exemplifies the
ideological and behavioral patterns characteristic of the Brahmanic model. Backward non-Brahmins and Untouchables, on
the other hand, may be placed on a continuum ranging from
conduct emphasizing the kingly model (for example, Maravars,
with their martial tradition; or Chettiars, with their business
interests) and ending with Untouchables, who have limited scope
for either.[36]

As forward non-Brahmins became increasingly urbanized, and
as modern occupational preferences and modes of political
organization penetrated the countryside, these elite non-Brahmins
invidiously compared their status in urban areas with their rural
status, their twentieth-century position with their position in the
pre-British era, and their opportunities with those of the Brahmins. In these contrasting situations, elite non-Brahmin capabilities were not commensurate with their expectations. As the idea
of the superiority of past Dravidian civilization spread, the present
position of non-Brahmins was declared a mockery of former
greatness. Finally, Dravidian-ness itself was seen as almost
necessitating achievement and excellence, so the present "downtrodden state" of non-Brahmins was ultimately held to fall short
of an ineffable, idealized ideological standard. Disjunctions
between the present and an ideological construct of what Dravidian-ness (and later Tamil-ness) requires became a more important
aspect of Dravidian movement and DMK politics during the
later cultural nationalist period.

Thus the politicization of traditional theological categories (that
is, Brahmin and Suddhra), construction of a non-Brahmin communal identity, and reification of ancient Dravidian life as a

model to be emulated were all interrelated processes growing out of early twentieth-century south Indian social change. The impact of British rule initiated processes that changed the position of Brahmins vis-à-vis non-Brahmin elites. Urbanization of elite non-Brahmins and their increased modernization became a threat to their caste identity and rank. During this early period we see two elite groups (Brahmins and elite non-Brahmins) moving in divergent ideological directions. Brahmin political involvement was predominantly in Home Rule organizations, and the nationalism propagated was territorial nationalism. Non-Brahmin elites, on the other hand, rejected Home Rule and territorial nationalism, emphasizing the primacy of Dravidian cultural authenticity, a common non-Brahmin identity and an incipient Dravidian cultural nationalism.

[1] The term "non-Brahmin movement" is loosely applied by Madrasis to all the organizations and activities associated with protest against supposed Brahmin hegemony during this early period.

[2] For a discussion of varna as well as a theoretical analysis of the Indian caste system, see Dumont, *Homo Hierarchicus*. Also see Selig Harrison, *India: the Most Dangerous Decades* (Princeton: Princeton University Press, 1960). Harrison also related the rise of the non-Brahmin movement to the cultural framework embodied in the southern varna system.

[3] Burton Stein, "Brahmin and Peasant in Early South Indian History," *Dr. V. Raghavan Felicitation Volume of the Adyar Library Bulletin* 31-32 (1967-1968), 244.

[4] *Ibid.*

[5] The term "forward non-Brahmin" subsequently became current in Madras politics. Generally it refers to landowning and business castes that formed an elite.

[6] *Ibid.*, p. 264. This special relationship involved specific ritual concessions. For an analysis of the stress created by attempts to terminate these special ritual concessions, also see S. Barnett, "Urban Is as Urban Does: Two Incidents on One Street in Madras City South India," *Urban Anthropology* 2 (Fall 1973), 129-160.

[7] T. V. Subramaniam, "The Tamil Brahmins: Some Guidelines to Research on Their Emergence and Eclipse," *Economic and Political Weekly* 4 (July 1969), 1133-1136.

[8] See Anil Seal, *The Emergence of Indian Nationalism: Competition and Collaboration in the Later Nineteenth Century* (Cambridge: Cambridge University Press, 1968), pp. 107-113.

[9] I am speaking of a general pattern. Of course there were non-Brahmins in urban professions and there were Brahmin landowners. Kathleen Gough, "The Social Structure of a Tanjore Village," in McKim Marriot, ed., *Village India: Studies in the Little Community* (Chicago: University of Chicago Press, 1955), states that the Brahmins there "own the land and have administrative rights in about 900 out of a total of 2,611 villages."

[10] Eugene Irschick, *Politics and Social Conflict in South India: The Non-Brah-

man Movement and Tamil Separatism, 1916-1929 (Berkeley and Los Angeles: University of California Press, 1969), p. 276. Also see Robert Hardgrave, Jr., *The Nadars of Tamil Nad: Political Culture of a Community in Change* (Berkeley and Los Angeles: University of California Press, 1969), pp. 43-70.

[11] Irschick, *Politics and Social Conflict*, p. 278.

[12] *Ibid.*, p. 279.

[13] *Ibid.*

[14] *Ibid.*, p. 280. Also see Rudolph and Rudolph, *Modernity of Tradition*, pp. 276-277 for more on J. H. Nelson.

[15] Irschick, *Politics and Social Conflict*, p. 281.

[16] Hugh F. Owen, "Mrs. Annie Besant and the Rise of Political Activity in South India, 1914-1919" paper presented to the Second International Conference Seminar of Tamil Studies, 1968, p. 1.

[17] *Ibid.*, p. 2.

[18] *Ibid.*, p. 4.

[19] *Ibid.*, p. 6.

[20] Recall that Mrs. Besant was an enthusiast of Brahmanic religion.

[21] India, Tamil Nadu Government, Government Order No. 22, January 27, 1919.

[22] For example, the central symbols of the movement might have been drawn from British Liberal thought. This was particularly likely since politics in the early twentieth century were conducted in an elite arena in which there was respect for and a desire to imitate the British political model.

[23] Ideological studies generally emphasize the function ideologies perform rather than their symbolic content. For a "revisionist" view that makes it clear that analysis of symbolic content is crucial for understanding function, see Geertz, "Ideology as a Cultural System," pp. 47-76 in David Apter, *Ideology and Discontent* (New York: Free Press, 1964).

[24] Interview with Sir P. T. Rajan, Madras City, 1968.

[25] *Justice Mirror of the Year 1927* (Madras: n.p., 1928).

[26] This was most dramatically true in cases where urbanization involved movement in new arenas where diverse castes came into contact with each other under circumstances in which correct social relations were ambiguous, for instance hostels and government offices.

[27] Samuel Stouffer, *The American Soldier* (Princeton: Princeton University Press, 1941). T. R. Gurr, *Why Men Rebel* (Princeton: Princeton University Press, 1970).

[28] Gurr, *Why Men Rebel*, p. 24.

[29] Robert K. Merton, *Social Theory and Social Structure* (New York: Free Press, 1963), pp. 234ff.

[30] Stephen A. Barnett, "The Structural Position of a South Indian Caste: Kontaikkatti Vellalas of Tamil Nadu" (Ph.D. dissertation, University of Chicago, 1970).

[31] See Steve Barnett, *From Structure to Substance: the Past Fifty Years of a South Indian Caste* (forthcoming), for a study of an elite non-Brahmin caste in rural and urban areas.

[32] For similar statements see S. Barnett, "Urban is as Urban Does." For a general analysis of transactions in Indian villages see McKim Marriott, "Caste Ranking and Food Transactions: a Matrix Analysis," in Milton Singer and Bernard Cohn, *Structure and Change in Indian Society* (Chicago: Aldine, 1969), pp. 423-452.

[33] The Madras Native Newspaper Reports are summaries and excerpts made by the British from vernacular newspapers. They are available in the Tamil Nadu Archives for the years 1916 to 1934.

[34] The quotation is from the article summary done by the government translator, who prepared the article for the Madras Native Newspaper Reports.

[35] See Dumont, *Homo Hierarchicus,* for an analysis of these two models.

[36] See S. Barnett, "The Structural Position of a South Indian Caste," conclusion.

CHAPTER THREE

Developing the Politics of Radical Social Reform

IN the preceding chapter, the rise of Dravidian ideology was related to the constraints facing a particular stratum of early twentieth-century Madras non-Brahmin society. From strains experienced by this stratum emerged the outlines of an ideology countering the Brahmanic Hindu tradition. With the founding of the Self-Respect League, these outlines were ramified into a more elaborate doctrine.

The Self-Respect League was officially organized in 1925.[1] The publication of *Kudi Arasu* in 1924 by E. V. Ramasami[2] was, however, the first sustained attempt to propagate radical ideas of social reform. The militant tone of the Self-Respect movement was set at that time by E. V. Ramasami, and he was responsible for the radicalization of Dravidian ideology. We cannot assume, however, that all members of the Self-Respect League, or even all those claiming to be strong adherents of the non-Brahmin or Dravidian movement, held the same radical positions on issues of caste, religion, *varnashrama dharma*, etc. Actually, two distinct positions emerged, both advocating rejection of Brahmanic Hinduism. the moderates (perhaps moderate radical would be a better term, although a neologism) criticized Brahmanic Hinduism from the vantage point of a "superior" non-Brahmin Saiva Siddhanta[3] tradition. This position had considerable appeal to elite non-Brahmin castes with a tradition of orthodoxy. Before turning to E. V. Ramasami and the radicalization of the Dravidian ideology, we will briefly explore the position of the moderates. By the mid-1930s, although the radicals saw the necessity of retaining an alliance with the moderates, they were reacting both to the perceived Aryan Brahmanic Hinduism of the Brahmins and to what they considered the too-modest reform proposals of the moderates.

SWAMIYAR KAIVAILYAM AND THE MODERATES

The moderate position is best represented in the writings of

Swamiyar Kaivailyam, a Saiva Siddhanta philosopher generally referred to as "Saint." Articles by Kaivailyam in the early volumes of *Kudi Arasu* indicate his basic views. For example, in a 1929 article entitled "Why the Self-Respect Movement Came into Existence" he wrote:

> The Self-Respect movement came into existence only to teach the real truth of the ancients; a truth that existed where there were no differences between people and justice existed between people. It comes only to save the society. Some cheats had taken advantage of the ignorance of our people; of the poverty of our people and instilled in them so many Shastras and Puranas, and told them that they were low caste. This movement comes only to assist the Shastras which said that there was only one God for all the Universe.

> The Self-Respect Movement comes to tell that God is common to all whether they are high or low caste people, whether they are strong or weak. [4]

Although Kaivailyam and the moderates trenchantly attacked *varnashrama dharma* and what they considered to be abuses of Hinduism, their main purpose was to reform Hinduism and eliminate "evil" Brahmin influences and "superstitious" practices.

The moderates (as well as the militants) challenged many traditional orthoprax customs and rituals. This type of reform engendered fairly widespread support from the Self-Respectors within orthodox, orthoprax forward non-Brahmin castes who found these ideas compatible with maintenance of religiosity. Religion and reform were compatible as long as reform was limited to ridding Hinduism of "disagreeable," "Aryan" customs. For many forward non-Brahmin adherents of the non-Brahmin and Self-Respect movements, it might be conjectured that destruction of the Brahmanic hierarchy would result in raising their own rank in a new Dravidian hierarchy. The ideological position adopted by Kaivailyam was consistent with that possibility.

Kaivailyam advocated a purging of corrupt practices and a return to the purity of pre-Aryan, i.e., Dravidian, beliefs and society. During the 1920s and 1930s some members of forward non-Brahmin castes began to eschew Brahmin priests (purohits) at weddings and other crucial life-cycle ceremonies. In their

place either non-Brahmin priests or elder members of the community were used. This had two major implications: (1) it denied
the necessity of Brahmin priests to legitimize life-cycle rituals;
and (2) it denied a key source of income to Brahmin purohits.
As a result of the Self-Respect movement, patterns of utilization
of Brahmin priests have changed for many orthodox forward
non-Brahmin castes.[5] This is another indicator of the particular
relevance of the movement to forward non-Brahmins (in contrast
to backward non-Brahmins), at least in its early stages. Brahmins
will not serve as priests for some backward castes, and certainly
not for untouchables. Hence many of the reforms advocated
at Self-Respect League Social Reform Conferences were primarily relevant to forward non-Brahmin castes.

E. V. RAMASAMI AND THE RADICALS

The more militant tone and position that came to dominate the
Self-Respect League was set by E. V. Ramasami. He was born
in Erode in 1879 to a Baliga Naidu family.[6] His father was
a wealthy merchant. In his biography, E. V. Ramasami recounts
childhood incidents to show he opposed "superstitious" caste
practices from "an early age." One incident is particularly
germane:

> I was sent to the village school when I was six years old.
> That school was a little away from Erode town. Around the
> school were houses of business Chettiars. They would be
> extracting oil there. Those who made mats and baskets out
> of bamboo had their huts in the ends of the street. There
> were also some huts of Muslims. Hence all around my school
> were Chettiars, Vedakaran, and Muslims. In those days, the
> other caste people would not eat anything in these people's
> houses. Hence, my people would not forget to tell me when
> I went to school. They would say: "we should not mix with
> those people. So do not drink water in their houses. If you
> want you can drink water in your teacher's house." Hence,
> once or twice I asked for water in my teacher's house. The
> teacher was a Brahmin. In their house a little girl would put
> a brass tumbler on the floor, pour water in it and ask me
> to lift it up and drink. [This is *not* the way a Brahmin would
> give water to another Brahmin.] After I drank she would

ask me to put it face down, she would pour water inside, wash it and take it outside. Also, since I did not know how to lift it up and drink [He means without touching the rim of the cup with his lips. This is the way in which Brahmins drink liquids], a part of it would spill on my nose and body and only a part would go to the mouth. I would cough and spill even the water I would drink. That girl would get angry and scold me. Hence, if I was thirsty, I would not ask for water in my teacher's house.[7]

Lest the issue of drinking water be thought trivial, we must remember drinking-water prohibitions are equivalent to general interdining restrictions and define caste rank.[8] Brahmins would not, of course, accept drinking water in non-Brahmin homes or from non-Brahmin hands. These transactions apply only to forward (Sat) non-Brahmins. Many backward non-Brahmin castes (and, of course, Adi-Dravidas) would not be allowed in the home of a Brahmin *or* forward non-Brahmin.

The following excerpt from the *Dravidan* of May 12, 1921, indicates the general significance of drinking water as a symbolic action around which elite non-Brahmin ire crystallized. The *Dravidan* of May 12, 1921, quotes a passage from the *Christian Outlook,* April 23, 1921, that shows a similar controversy involving drinking water in government offices. The *Christian Outlook* stated:

Admission into the water shed is restricted only to Brahmans. As the water Brahman [Brahmin in charge of water supplies] employed at government expense is generally conspicuous by his absence, a non-Brahman clerk requiring water is frequently at the mercy of his Brahman co-clerks for a supply of the same, while the Brahman can himself enter and satisfy his thirst. There have been cases in which non-Brahman clerks, who tired of waiting outside for water went in and helped themselves, had to pay dearly for it as the water Brahman subsequently broke the pots and recovered the cost from them. Further, it is not proper to allow the Brahmans, many of whom are filthy and suffering from loathsome diseases, to dip their hands deep down into the water pots while those infinitely cleaner in dress and habits, are forced to wait outside and drink the contaminated water.[9]

To continue with E. V. Ramasami's account of his drinking water episode:

> The children of business Chettiars did not ask for water in the teacher's house. If a Chettiar is thirsty, the teacher would say, "Go home and come back." He would run to his house or if his house was very far, he would go to any other Chettiar's house and drink water. One day I thought that I would go with him and drink water. . . . He and I went to his house though the back door, he ran inside and brought me water in a tumbler. I put my mouth on it [here Periyar is rejecting the Brahmin custom of not allowing the lips to touch the rim of a tumbler] and drank as I would at home. . . .
>
> Gradually this led me to eat in their houses. [10]

E. V. Ramasami, therefore, violated the rules of caste purity at a very early age and in an extreme manner. In the 1880s intercaste dining was a rare thing indeed. For a *child* in rural Madras Presidency to violate such mores is almost inconceivable!

Continuing with Naicker's biography: E. V. Ramasami's father ended his education at the age of ten years because of his associations with lower-caste boys. Among other measures, his parents shackled his feet in response to his violation of caste customs. At the age of ten, he was taken into his father's business (general merchant), and out of school.

By twenty-five, E. V. Ramasami had amassed a considerable fortune of his own and also a reputation as a shrewd businessman. At twenty-five, he decided to renounce the world and became a saddhu. As a saddhu, he wandered to Calcutta and Benares before returning to Erode to resume his position in his father's business. The fact that he "took up the saffron robe" is a further indication of the continuing psychological sense of marginality that characterizes his life. E. V. Ramasami returned to Erode, disillusioned with both Brahmanical society and the ascetic mode of life. Those who practiced priesthood (in society as Brahmins or as renouncers, saddhus) failed to live up to his ideal.

E. V. Ramasami began his political life as a staunch Congressman. He gained wide publicity from his participation in the satayagraha in Vikom, Kerala, to open certain roads to Untouchables. [11] As a result of this satyagraha, he became widely known as the Hero of Vikom.

In 1924, E. V. Ramasami resigned as secretary of the Madras Presidency Congress Committee over an incident in which Brahmin and non-Brahmin eating facilities were segregated in a school (gurukul) run under Congress auspices. In 1925 he left Congress, and declared, "hereafter my work is to dissolve the Congress." [12] His biographer claims that his dissatisfaction with Congress resulted from the attitudes of Brahmins to non-Brahmins in Congress; that it was solely a matter of principle, and that his strong political opposition to what he termed Brahmin dominance in public life dates from this period. Another interpretation is that E. V. Ramasami and a number of other leaders were involved in an unsuccessful power play within the Congress and left after their defeat. [13]

Although it is always difficult to impute motives to leaders, we can place E. V. Ramasami's exit from Congress in the context of the development of his social and political ideas as well as of his life style during this period. When E. V. Ramasami became a Congress adherent, he did so in a thoroughgoing, dedicated fashion. He wore khaddar (hand-woven cloth) and even had his entire family (including his eighty-year-old mother) do likewise. At one time, he lost 50,000 rupees indirectly because of his Congress work when he cut down five hundred coconut trees used in preparing alcoholic toddy. [14] According to his biographer, his devotion to Gandhi and to Congress was total and shaped his young adulthood.

As early as 1922, while still a member of Congress, E. V. Ramasami advocated burning the *Manu Dharma Shastras* and the *Ramayana*. While a saddhu, before his political activities, he advocated abandoning Hindu mythology because it represented a corrupting influence. By the time he joined Congress, therefore, his religious militancy was established and, as we saw from the story of his breaking caste restrictions on interdining and his early association with people from all castes, the outline of a radical position on social matters had taken shape at an early age. His participation in the Kerala satyagraha and the subsequent accolade as the "Hero of Vikom" were important in crystallizing his commitment to social reform. The Kerala satyagraha took place in 1922, the year in which E. V. Ramasami began to criticize publicly the central mythologies of the Hindu religion. In 1924 he began *Kudi Arasu* to propagate principles of social reform. The depth of his commitment to social reform was beginning to run parallel to (and rival) his commitment to Congress.

Therefore, E. V. Ramasami's exit from Congress must in some sense be interpreted in terms of his increasing commitment to social reform and his redefinition of its priority vis-à-vis attainment of Home Rule or independence. E. V. Ramasami, the radical "Self-Respector," had already emerged by 1924, while he was still in Congress. The gurukul (school) incident was a catalyst setting off a predictable chain of events that ended with E. V. Ramasami outside the Congress. In fact, by 1927, his attitude toward Gandhi had come full circle from devoted disciple to hostile opponent on the crucial issue of *varnashrama dharma*.

After returning from a trip to the Soviet Union, E. V. Ramasami added a version of Marxism to the Dravidian ideology. An article entitled "What is Our Aim? Capitalism and Religion Should Be Destroyed," [15] expressed the radical tenets of his ideology. Note the profound difference between E. V. Ramasami and Kaivailyam. The article begins by noting, "It is well known that in the beginning of the self-respect movement we were condemning not only the Shastrams and ritual celebrations but also the political Brahmins. Afterwards, the self-respect movement began to . . . attack the Gods, religions and Shastramas. . . . The movement is propagandizing communist principles. Many think some danger will come to them [because of this]." A central question raised by the article is what should be the purpose of the movement and the methods used to attain it. "Some persons are of the opinion that the self-respect movement should not enter into politics but should only make rational propaganda. Some think that . . . we should engage in communist propaganda and enter politics. Some others think it is enough to insult the Brahmins and get offices for non-Brahmins." [16] The article concluded that the correct path for the Self-Respect movement was to "take as our problem the destruction of the cruelties of capitalists and the cruelties of religion. Whoever accepts these principles should be included in our movement. That is the only way to solve these problems." [17] And so with atheism, communism, non-Brahmin political prominence, and ritual and social reform, E. V. Ramasamis radicalism was complete.

Having examined the radicalization of the Dravidian ideology and the ideological cleavage between radicals and moderates, it is useful to view these processes in the context of the politics of non-Brahminism.

POLITICAL CLIMATE FOR SOCIAL REFORM: THE POLITICS OF
NON-BRAHMINISM

A crucial facet of the political climate in the 1920s and 1930s
was the relations of the Justice party and non-Brahmins with
the British. Although the subtle intricacies are too complex to
describe here in detail, pertinent evidence on the British view
of the Justice party is provided by Government Order (GO)
122 (October 17, 1919), Local and Municipal Department. The
specific question raised by the GO was the ability of non-Brahmins
to withstand Brahmin influence in electoral contests. The Justice
party claim of being in some way underprivileged and in need
of special protective electoral mechanisms was being seriously
considered. In untangling this question, the GO examined a
number of factors in the complex Madras Presidency equation—
the Brahmins in Congress and the Home Rule parties, and
non-Brahmins in the Justice party and the Madras Presidency
Association. [18] The Madras Presidency Association was formed
in 1917 by non-Brahmins who were nationalistic, but nevertheless
felt the need for a non-Brahmin organization. About the MPA
and Justice party, the Government order said:

> Doctor Nayar's party have consistently drawn a clear distinc-
> tion between the non-Brahmans of their party and those whose
> political opinions are similar to the views of the Home Rule
> League and Congress party. They have emphasized that the
> Madras Presidency Association is an organism formed by Home
> Rule and Congress interests with a view to create the impression
> that non-Brahman feeling is in harmony with the attitudes
> of the advanced Brahman, and is at least not opposed to the
> method of communal representation which consists in the
> reservation of seats for non-Brahmans in plural constituencies.
> Dr. Nayar's party [Justice] has strenuously opposed this
> method on the ground that it would merely result in the return
> to the legislative Council of non-Brahmans which [sic] political
> sympathies in no way represents the views of the non-Brahman
> members of the South Indian Liberal Federation." [19]

So here the British are overtly concerned that the Justice
party supported them, while the Home Rule and Congress parties
did not. The Justice party argued that social reform should precede
Home Rule, since Home Rule under present circumstances would

be merely Brahmin rule. The British were naturally concerned that non-Brahmin representation favored continuation of the British connection.

The Government Order then analyzes a number of specific electoral contests. Here is the breakdown for one constituency:

> This constituency with 507 voters including about 114 Brahmans furnishes the only genuine illustration of the success of a non-Brahman against a Brahman. There were four candidates, of whom two only secured 8 votes, 241 were cast for the non-Brahmin, Mr. Sivagnanam Pillai and 167 for the Brahman outgoing representative, Mr. K. Rama Ayyangar. I should say that there is little doubt that this result was attributable to the influence of the Vellala community in the Tinnevely district in which nearly 36 per cent of the voters were resident. *It is notorious that in this district the position of the Vellala is such as to enable him to compete on level terms with a Brahman* (emphasis added). [20]

In the nine groups of constituencies taken together in this analysis, the GO stated that of the 3,640 registered voters, 752 were Brahmins. The actual poll came to 2,900 votes, of which 1,457 votes were cast in favor of Brahmins, 355 in favor of non-Brahmins affiliated with the Madras Presidency Association, and 1,088 in favor of Justice party non-Brahmins. The GO concluded, as is evident from the data, that there were non-Brahmins voting for Brahmin candidates and also for non-Brahmins of nationalist views.

This GO indicates a British position regarding the Justice party that was a kind of pragmatic, "tit for tat." The British consequently instituted reforms in administrative recruitment that incorporated Justice party suggestions. The communal Government Order in effect established a quota system giving a certain percentage of all administrative jobs to non-Brahmins. A communal rule was established that stated that for every twelve appointments the caste distribution would be as follows: Brahmins 2, non-Brahmins 5, Muslims 2, Christians 2, others 1. These reforms had mixed results. [21]

The Justice party took office in 1920 and attempted to work the new system of dyarchy introduced by the Montagu-Chelmsford reforms. [22] After taking office it began a conservative transformation. When the Justice party was first organized, the term "non-Brahmin" provided the broadest base for unified political action because it included Muslims, Untouchables, and Anglo-Indians—in fact, all non-Brahmins. After the Justice party assumed office, both the Muslim press and the Untouchable elites affiliated with the Justice party accused the party of reserving all the newly opened jobs provided by the communal reforms for high-caste Hindus, and reneging on promises of social reform. At the same time that relations among the various caste groups in the Justice party became strained, the radicals in the party were becoming alienated from the moderate-party office holders. Untouchables became particularly disenchanted with the Justice party.

In 1923, M. C. Rajah, the most prominent Untouchable in the Justice party, withdrew, taking a number of Untouchable leaders with him.[23] These Untouchables made a number of charges against party policy: that higher castes had appropriated all the posts in the British administration for themselves; that Adi-Dravidas were not represented on municipal boards in proportion to their numbers;[24] and that the Justice party had not:

a. initiated house building schemes;
b. given the Adi-Dravidas economic help;
c. developed free education;
d. instituted land distribution and reform;
e. visited Adi-Dravida villages to hear their grievances.[25]

A prominent member of the Justice party reported a conversation that adds insight to the atmosphere in which these charges were made. M. C. Rajah was complaining in a party strategy meeting that the party had done nothing for Untouchables. "What," he asked, "has the Justice party done for the Adi-Dravidas?" An important caste Hindu leader of the party responded, "it enabled a Paraiyan to meet the Queen." This is significant for a number of reasons. Not only is it arrogant and patronizing, but the use of the word Paraiyan was an insult, since Untouchables had continually petitioned the legislative assembly to substitute the term Adi-Dravida (adi-first—therefore "first Dravidians" would be substituted for the hated word "Paraiyan").

The case of Untouchables versus the Justice party in power,

while enriching the analysis, provides a seemingly paradoxical or even contradictory example: if the ideology attacks caste *(varnashrama dharma)* and advocates social reform, why is actual behavior so different? The answer to this question is consistent with the notion of a radical/moderate cleavage. The moderates dominated the Justice party government. Recall that the initial Dravidian ideology was an elite response to social strain, and was forged in a universe where Brahmins and elite non-Brahmins were preeminent. Early moderate non-Brahmin adherents may have desired basic changes, but those changes would not have destroyed the system; rather the effect would have been to destroy the then present hierarchy headed by "Aryan" Brahmins. A "Dravidian" society might conceivably have been dominated by elite non-Brahmins. The radicals, in contrast, demanded more thoroughgoing systemic change. These differences between radicals and moderates are crucial to understanding the interplay between the radical-dominated Self-Respect League and the moderate-dominated Justice party. [26]

THE JUSTICE PARTY AND THE SELF-RESPECT LEAGUE

The appellation "Self-Respect" is rich in meaning. The Justice party, the common name for the South Indian Liberal Federation, was derived from the paper *Justice*, and referred to the idea of justice for non-Brahmins. The call for self-respect was a stronger manifestation of the attempt not only to secure political "justice," but to achieve structural change in south Indian society. Self-Respect meant Self-Respect for the (culturally and politically) downtrodden Dravidians, and freedom from the "slavery of the mind."

Understanding the Self-Respect movement as an attempt to develop viable Dravidian cultural alternatives is crucial for analysis of the later periods in Tamil Nadu politics. Essentially cultural functions of the Self-Respect movement were combined with a strong emphasis on social reform. The Self-Respect movement combined many strands of opinion, ranging from mere religious reform to social radicalism. What united the Self-Respect movement and defined the pattern of cooperation between the Self-Respect League and the Justice party during the 1920s and 1930s was the overriding goal of extending, transforming, and radicalizing social and political consciousness among non-Brahmins.

In the early stages, the relationship with the Justice party was very close. P. T. Rajan, a key Justice party leader, defined his understanding of the Self-Respect movement while inaugurating the first provincial Self-Respect conference: "The Self-Respect movement wants to do away with a social system that keeps man and man apart, community and community aloof—a system that puts premium on the accident of birth, a system that makes it possible for large sections of the community to be treated as chattel. It aims on its side at giving equal opportunities to all, at making men and women all equal in the eye of the law, GOD-made as well as man-made, affording the freest and fullest scope for self-development to one and all."[27] At the same conference Dr. P. Subbarayan, former Justice party member and chief minister and zamindar of Kumaramangalam, argued for the priority of social reform and social awakening:

It is time we realized that we cannot be a self-respecting people politically unless we ourselves respect socialism. The truth must be admitted that customs and beliefs which restrict freedom of people in the social sphere cannot prop up a free nation. As long as such customs and beliefs continue, it is not possible to erect a free and democratic state on a society hopelessly given over to all that is antiquated, superstitious and unprogressive. A people who are dominated by priests in their social life cannot escape subjugation to a bureaucracy and it is not surprising that the priest is the person who most easily transforms himself into the bureaucrat. All he has to do is to employ, in the political sphere, the talents he has perfected and the knowledge of our weaknesses that he has acquired in the social sphere and his success is assured.[28]

Reference to priests in this quotation is to Brahmin priests. Subbarayan further stated that "A social system that tolerates enumerable castes can never produce a unified people required for the working of democracy. A society that denies to its members social justice will not produce leaders capable of fighting for economic and political equality."[29]

These statements of prominent Justice party leaders delineate the areas in which the Self-Respect movement was able to mobilize the most generalized support. The theory of a pre-Aryan, casteless society was articulated at this same conference by W.P.A. Soundrapandian, another Justice party leader.

> Let us contemplate for a moment the condition of ancient Tamilian society. Saint Tiruvalluvar has said: "Birth is common to all, but intrinsic worth differs according to the various deeds in which people are engaged. . . ." Untouchability, unapproachability, unseeability and other monstrous customs were unknown to our ancients. Caste distinctions, religious dissensions and class disputes were absent. The word Jati which connotes caste, is not of Tamil origin. Every human being had equal rights of access to tanks, temples, Choultries, etc. People regulated their lives in a spirit of brotherliness towards their fellow beings. Love was their watchword and hatred never found a place in their hearts. They worshiped nature and led a life of utter simplicity resulting in true happiness. Ever since the days when the Aryans penetrated the South and attempted to strengthen and consolidate their position a great calamity overtook the country.[30]

In the remainder of his speech, Soundrapandian reiterated the idea that the non-Brahmins had fallen to a deplorable condition, their solidarity destroyed by the advent of the Aryans.

As we see from these statements of Justice party leaders, the relationship between the Justice party and the Self-Respect movement included much overlap in leadership as early as the 1920s. Ideologically, this overlap included reformist and at some points, radical attacks on Hinduism. It is significant that the Justice party's chief minister of Madras Presidency and two of the most powerful and important Justicities were outspoken, as the quotations above indicate, in favor of the cause of social reform. Somewhere between the extreme position of viewing the Justice party and the Self-Respect League as all the same thing (as many Tamilians do), on the one hand, and seeing them as totally different, on the other, is a view of them in a symbiotic relationship. While the Justice party contested elections, the Self-Respect League excelled in propaganda. In 1944 the two organizations were joined, forming the Dravida Kazhagam. That union was only achieved, however, after many moderates had defected to Congress.

THE POLITICS OF RADICAL SOCIAL REFORM AND
NON-BRAHMINISM VERSUS THE POLITICS OF
INDEPENDENCE

While the pattern of Justice party–Self-Respect League interaction was one of increasing cooperation, what was the relationship between these organizations and the Congress Party? between social reform ideology and independence demands? between budding Dravidian cultural nationalism and support for Congress territorial nationalism? We might begin with the activities of non-Brahmin advocates of Home Rule and independence through the Madras Presidency Association. The establishment of the Madras Presidency Association (henceforth MPA) grew out of a meeting called by non-Brahmin Congress supporters in 1917 to discuss how to protect non-Brahmin interests in light of upcoming changes in representation under the new Montagu-Chelmsford Act of 1918.[31] It is particularly significant that as early as 1917 a Congress non-Brahmin wrote in a letter to *New India* that "although there was no point in keeping Brahmans out of a political organization there must be some organization limited to non-Brahmans which would voice non-Brahman opinion within Congress in opposition to the claims of the Justice Party.[32] One major effect of the Justice party, therefore, was to create a political category, "non-Brahmin," which so fundamentally altered perceptions about the Madras political arena that non-Brahmins in Congress felt the need to organize around that affiliation. The importance of this fact cannot be overemphasized. In one sense, perception of political reality in Brahmin–non-Brahmin terms was half the battle. It meant legitimization of the category "non-Brahmin," and imputation of at least some common interests to this amorphous unit. The Justice party accused the MPA of being a tool of the Brahmins. This accusation, interestingly enough, is not accurate. The MPA did oppose the Justice party, but on Justice party grounds—as one non-Brahmin party seeking to protect non-Brahmin interests opposing another non-Brahmin party with similar but not identical interests. This perception of the Congress movement in Brahmin–non-Brahmin terms meant that internecine (that is, intra-Congress) factionalism was often recast in a Brahmin versus non-Brahmin framework.

By 1920, there were some suggestions that in the matter of communal representation, the MPA and the Justice party should

join forces. P. Kesava Pillai, president of the MPA, was the
first to make this suggestion.[33] In this regard, Irschick cites
a very revealing letter written by an Indian Christian member
of the MPA who "claimed that the M.P.A. had been under
the impression that the Brahmans in the Madras Congress
organization supported their demand for special treatment in
the electorates of Madras Presidency but . . . was disgusted
by the way in which both the Justice Party and the M.P.A.
representatives had been treated, especially at the second conference; in particular he cited the growing Brahman intransigence
over the question of granting a larger number of seats to
non-Brahmans."[34] By 1920, after the establishment of Merton's
communal award,[35] the purpose of securing reserved seats had
been accomplished, so MPA leaders turned their attention elsewhere. The MPA, while it existed, reflected intra-Congress elite
non-Brahmin–Brahmin cleavage. The development of a wing
within Congress that to some extent was loyal to a parochial
regional identity originated with the MPA and provided the
framework within which later "Tamilization of the Congress"
must be viewed.

MPA non-Brahmins combined acceptance of non-Brahmin
identity with support for political independence and Congress.
They focused primarily on the conflict between Indian and
Englishman, but also supported non-Brahmin quotas in the British
administration and reservation of seats in the legislature. Always
a small minority among non-Brahmins, after 1920 the MPA was
disbanded. However, greater non-Brahmin support for independence developed during the late 1930s and 1940s. It is crucial
to understand the context in which the Congress and the Swarajists enhanced their appeal among non-Brahmins, and in which
the goal of independence gained greater widespread support.
There was a push-pull factor involved here. On the one hand,
the emergence of agitational politics (introduced by the Swarajist
wing of the independence movement) and growing Congress
militancy against the British had a positive appeal, a "pull";
the decline of the Justice party as a source of political influence,
patronage, and emotional allegiance had a "push" effect.

DECLINE OF THE JUSTICE PARTY

The reasons for the Justice party decline are complex, with
two major causes. First, they lost Muslim and Untouchable

support after taking office. Second, as the Self-Respect League became more radical, it tended (in conjunction with the other variables influencing Madras Presidency politics) to divide elite non-Brahmins into three categories: (1) Those accepting radicalization and strongly supporting the Self-Respect League, who lost interest in Justice party political activities. These non-Brahmins tended to be most upset by what they considered the failure of the Justic party to pass sufficient legislation for social reform while in power. (2) Those non-Brahmins who accepted the general goals of the Self-Respect movement but were reformist rather than radical on matters of social reform. They supported the moderate wing of the Self-Respect League, and became increasingly alienated as the radicals gained prominence. Many maintained their Justice party affiliation as late as 1944. (The contemporary Justice party "rump" that still identifies with the party is composed of moderates of this sort.) (3) Those non-Brahmins who accepted the minimal ideological redefinition of political, cultural, and historical reality advocated by the Dravidian movement organizations, but who were concerned with the issues of political power rather than social reform. For these non-Brahmins, the non-Brahmin wing in congress was increasingly attractive when it became obvious in the late 1930s and 1940s that independence would be achieved and Congress would be the ruling party in an independent India. This group of "pragmatists" deserted the Justice party in increasing numbers after 1926, when the Swarajists won 41 out of 99 seats in the Madras Presidency legislative elections.[36] They never became involved in the radical activities of the Self-Respect League.

These categories provide an insight into political affiliations in the late 1920s and 1930s. The radicals became involved in Self-Respect League non political activity, while the moderates supported the Justice party, and the pragmatists were drawn to Congress. By the early 1930s, the Congress was making a sustained attempt to attract non-Brahmins. In 1927, the Justice party passed a resolution permitting Justice party members to enter Congress. V. Ramdas, an Andhra Congress member, predicted little change in the Tamil and Telegu areas because

the leading non-Brahmin communities of Kammas and Kapoos were already largely pro-Congress and the anti-Congressmen among them were still dominated by leaders like K. V. Reddi who do not favour Congress entry.

In Tamil Nadu, non-Brahmins will enlist as Congressmen in large numbers; and it is not unlikely that serious efforts will be made to alter the present composition of the Congress organization in . . . Tamil Nadu, especially of the provincial Congress committee. [37]

Ramdas proved correct. During the 1930s many changes occurred in Congress, and non-Brahmins entered Congress in larger numbers.

In 1928, the Rajah of Panagal, an important Justice party leader, died. Although the party won control of the government between 1930 and 1936 after 1929 its decline was precipitous. In his study of the Justice party, Eugene Irschick takes 1929 as the date of the effective demise of the Justice party.

SOCIAL SUPPORT FOR CONGRESS

In 1936, Congress won the elections under the Government of India Act of 1935, and C. Rajagopalacharia became the premier of a Congress government in Madras Presidency. The fact that Congress won in 1936 does not in itself, however, constitute proof that they had majority support. During the 1930s, the political arena was still largely limited to Brahmin and non-Brahmin elites. While Brahmins in large measure supported Congress, the position among non-Brahmins is unclear. Non-Tamil groups, such as Reddiars, Kammas, and so on, supported Congress, but it is difficult to gauge support among important Tamil castes. The fact that the radical adherents of the Self-Respect League were encouraged neither to vote nor to contest office negates voting returns as a reliable measure of majority support even among those eligible to vote. One important indicator of Congress support in pre-Independence Madras Presidency comes from records the British maintained on demonstrators arrested during Congress agitations. Table 3-1 is a record of prisoners detained in the 1942 Quit India movement. The 1942 Quit India movement was one of the largest and most effective movements organized by Congress as part of the independence campaign. Therefore this chart indicates Congress support at its peak.

From table 3-1, it is evident that Brahmins, 3 percent of the population of Madras Presidency, provided 20 percent of the prisoners. Next came the Reddiars, a landowning Telegu-speaking

TABLE 3-1
Male Political Prisoners Detained under Defense of India Rules
Report for Year Ending March 12, 1942

(N = 504)

Caste	Number	Percent
Brahmin	98	19.5
South Indian forward non-Brahmin[a]	175	33.9
Major south Indian backward non-Brahmin[b]	33	4.9
Service castes[c]	3	.5
Non-Hindu religious sects[d]	19	3.4
Major north Indian castes[e]	11	1.8
Untouchables[f]	2	.4
No specific mention of caste	146	29.1
Other castes	17	6.5
	504	100.0

Source: GO 428, August 2, 1943. Subject: Political Agitation Security Prisoners Detained under Defense of India Rules. Report for Year Ending March 12, 1942. 504 Prisoners Detained in: The Central Jail, Vellore; the Penitentiary, Madras; the Borstal School, Palamcottah; The Central Jail, Salem; and the Central Jail, Rajamundry.

[a] Reddiar, Vellala, Naidu, Mudaliar, Nair, Chettiar, Kshatriya, Pillai, Vaisya.
[b] Naicker, Gounder, Nadar, Gramani, Thevar, Maravar, Agambadiya, Servai.
[c] Odiya, Archari.
[d] Jains, Lingayat, Buddhist, Christian, Muslim.
[e] Marwari, Maratha, Rajput, Jat, Sourashtrian, Sikh.
[f] Thiya.

caste of forward non-Brahmins, with 13 percent representation. Vellalas, Naidus, Mudialiars, Nairs, Chettiars, Pillais, ranked in order after Reddiars with 4 percent, 4 percent, 3 percent, 2 percent, 2 percent, and 2 percent representation. Except for Naidus, who are mainly Telegu-speaking, and Nairs, who are Malayali speakers, these represent dominant Tamil-speaking landowning castes. Nairs stand next to Brahmins in the Malabar caste hierarchy, and Naidus are an important commercial and landowning Telegu caste.

We have already noted that Brahmins constituted 20 percent of the prisoners. It is also fruitful to ask which caste or communal groups were under-represented. First, no major Tamil Untouchable groups (Paraiyans, Tottis, etc.) are listed, and only one major Untouchable group is represented, a Thiya. Since Untouchables are approximately 20 percent of the Madras Presidency population, this shows a marked lack of interest and mobilization. Even if these groups were sympathetic, that they were not arrested indicates they were not willing to place themselves in vulnerable positions. Second, there is a dearth of service castes; potters are represented by one person, goldsmiths by two, and in general there are disproportionately few backward castes. The Maravars, Thevars, Agambadiyas, and Servais are vastly under-represented, in spite of their large numbers in the southern Tamil districts of Madurai, Ramnad, and Tirunelveli. Padayachis and Gounders are also under-represented, as are Christians. No Anglo-Indian was arrested. Muslims are present with, 2 percent representation, as are small esoteric religious groups such as Jains and Buddhists.

In general, then, the most significant factors are the extreme over-representation of Brahmins; lack of representation of Untouchables; over-representation of forward non-Brahmins, and under-representation of backward non-Brahmins.

SOCIAL SUPPORT FOR THE SELF-RESPECT MOVEMENT

Social support for the Self-Respect movement is difficult to gauge accurately. We know that forward non-Brahmins supported the movement. We must consider that during this period (the 1930s) there was no large-scale mobilization of backward non-Brahmins or Untouchables and, therefore, that support for the Justice party and Self-Respect movement came from roughly the same groups, Tamil forward non-Brahmin caste Hindus.[38] Although most castes had "caste associations" as early as the 1920s, the existence of restrictions on voting, the petitional style of politics, the dominance of the wealthy and educated in political life, and the use of English as the language of politics meant that relatively few members of backward castes (that is, caste Hindus of low ritual rank and educational and income status) or Untouchables were politically active or politically mobilized.

Of course, the Dravidian movement organizations were important instruments for expanding political consciousness and increasing political mobilization. An important vehicle for this was the advent of vernacular newspapers, which appealed to a large segment of the population. We must recall, however, that this was a cumulative process. The early movements were certainly supported largely by forward-caste Hindus. As the movements developed into the 1940s, larger and larger numbers of backward castes became involved in politics and became politically mobilized.

Perhaps the best evidence suggesting that the early Self-Respect movement was not a mass movement with broad appeal was the attempt by E. V. Ramasami to reorganize the Justice party and the Self-Respect League precisely to attract mass support. In the last analysis, what we know for certain about social support is (1) that there was overlap between support of the Justice party and the Self-Respect movement; (2) that the articles in *Kudi Arasu* were unlikely to be understood by poorly educated people, even though *Kudi Arasu* was a vernacular paper; (3) the English journal *Revolt* was clearly aimed at an educated elite; (4) there was a property qualification on voting that limited effective interest in politics and social matters to the upper classes; (5) methods of political communication and participation of the Self-Respect movement and Justice party were essentially those that involved skills acquired through education and that were based on British liberal assumptions.

DRAVIDA NADU: THE DRAVIDIAN INDEPENDENCE MOVEMENT IS BORN

In the 1936 elections, Congress made a clean sweep, gaining a majority in the Legislative Assembly and taking over the municipalities, district boards, and panchayats. In the biography of E. V. Ramasami, Sitambaranar states, "All the big shots who stood against the Congress were defeated. Because of this many people went away saying that they did not want public life. Some of them joined the Congress."[39] Hence the elections of 1936 represented something of a low point in the fortunes of the Justice party.

Up to this point the Dravidian movement had not engaged in agitational politics. The Congress party, through its inauguration of liquor store picketing, individual satyagraha, salt satyagrahas, protests against untouchability, and so on, had succeeded in introducing agitational politics into Madras Presidency.

The issue that produced the first Dravidian movement agitation was the introduction of Hindustani in certain schools as a compulsory subject. *Kudi Arasu, Revolt,* and *Justice* had opposed both Hindi and Hindustani as northern, Aryan languages as early

as the 1920s.[40] This opposition stemmed logically from their
theory of a Sanskritic, Aryan culture which was Brahmanic and
fundamentally opposed to a non-Brahmin Dravidian culture.
Furthermore, the language issue provided a convenient political
rallying point after the 1936 election debacle.

The introduction of compulsory Hindustani in 1938 was followed by intensive agitation, taking a number of forms. The
residence of the chief minister of Madras (then called the premier)
was picketed, and also certain high schools. A number of meetings
and processions were also held.[41] According to the 1939 Home
Department Administration Report, 536 persons had been arrested
and convicted for participation in the agitation by the end of
1938.[42] This report indicated that "the anti-Hindustani agitation
which had started in June 1938 continued to the outbreak of
the war, but not with the same amount of enthusiasm as in
the previous year." One of the chief non-Brahmin unifying
slogans was, significantly, "Down with Brahmin Raj."[43]

Government Order 597 (April 13, 1940) gives some pertinent
data on the number of people arrested (table 3-2). As can be
seen from this table, the anti-Hindustani agitation was substantial.
Recalling that Madras Presidency contained Telegu, Kannarese,
and Malayam-speaking districts as well as Tamil-speaking districts, it is significant for understanding later political developments that North Arcot, Salem, Trichinopoly, Tanjore, Madurai,
Ramnad, and Tirunelveli had the greatest anti-Hindustani activity. These are all Tamil districts. In Madras City, the anti-Hindustani agitation gained new impetus after the Tamilnadu Women's
Conference was held in November. There E. V. Ramasami was
given the title "Periyar." It was also during the 1938 anti-Hindustani agitation that C. N. Annadurai gained a widespread reputa-

TABLE 3-2

Number of Persons Arrested and Convicted for Picketing up to
January 1, 1939

	Males	Females
In front of premier's residence	173	0
Hindu Theologial High School	449	36
Hindu High School, Triplicane	25	0
	647	36

Also 9 ladies with children

tion as a skillful agitator, propagandist, and organizer.

Perhaps the most important event accompanying the agitation was the demand for a separate Dravida Nadu. This issue united many who were divided on the question of radical social reform. C. Natesa Mudaliar, a moderate conservative, and E. V. Ramasami, a radical, joined in demanding a separate land for the Dravidians.[44] On July 1, 1939, the first "Dravida Nadu Separation Day," speeches were given explaining the genesis of the demand for separation. At the time E. V. Ramasami made the connection between the language issue and the need for separation. The language issue was portrayed as a superficial manifestation of the sinister penetration of Aryan ideas into Tamil culture through the political control of the Brahmins.[45] The slogan "Dravida Nadu for Dravidians" symbolically united the moderates and radicals in the Dravidian movement, as well as galvanizing many sympathizers outside movement organizations.

The Second World War interrupted the anti-Hindustani agitation and diverted attention. The Congress party did not support the Bristish war effort, and organized instead agitations demanding that the British "Quit India." On the other hand, E. V. Ramasami did support the war. His paper was used for propaganda purposes, and was subsidized by the British government during the war years.[46] Between 1939 and the formation of the Dravida Kazhagam in 1944, E. V. Ramasami sought to gain mass support for the Justice party (with marked lack of success, even though most of the major Congress leaders were in jail). In 1939 he met with Sir Stafford Cripps and emphasized the need for a separate Dravida Nadu; in 1943 he met with Jinnah and Dr. Ambedkar, and among other things explained his plan for partition of an independent India.[47]

CONCLUSION: IDENTITY AND DEVELOPING THE POLITICS OF RADICAL SOCIAL REFORM

Radicalization of the Dravidian ideology occurred mainly in the 1930s, but had its roots in activities of E. V. Ramasami, reaching as far back as the 1924 founding of *Kudi Arasu*. During the 1930s, despite increasing Congress popularity as manifested in the 1936 electoral victory and the cleavage between radicals and moderates in the Dravidian movement, "Dravidian" political identity remained salient.

For many moderates, however, their goals had been at least partially achieved with increases in non-Brahmin political power, representation in the British bureaucracy, and reforms in their caste ritual practices. They still continued to demand reform, but rejected radical demands for a total restructuring of society. Although many moderates supported Dravida Nadu separation, they rejected atheism, communism, and the abandonment of Hinduism. Many non-Brahmins did so for pragmatic reasons, while still retaining a strong sense of non-Brahmin comradeship and a self-definition as Dravidians.

The radicals, however, continued to develop the Dravidian movement. In the next chapter we will examine the scope, dimensions, and impact of radical social reform politics.

[1] Sitamparaṇār, *Tamiṛar Talaivar* [Ṭamilian's Leader] (Erode: Kudi Arasu Press, 1939).

[2] *Kudi Arasu* was a Tamil vernacular newspaper that Ramasami used to propagate social reform ideas. Ramasami's surname was Naicker, but he refused to use caste names. He was given the title Periyar ("esteemed") during a 1938 women's conference.

[3] A variant of Hindu philosophy developed by non-Brahmin philosophers. See the *Srila-Sri Arulnandi Sivacharya Swamigal Sivagnana Siddhiyar Endowment Collected Lectures on Saiva Siddhanta 1946-1954* (Annamalai Nagar: Annamalai University: 1965). Also, V. Paranjoti, *Saiva Siddhanta* (London: Luzac, 1954).

[4] *Kudi Arasu*, July 27, 1929.

[5] Interviews with Justice party leaders and supporters.

[6] Information in this section comes from Sitamparanar, *Tamiṛar Talaivar*.

[7] *Ibid.*

[8] Interview with Sir P. T. Rajan.

[9] Madras Native Newspaper Reports, 1921.

[10] Sitamparaṇār, *Tamiṛar Talaivar*.

[11] Literally "zeal for truth," satyagraha involves passive defiance of law, civil disobedience. Travancore-Cochin, now Kerala, was an area where extreme forms of untouchability were practiced.

[12] Sitamparaṇār, *Tamiṛar Talaivar*.

[13] This was suggested by a number of informants.

[14] Gandhi and Congress opposed all forms of alcoholic beverages and requested followers to eliminate the products from which these beverages could be made.

[15] *Kudi Arasu*, May 11, 1933.

[16] *Ibid.*

[17] *Ibid.*

[18] The Madras Presidency Association grew out of a meeting by Congress non-Brahmins held on September 20, 1917. The purpose was to develop a proposal to give non-Brahmins full communal representation under the Montagu-Chelmsford reforms. See Irschick, *Politics and Social Conflict*, p. 61.

[19] India, Tamil Nadu, Government Order No. 122, October 17, 1919.

[20] *Ibid.* This analysis by the Government of India of the 1919 elections tends, parenthetically, to support the earlier assertions concerning the centrality of

non-Brahmin elites. The Tirunelveli Vellalas described above are both a dominant land-owning caste and highly orthodox.

[21] See Appendix A for data on appointments by caste and year.

[22] The Montagu-Chelmsford Report, published in July 1918, committed the British government to the principle of increased participation by Indians in the administration of India by means of dyarchy. This concept created a division of functions in the provinces between the official half of the government, and the non-official half, responsible to an Indian elected majority in the Provincial Legislative Councils. The Justice party worked these reforms. (See Irschick, *Politics and Social Conflict*, pp. 89ff.)

[23] *Ibid.*, p. 192.

[24] See *Andhra Patrika*, April 6, 1923, for example. Also *Sudarsini*, June 15, 1923.

[25] *Andhra Patrika*, May 3, 1923. The term Adi-Dravida is used for all Untouchables by adherents of the Dravidian movement.

[26] For a complete discussion of the history of the Justice party in power, see Irschick, *Politics and Social Conflict*.

[27] *Revolt* 1, No. 16 (February 20, 1929).

[28] *Ibid.*

[29] *Ibid.*

[30] *Ibid.*

[31] Irschick, *Politics and Social Conflict*, p. 60.

[32] *Ibid.*

[33] *Ibid.*, p. 163. Pillai joined the Justice party in 1920.

[34] *Ibid.*

[35] Non-Brahmins, however, were not satisfied by the number of seats granted by this award. See Irschick, *Politics and Social Conflict*, p. 164-166 for a discussion of Merton's award.

[36] Great Britain, Indian Statutory Commission, Vol. 6, Memorandum submitted to the Statutory Commission by the Madras Government, p. 17. Quoted in Irschick, *Politics and Social Conflict*, p. 313.

[37] *Ibid.*, p. 320.

[38] Interviews with Self-Respect leaders confirm this interpretation. To the extent that backward non-Brahmins and Untouchables were involved in politics, most groups did tend to support the Self-Respect League rather than Congress.

[39] Sitamparaṇār, *Tamirar Talaivar*.

[40] See the Madras Native Newspaper Reports for the 1920s.

[41] India, Tamil Nadu, Government Order 3755. Home Administration Report for 1939.

[42] *Ibid.*

[43] *Ibid.*

[44] Pannerselvam, Rajan, Ramasami, and C. Natesa Mudaliar all supported the Dravida Nadu demand.

[45] See E. V. Ramasami's speech at the First Dravida Nadu Separation Day, reported in Sitamparaṇār, *Tamirar Talaivar*.

[46] India, Tamil Nadu, Government Order 2489, October 19, 1945.

[47] Sitamparaṇār, *Tamiṛar Talaivar*.

CHAPTER FOUR

The Dravida Kazhagam, the Dravida Munnetra Kazhagam, and Radical Politics in a Changing Political Arena

MOBILIZATION OF THE BACKWARD CASTES

RADICAL Dravidian movement politics must be analyzed within the contex of the transformation of the political arena that took place during the 1940s in Madras Presidency. What emerged was a pattern of slow transformation of politics in Madras Presidency from the 1890s through 1940s. During the late nineteenth century, politics was very much a Brahmin enterprise that included a few forward non-Brahmin elites. While Brahmins became politically mobilized in the later nineteenth century, most forward non-Brahmin castes did not aggressively enter the political arena until the 1920s. Only during the 1940s did significant numbers of backward non-Brahmin castes demand a greater share of government appointments, power, and influence. And during the 1940s, the advent of universal manhood suffrage gave impetus to mass political participation.

Prior to the 1940s backward castes in Madras Presidency could be divided into three categories, according to political activity. First are those castes that had an active caste association composed of educated members able to represent the caste politically. This category included castes such as the Nadars, Naickers, and Viswakama "Brahmins" (Acharis—Viswakama "Brahmins" claim Brahmin status but are really a backward service caste). Second are those castes with ineffectual associations, but with leaders in important positions. Figuring most prominently in this category is the Muukoolathur cluster of castes, composed of Maravars, Thevars, Kallers, and Agamudiars.[1] In the third category are the vast majority of backward castes, with weak associations, and about whose political activity and support one knows very little during this period. This includes most of the service castes.

Linked to the increasing mobilization of the backward castes in the 1940s is an equally important change: the breakdown, for political and administrative purposes, of the "non-Brahmin" category into two distinct segments, forward non-Brahmins and backward non-Brahmins. Increasingly, backward non-Brahmin caste organizations used some of the same arguments against under-representation that had been used in the 1920s by forward non-Brahmins against Brahmins. This dichotomization left the forward, or elite, non-Brahmins in a difficult minority position. The Madras Provincial Backward Classes League claimed that backward non-Brahmins constituted fifty per cent of the Presidency population. Whether or not this was correct, it is nevertheless true that separate mobilization of the backward non-Brahmins left the elite, or forward, non-Brahmins somewhat politically isolated. With the increasing mobilization of the backward castes, therefore, non-Brahmins, as a political community, seemed threatened by fragmentation. The term "non-Brahmin" masked economic, social, and cultural heterogeneity that was difficult to bridge.

However, the concept of a Dravidian community and a Dravidian identity, present in nascent form since the 1900s, was reinforced, elaborated, and linked to linguistic politics by the 1938 anti-Hindustani agitation. That agitation was organized by C. N. Annadurai, but sanctioned by E. V. Ramasami. During the 1938 agitation, the Dravida Kazhagam demanded Dravida Nadu as a separate, independent home for Dravidians. This was a meaningful goal for both forward and backward non-Brahmins. It was also the basis for the broader cultural nationalist appeal and expanded mobilization that characterized the 1960s.

This chapter examines the emergence of the Dravida Kazhagam and Dravida Munnetra Kazhagam and their attempts to increase support for radical goals in the changing political arena of the 1940s and early 1950s. The manner in which they chose to do so shaped the way Dravidian political identity was internalized by masses of Tamilians.

It becomes important to know who these backward non-Brahmins were, and to outline how they perceived themselves and their relationship to Dravidian ideology and political identity. "Awakening" of the backward classes began in the 1930s. The Madras Provincial Backward Classes League was formed in 1934 to present grievances to the British government. From that time, they held regular meetings, conducted conferences in different parts of the province, and sought concessions and facilities for the educational, economic, and other advancement of the backward communities.[2] Although backward caste associations were formed, participation largely consisted of the elites of these castes.

There was not overwhelming involvement among the backward classes in the Congress movement, however the debates of that period and the Congress agitations created a heightened awareness, not only of politics, but of a new concept in politics: the importance of numbers rather than wealth or ritual status. The first issue that immediately involved the backward castes was the Communal Government Order and its distribution of reserved places in the administration.

SOCIAL, CULTURAL, AND POLITICAL PERSPECTIVES OF THE BACKWARD CASTES[3]

In view of the importance, of backward castes, it is pertinent to look closely at the way they perceived the political arena of the 1940s. A most revealing document is a Government Order containing the speeches delivered to the 1943 Madras Provincial Backward Classes League.[4]

The welcome address to this conference stated:

The first and foremost thing that is required at present is the unification of the different Backward Classes of this province and setting our organization on a proper footing and strong basis through sustained effort of the leaders of the various Backward Classes.

The educational advancement of the Backward Classes should constitute the main plank in the programme of our ameliorative endeavors. No effort should be spared in this direction, as it is education that gives consciousness of power and strength which is highly essential for any assertion of rights and claims. The next thing that should engage our attention is the representation of Backward Classes in public services. The arrangement embodied in the communal G.O. gives undue and over-representation to certain communities far out of proportion to their population. There is an urgent need therefore for an immediate revision of the communal G.O., making special provision for the Backward Classes, treating them as a separate entity. The fact that *out of about 2100 gazetted appointments in the Madras government* only about 50 or 2 per cent are occupied by the Backward Classes will speak volumes. [My emphasis.][5]

This demand for a readjustment in communal representation is extremely enlightening. In an earlier memorandum, backward caste leaders had strenuously objected to being classified with "forward" non-Brahmins in the allocation of jobs and seats in universities:

We may be permitted to point out that most of the Backward Classes are not in any way better than the scheduled Classes and some of them such as certain hill tribes are more backward than scheduled classes themselves. It will therefore be seen that the grouping of the backward communities along with the forward non-Brahmin communities has been disadvantageous to the Backward Classes since most of the seats allotted for the non-Brahmins are taken up by the forward non-Brahmins such as Malayalis, Mudaliars, Naidus, Reddys, etc.[6]

The Madras Provincial Backward Classes League attached a table (table 4-1) to their memorandum to strengthen their case.
The crux of their complaint concerning administrative posts

TABLE 4-1
Communal Representation in the Madras Presidency
Administration, 1944

Communities	Population in lakhs	Percent of population	Number of posts	Percent of posts
Brahmins	15	3	820	37
Christians	20	4	190	9
Muhammadans	37	7	150	7
Depressed classes [Untouchables]	70	14	25	1.5
Forward Non-Brahmins	113	22	620	27
Backward Non-Brahmins	245	50	50	2

Source: Table attached to GO 190 Containing Memorandum from Madras Provincial Backward Classes Association, 1944. One Lakh = 10,000. Table does not include figures for Europeans and Eurasians.

was that both the forward non-Brahmins and the Brahmins were advanced communities, and that it was the backward non-Brahmins who really suffered discrimination. Furthermore, attempts to remedy Brahmin domination in the services had only led to creation of more jobs for elite non-Brahmins.

Given that position, we can understand their attitude toward the major political parties in the presidency. The association leaders were positively oriented toward the British (at a time when Congress support was at its pre-Independence peak) and expected British support and sympathy: "Illiteracy and the caste system have shunted our people to a remote corner; there they sit lamenting over their fate. But I believe we have no reason to be despondent. We may count on the British to come to our aid and they will help us, even as they have helped the depressed classes [Untouchables] to come forward. . . . We can get the same help, provided we agitate constitutionally." They were ambivalent about the Congress:

How are we to attain our political salvation? Are we to work it out alone, or are we to ally ourselves with the political parties which now hold the field? The depressed classes [Untouchables] have organized themselves sufficiently well and their voices are sufficiently heard by government. . . . As for the Congress party, I am afraid we cannot ally ourselves with it at the present moment. . . . They are extremists. Government have been viewing all their activities with suspicion, and the Congress people suspect every move of the government. *I cannot definitely say that they as a body are in sympathy with the aspirations of the Backward Classes.* For example, when the time was ripe for dealing a death blow to the Deva Dasi[7] system of South India, the Madras Congress Cabinet made only a feeble attempt to promote this long-pending legislation (emphasis added).[8]

The Justice Party received somewhat less harsh treatment: "As for the Justice Party, it is practically not functioning because the high idealism of leaders like Dr. T. M. Nair and the Raja of Panagal were [sic] soon lost sight and ultimately it degenerated into a job-hunting party." However, both the Justice party and the Congress were perceived as having failed the backward classes. The Self-Respect movement too, was not spared: "As for the Self-Respect party, *Ramasami Periyar who had the rare opportunity of bringing about social reconstruction in South India drifted himself into politics and allowed himself to be dragged on by the chariot wheel of the Justice Party. The result is that he is neither here nor there.* [My emphasis.][9]

The conclusion of this discussion of the strength and weaknesses of the major parties was that "Under these circumstances, it is neither wise nor safe for the vast body of the Hindu Backward Classes to ally themselves or cast their lot with any of these political parties. It follows that we have to work out our salvation independently of all these parties." As an alternative, it was suggested that

> I believe you will all agree with me that we should be satisfied for the present, with Dominion status within the British Commonwealth. If this is our goal, we should organize ourselves as an independent nationalist party, devise ways and means from now on to send duly qualified representatives to the legislatures as soon as the new political structure is framed, whatever may be its form or scope in the new era. When once we accept this as our goal, *it should not be open to the members of the Backward Classes to play the truant and join this or that party according to their whims and fancies. We should all sink or swim together.* [My emphasis.][10]

After Independence, political parties appeared composed almost entirely of one or more backward class groups. The foundations for this development were laid in the 1944 conference. "Backward" classes represented the greatest single political plum in a system of universal manhood suffrage.

Among the communities that joined together in the Backward Classes Association were two prominent caste clusters, the Vanniya Kula Kshatriyas, and the Muukoolathur.[11] Also involved were Nadars, Gramanis, service castes (such as Viswakama "Brahmins" [Acharis], and Ambattans), and many other small castes.[12] Since the two most important caste clusters were the Muukoolathur and Vanniya Kula Kshatriya groups, I shall focus on them briefly.

The Vanniya Kula Kshatriya[13] consists of Vanniyas, Padayachis, Gounders, and Naickers. These castes are concentrated in the districts of North Arcot, South Arcot, and Salem, where they are the local majority. They are by and large landless agricultural workers or small landowners, with low ritual status.

Padayachies are ranked above the other castes in the Vanniya group. Traditionally, they had no special ritual relationship or alliance with Brahmins. The districts where the Vanniya Kula Kshatriyas predominate are areas where nonvegetarian Mudaliars (Arcot Mudaliars) and Naidus (a Telegu-speaking upper non-Brahmin caste) tend to be important landowners, while Muslims predominate in commerce.[14]

In the 1940s the Vanniya Kula Kshatriya castes had not attained a degree of education comparable to the elite non-Brahmins discussed earlier. Furthermore, there is no indication that Vanniya Kula Kshatriya urbanization was a threat to their caste identity; in fact, it may well have represented an opportunity for advancement and enhancement of their status. And most importantly, because they had no special traditional ritual relationship with Brahmins, the symbol "Suddhra" was not a central emotioal rallying point for them.

The Muukoolathur cluster is in many ways similar to the Vanniya Kula Kshatriyas.[15] They predominate in the southern districts of Madras Presidency, particularly Ramnad, Madurai, and to some extent Trichy and Tirunelveli and are composed of Maravar, Kallar, Thevar, and Agamudiar castes. A 1957 Government Order, written as a result of several clashes between Maravars and Untouchables, conveys the flavor of the Muukoolathur ambience. This description of Maravars in one taluk (administrative subdivision of a district) could easily apply to large areas in the southern part of the presidency.

> Maravars form the majority community in the Mudukulathur [taluk] area with about 45 per cent of the total population. The Harijans are next in importance with about 20 per cent. Harijans, Chaklis, Dhobies and other minority communities having been subordinate and subservient to the Maravars and live in eternal fear because of the Maravar reputation for being ruthless, aggressive, unreasonable and violent.
>
> Every Maravar in this area considers himself superior to any other non-Marava and take offense if he tries to be on equal terms with the Marava. Local officials also fear . . . the Maravars because either the officers' lives are in danger if they offend the Maravas and also cases are easily concocted

against them and evidence is arranged. Maravars in this area are poorly educated, lethargic and mostly criminals.[16]

The report goes on to quote Thurston's *Castes and Tribes of South India:* "The Maravars of today, as members of a caste which is numerous and influential, as a man of superior physique and bold independent spirit, thief and robber, village policeman and detective combined, is an immense power in the land."[17]

The GO then describes the Maravars as fighting to maintain their position:

> They are proud of the caste heritage and would brook nobody else other than a Marava holding sway in the Maravanad. Their education being poor they are not able to reconcile with the present democratic conditions, and cannot accept the disappearance of a feudal system.
>
> . . . With the increasing education and association with the Missionaries, large numbers of Harijans having been converted to Christianity, have become conscious of their rights. They are increasingly demanding their rightful place in society and nowadays refuse to be cowed down by the Maravars. The Maravars have become infuriated with the open defiance by Harijans and their refusal to pay the customary homage to the Marava, i.e., to remove the shoes, walking with barefoot and remove the upper cloths whenever he saw a Marava. . . . In short the Maravar is fighting hard to retain his slowly dwindling dominant position in the local society and clings to the last vestiges of feudal rights.[18]

This description conveys a vivid picture of the Muukoolathur. Although this GO was written in 1957, the situation was already developing in the 1940s. The activities of the missionaries in the southern districts date back, in fact, at least a century. Robert Hardgrave reports that the Maravars and the Nadars (at that time a low-ranked caste of toddy tappers) had a history of communal clashes in the early part of the nineteenth century.[19] The Maravars, then, represent a different kind of dominant caste, the numerically dominant caste that uses force to maintain its position. As we can see from these reports, the orientation of the Maravars was to maintain their position vis-à-vis castes below them. In the districts where the Muukoolathur are located, the ritually superior non-Brahmin castes are Nairs, some Mudaliars, Pillais, Chettiars, and, of greatest importance, the highly ranked Tirunelveli Vellalas. In business and commerce, the Chettiars, traditionally a wealthy merchant community, and some newly-rich Nadars are important (in recent years the Nadars have progressed dramatically. One segment of the caste, "business Nadars" are generally considered economically prosperous).

As in the Vanniya Kula Kshatriya case, the symbol of "Suddhrahood" was not of central emotional importance to the Muukoolathur. They had not traditionally allied with Brahmins, and did not see them as a relevant reference group.

Most backward castes were agricultural laborers or small landowners. Where dominant, their preeminence rested on other backward castes below them, particularly Untouchables. Modernization and social change brought immediate threats from below. As backward castes became more educated and politically mobilized, they saw a dual challenge: preserving their traditional superiority to Untouchables, and displacing forward non-Brahmins in the British administration.

Although the case of the Muukoolathur groups stands out because of their frequent resort to violence, the position of the Vanniya Kula Kshatriyas is not essentially different.[20] They, too, are concerned about maintaining their superiority to untouchables and to those service castes below them. Although it is difficult to get information for every backward caste, generally their positions are similar.

We can see from these summary descriptions of the Vanniya Kula Kshatriyas and the Muukoolathur the sense in which backward castes were backward. Not unlike the ideological label "non-Brahmin," the label "backward" masks a complicated social reality. First, among backward castes there are wealthier individuals or even wealthier subcastes and segments within the caste.[21] In a given district, a backward group may also in fact be a dominant group, such as the Muukoolathurs. All of these castes (taken as a whole) are ritually low ranked, less wealthy, and poorer educated than the elite non-Brahmins and Brahmins discussed earlier. However, perception of oneself as "backward" and linked to other "backward" individuals represents a widening of horizons and perceptions about social structure, since "backward," like "forward" and "non-Brahmin," are relative, not absolute categories, and are more inclusive than single caste titles. The distinction of "forward" from "backward" can also be seen in the differential concern over the label "Suddhra," and concomitant involvement in the advancing fortunes of upper and lower castes. But the problem for the Dravidian movement was how "backwardness" could be articulated into the concept of Dravidian political identity.

The perceptions and propensities of the backward non-Brahmins set the stage and provided the critical context for a post-Independence politics based on universal manhood suffrage. Increased backward caste political awakening during the 1940s was another indication to members of Dravidian movement organizations (Justice party and Self-Respect League) that henceforth effective political associations and parties would have to be organized on a mass basis.

FORMATION OF THE DRAVIDA KAZHAGAM

E. V. Ramasami was elected president of the Justice party while serving a jail term for his activities in the 1938 anti-Hindustani agitation. Although the Dravida Kazhagam was organized in 1944, its roots lay in the decline of the Justice party during the late 1930s and the hope for rejuvenation of the Dravidian movement after the 1938 anti-Hindustani agitation.

Under E. V. Ramasami's leadership, the Justice party was not successful in mobilizing mass support or in changing the image of the party. In some ways this reflected the continued presence of conservatives in the party, but also involved E. V. Ramasami's perspective, shaped by turn-of-the-century issues and methods. Hence in 1940, well past the period when petitions to the British government were an effective means of political action, and after the Justice party had successfully established the principal of communal representation, E. V. Ramasami was still writing the governor of Madras complaining that the communal rule had not been observed and that Brahmins were over-represented in the services.[22] By the mid-1940s, it became obvious to key leaders in the Justice party and Self-Respect movement that a new effort was needed to rejuvenate the Dravidian movement and to gain mass support.

The Dravida Kazhagam grew out of the 1944 Salem Conference of the Justice party. At that conference Annadurai proposed four resolutions:

1. Those who had received titles of honour such as Rao Bahadur, Diwan Bahadur, Sir, Saheb, etc. which were conferred by the British, should immediately abandon these titles, and nobody should receive these titles in the future.

2. Those who hold positions of honour such as Honorary Presidency Magistrate, leader of the local Panchayat, etc. should immediately resign these posts forever.

3. The suffix to names which connote caste should immediately be abandoned and in the future nobody should use these special names.

4. The South Indian Liberal Federation (Justice Party) should be changed into Dravida Kazhagam forthwith.[23]

The DMK official history is remarkably candid in explaining the reasons for those resolutions and their relationship to formation of the Dravida Kazhagam:

The opposition had hitherto created a wrong impression in the minds of the people, that the Justice Party was a rich man's party, that the party had underhand dealings with the British for whose benefit it was functioning and that the entire structure of the party was incompatible with any idea or notion of freedom. Aringnar [genius] Anna [Annadurai] worked ceaselessly to allay these fears of the people and to erase the misapprehension. His strenuous efforts culminated in the drafting of novel schemes for the uplift of the non-Brahmins.[24]

It seems obvious from the above passage that the formation of the Dravida Kazhagam (or, more precisely, renaming the old Justice party) was at least partially a public relations move, an attempt to create a new image. There were both external (public relations) and internal (organizational) reasons for this. Internally, the Annadurai resolutions represented a direct challenge to the wealthy, titled conservatives in the party. While E. V. Ramasami wanted these people out to "purify" the party, we can postulate that Annadurai wanted them out to improve the party's image. Externally, the change in name and image was an attempt to identify with increasingly popular anti-British feelings without going as far as demanding independence. Destruction of the image of a privileged elite was designed to make the party appealing to newly mobilizing social groups, particularly backward castes.

Those who initiated the Salem coup were agreed on the desirability of a new image and a mass movement. However, a "mass" movement apparently meant different things to different people. When E. V. Ramasami was made president of the Justice party in 1939, conservatives supported the move because they hoped he could revive the party enough to lure back members who had left after the 1936 Congress electoral victory. For many conservatives, support of the "masses" implied the majority of the elite rather than the majority of the people.

For Annadurai, a mass movement meant the majority of the people, and he therefore was most concerned with developing support among the backward castes. He wanted to enter elections and achieve his goals through parliamentary politics.

E. V. Ramasami's conception of a mass party was distinct from either the conservative or the majoritarian (Annadurai) position. It is useful to look at Periyar's views on the 1936 elections to explicate his esoteric perspective. In a speech before the elections he stated, "I will feel happy if the Justice Party is defeated and I feel that the propaganda for the movement would be stronger, since we would have the support of the non-Brahmins for the Self-Respect movement. If the Justice Party wins, the leaders and those who attained positions might neglect us. Hence the defeat of the Justice Party would be a tool to get the scattered non-Brahmins together and work hard."[25]

Then in *Kudi Arasu* (April 25, 1937), after the elections, E. V. Ramasami discussed those who left the party to join the Congress:

Now many people change from party to party . . . . Since the recent foolish election has shown that all those who want jobs and posts should join the Congress, now the people who want positions and those who will not have any respect if they do not have these positions and those who have no other goal in life are fast joining the Congress.

It is a problem whether we are to feel happy or sad about this. It is my opinion that we should feel happy about this.

All those in the Justice Party, who had positions and power
and administered, earned a bad name for the party and were
the cause of the defeat of the party and just when we were
unable to push them away from the party, they themselves
are going away, hence what other proof do we need to show
that the Justice Party is being purified.[26]

So for E. V. Ramasami, the relevant "mass" was ideologically
defined. He wanted a party of those firmly committed to social
reform views, who would then convince the rest. Until social
reconstruction was achieved, elections were an anathema to him.
This distinction between Annadurai and E. V. Ramasami is central
to understanding the internal factionalism of the Dravida Kazhagam, as well as the divergent paths the two Dravidian movement
organizations (the Dravida Kazhagam and the Dravida Munnetra
Kazhagam) took after the split in 1949.

The conflicting political perceptions inherent in the Dravida
Kazhagam from its inception erupted in 1947 over the issue
of the party's position on achievement of Indian Independence.
E. V. Ramasami declared August 15 (Independence Day) a day
of mourning. Annadurai publicly disclaimed identification with
E. V. Ramasami's stand. Some party papers supported Annadurai's position, others E. V. Ramasami's. Annadurai explained
his viewpoint in *Dravida Nadu*:

We the Dravidians, have been emphasizing that we should
not be under the British rule ever since 1939. Even at a time,
when the country was in ferment with anti-Hindi agitation,
in the Madras conference, we demanded complete freedom
and autonomy for us. For years, it has been our endeavor
and our cherished wish also, that we should be free from
foreign yoke. But today, after abolishing alien rule, the
Congress is trying to impose Aryan domination. We oppose
the Congress solely on this ground.[27]

Annadurai also resolved to emulate the Congress example in
the fight to gain Dravidam for the Dravidians, and then added,
"to be worthy to emulate them it is only fair and proper that
we respect them and pay our homage."[28]

In a sense, by 1947 the Salem chickens had come home to
roost for E. V. Ramasami. He had been too closely involved
with the British to support Congress achievement of Indepen-

dence without separation of Dravida Nadu and without radical social reform. His position had been that reform should precede independence. His identification with the British was implicitly criticized in the Salem resolutions, but he accepted it to rid the party of dead wood. The 1944 Salem resolutions, although attempting to capitalize on the popular opposition to the British, did not call for direct support of the Independence movement. By 1947, however, it was no longer feasible for Annadurai (who wanted to mobilize large numbers) to take a middle-of-the-road position: it was politically imperative for him to go on record in support of Independence.

Although the Dravida Kazhagam split did not occur until 1949, tensions in the party persisted after the 1947 incident. Lines of opposition were drawn, and it was only a matter of time before a formal split. Meanwhile, the Dravida Kazhagam was slowly developing support. From an initial membership of 7,369 in 1944, it increased to 49,574 in 1946 and 75,000 by 1949.

FORMATION OF THE DMK

After the August 15, 1947, incident, when E. V. Ramasami and C. N. Annadurai publicly disagreed over party policy on Indian Independence, Annadurai curbed his party activities. He even failed to attend the important Dravida Kazhagam conference on Dravida Nadu separation held in October 1947. Between October 1947, and October 1948, however, E. V. Ramasami and Annadurai managed to achieve at least a partial reapproach-ment, and at the 1948 Dravida Kazhagam conference at Erode, Annadurai was announced as E. V. Ramasami's successor. At that conference, E. V. Ramasami said:

I have been in public life for well over forty years and I am over seventy years old. How long can I go on serving? My health is failing, but at the same time our Kazhagam is ever growing beyond the limits envisioned by us. So long I had taken upon myself the sole responsibility of conducting the affairs of the organization and I do not want this to continue any longer. There are many people in the organization who are prepared to render relentless service for the organization. Why, Annadurai alone is enough. He is educated, endowed with good intellect, a prolific writer, a great orator and above

all one who has captivated all of you, he is young and he
alone is enough to lead us. So far as I am concerned, I have
become aged and it is only proper that I entrust my responsibilities to another, like a father to a son. Therefore, in your
august presence, today, I hand over the keys of the organization
to Anna.[29]

In spite of these compliments, in early 1949, as a result of
new intraparty friction, E. V. Ramasami changed his mind. In
the June 28, 1949 *Viduthalai,* he announced his impending
marriage (at 71) to a 29-year-old party worker, and named her
as his new successor. His comments on that occasion were very
revealing.

I have completely understood the psychology of the masses
especially in the lower rungs. Even though for all practical
purposes, I will agree to everything, I will be stern regarding
policies and ideals. Though this attitude of mind has earned
me the displeasure of many of my friends, I am able to conduct
the organization smoothly only because of this tendency
irrespective of what other people think about me . . . . Since
I consider it unnecessary at this stage to convince those who
have no faith in me or in my actions, I am not going to dwell
on this subject now. Therefore, as has been explained by
me for the last four or five months in various public meetings,
in my writings and in line with my talks with C. R. Achariar
[C. Rajagopalacharia]. . . I have decided to make Maniammal
with whom I have been in close association for the last five
or six years and who has also identified herself with my own
interests and the interests of the movement, as my legal
successor.[30]

There are a number of interesting aspects to this excerpt.
First, it indicates E. V. Ramasami's autocratic approach to party
leadership. His autocratic control over the party was a major
complaint of Annadurai and other junior leaders, and their
complaint seems to be at least partially justified.

Second, it is notable that E. V. Ramasami states that C.
Rajagopalacharia, a Brahmin, former premier (chief minister)
of Madras Presidency, and the person against whom the 1938
anti-Hindustani agitation had been directed, was his advisor

in this matter! C. Rajagopalacharia was E. V. Ramasami's lawyer, and remains his friend. Although this disjunction between personal conduct and public ideology seems inconceivable, it reveals an extremely important fact about the Dravida Kazhagam. One must take very seriously the party's stated desire to destroy the caste system and not Brahmins per se. E. V. Ramasami repeatedly reiterated that his goal was destruction of the caste system, and not attacks on specific Brahmins. Although other leaders were more vitriolic and specifically anti-Brahmin, E. V. Ramasami is a more complex personality. I interpret statements like "If you see a Brahmin and a snake on the road, kill the Brahmin first" as metaphoric devices meant to encapsulate the complex ideas of the movement for mass appeal. These were ways of personalizing this abstract cultural and ideological struggle, E. V. Ramasami's belief that he "completely understood the psychology of the masses especially in the lower rungs," is indicative of his theoretical orientation toward gaining support from different elements in society.

His statement in a *Hindu* article gives some insight into his views on Brahmins and Brahminism. E. V. Ramasami wrote:

"The Dravidians have a distinct origin in society, their languages are independent and belong to a separate class. The terms 'Aryan' and 'Dravidian' are not my inventions. They are historical realities. They can be found in any school boy's textbook. That the Ramayana is an allegoric representation of the invading Aryans and the domiciled Dravidians has been accepted by all historians including Pandit Nehru and all reformers including Swami Vivekananda. My desire is not to perpetuate this difference but to unify the two opposing elements in society. I am not a believer in the race theory as propounded by the late Nazi leader of Germany . . . . None can divide the South Indian people into two races by means of any blood test. It is not only suicidal but most reactionary. But the fundamental difference between the two different cultures, Aryan and Dravidian, cannot be refuted by anyone who has closely studied the daily life, habits and customs and literature of these two distinct elements in South India."[31]

Unlike others of his era, and in fact, unlike many contemporary

Tamilians, E. V. Ramasami was not arguing that the Brahmins were a separate race. Until recently the belief that Aryan and Dravidian were racial differences was widespread.

An important feature of the 1949 *Viduthalai* article was E. V. Ramasami's assertion that he would be stern regarding policies and ideals. This is pertinent to the conflict over entry into electoral politics. As we have seen, as early as 1936, while in the Justice party, he felt that office holding and elections had an adverse effect on the party. He supposed that inevitably the ideology of the organization would have to be modified in order to compete successfully in elections.

It should not be assumed that because Annadurai was willing to contest elections and wanted to use a different political style that he was ideologically more conservative than E. V. Ramasami. Annadurai's speeches and writings from the 1930s, 1940s, and part of the 1950s are extremely radical. Perhaps the best example of Annadurai's work as a propagandist is *Aryan Illusion (Ā-riyamāyai)*. Written in 1943, it eventually became one of the key books stating the ideology of the movement. Even for nonmembers of Dravidian movement organizations, *Aryan Illusion* has become a minor classic in modern Tamil.

Although the general outlines of the *Aryan Illusion* argument have been presented elsewhere, it is useful, given the importance of Annadurai's radicalism, to examine his ideological approach. In *Aryan Illusion*, Annadurai undertakes a thorough explication of the cultural foundations of the Dravidian movement. He was critical of the Puranas and other Hindu epics, and argued that Dravidians should not call themselves Hindus, because (among other reasons) "we are not prepared to admit that the obscene anecdotes in the Puranas are the playful activities of our Gods." About Tamilians and Aryans, he had this to say:

> It is an indisputable fact that in ancient times, the Tamilians excelled in intelligence, efficiency, business and cottage industries. The history of many countries bears evidence of this. But the Aryans, who came in the middle polluted the Tamilian culture and resorted to many devices to perpetrate their own glory and their own supremacy, pushing to the background the Tamilian civilization.

> In the course of time the false propaganda resorted to by the Aryans that the Aryans conquered the Tamilians in battle,

that they were driven beyond the Vindhyas to the South and that it was only after the advent of the Aryans that civilization and culture began to spread into India gradually gained prominence. There is no concrete evidence to prove that the Aryans invaded India and destroyed the Dravidians. The Aryans show the Vedas, their own creation as an evidence to substantiate this point.[32]

The Indus Valley excavations are cited as grounds for construction of a different historical interpretation.

From the findings of the Indian plains and Mohenjodaro, it is evident that even before the Aryan civilization, there was another civilization. It is therefore a matter for serious consideration whether there is any truth in the contention that civilization could have spread from the South to the North or from the East to the West or vice-versa. When viewed according to the old evidence we have only to say that the Aryans came to India only at a very late stage.[33]

On the nature of the ancient Dravidian civilization: "If we believe the customs and practices of the South Indians, we come to know that there was a subcontinent in the South, a major part of which has corroded into the sea and that in those regions there flourished a wonderful civilization."[34] On the irony of Aryan superiority today: "By the irony of fate, the people who came here with their cattle, badly in search of a place for living, have today become our rulers and masters; the Aryans by intoxicating us with their stories of imagination, have perverted us and have plunged us into desolation and the gloom of Brahminism."[35] And, finally, a call to action: "Our people will be liberated from ignorance only on the day we are freed from the Aryan Illusion! Success is ours!"[36]

Annadurai's ideological approach addresses itself to four concerns: description and statement of the nature of the oppression; statement of reasons for the oppression; elaboration of an alternative, "the good society"; and, finally, suggestion of a program and a call to action. The *Aryan Illusion* deftly handles these four questions. The key oppressive structure is the Hindu caste system; the main reason for the maintenance of caste oppression is the "false consciousness" of the Dravidians, that is, belief in the "Aryan Illusion," hierarchical Hinduism. The alternative is an egalitarian society replicating the idealized ancient Dravidian one; the prerequisite is rejection of the Aryan Illusion, including belief in Hinduism and Aryan (Brahmin) superiority. For these purposes "rational" propaganda must be spread (anti-caste, anti-Hinduism), and a separate Dravida Nadu secured, where Dravidians could organize a "rational" society.

After formation of the DMK, Annadurai repeatedly affirmed adherence to DK principles. However, the question of his radicalism and sincerity (and by implication the commitment of top DMK leaders) is too crucial simply to accept public statements. One political scientist believes, in fact, that Annadurai was insincere about Dravida Nadu.[37] I shall return to the Dravida Nadu question later; here the key issue is radicalism. Dravida Nadu was demanded (at least initially) to facilitate achievement of social reform. Partition of a nation need not fundamentally change cultural models or behavior patterns. In contrast, the call for social reform—abolition of caste, nonadherence to Hinduism, restructuring of philosophical beliefs and historical assumptions (such as the introduction of egalitarianism into a hierarchical society)—was revolutionary. So, the issue of commitment in 1949 revolves around the question of social reform.

Convincing evidence comes from two political leaders who would have no motive in presenting a false picture of leadership commitment to social reform but, in fact, might have an interest in discrediting motives of DMK leaders. They were both top leaders of the party until 1960 or so, and left after intraparty conflict. The first is E.V.K. Sampath, nephew of E. V. Ramasami, and in 1949, a follower of Annadurai and second in command in the DMK. He states that the "DK and DMK had the same principles,"[38] and that "the DMK was criticizing all the same things as 'Periyar' but using gentler words and a gentler approach."[39] Asked if the DMK criticized Hinduism, he said, "the DMK was critical of Hinduism itself, in the same way as Periyar."[40] Asked if the leadership started to deemphasize social reform as early as 1953-1954, he stated that "no, even as late as 1959 and 1960, the DMK had a strong idea of social reform."[41]

Another, perhaps better, corroboration comes from V. P. Raman, a Brahmin who joined the DMK in 1957. Since Raman was not among the founders of the DMK, he would not even have that reason for distorting their views. This exchange comes from an interview:

> *Question:* What about social reform, were they [DMK leadership] serious about that?
>
> *Raman:* If the DMK Leadership had clear ideas about anything, they had clear ideas about social reform. They were clear about two things; they were keen on the abolition of caste and the development of a rational approach—the abolition of superstition. Most of the leaders were powerful writers and were doing a lot of good work in this field.[42]

Formation of the DMK took place after E.V.K. Sampath reconnoitered Madras Presidency in 1949, assessing potential support. Recalling that period, in an interview, Sampath stated,

> For forming the DMK I was the main force in those days. No one was bold enough to rebel against Periyar and organize a party. Actually Annadurai pleaded with me to go to the U.K. for higher studies and he said he would devote his time in the cine field. It was me who insisted that we should organize a party and teach Mr. Periyar a lesson. I undertook the job of scouting the important centers to see if we could start a party. Only after my personal survey throughout the state we decided to continue in politics. This survey was in 1949.[43]

The final split was caused by divergent views on electoral participation and political style. Annadurai was loath to antagonize; E. V. Ramasami freely used ridicule and cruel satire. Other important issues included the question of a successor and E. V. Ramasami's alleged authoritarianism, as evidenced by the handling and accountability of party finances. E. V. Ramasami placed his party leaders on sparse budgets and held them strictly accountable, at the same time refusing to reveal the overall financial position of the organization. However, publically, at least, DMK leaders claimed they were leaving because E. V. Ramasami's marriage at 71 to a woman of 29 was a transgression of rationalist social reform ideals.

When the final split came, approximately three-quarters of the 75,000 DK membership joined the DMK. The formation

of the DMK was accompanied by angry oratory and bitterness.
E. V. Ramasami called those that left the "tears," and predicted
they would have little or no success. Annadurai emphasized
(in reference to the financial issue) that those who left had
"nothing but the towels flung over their shoulders." More
importantly, he constantly reiterated that the DMK and the DK
would be a "double-barreled shotgun." When the party was
formed after a meeting held September 17, 1949 in Royapuram
(Madras City), Annadurai was emphatic that he had not left
the D.K. because of a disagreement over policy, but over E.
V. Ramasami's marriage.[44]

THE EMERGING PROMINENCE OF C. N. ANNADURAI

If the DK and the DMK were going to pursue the same goals,
one might ask why 75 percent of the rank and file membership
left with Annadurai. There are a number of reasons: many were
genuinely upset by E.V. R.'s marriage. Among those who were
more sophisticated, many refused to accept Maniammal as E.
V. Ramasami's successor. Among the highly sophisticated, the
issue of electoral politics had filtered downward, and many agreed
with Annadurai that the way to achieve social reform was through
use of politics as a way to expand consciousness or to seize
power through control of the Legislative Assembly. Some left
E. V. Ramasami because of his authoritarianism. Crucially, many
were attached to Annadurai, and left simply to follow him. In
addition to being charismatic, Annadurai was a talented writer,
dramatist, actor, and propagandist. He had been instrumental
in attracting many younger members of the Dravida Kazhagam,
and it was mostly these younger members that followed him.

In 1949, the DK and the DMK had the same ideology, but
differed in organizational structure. E. V. Ramasami was authori-
tarian in his approach to party organization, while Annadurai
emphasized, in theory, intraparty democracy. In the newly formed
DMK the presidency was left open (for E. V. Ramasami—if
he changed his attitudes), and Annadurai became DMK general
secretary. Decision-making power was vested in the General
Council, to be elected indirectly. The primary organizational
unit of the party was the branch. In practice, Annadurai was
party strategist and the focal point in party decision making
and E. V. K. Sampath was second in the party hierarchy.

Early in DMK history, most leaders were too involved with propaganda activities to become effective organizers. Speeches would be made, party interest aroused, but little effort given to organizational follow-up. Many branches were organized by individuals who, on their own iniative, recruited twenty-five members and sent in the requisite dues. Mu. Karunanidhi, present chief minister of Tamil Nadu and an exception to this pattern, appreciated the value of sound grass roots organization and early capitalized on the interest aroused by public meetings, dramas, and so on to organize branches.

DMK POLITICAL BAPTISM: THE VANNIYA KULA KSHATRIYA "DOUBLE CROSS"

In the 1946 elections, the Congress achieved a sweeping victory in Madras Presidency, winning 165 of 205 seats. There was opposition to C. Rajagopalacharia resuming the premiership (he had been premier in 1936), so Sri Prakasam assumed the office. Although Prakasam held the premiership, Kamaraj Nadar controlled the Tamil Nadu Congress Committee. This split between the Congress party in government and the Congress organization was one reason for the succession of leaders of the Congress legislative party between 1946 and 1952. Prakasam was replaced by O. P. Reddiar in 1947, and he was replaced in 1949 by P. S. Kumaraswami Raja.

During this period of Congress party tensions, Kamaraj Nadar became known as the (Madras Presidency) "kingmaker" because of his role behind the scenes in choosing leaders. Apart from the conflict between government and organization, there was also continued factionalism within the Congress. Kamaraj Nadar controlled the most powerful faction in the party, in opposition to C. Rajagopalacharia. This intra-Congress factionalism was personal, and dated from an earlier conflict between Satyiamurthi, a prominent Brahmin Congressman (and political mentor of Kamaraj Nadar) and C. Rajagopalacharia.

The new constitution for independent India came into force in 1950 and elections were held in 1952, the first with universal manhood suffrage. If we recall that the pattern of social support for Congress in the 1940s was skewed toward upper castes, it is not surprising that in the 1952 elections Congress did not sustain the decisive political victories of 1936 and 1946. Six ministers in the Kumaraswami Raja ministry were defeated, and Congress party strength was reduced from 165 of 205 seats in 1946 to 152 of 375 in 1952. Congress was still the largest party, but no longer had a majority. The opposition consisted of the Communists with 59 seats, the Kisan-Mazdoor Praja party with 35, the Socialists with 13, and the Krishikar Lok party with 15, the Tamil Nad Toilers with 19, and the Commonweal party with 6. There were also 63 independents elected.

The DMK did not enter the 1952 elections directly. They were not sufficiently well organized. Since 1949, party effort had gone into social reform propaganda and simply developing a basic structure. Also, the leadership did not want to justify E. V. Ramasami's criticism about the lure of elected office. Instead of entering directly, the DMK supported candidates willing to sign a pledge that they would support and work for the ideals of the Dravida Munnetra Kazhagam (including Dravida Nadu) in the assembly. The DMK worked particularly hard for candidates from the Commonweal and Tamil Nad Toilers parties. These parties had their greatest strength in North and South Arcot districts, and were essentially "caste" parties composed mainly of the Vanniya Kula Kshatriya.[45]

After the 1952 elections, Kamaraj favored giving the disparate opposition parties in the United Democratic Front an opportunity to govern.[46] He was, however, overruled by other party leaders, and Rajagopalacharia ("Rajaji") returned from self-imposed retirement to become chief minister. Among other measures to strengthen Congress support, Rajaji took Manikavelu, leader of the Commonweal party, into his cabinet. When Kamaraj Nadar later took over as chief minister, he recruited S. Ramasami Padayachi, leader of the Tamil Nad Toilers party, into the cabinet and retained Manikavelu. Thus Kamaraj was able to raise the strength of the Congress legislative party and its associates to 142 in a reorganized House of 231. In post-Independence politics, as Kamaraj well understood, the center of political gravity had shifted from Brahmins and forward non-Brahmins to the numerically strong backward castes. So winning support of these parties was a double victory. It gave the Congress governmental stability, and at the same time provided an opening into this powerful backward caste bloc. However, the DMK considered the entire affair a clear double cross. The preelection pledge was easily forgotten, and DMK efforts seemed to have been in vain.[47]

This set the emotional stage for the 1956 party decision to enter elective politics.

Another factor that positively influenced the rank and file toward direct participation in politics was alleged unfair treatment by the government. DMK leaders were involved in a number of court cases involving party publications. *Aryan Illusion*, for example, was banned in early 1952 as inflammatory, and both Annadurai and the publishers fined. Most decisive in developing a sense of unjust treatment was the feeling of government suppression of the DMK during the Three Corner Agitation.

THREE CORNER AGITATION

In July 1952, the Rajagopalacharia Congress government began a study of educational resources in Madras state to provide the basis for a program of universal primary education. As a result, Rajagopalacharia proposed an educational system in which children would attend school half a day and work at their father's occupations half a day. Supposedly the purpose of this shift system was to allow all children to acquire a minimal primary education as quickly as possible within existing educational facilities. At that time only fifty per cent of school-age children were in school. However, by introducing the notion of allowing children to pursue the traditional occupations of their parents, Rajagopalacharia provided the ammunition that his opponents both inside and outside the Congress used to force his temporary political downfall.

E. V. Ramasami and Annadurai were at the forefront of the campaign against what became known as "caste-based education." E. V. Ramasami, critical of Rajagopalacharia's return to power in Madras partly because Rajagopalacharia is a Brahmin, was especially vehement, linking his attack to his more generalized attacks on *varnashrama dharma.*

In 1953, the DMK launched their first major agitation. This program had three objectives; the first was opposition to the government's "caste-based education"; the second was to change the name of a Trichy district town from Dalmiapuram to Kallakudi (Dalmiapuram was named after a north Indian cement magnate, while Kallakudi had been the original Tamil name of the town). This aspect of the agitation symbolized party opposition to northern domination of the south. The third objective was to dramatize party indignation over certain derogatory remarks Nehru allegedly made about the DMK.

On the first day of the protest, five top DMK leaders were placed under house arrest. In spite of this, the agitation was launched; trains were stopped by party activists, and protest demonstrations were held in key places throughout the state. As a result of the "three corner agitation," and government attempts to curb it, hundreds were injured and at least nine demonstrators were killed.

Although both the DK and the DMK launched massive demonstrations against the government's educational policy, the decisive blow to the Rajagopalacharia government came from within the Congress party. He was more the victim of intraparty factionalism than of the efforts of the opposition. Opposition to the educational plan provided an opportunity for the Kamaraj faction finally to oust Rajagopalacharia from party prominence. In 1954, as time for the election of the leader of the Congress legislative party drew near, some members started collecting signatures for a change in leadership. Rajagopalacharia, realizing that he was in an untenable position, resigned.

After Rajagopalacharia's resignation in 1954, Kamaraj reportedly tried to find a prominent non-Brahmin leader who would assume the leadership, but was unsuccessful. Finally, encouraged by the advice of E. V. Ramasami, he became chief minister of Madras himself. The rise of Kamaraj Nadar to the chief ministership inaugurated a new era in Madras politics. Unlike previous chief ministers, he was not well educated, not fluent in English, and came from a backward caste community. After Kamaraj became chief minister, E. V. Ramasami called him a "pukka Tamizhan" (pure Tamilian), and applauded the lack of a Brahmin in the Kamaraj cabinet. Subsequently, E. V. Ramasami indirectly supported what he termed the "Kamaraj Congress." Kamaraj was in power from 1954 to 1963, and throughout this period was supported by the DK.[48]

Reasons for DK support of the "Kamaraj Congress" are not easy to discern. E. V. Ramasami stated that he was supporting Kamaraj, not Congress, since Kamaraj stood for social reform. Although this is probably genuine, there were extenuating circumstances. E. V. Ramasami was undoubtedly acting in anticipation of the DMK entry into elective politics, and may have hoped to strengthen Kamaraj's hand against his old rival Annadurai. A second reason might be his contemptuous attitude toward party politics. He viewed himself as a man outside and above politics and politicians. Kamaraj's deference to E. V. Ramasami reinforced this self-image.[49] Publicly, Kamaraj denied knowledge of E. V. Ramasami's support and refused to speculate on it.

The apparent strength of the Congress political position may also have influenced E. V. Ramasami. In 1954, Congress was firmly entrenched in power. The opposition was badly splintered and seemingly effete. The major caste parties had been co-opted into the Kamaraj cabinet. The Communist party, the second most important party in Madras state (excluding the DK and DMK, which did not contest the 1952 elections), did not appeal to E. V. Ramsami. He supported them in the February 1952 elections, but by December 1952, he was decidedly negative.[50]

BUILDING A SUPPORT BASE DURING THE RADICAL PERIOD

Methods used to build a support base during the radical period presaged the DMK's later successful use of political communications, particularly vernacular media. On October 17, 1950, according to police reporters, Annadurai told an enthusiastic audience of about six thousand:

Our party does not have as its objective changing the Congress administration and establishing our rule. At the same time our party is not a party which asks the people to act in an irresponsible manner. Our movement is not a job hunting body which says the Omandurar or Prakasam may be brought as the Chief Minister. We wish to see a new constitution in this land—a new society, a new societal order in this land. We are preparing the people only for it. We are making the people heroes for only that purpose. We desire that those having an inferiority complex should walk erect again. We are making the ranks which have become disorganized stand again in a disciplined and orderly manner. Whenever we speak thus of a righteous war, Kumaraswami Raja, Chief Minister, seems to think that we have come bringing battalions, that we are standing at the entrance to the fort and we have come to wrest Bharatamata's citadel from them. *Ours is not a movement*

*having force or battalions as its basis but finding that the
ranks of the intelligentsia in the land have become disorganized,
we are only asking our comrades to set right those ranks again*
(emphasis added).[51]

Annadurai's reference to intellectuals is an important indication
of the DMK's method of penetrating the mass media. The DMK
had a strong appeal for non-Brahmin intellectuals.

The party attracted many Tamil scholars, its major leaders
made a point of speaking in scholastic (poetic) Tamil, and all
leaders were skilled in Tamil oratory. In fact, some of the top
leaders themselves were Tamil scholars. Consequently the DMK
won strong support in academic circles. The emphasis of DMK
leaders on scholarly studies of Tamil helped renew interest in
Tamil literature and linguistics, and contributed to a renaissance
of Tamil literature. The DMK increasingly combined political
and literary conferences, often sponsoring poetry contests on
political subjects.[52]

There were numerous party papers published by DMK leaders.
Of these, *Murosoli, Nam Nadu, Dravida Nadu,* and *Manram*
were the most important. In fact, so popular were DMK magazines
and party papers that almost every major leader published either
a paper or a journal, and sometimes both, as well as party
pamphlets. In spite of Congress political hegemony, political
propaganda in post-Independence Madras State gradually came
to be heavily influenced by the DMK.

Radio dramas and speeches were given by Annadurai and
the more important second-rank leaders. Traveling companies
presented the party's ideas in dramatic dialogues. Of all media,
perhaps films were most important. Annadurai, Karunanidhi,
and many lower-level leaders were connected with film making.
Some of the most famous Tamil films (including musical scores)
have DMK themes (for example, *Parasakti,* written by Mu.
Karunanidhi in 1952 starred Shiviji Ganesan, who became famous
as an actor through his participation in DMK plays and films).[53]

Parasakti, for example, opens with a long monologue bewailing
the plight of Tamilians who had to leave their native country
because of poverty, to "toil and suffer" in foreign lands.[54] Every
opportunity is taken to criticize religious "superstition," and
the corruption of temple priests is ridiculed. The government
is scathingly characterized as unfeeling; the fate of Tamilians

who had to sleep in the streets because they had no homes was elaborated. (I saw *Parasakti* in 1968 when the DMK was in power, and these scenes were still being cheered). In other films and dramas Dravida Nadu provides a major or supplemental theme. In almost all DMK-influenced films the characters at some point speak of the plight of the poor, of people living in the streets, of starvation, of political corruption, all linked to the ineptitude of the Congress government. Such political communication was intensive, creative, and highly effective. The DMK used films for propaganda when cinema houses were just being extended to the rural areas of Madras.[55] It was common for people to walk as much as five miles to see a film, and films were (and still are) seen repeatedly. Children reenact film parts in play and both adults and children memorize and sing film theme songs.

DMK ideas therefore reached every area of life in Madras either through films, books, pamphlets, speeches, dramas, poems, songs, or newspapers. Apart from these, committed young people often went to the remotest corners of the state to spread DMK ideas and to establish reading rooms and DMK branches. Hence, during the movement phase of DMK development, the ideology of the party was widely spread and began to take hold as large numbers of people restructured their conceptions of political and social reality. What was internalized, however, was not always the radical ideas (such as Atheism, DMK communism, and so on), but the cultural definition of what it meant to be a Dravidian, that is, Dravidian political identity linked to the past.

CONCLUSION

Mass mobilization of the backward castes during the 1940s transformed the character of the Madras Presidency political arena and determined the essential constraints on radical politics. The orientation of backward castes was toward maintaining their position in the face of competition from Untouchables and other backward groups. This status was not threatened by the wealthy landlord or the proud and orthodox Brahmin, but by the previously subservient Untouchable. The social base of the radical Dravidian ideology during its period of origin in the early twentieth century was the elite non-Brahmin groups who felt a sense of relative loss. The symbols of oppression (particularly the symbol, "Suddhra"), so important in shaping a radical support structure for the Dravidian movement, were irrelevant for the backward castes. That is not to say it would have been impossible to develop a radical movement around symbols relevant to the backward castes. Their economic relationship to the forward non-Brahmins and Brahmins is an obvious issue. For the Dravidian ideology, however, economic oppression was subsumed to ritual and cultural oppression. Although economic egalitarianism was emphasized, as stated earlier, issues of hierarchical Hinduism and caste domination were of prime importance.

During the radical period, the DMK and the DK attempted to penetrate public political consciousness in numerous ways. Films, oratory, pamphlets, books, and so forth were all used in an attempt to develop new forms of political and social consciousness. These efforts were successful in creating an awareness of Dravidian identity. It is this awareness that laid the foundation for the politics of cultural nationalism.

[1] For more on these castes see Louis Dumont, *Une Sous-Caste de l'Inde du sud: organisation sociale et religeuse des Pramalai Kallar* (Paris: Gallimard, 1957); and Rudolph and Rudolph, *Modernity of Tradition*, pp. 98–103.

[2] India, Tamil Nadu, Government Order 690, March 14, 1945.

[3] The next few pages constitute an overall sketch of lower non-Brahmin mobilization. For more on the role of backward castes in south Indian politics, see Rudolph and Rudolph, *The Modernity of Tradition*, and Robert Hardgrave, Jr., *The Nadars of Tamil Nad: Political Culture of a Community in Change* (Berkeley and Los Angeles: University of California Press, 1969).

[4] India, Tamil Nadu, Government Order 190 (GO 190), January 20, 1944.

[5] *Ibid.*

[6] *Ibid.*

[7] Deva dasis perform at temple functions and are often concubines.

[8] GO 190.

[9] *Ibid.* Recall that in the late 1930s, the Self-Respect movement became involved in propaganda work for the Justice party. This involvement stemmed from two factors: first, E. V. Ramasami became president of the Justice party in 1939 (he was elected while in jail for activities in the anti-Hindustani agitation). And second, E. V. Ramasami believed that the Justice party was worth sustained support as the only political party that represented non-Brahmins. Paradoxically, even though he participated in political activities and supported the Justice party, E. V. Ramasami also looked upon the Justice party as a negative didactic experience for his followers. Through involvement, they would learn the futility of trying to use politics to achieve social revolution and therefore self-serving political office-seekers would be driven away, purifying the party.

[10] GO 190.

[11] The Vanniya Kula Kshatriyas consist of Naicker, Padayachi, and Vanniya

castes. The Muukoolathur consist of the Kallar, Thevar, Agamudiar, and Maravar castes. See Rudolph and Rudolph, *Modernity of Tradition*, for a discussion of Vanniya politics.

[12] See GO 190 for a complete list of these castes.

[13] They also are known as Pallis. In the districts of North Arcot, South Arcot, and Salem sporadic political activity of the Vanniyas can be traced as far back as 1900. However, it was not until 1952 that a Madras-wide Vanniya Kula Kshatriya Sangram (association) was formed.

[14] Interviews with A. P. Janarthanam and Sri Manikavelu, former leader of the Commonweal party, which was primarily composed of Vanniyas. Madras, 1968.

[15] Also see Rudolph and Rudolph, *Modernity of Tradition*, pp. 98–103.

[16] India, Tamil Nadu, Government Order 3663, December 1957.

[17] Quoted *ibid.*

[18] *Ibid.*

[19] See Hardgrave, *The Nadars of Tamil Nad.*

[20] There are also reports of Naicker-Harijan conflicts in North and South Arcot.

[21] Rudolph and Rudolph, *Modernity of Tradition*, argue that in the face of internal differentiation and elongation of the Nadar community on a socio-economic continuum, "the Nadar Mahajana Sangam [its principle caste association] has increasingly adopted a non-partisan strategy" (p. 95).

[22] India, Tamil Nadu, Government Order 527, March 11, 1941. The papers on E. V. Ramasami's Naicker letter are very illuminating. In response to his charges it was stated: "Mr Naicker is under the wrong impression that the longer the high percentage of Brahmins persists, the longer it will take to vanish. This is not correct. If, for instance, a service of 100 places start in 1930 with every place filled by a Brahmin aged 25 and there are no casualties for the next 30 years, then all through the period the percentage of Brahmins keeps without any fall at 100 yet in 1960, the percentage will drop down to 16-2/3 through recruitment under the communal rule, except to the extent that other communities cannot supply adequate number of recruits."

[23] T. M. Partasārati, *Ti Mu Kaḻaka Varalāṟu* [DMK History] (Madras: Pari Nilayam, 1961).

[24] *Ibid.*

[25] Sitamparaṇār, *Tamiṟar Talaivar* [*Tamilian's Leader*].

[26] *Ibid.*

[27] C. N. Aṇṇaturai, *Dravida Nadu*, August, 1947.

[28] *Ibid.*

[29] Partasārati, *Ti Mu Kaḻaka Varalāṟu.*

[30] *Ibid.*

[31] *Hindu*, August 15, 1947.

[32] C. N. Aṇṇaturai, *Āriyamāyai* [*Aryan Illusion*] (Trichy: Dravidappani, 1943).

[33] *Ibid.*

[34] *Ibid.*

[35] *Ibid.*

[36] *Ibid.*

[37] Hardgrave, *The Nadars of Tamil Nad*, p. 196.

[38] Interview with E. V. K. Sampath, Madras, 1968.

[39] *Ibid.*

[40] *Ibid.*

[41] *Ibid.*

[42] Interview with V. P. Raman, Madras, 1968.

[43] Interview with E. V. K. Sampath, Madras, 1968.

⁴⁴ Partasārati, *Ti Mu Kaḷaka Varalāṟu*.

⁴⁵ Rudolph and Rudolph, *Modernity of Tradition*, pp. 53–58.

⁴⁶ V. K. Narasimhan, *Kamaraj, a Study* (Bombay: Manaktalas, 1967).

⁴⁷ As we shall see, the DMK reaped some benefits from their 1952 efforts in the 1957 elections.

⁴⁸ See Lloyd I. Rudolph, "Urban Life and Populist Radicalism," *Journal of Asian Studies*, 20 (May 1961), 283–297, for more on Congress-DK collaboration; see also André Beteille, *Class, Caste, and Power* (Berkeley and Los Angeles: University of California Press, 1965) and Harrison, *India: the Most Dangerous Decades*.

⁴⁹ Also it is alleged that Kamaraj allowed E. V. Ramasami to influence the choice of certain members of his top administrative staff.

⁵⁰ Harrison, *India: the Most Dangerous Decades*, p. 186, reports the following comment by Periyar in an interview December 14, 1952. "The Communists have their office at a foreign place, Bombay or Delhi, and they are just as interested in exploiting our country as any of the other foreign-controlled parties. Besides, most of the Communists leaders are Brahman. Ramamurthi is a '*pucca Brahman.*'"

⁵¹ India, Tamil Nadu, Government Order 360, February 1952.

⁵² For a list of the exhausting schedule of the party leaders, see *Dravida Nadu* for these early years. It lists every conference, drama event, and so on.

⁵³ For an interesting view of Shivaji Ganesan and the film industry, see Susanne Hoeber Rudolph, "From Madras, View of the Southern Film," *Yale Review* (Spring 1971). Also see Robert Hardgrave, Jr., "When Stars Displace the Gods: the Folk Culture of Cinemas in Tamilnadu" in Charles Leslie, ed., *Asian Films and Popular Cultures* (forthcoming).

⁵⁴ There are substantial numbers of Tamil-speaking workers in East Africa, Ceylon, and Malaya. Also there are large film markets in these areas.

⁵⁵ It is ironic that the DMK ability to extend its influence through the cinema was made possible by the Congress electrification campaign.

PART TWO

The Politics of Emergent Nationalism

CHAPTER FIVE

The DMK and Emergent Cultural Nationalism

THE late 1950s and early 1960s mark the emergence of the politics of cultural nationalism and the mass internalization of Tamil identity. Not only did the DMK change from a political movement to a full-fledged party, contesting elections; the ideology changed from a radical challenge to core values underlying Hindu society and demands for establishment of a territorially separate polity to emphasis on reform within the existing (social, cultural, and political) system. Radical ideas of social reform (such as abolition of the caste system and destruction of Hinduism) were transformed to promoting "rationality"[1] in ritual observances and theology, "one God, one caste," eradication of "superstition," and uplift of the backward castes. Voltaire and the rationalist school of French philosophy became important models for some leaders. Others, mainly Untouchable leaders,[2] contrasted the humanitarian aspects of Buddhism with what they terned the cruelties of caste in Hinduism. Speakers and propagandists ceased to attack Brahmins and focused only on anti-Brahminism as an ideological stance. Speeches, dramas, and films continued to be made with what were termed "rational" themes, but they were less ascerbic, and by the 1960s almost completely theistic (one God, one caste) rather than atheistic.

This ideological deradicalization and the muting of the goal of fundamental structural change (the destruction of Hinduism, for example) is of crucial importance to the emerging ideological priority of cultural nationalism. Cultural nationalism is not an autonomously legitimate ideology; it can occur only within a certain context. But promotion of radical social reform and the propagation of the idea that the old societal structure was illegitimate created the groundwork for a new consciousness.

Another important component of DMK ideological change was the abandonment of territorial aspirations, informally in 1961 and formally in 1963. Abandonment of the Dravida Nadu demand was a manifestation, not a cause, of the development of a political, social, and cultural climate more hospitable to cultural nationalism than to territorial separation and radical reform.

Organizationally, the DMK developed a complex infrastructure during these years. The decision to contest elections was an important factor in forcing the party to rationalize its bureaucracy and to readjust its functional priorities from propaganda designed to change attitudes to propaganda and organization designed to develop and sustain political commitment and organizational adherence. Ideological and organizational changes during this radical period took place while the DMK was building support among lower-caste non-Brahmins, and are related to the constraints of the party's expanded support base.

In 1956 the DMK formally and publicly decided to enter electoral competition. This decision was taken at a conference held in Madras City, attended by over 50,000 party members.[3] The question of electoral participation was submitted to a vote of the attending rank-and-file membership and was overwhelmingly approved. As we saw from the previous chapter, the "Vanniya double cross" and the events surrounding the three-corner agitation had already set the stage for rank-and-file support of a change from movement group to political party. Among the rank and file, the only argument against electoral participation (first suggested by E. V. Ramasami and still held by some members of the DMK) was that electoral participation would result in a loss of radical ideals. Annadurai and other top leaders had earlier rejected and subsequently criticized that assumption. Annadurai saw a situation in which democratic majoritarian politics were a distinct possibility. The political arena was rapidly expanding, in the sense that backward-caste and lower-class political participation had been increased by universal manhood suffrage. In addition, the ranks of the educated classes were also increasing rapidly. Even when Annadurai was in the Dravida Kazhagam, he was optimistic about the possibility of using democratic electoral competition for radical social reform. It was also fleetingly supposed that Dravida Nadu could be achieved by parliamentary means—winning an Assembly majority and then demanding separation.

Also important in shaping rank-and-file opinions on electoral participation was the political climate after 1954. E. V. Ramasami had begun to support the "Kamaraj" Congress, thus providing legitimacy for Congress claims of social reform. And at the 1955 Avadi session, the Congress party had committed itself to a "socialist" pattern of society. The Congress could (and did) claim, therefore, that they, too, were striving for a casteless and classless society.[4] In this sense, changes within the Congress party, both ideological and organizational, shaped the political environment in which the DMK functioned. But change within the Congress is not a sufficient explanation of the DMK's decision to contest the 1957 elections.

Electoral competition seemed at the time to offer the possibility of some success. The DMK could hope to secure an immediate base of support from those that balked at following Periyar E. V. Ramasami's lead in supporting the Congress, and from those previously supportive of independent candidates of Dravidian persuasion.

After the 1952 elections, members of the Legislative Assembly sympathetic to the ideological goals of the Dravidian movement had formed a Dravida Assembly party. This group of legislators enjoyed the support and advice of E. V. Ramasami up to 1954, and were an important vehicle for expression of these ideas in the Assembly. By 1954, however, serious strains and a sense of directionlessness appeared in the Dravida Parliamentary party. In that year, the Dravida Parliamentary party announced it might henceforth contest elections under its own name. E. V. Ramasami disapproved, since the DK had already quietly begun to support the "Kamaraj" Congress. Without E. V. Ramasami's guidance and support, the Dravida Parliamentary party weakened, and it was even proposed that members of the Dravida Parliamentary party join Congress and then ally with both E. V. Ramasami and the "Kamaraj" Congress.

The central political question for the DMK was how to deal strategically with the dominant position of the Congress party. When, in the mid-fifties, Kamaraj assessed the political picture in Madras state, he must have been quite optimisitic. Support for the Communists had waned; the Dravidian movement was split, with the DK supporting the "Kamaraj Congress" and the DMK untested at the polls. Most of the followers (and leaders) of the DMK were extremely young. (Some political leaders even made jokes about the "rag-tail army of infants that followed the DMK") The only area of the state in which Kamaraj lacked support was in the extreme southeastern Muukoolathur areas, where Mutharamalinga Thevar's Forward Bloc was dominant; and even there Congress was winning support among ex-Untouchables. Inside the Congress, although some of the top leaders were unhappy about DK support and openly condemned the DK as communal, Kamaraj retained a firm hand.[5]

After the 1949 split in the DK, E. V. Ramasami continued his propaganda efforts for radical social reform.[6] In fact, during the 1950s many government reports record more concern about his activities than those of the DMK. DK protest continued to be dramatic and ascerbic. E. V. Ramasami continued to give performances of the Ramayana in which Ravana was the hero and Rama and Sita were "despicable characters."[7] Temple idols were broken and Untouchables taken into temples in large numbers. At frequent public meetings organized by E. V. Ramasami, as many as five or ten thousand people would hear his excoriation of the Brahmins, Brahminism, and Hindu ritual and theology. DK agitations against hotels (or restaurants) with the appellation "Brahmin" on outdoor signs was highly successful. The DMK joined these as well as the agitations against north Indian businessmen. Hence in the early 1950s, although a large percentage of the Dravida Kazhagam had left to join the DMK, it was not clear that DK influence would ebb.

By becoming a political party, the DMK could hope to galvanize, or at least compete for support from, those with a Dravidian ideological perspective. Continuation as an interest group allowed E. V. Ramasami's DK plus a variety of independent candidates, to gain the electoral benefits of Dravidian movement propaganda efforts. For rank-and-file political supporters, as well as for party leadership, the dilemmas of the DMK entering the political arena were all too obvious. The decision to contest elections was made in the context of the complex political conundrums in Madras of the 1950s. It also rested on Annadurai's belief in the legitimacy of electoral competition as a way to achieve radical movement goals.

SYMBOLIC IMPORTANCE OF DRAVIDA NADU

The 1957 electoral campaign of the DMK stands out in contrast to later elections. Candidates were chosen for their abilities as party propagandists. Often the caste of a candidate was not strategically consistent with caste majorities in a constituency or the caste of other probable candidates. DMK candidates and propagandists stressed ideas of social reform (although extreme anti-Brahminism was silenced and atheism soft-pedaled). Primary focus was placed on the demand for a separate Dravida Nadu.

The stress on Dravida Nadu represented a thorough change in ideological priorities. The primary impetus of the Dravidian movement (particularly the DK) had been on social-reform propaganda, with Dravida Nadu as a secondary, although instrinsically related, issue, growing out of the 1938 anti-Hindustani agitations. In the DMK, however, Dravida Nadu had gradually increased in ideological importance. As early as 1954, Dravida Nadu was used as a metaphoric device to facilitate expression of radical movement goals. All good things would come with Dravida Nadu. An article in *Murosoli* provides an example of this appeal. The article declared that the DMK was a freedom movement engaged in a struggle for Dravida Nadu. It described what life would be like in an independent Dravida Nadu: "In the Dravida Nadu that we are going to get there will be absolute equality and it will be marked by social reformation. Food, clothing, and housing will receive foremost consideration. The landed property will be considered as national property, and produce will be divided and distributed to all the people. To attain this Dravidam, all Dravidians should unite."[8]

The DMK argued that only with an independent Dravida Nadu were these goals possible for the Dravidians. They argued that India was too large and Aryan domination too entrenched for them to be achieved within the Indian state. The party still attacked what they termed "superstition" in the name of rationalism throughout the movement period. Every feature of Hindu society considered offensive, from polytheism to social practices, was criticized. After 1957, however, ideas of social reform were played down in general.

In a paradoxical sense (considering later events), the increased emphasis on Dravida Nadu as a political symbol was also related to the party's decision to contest elections. A party contesting elections must appear to stand for something concrete, or it must claim to be a superior representative of the interests of the constituency. It would be difficult to contest an election only on the basis that caste prejudices and religious "superstition" should be eliminated. For one thing, in 1957 no one would disagree publicly with that position; the Congress government had already, in fact, made untouchability illegal. Nehru was a staunch advocate of secularism, and Kamaraj Nadar had declared himself and his government dedicated to the uplift of the scheduled castes (ex-Untouchables) and backward classes.

But the social reform advocated by the DMK and the DK should not be equated with these programs. Gandhi's social reform program was based on his interpretation of Hinduism; Annadurai's and E. V. Ramasami's social reform programs were based on the rejection of Hinduism in all forms. Congress' version of social reform did not offend the beliefs of a deeply religious population; it was not even the policy of the Madras State Congress party to eradicate the caste system through government action.[9]

In electoral terms it seemed (as E. V. Ramasami continually reiterated) that the kind of social reform advocated by the DMK could not be achieved by election to the Legislative Assembly. To all but the most sophisticated, the important differences between the DMK and Congress notions of social reform would be lost. Dravida Nadu, however, was concrete, directly related to candidacy for public office, and a convenient focal point for elaborating DMK ideas about social reform.

THE 1957 ELECTIONS

DMK showing in the 1957 elections was not impressive; the party won 15 seats of 120 contested. It is difficult to say how much E. V. Ramasami's support of Kamaraj Congress helped the Congress in 1957. It is true that in 1954 his support of the Congress had been considered instrumental in producing success in certain by-elections. But however much E. V. Ramasami was responsible, the Congress victory in the 1957 elections was decisive. Between 1952 and 1957 Congress substantially strengthened its position in almost all districts. (See table 5-1 and figure 1).[10] The decrease in Tirunelveli and Ramnad of seats won by Congress (the only districts where the number of seats decreased) was probably due to the activities of Muthuramalinga Thevar's Forward Bloc. The Communist Party of India (CPI) fell from second to third place (behind the DMK), with fourteen seats in the Legislative Assembly. Table 5-2 shows that Tanjore was the area in which the CPI lost most of its seats. There the Self-Respect movement has always had a strong base of support, and had done a good deal of organization among the Adi-Dravidas. E. V. Ramasami's support of Congress might have been crucial here, if not elsewhere.

TABLE 5-1
Congress Vote in 1952 and 1957 Elections
(Percent)

District	1952	1957	Difference
Chingleput	46.27	32.10	+14.17
Nilgiris	49.90	39.08	+10.82
Salem	46.83	36.64	+10.19
Trichy	43.73	33.92	+ 9.81
Tanjore	48.25	40.04	+ 8.21
N. Arcot	43.19	36.09	+ 7.10
Tirunelveli	48.47	42.67	+ 5.80
Coimbatore	48.09	43.67	+ 4.42
Madurai	48.09	44.22	+ 3.87
S. Arcot	41.21	40.03	+ 1.18
Ramnad	37.63	39.57	− 1.94
Madras City	42.98	31.57	+11.41

Note: Only those districts included in Madras State after 1956 States Reorganization are included here.

The extent of Communist party loss in the 1957 election, although surprising to many, was related to the success of the Dravidian movement in setting the ideological tone for Madras politics. Many young people otherwise attracted to the Communist party turned to the DMK. Both E. V. Ramasami and Annadurai

TABLE 5-2
Communist Party of India Electoral Support 1952–1957

District	Seats
Tanjore	Lost 6
Salem	Lost 2
Trichy	Lost 1
Chingleput	Same 0
S. Arcot	Same 0
Tirunelveli	Same 0
Ramnad	Same 0
Madurai	Same 2
Coimbatore	Increased 1
N. Arcot	Increased 1
Madras City	Lost 1

Note: Only those districts included in Madras State after 1956 States Reorganization are included here.

FIGURE 1

CHANGE IN NUMBER OF SEATS WON
BY CONGRESS IN 1952* AND 1957

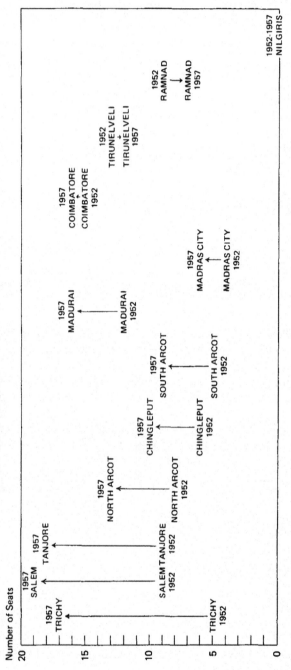

*Only the districts included in Madras State after 1956 states reorganization are included here.

advocated economic egalitarianism, and both accused the Communists of not working to propagate atheism and radical social reform.

By 1957 the *Janasakthi*, a Communist journal, admitted after the election that the DMK had been highly successful in creating the impression among the Tamilians, and especially among the youth, that it (the DMK) was the only party really interested in their welfare.[11] In the 1957 elections, the Communists directed their campaign against "anti-national" interests, realizing that their competition was both Congress and the DMK. By this time, however, the DMK had already begun to entrench itself in what would have been a very promising constituency for the Communist party, the educated youth. Even after 1957, the Communist party never gained a strong place in Madras politics, and class analysis was preempted by the Brahmin-non-Brahmin interpretation of conflict. In one issue of *Murosoli,* the DMK said it would join with the Communist party and change its name to the Dravidian Communist party if the Communist party would add Dravidian to its name.

Although it is difficult to gauge how much support the DMK diverted from the Communist party, it is clear that in 1957 the DMK gained at the expense of both independent candidates[12] and the CPI. In this election the DMK support came largely from North and South Arcot (Vanniya Kula Kshatriya strongholds) and from the cities. This pattern reflected intense DMK propaganda efforts in 1952, which were oriented towards the Vanniya areas. It also reflected the emotional appeal of the DMK party involvement in drama, literature, and film; the compelling nature of both the Dravidian ideology and the emphasis on language, history, and culture were all important in mobilizing the urban lower middle class. It was among urban youth, the lower middle classes, and among the backward castes that the DMK hoped to develop a strong mass base.

1957 IN PERSPECTIVE

What were the reasons for the poor showing of the DMK in the 1957 elections, and what were the longer-range implications?

First, of course, was the popularity of Congress. In 1957 Congress under Kamaraj Nadar's leadership developed a broad base of support. Brahmins and many elite non-Brahmin castes had begun to support Congress during the 1930s. After independence, Congress was able to win votes among Adi-Dravidas (ex-Untouchables) by indirect patron-client mobilization—largely through the Pannaiyal agricultural system. In Madras, Pannaiyals, or agricultural workers, have a relationship with the landlords economically and sociologically similar to the feudal master-servant bond. This dependence was politically exploited by landlords who delivered the vote of their agricultural workers.[13] Most of the landlords were from the elite non-Brahmin castes that had shifted their allegiance to Congress during the late 1930s and 1940s. Hence, in rural areas the Adi-Dravida vote went largely to the Congress.

Kamaraj's alliance with E. V. Ramasami netted the Congress extra votes. The Self-Respect movement had always been particularly strong in Tanjore and Salem, and there E. V. Ramasami's support was undoubtedly useful. The alliance with the Commonweal and Tamil Nad Toiler's party led to some increase in support among Vanniya groups. Finally, many people were attracted to Congress because Congress had achieved independence and was pursuing many policies that were popular.

Apart from the popularity of Congress, the poor performance of the DMK is also related to the manner in which the party waged its campaign. It displayed a marked lack of sensitivity to the politics of the caste-balanced ticket. Even more important was the realization after 1957 that there was no immediately useful base of mass support for radical social-reform policies.

What were the possibilities for the DMK to build a *mass* support base for radical social reform in 1957? If we review the caste and class make up of Tamil Nadu in the 1950s, we sense the constraints involved in trying to develop the basis for a radical social-reform movement. Beginning with the top, the Brahmins who had a consciousness of the need for social reform were surely not likely to join the DMK, when Congress offered a much less threatening alternative. Most Brahmins considered the DMK anti-Brahmin in spite of Annadurai's protestations.

Elite non-Brahmins who remained oriented toward social reform were divided between the DMK and the DK. E. V. Ramasami's support of Congress made it consistent for many of these elite non-Brahmins to support the party in power and yet maintain at least symbolic commitments to social reform.

Other elite non-Brahmins continued to support the Justice party (which had continued after 1944 as a rump organization), and some were also attracted to independent candidates.

Although Adi-Dravidas might have provided an effective central organizational basis, the problem was to detach them from the effects of the politicization of the Pannaiyal system. In 1957 it seemed unlikely that Adi-Dravida support could be gained without enormous effort. Furthermore, the All-India Congress government had taken great pains to woo ex-Untouchable support. Untouchability had been made illegal, and certain concessions were granted to Untouchables, including reserved places in the services and the universities, schools, and the legislature. Dr. Ambedker, the Untouchable leader, had been taken into the Nehru cabinet (he later resigned) and efforts were made to identify the Congress with a new and better deal for Untouchables. Some Untouchables therefore no doubt supported Congress enthusiastically, although before Independence many Untouchables in Madras had supported (through their leaders at least) the British raj.

That left the backward castes as the best potential base of support. The orientation of the backward castes was toward maintaining their position in the face of competition from Untouchables and other backward groups below them. Their status was not as threatened by the wealthy landlord or the orthodox Brahmin as by the previously subservient Untouchables. Backward castes in Madras accepted social reform as a relevant social goal, but social reform did not have the radical connotations of Dravidian ideology, that is, atheism or anti-Hinduism. Social reform, as it came to be defined in the 1950s, meant uplift of the scheduled and backward castes. Instead of the destruction of the caste system and implementation of a new principle of societal organization, social reform came to mean betterment of the condition of those groups at the bottom *within* the old system. Since the scheduled castes were granted certain benefits, such as reserved seats in the legislature and some specific statutory protections, the backward castes felt neglected.

Between 1957 and 1962, the DMK began to talk more about this "neglected" segment, "neither the very bottom nor the very top of society." It was this "common man" that Annadurai claimed to represent. The appeal to the common man was directed toward the rising urban lower middle class, the educated unemployed youth, and the middling (film-going) farmer in the backward castes. Furthermore, it was from these backward caste groups, this urban lower middle class and middling farmer category, that the new educated classes were largely being drawn.

In general, then, we can say that the 1957 political arena in Madras State was inhospitable to radical social reform as the basis for a mass political organization seeking election victories. There was a contradiction between radical social reformation, a policy desired by only a small number of people, and a mass political arena based on universal manhood suffrage. For the DMK, the contradiction was politically excruciating: majoritarian politics demanded modification of their views of radical, atheistic social reform.

IDEOLOGICAL ROOTS OF MOVEMENT TRANSFORMATION

Before proceeding, it is important to discuss an additional factor in the DMK's modification of their ideology of social reformation. As the persistence of E. V. Ramasami's DK indicates, the DMK could have survived, with Annadurai's talents, as a nonelectoral interest group. But continuation as an interest group clearly would have meant fighting enervating criticism by political parties. As it was, before 1962 the DMK was considered an organization of undesirable, if not dangerous, socially under-class persons. Some families would not marry their daughters to DMK men; employers reportedly discriminated against DMK followers; and even in law cases DMK adherents were afraid to acknowledge their affiliation.

Still, survival as an organization was possible. What was incompatible with interest group continuation was mass support, and the possibility of dramatic, immediate success. Nevertheless, had the DMK had an ideology of denial, or an ideology that predicted inevitable long-run success, they might have been prepared to pay the immediate price for long-term benefits. Hence, I would argue that one final factor in tipping the balance toward modification of social-reform ideas was the substance of the Dravidian ideology.

Dravidian ideology did not argue that the victory of the culturally oppressed was inevitable, or that social reformation was inevitable because of some intrinsic structural logic of the system. Rather the DK, for example, saw the adherents of the

Dravidian ideology as a small group propagating ideas of rationality in an otherwise superstitious world. Furthermore, the Dravidian ideology had no theory about the inevitability of the rise of its own movement. When one asks adherents how the Dravidian movement originated, the response typically comes down to the leadership of Periyar. The accuracy of this is not important here—what is at issue is the absence of belief in historical inevitability. Had Periyar not been born, such ideas might not have arisen at all, according to this logic. Perhaps the best manifestation of the party pessimism is the reported belief of E. V. Ramasami in 1967 that hope for total reformation was lost. He is reported to have believed (in the manner of Louis XIV), "after me, the deluge."[14]

Instead, adherents of both the DK and the DMK were discouraged by the results of the movement phase of the party.[15] They were somewhat indecisive and lacked self-confidence. Unlike Castro, who firmly announced during what seemed to be the nadir of the Cuban liberation movement that "history would absolve him," the Dravidian ideologues believed, rather, that if their organization went under, other parties with social-reform ideals might not rise again for another hundred or perhaps thousand years. This attitude created an obsession with protecting the organization, and it inspired cautiousness and a lack of political confidence. These characteristics underlie DMK party history.

For many, therefore, entering elections seemed the obvious choice for the DMK in 1956. Between 1957 and 1962, maintaining and enhancing the DMK electoral position seemed to be an important means for attaining party goals. It was with this end in view that the social-reform ideology was modified. What I am suggesting is that ideological structures can contain the seeds of their own destruction. The pattern of ideological development in a movement depends on three factors: first, the strategy and inclinations of movement leaders; second, the political and social environment; and third, internal ideological structure.

Although the DMK continued to conduct social-reform dramas until 1961, moderation and transformation of the DMK social-reform ideology began in 1957 and was virtually complete by the 1962 elections. The term "social reform" remained, but the meaning changed to the uplift of backward classes. Between 1957 and 1962 the DMK drastically reduced the number of social-reform conferences held, discouraged radical atheistic articles in the party press, and asked party speakers to tone down their speeches. The DMK also took particular pains to distinguish itself from the DK on anti-Brahmin as against anti-Brahmanism, as well as on methods of propaganda. It accused the DK of carrying on a campaign against the Brahmin community in Madras.

The theory of racial differences between Brahmins and non-Brahmins in Madras also underwent a change. In a 1958 *Homeland* article entitled "Kamaraj and the D.K.," the author stated, "While on the one hand the D.K. reviles Northern and Aryan domination, it carries on a relentless tirade and campaign against the Brahmin community as such in Madras. The illogical nature of this agitation, which ignores that the non-Brahmins of the North are as Aryan as the Brahmins of the North, and that the Brahmins of the South are as Dravidian as the non-Brahmins of the South, has never been analyzed."[16] It is important to emphasize at this point that the demand for Dravida Nadu was not abandoned in 1957. The circumstances under which this demand was given up were very different from the circumstances surrounding modification of social-reform principles, These will be discussed later in the chapter.

CHANGES IN DMK POLITICAL ACTIVITY AND PROPAGANDA

Party political literature between 1957 and 1962 reflects the DMK transformation from movement to party. Although the theme of northern prosperity and southern neglect had been discussed since 1947, between 1957 and 1962 articles on this subject were more detailed, appearing with increasing frequency in party speeches and in the party press. The following article is an example of this genre, although less antinorthern than many other articles. It is entitled "North-South."

The D.M.K. has been explaining to the people often very nicely that the south has been purposely neglected and driven to a state of perpetual backwardness by the Delhi government and we have always proved our contention by authenticated references and often with the help of statistics provided by the government itself.

On the other side, the press is saying that the south is not disintegrating, but growing. We would like to bring the following few facts for the consideration of these so-called national newspapers. To insure good living for the slum dwellers, the government launched various schemes bestowing benefits on the slum dwellers. . . . For this the central government has given very meager assistance. But this same central government has come forward to provide about three crores of rupees to the Bombay and Calcutta Corporations for the purpose of slum clearance. The same central government has allotted Madras and Bangalore Corporations only rupees of one crore. Is it not fair that this assistance should be allotted in a fixed proportion to all the states?[17]

Given the amount and quality of south Indian representation in the central cabinet, it is difficult to maintain the position that the south was being neglected by the central government. However, these claims structured a perception of north and south that persists in some measure to this day. Their argument in 1959 was that competing regional interests, specifically those of the north and the south, were intrinsically incompatible and could not be balanced in a way that would allow the cultural, economic, and political development of the south.

DMK party press and speeches also continued to argue for Dravida Nadu, criticize the caste system (although in temperate language), speak for the backward classes, criticize government language policy, and, of course, extol the greatness of Tamil culture. Increasingly, however, the party press and leadership focused on analysis of specific political issues and suggestions for alternative solutions to concrete problems, rather than on systemic demands.

Party agitational activity generally focused on three types of demonstrations: minor language agitations, agitations against businesses owned by north Indians, and a consistent program of showing black flags to various political leaders.[18]

More important than agitations were the changes in organization and leadership of the DMK party as it gained experience functioning as an opposition party during this period. Some of the credit for the DMK's increase in parliamentary skills and responsibility must be given to the wisdom of the Madras Congress party. The Congress made deliberate attempts to develop viable political conventions. In doing so, they undertook to socialize the opposition parties, including the DMK. This entire process had a profound effect on the development of the DMK as a skillful parliamentary organization.

An illustrative instance is the 1958 agreement between the Congress and all opposition parties on the noninvolvement of students in party politics. In a government order in which the Madras government reported the results of this agreement to the Delhi government, one of the Union ministers, obviously surprised at what he termed a "miracle," asked the Madras government how it was possible for them to bring the representatives of political parties together on this question. The GO explains, and in doing so elucidates, the Tamil Nadu Congress strategy in dealing with opposition parties:

The simple answer seems to be that government sought the cooperation of all the opposition parties in the Legislature openly and in full view of the public; and made it clear in private discussion they were sincere and earnest in doing so. It should also be added that such an approach has been adopted systematically over a number of different issues during the last three years; and this had a cumulative effect in building up healthy relations between the party in power and the opposition parties in the Legislature.

The first attempt was made when the official language commission visited the State. Government took the opposition leaders into their confidence and discussed with them not only the general line but the detailed draft of the memorandum which was later presented to the Commission. Subsequently, when the flood-gates of controversy were opened by the report of the Commission, the same procedure was gone through again with eminently satisfactory results.

The next important occasion was provided by the white paper on education. A legislative committee consisting of leading members of our parties went into the detailed story thoroughly and reached a decision on many highly debatable issues, arising out of article Five of the Constitution and the report of the Secondary Education Commission. The resulting agreement was so complete the final decision of the Legislature was based on a motion moved by the leader of the opposition.

A similar procedure is being followed at the moment in

respect to the overhaul of the entire organization of local administration in the State, including the important new departure involved in the Constitution of Panchayat Union for development blocs. Very important proposals have been formulated by a sub-committee of which the chairman is the leader of the opposition in the Legislative assembly. Thus the ground had been prepared already for legislation to be undertaken in the near future for reform of local administration in the State. And, that is good reason for entertaining the hope that the reforms will be accepted as an all-party decision. . . .

In brief, the government of Madras has been taking the initiative during the last three years in an attempt to develop party political conventions. Such unwritten conventions must necessarily supplement to the written law of the land in order that the mutual relations between the party in power and parties in opposition will be regulated in the light of the larger public interests which all of them seek to serve.

In an attempt to establish healthy relations between political parties on the one hand and educational institutions on the other has met with a measure of initial success in this State mainly because it has been preceded by a sustained effort to bring about and maintain healthy relations between the political parties among themselves.[19]

DMK ORGANIZATIONAL AND LEADERSHIP TRANSFORMATION

Organizational regularity in the DMK accompanied increased electoral participation. After the 1957 elections, the next campaign waged by the DMK was for the municipal elections of 1959. These corporation elections yielded the first major DMK victory. In cooperation with the Communist Party of India (a marriage of convenience), the DMK was able to elect one of its own party men as mayor of Madras. At that time the Madras corporation came under DMK political control.

Contesting elections required formal organizations and coordination on the local level throughout the state. No longer could DMK leaders make propaganda speeches and simply move on. Committees had to be set up to raise funds, conduct propaganda, hold meetings, and recruit people for canvassing and other necessary activities. Increasing emphasis was placed on adherence to the party constitution in setting up branches.

A noticeable change took place in the attitudes of legislators between 1957 and 1962. In 1957 the DMK adopted a moral stance. It pictured itself as in the legislature to convince the world of its "just" cause. "We will go to Delhi and explain the movement," was the attitude of Sampath and Anbil Dharmalingam, the first elected DMK members of Parliament. The attitude toward the Madras Legislative Assembly was that it was a testing ground (possibly for legislative participation in an independent Dravida Nadu).[20] Since the DMK still considered itself a freedom movement, the Madras Legislative Assembly was viewed as a means, not an end in itself. By 1967, of course, election to the Legislative Assembly and formation of the government was the end in itself.

Experience in the Madras Legislative Assembly and Lok Sabha led the top leadership to emphasize the problems debated in these bodies. Mere presence in the legislative chambers necessitated acquisition of at least some knowledge of and respect for procedure, as well as awareness and emphasis on the issues under discussion. This led to a growing gulf between the legislators (who were the top party leadership) and lower-level cadres.

During the movement years, lower-level leaders had been politically trained by courses organized for public speakers. Nedunchezhian and other DMK leaders would run these "schools," in which the ideals of the movement and their justification would be fully explained.[21] Speakers were instructed in the most effective arguments for separation, social reform, and economic egalitarianism.

Both ideological arguments and instruction in use of "chaste and pure Tamil" were part of the curriculum of these leadership schools. The schools also afforded an opportunity for close contact between the secondary leadership and the top leaders. Because of the increasingly busy schedules of the top leaders after 1957, these schools were gradually discontinued. Furthermore, the heavy legislative schedules of top leaders, plus their party duties, meant that many of them had less time to devote to their publications. This leadership gap, within the context of party ideological and organizational transformation, is crucial to understanding the complex factional quarrel in the DMK in 1961 and the resulting split.

FACTIONALISM IN THE DMK

In 1955, the selection of Nedunchezhian as general secretary of the DMK, replacing C. N. Annadurai, was the outcome of a minor struggle between E.V.K. Sampath and Karunanidhi. E.V.K. Sampath, E. V. Ramasami's nephew and a talented propagandist, had been a valuable addition to the newly formed DMK in 1949. Initially, E.V.K. Sampath (along with Nedunchezhian, Mathiazhagan, N. V. Natarajan, and Karunanidhi) was one of the top leaders of the party. Although Nedunchezhian was chosen general secretary in 1955, Sampath was considered by many to be the party's number two man.

When the DMK was founded, Annadurai had announced that the general secretaryship would be rotated among the top leaders to avoid the kind of "totalitarianism" that supposedly characterized the DK. From 1949 to 1955 Annadurai was general secretary. In 1955, when Annadurai sought to implement his rotation plan, both E.V.K. Sampath and Mu. Karunanidhi actively sought the general secretaryship. Nedunchezhian was agreed upon as a compromise candidate. At this point, however, factions and factionalism did not exist in the party. The struggle remained a struggle among individuals rather than among organized, cohesive groups.

The roots of DMK factionalism can be traced to the founding of *Murosoli* by Karunanidhi in 1954. As he organized news agents in remote villages, Karunanidhi also organized party branches and a support structure for himself. Gradually he began to ask his branches to support certain candidates for taluk and district offices, and for the General Council. He did favors for many people in the party, and thus earned their loyalty. Karunanidhi tended to gather around him the pragmatic elements of the party. At intraparty meetings he would allegedly state that "politics is a business like any other business." At any rate, Karunanidhi's reputation for pragmatism and favor-granting meant that those who wished to earn money through the party found shelter under the Karunanidhi umbrella, especially through party connections with the film industry. The relationship between the film industry and the party was more symbiotic than parasitic. The party disseminated valuable propaganda and developed additional organizational infrastructure through its film connections, while specific films and actors gained increased popularity through DMK connections.

The other major faction developed before 1961 was associated with Sampath.[22] The organization of the Sampath faction did not extend much below the General Council and top leadership levels except for a student component. Sampath did not have the magnitude of grass-roots support possessed by Karunanidhi, but at certain crucial points he had the majority support of the General Council and the Executive Committee of the General Council.

By 1961 Sampath, however, had left the party. He argued that "non-political" personages (cinema actors and dramatists) played too important a role in party affairs; that they were often given precedence on party platforms; and that audiences were often more interested in seeing and hearing film stars than political speakers. Sampath argued that emphasis on film actors and those connected with the cinema field would "cheapen" the party, and his position was probably based on more than the fear of film stars upstaging DMK party regulars. Karunanidhi was prominent in the cinema field (as was Annadurai), and had recruited cinema personalities for party work. Most of the cinema people connected with the party were in the Karunanidhi "group."[23] Those not in this group were followers of Kannadasan, a poet and cinema song writer whose quarrel with Karunanidhi in the film industry carried over into party work. Kannadasan followers subsequently became identified with the Sampath faction.

A second issue related to the first was the question of party bureaucratization. Sampath was adamant that the DMK should devote itself solely to politics. In this, he had undoubtedly been influenced by his tenure in the Delhi Lok Sabha. He was dissatisfied with the DMK as both a social-reform movement and a political party. The DMK sponsored many cultural activities and had been involved in social-reform activities, and Sampath felt that these activities were not political. He also felt that the degree of DMK entanglement with the film industry mitigated against development as a full-fledged political party. For Sampath, at least at this time, the Congress set the standard of what a political party was and how it should be organized. But Karunanidhi (and Annadurai) were loath to tamper with what had become a successful party formula. They were not opposed to the increased routinization of the party, but they disagreed over the methods and speed of the transformation.

The third issue was party ideology. Among lower-level party cadres, Sampath was seen as upholding the radical ideological goals of the party against the pragmatic Karunanidhi. At least some lower-level leadership support of the Sampath faction was based on this misapprehension about his intentions. Many party members who opposed the direction of party change away from radical social reform blamed that change on the influence of Karunanidhi, and took this opportunity to oppose him. This view of Sampath's position, however, was incorrect. Among the top-level leadership the key ideological question was what to do about the Dravida Nadu demand, and Sampath argued the issue should be immediately dropped. He personally felt that Dravida Nadu was not feasible, and that if the Delhi government made separatist parties illegal, as seemed likely, the DMK would be destroyed.[24]

Within the ranks of the very top leadership, the idea of achieving a separate Dravida Nadu had already been seriously undermined. The central role in this process had been played by V. P. Raman, a Brahmin who had joined the party in 1958 and rapidly acquired a leadership role. Raman was a wealthy, talented lawyer, fluent in English. Because of his talent and his symbolic value as a Brahmin adherent, Raman was given more and more party duties, particularly writing articles for the English press.

After 1958, Raman's spacious home in Madras became a mecca for moffossil (rural) leaders as well as those from Madras City. Nightly, top leaders would gather there for conversation. (At that time the party did not have a headquarters which could serve as a gathering place. Annadurai lived and worked in Kancheepuram). Raman continually questioned the feasibility of achieving Dravida Nadu at these sessions. He argued that since Kerala, Mysore, and Andhra Pradesh failed to support the idea it would be impossible to achieve. Furthermore, if Dravida Nadu was impossible and an attempt were made to achieve a separate Tamil Nadu, although it would be more popular, it might not be economically and militarily viable.

His reasoning eventually convinced enough leaders to lay the foundation for a meeting in his home in November 1960 to discuss the entire issue. Annadurai did not attend and, in fact, did not know the meeting was taking place. The consensus at the meeting was that the Dravida Nadu demand should be publicly abandoned. The top leaders of the DMK—Karunanidhi, Nedunchezhian, Sampath, Raman, and Mathiazhagan—were all present and in agreement. Mathiazhagan, however, was uneasy due to Annadurai's absence, and called him at Kancheepuram after the meeting. Annadurai immediately came to Madras, and another meeting was held at Raman's house. Here Annadurai pointed out that since the party cadres had been developed on the separation demand, the party could not simple drop this demand and maintain credibility in the eyes of the lower-echelon leadership. But he vowed gradually to prepare the party for dropping the Dravida Nadu demand.

Distorted rumors of the meeting at Raman's house and the discussion about Dravida Nadu seeped out, creating confusion in the party. Sampath picked this time as propitious for calling for internal reforms. This was also the time of elections for general secretary, so the issues emerged in a contest between Sampath and Karunanidhi for general secretary of the party. Karunanidhi, seeing an opportunity to discredit his dangerous rival, cautiously began to oppose Sampath. First Karunanidhi came to the defense of the movie actors and others connected with the film industry. Tempers flared so high that Sampath was attacked at a DMK meeting by thugs allegedly hired by one of Karunanidhi's lieutenants, Madurai Muthu.

For those idealists who saw the party degenerating after 1957, Sampath promised revitalization. Many believed Sampath was a radical on the issues of Dravida Nadu and social reform. Within student groups (as well as in a few DMK labor unions) Sampath supporters openly declared themselves, and Sampath factions organized. At least some of the student support of Sampath was derived from student ire over the 1958 decision (discussed in GO 240) in which Annadurai agreed with Congress proposals to limit student political activity. T. K. Ponnuvelu, the leader of the Dravida Manaver Munnetra Kazhagam (Dravidian Students Progressive Association), had been bitterly opposed to this limitation. Eventually, however, he had acquiesced. Other student leaders were less easily convinced, believing the pact was in conflict with DMK interests, since it was the DMK that had the fastest-growing student organizations.

The upsurge of Sampath support (which resulted from the misunderstanding about Sampath's position on Dravida Nadu and other issues) had begun to concern Annadurai. Annadurai had remained pretty much outside this factional dispute, and had been silent on the choice of general secretary. Nedunchezhian's tenure had shown how meaningless it was to have someone other than Annadurai as general secretary, since major decisions continued to be made by Annadurai. Annadurai probably knew that the total effect of Sampath's proposals would be detrimental to the party since he, more than anyone, appreciated the emotional and symbolic importance of Dravida Nadu and the importance of tactfully handling its abandonment. Annadurai, therefore, quietly began to oppose Sampath. Karunanidhi immediately assimilated the possibilities of the situation and maneuvered an over-confident Sampath into directly challenging Annadurai.

Once Sampath was placed in the position of challenging Annadurai, and once Annadurai himself abandoned neutrality (which he did in a series of articles in his journal, *Dravida Nadu*, entitled "All Are Kings in This Country")[25] Sampath had lost. On February 23, 1961, Sampath went on an indefinite fast to bring about unity in the faction-ridden Dravida Munnetra Kazhagam. Along with V. Munusami (mayor of Madras at the time and a member of the Sampath faction), Sampath erected a pandal (covered platform) near a local high school and decorated it with the black and red Kazhagam flags and began his fast. Since he was a member of Parliament at the time, the fast drew considerable press coverage. In the English papers the DMK had previously received very limited space. Now, however, both the *Hindu* and the *Mail*, the two most important English papers in Madras State reported the DMK factional quarrel. Annadurai and other top leaders of the Kazhagam were "forced" to come to Sampath in order to try to solve the party problems. DMK leaders Mathiazhagan, Natarajan, Asaithambi, and Nedunchezhian, all of whom were in the Sampath camp or were sympathetic to Sampath, worked hard during the period of the fast to reach an agreement. Annadurai professed concern and visited Sampath often.

As the result of this infighting, there were clashes within the city Corporation Council (which the DMK had controlled since 1959), and even a shoving match in the Madras Legislative Assembly between members of the DMK in opposite factions. On the third day of Sampath's fast, Annadurai assured him that "every effort would be made to locate evil forces within the

organization and root out such elements without fear or favor."[26]
He also deplored "tendencies to resort to violent conduct to
ventilate political differences." "I am," he said, "as keen as
Mr. Sampath to preserve not only the integrity of the party,
which we built up with tears and toil, but also to see that the
organization is maintained with the highest standards of purity
and discipline. I have also been able to see today indications
of a change of heart that Mr. Sampath desired."[27] That was
in February. But soon the surface unity collapsed. Karunanidhi's
and Sampath's followers continued to criticize each other vehe-
mently, and finally Karunanidhi and Sampath renewed their
attacks. Annadurai wrote his series of articles criticizing Sampath,
and the issue of Dravida Nadu was resolved by Annadurai
deciding not to abandon the secession demand. Annadurai had
firmly joined the Karunanidhi camp, forcing Sampath to submit
or leave.

For his part, Sampath was apparently deceived into thinking
that more members would bolt the party with him than were
in fact ready to do so. Asaithambi, nephew of K. Kamaraj and
editor of a Tamil journal, was a Sampath supporter, as was
Kannadasan, who was also editor of *Thenral*, A tamil journal.
T. K. Srinivasan, frequently a contributor to *Dravidam*; C. P.
Arasu, an editor of a Tamil journal; Anbazhahan, an exprofessor,
Tamil scholar, and powerful speaker; T. K. Ponnuvelu, an
important student leader; and Mathiazhagan, one of the major
founders and leaders of the party were numbered among his
followers. But when Sampath left the party, only Kannadasan
left with him. V. Munusami, who was mayor of Madras, left
temporarily but quickly returned when faced with the prospect
of a long period in the political wilderness building up a new
party.

Why did these important leaders desert Sampath? What does
this incident tell us about the DMK party leadership in 1961?
First, those leaders just mentioned knew exactly what Sampath
stood for ideologically. They were either in attendance at the
meetings at V. P. Raman's house or knew from reliable sources
what had taken place. They also knew what Sampath's notion
of party revitalization was, and that the ideological differences
between Sampath and Annadurai or Sampath and Karunanidhi
were not central. The issues were tactical—when and how
officially to abandon Dravida Nadu as a demand. Another issue

was the role of the film community in the party and the use of drama as a vehicle for party political propaganda. These issues were not sufficiently potent to drive them out of the party, even under the umbrella of a politician of Sampath's stature.

Second, by 1961 the DMK was sufficiently institutionalized, and enough leaders had developed concrete interests in the party, that the organization was a countervailing force against centrifugal factional tendencies. Many of the top leaders who supported Sampath were reluctant to abandon the party that they had been instrumental in developing.

Pragmatic explanations, however, are not sufficient. There was also a profound attachment to Annadurai. Many top leaders, although temporarily at odds with Annadurai, were loath permanently to rupture that relationship. He was still "Anna" (elder brother) to many of them (who were his Thambis—younger brothers). For others, Annadurai represented the last faint hope for achieving ideological goals. Having material and opportunistic interest in the party does not preclude also having latent or even manifest attachment to ideological goals.

About ten thousand DMK members left the party with Sampath.[28] Among these lower-level party adherents there was much confusion about exactly what Sampath stood for. There was an erroneous impression that Sampath was going to lead agitation for the achievement of Dravida Nadu. Sampath left the party on April 10, 1961, and immediately organized a new party, the Tamil Nationalist party (TNP). On July 30, he explained the aims of the party, calling for a separate, sovereign Tamil Nadu *within* the Indian Union: "if any State is unable to function satisfactorily because of controls by the central government, that state had the right to become separate and sovereign. Such states should have absolute power to collect taxes and spend the money as it deems fit."[29] Explaining why the members of his party had left the DMK, he said "the demand for a separate Dravida Nadu was not practicable, it was just a dream."[30] He also accused the Kazhagam of raising false hopes in the public, and said that it had no support in neighboring states of Kerala, Mysore, and Andhra Pradash. Note that even when Sampath abandoned the demand for a separate Dravida Nadu, he did not call it undesirable, only "not practicable."

When it finally became clear that Sampath stood for abandonment of the demand for Dravida Nadu altogether, many who

left the party returned, and so the TNP never really got off
the ground. Its major activity was to expose the DMK leadership
on the Dravida Nadu issue. The TNP eventually merged with
the Congress in 1964, joining the Kamaraj faction, where a number
of followers of E. V. Ramasami (Sampath's uncle) were already
ensconced.

GOAL TRANSFORMATION[31]

I have argued that the transformation of radical social-reform
goals (anti-Hinduism, atheism, and so on) must be distinguished
from intraparty (and eventually public) rejection of Dravida Nadu.
While radical social reform was modified and redefined because
of perceived public hostility, Dravida Nadu was dropped because
it was thought not to be feasible. As early as 1958 there were
rumors of Government of India action against secessionist parties,
and all top leaders were privately committed to saving the party
from destruction, even if it meant abandoning Dravida Nadu.

Mobilization of the lower castes changed the nature of the
effective political community, and made propagandization of
radical social reform (such as atheism and anti-Hinduism) no
longer viable for a party seeking mass support. We can not,
however, understand the rejection of Dravida Nadu as a party
response to social, economic, or cultural change. In fact, the
separation demand came up again in 1968, and remains an
undercurrent of contemporary Tamil Nadu political life. Removing the underlying current of separationist sentiment would
involve formidable change, since Dravida Nadu (and/or Tamil
Nadu) separation is one way of expressing or symbolizing
Tamil/Dravidian political identity.[32] The rise of Tamil cultural
nationalism occurs in this context. Separationist sentiment has
been vitiated but not eradicated.[33]

CONCLUSION

As the DMK was in transition from movement to party, its
base of support was also increasing among lower-caste non-Brahmins, the urban lower middle class, and particularly among the
youth. Annadurai and the DMK appealed to lower-caste non-
Brahmins by defining the DMK as the party of the "common

man," the middleman," the ordinary Dravidian. The concept
of social reform was redefined and transformed from meaning
attacks on religion and Hinduism to the uplift of backward castes.

More important, the concept of "backward non-Brahmins"
did not become an alternative to Dravidian political identity,
as it might have. The concept of "non-Brahmin" as a political
entity faded from public usage after its fragmentation into
"forward" and "backward" segments, and was replaced by
Dravidian political identity. The "common man" was the embodiment of "Dravidian-ness" in the DMK formulation. This vitiated
any ideological opposition between "backward" and "forward"
castes and, needless to say, this way of perceiving political reality
subsumed class conflict to Dravidian nationality. Annadurai even
did an about-face, including Brahmins in Dravidian nationality.

The factional quarrel that ruptured the party in 1961 was a
manifestation of the turmoil accompanying organizational and
ideological transformation. Transformation from movement to
party was a multidimensional process involving routinization of
the party bureaucratic structure, political socialization of party
leadership, and goal transformation. Ideological and organizational transformation posed new problems for the party. The
dilemma of the 1940s and 1950s was how to attract mass support
and extend commitment to the party ideology and to Dravidian
political identity in a changing political arena. The problem of
the 1960s was how to maintain and extend support after the
key goal of Dravida Nadu separation was abandoned, and after
transformation to a political party. The next chapters pursue
this theme.

---

[1] Of course, the Dravidian leaders emphasized that they represented the forces
of rationality, but rationality had previously been symbolically identified with
atheism and anti-Hinduism.

[2] For example, Satyiavani Muthu, minister for Harijan affairs in the DMK
government formed after 1967, who comes from a family involved in the Buddhist
wing of the rationalist movement.

[3] T. M. Partasārti, *Ti Mu Kalaka Varalāru [History of the DMK]*.

[4] From the DMK ideologues' point of view, of course, Congress social reform
was form and not substance, since it did not envisage the eradication of Hinduism.

[5] See Beteille, *Class, Caste, and Power*, pp. 180-181 for a lengthier discussion
of Brahmin reaction to DK support of Congress. In later years Brahmins become
more and more hostile to the Congress because of DK support. This alienation
bore bitter fruit for the Congress after the formation of the Swatantra party,
when Rajagopalacharia came out of the political retirement forced on him by

the events of 1953 to form the Swatantra party. Many Brahmins became Swatantra supporters.

[6] In fact, the radical goals of the Dravida Kazhagam have never been transformed. Although the organization has lost ground, E. V. Ramasami retained a good deal of power and influence until his recent death.

[7] The "rationalist" performances of the Ramayana are among the most famous Dravida Kazhagam activities. About the Ramayana, one of the central Hindu religious mythologies, E. V. Ramasami has said: "The Ramayama is not based on any historical truth. It is a fiction. According to it, Rama was not a Tamilian nor did he belong to Tamil Nad. He was a Northerner. Ravana who was killed by him was the King of Lanka, i.e. southern Tamil Nad." E. V. Ramasami, *The Ramayana: A True Reading* (Madras: Rationalist Publications, 1959), p. iii.

[8] *Murosoli*, April 16, 1954.

[9] See, for example, the 1950 exchange between Gopala Reddy and M. S. Abdul Majid: in Tamil Nadu, Government Order 1821, June 12, 1950:

"M. S. Abdul Majid: Is it not a fact that the age-long caste system in this country is based on the laws of Manu, and may I know whether it is the intention of the government to go against the very Laws of Manu?

"Reddy: What is desirable for a community must be decided by the community itself. As I said, *government action is not called for in this matter.* [My emphasis.] People are not anxious to follow Manu. They are certainly at liberty to abolish the caste system."

[10] Information for these tables come from H. K. Ghazi, *I.A.S. Report on the Fourth General Elections in Madras, 1967* (Madras: Government of Madras, 1968), vols. I,II, III.

[11] Quoted in *Murosoli*, March 29, 1957.

[12] Some independent candidates held a Dravidian ideological perspective. The DMK was most successful in aggregating support from this type of independent.

[13] See Rudolph and Rudolph's discussion of vertical mobilization in *Modernity of Tradition*, pp. 24-27. They compare and contrast vertical, horizontal, and differential mobilization.

[14] Interviews with DK adherents and leaders, as well as others now out of the DK but still close to E. V. Ramasami, all indicate this pessimism on his part.

[15] This section on the attitudes of party adherents is based on interviews.

[16] *Homeland*, 1958.

[17] *Dravida Nadu*, September 13, 1959.

[18] One of the most widely discussed demonstrations during this period was the 1958 black flag demonstration against Nehru. This account is based on Tamil Nadu, Government Order 519, May 17, 1958 and Tamil Nadu, Government Order 793, March 12, 1959.

[19] Tamil Nadu, Government Order 240, February 15, 1961.

[20] See the party press during the years 1957 to 1958. For example, in 1958 *Homeland*, an article appeared entitled "Lincoln in the Legislature." In that article, the author wrote that "the words 'Dravida Nadu' were on the lips of practically all the legislators, who participated in the debate on the Governor's address in the Madras Assembly last week. This was the special feature that characterized this session and we welcome this development."

[21] Although called schools, they were one-shot meetings in which top leaders spoke on specific topics.

[22] Information on the Sampath faction and on DMK factionalism comes from interviews, newspapers, and press reports.

[23] DMK party members often refer to different factions in English as "groups."

[24] The possibility of outlawing separatist parties had been "in the air" almost since Independence, and was being discussed with increasing seriousness after States Reorganization in 1956 was seen as a threat to national integration. The phrase "emotional integration" also achieved increasing currency after 1956.

[25] C. N. Aṇṇaturai, "Ellōrum Innāṭṭu Mannar" [All Are Kings in This Country] *Dravida Nadu*, November 1961. Annadurai did not publicly denounce those who wanted to drop the Dravida Nadu demand, since that discussion was never made public. Even within the party only the top leaders knew the real source of conflict.

[26] *Mail*, February 12, 1961 and thereafter.

[27] *Mail*, February 26, 1961.

[28] Total DMK membership at the time was 450,000 in 4,800 party branches. (*Mail*, July 9, 1961). The figure of 10,000 comes from interviews. It has also been estimated that as few as 5,000 members left. However, some DMK leaders have indicated that the 10,000 figure may be closer to the truth, although they argue that almost all quickly returned to the DMK.

[29] *Mail*, July 30, 1961.

[30] *Ibid.*

[31] For a schematic analysis of types of goal transformation, see Mayer N. Zald and Roberta Ash, "Social Movement Organizations: Growth, Decay and Change," *Social Forces* 44 (1966), 327-341.

[32] As we shall see, this does not mean that a vast majority of Tamilians are ready to separate from India. The argument is, rather, that the links between separation and political identity are complex.

[33] For another view of goal transformation in the Dravidian movement, see Robert Hardgrave, Jr., *The Dravidian Movement* (Bombay: Popular Prakashan, 1965).

CHAPTER SIX

Politics of the Loyal Opposition

BETWEEN the 1962 and the 1967 general elections, the DMK increased its electoral support and enhanced its image as a responsible opposition. In the 1962 elections the DMK secured fifty seats in the Legislative Assembly, thus becoming the major opposition party. By 1967, the party captured the state government.At the same time that DMK support was increasing, the Congress party in Tamil Nadu was losing some of its capacity to mobilize or ally with emerging social and economic groups. The language issue in general, and the 1965 language riots in particular, were important factors discrediting Congress and increasing DMK support. But the way had already been paved for DMK expansion into rural areas and southern districts. During the movement phase and afterwards, party volunteers journeyed throughout the state, holding public meetings to familiarize Tamilians with DMK ideology. The heavy party involvement in the film industry meant numerous films with DMK themes and with overt and often heavy-handed display of party symbols. Furthermore, DMK ability to win control of the state government after only ten years (from 1957 when it first contested the general elections to 1967) must be understood in terms of the long history of the Dravidian movement.

THE 1959 CORPORATION ELECTIONS: PRELUDE TO THE
1962 STATE ASSEMBLY CONTEST

In February 1962, the third general elections were held in Tamil Nadu. Preparations began as early as 1959, when DMK optimism was buoyed by the party victory in the Madras Corporation elections. In 1959, Congress changed the pre-Independence precedent of nonpartisan Corporation elections and contested these elections on a partisan basis. This maneuver probably reflected the Congress hope that they could gain control of the Corporation.

The Madras Corporation is divided into 100 divisions. Each division elects one representative. The DMK contested 90 divisions in 1959, while Congress contested all 100. The Congress campaign reflected party self-confidence based on twenty years of Corporation control. In contrast, the DMK saw the election as an opportunity for building the party and consolidating support, but hardly believed it would be possible to defeat the Congress. DMK campaigning consisted of daily meetings and processions, street dramas, and other activities that were lively mixtures of entertainment and politics. Red and black rising sun symbols (the DMK electoral emblem) appeared all over Madras City. Meanwhile, Congress concentrated on door-to-door canvassing. As table 6-1 indicates, while the DMK won 45 of 90 contested seats, the Congress won only 37 of 100.

In the Coimbatore City elections, the Communist party won the second largest number of seats, while the Congress had a plurality but not a majority.[1] The DMK and the Communist party then reached an understanding: the Communists and their allies agreed to support the DMK candidate for mayor of Madras, while the DMK agreed to support the Communist party candidate in the Coimbatore mayorality election. Success in the 1959 Corporation elections and election of a DMK mayor were significant victories. Madras party cadres greeted this event with enthusiastic emotional displays and impromptu public processions. DMK control over the Madras Corporation has persisted to the present.[2]

1960 ANTI-HINDI AGITATION: PRELUDE TO THE 1962
STATE ASSEMBLY CONTEST

The 1959 Corporation victory was followed in 1960 by a successful DMK propaganda effort on the language issue. The occasion

TABLE 6-1
Results from 1959 Madras Corporation Elections

Party	Number of seats won	Number of places contested
DMK	45	90
Congress	37	100
Independents	13	147
Communist	2	17
Praja Socialist party	2	4
Socialist	1	18
Jana Sangh	0	8

for DMK activity was a Government of India directive concerning the institutionalization of Hindi as the language of administration by 1965. In the Working Committee meeting of the DMK, a resolution was passed criticizing this directive, stating that if it were not withdrawn before September 30, 1960, the "DMK will be forced to launch an agitation."[3] A copy of the directive was sent to the president of India. E.V.K. Sampath also forwarded a letter to the president, saying "if you do not modify or deny your intention to impose Hindi on the South, we will launch an agitation." About the president's scheduled visit to the south, he warned, "We are sorry to learn of your proposed visit at the most inauspicious and inappropriate time. Dravidam which is fully conscious of the evil effects of your directive now anxiously looks forward to your order of withdrawal of the directive. The whole Dravidam is disgruntled at your directive imposing Hindi."[4]

Later, when the visit was confirmed, an anti-Hindi agitation conference[5] was convened and a decision taken to display black flags on his arrival.[6] Annadurai was president of the conference. His speech on that occasion is useful for understanding the interrelation of agitational politics, Tamil linguistic nationalism, and the DMK political role as the "responsible" opposition:

> Ever since the inception of this organization, at no time has there been a craving in me for conducting any agitation, because the party was never dependent on conducting of agitations for its sustenance. The DMK has grown up to undreamt-of heights and has carved out for itself a special status of its own. And, the DMK will never lose its grip by unnecessarily engaging itself in agitations.
>
> Whenever my brothers in the party demand that we should agitate, I have pacified them, saying "Wait" and I am not ashamed openly to acknowledge this here and the fact that my words were obeyed only indicates the support that a leader receives from his party men.
>
> We decided on this agitation because all the doors for an honorable reconciliation, an acceptable compromise, have been closed to us, and if we do not act fast, our self-respect and honor will be in jeopardy. We do not consider agitation as a plaything.[7]

Annadurai was sincere here about his own reluctance to sanction agitations. In the 1960 anti-Hindi stir, however, younger elements in the party determined policy. DMK students were particularly anxious for the party to back up its flamboyant and dramatic rhetoric.

The DMK action provoked a quick response. C. Subramaniam stated that he was confident that he could get the DMK to withdraw its ultimatum; that he never considered language the issue of one party, and that the "government has consulted in every one of the meetings on this issue and has always arrived at a unanimous decision."[8] (He meant here that the government had consulted with the opposition parties.) Home Minister Pandit Pant devoted a lengthy speech in Parliament to the language question and Nehru's assurances; newspaper articles described the president's directive, which previously received little coverage. Answering Sampath's letter, Nehru stated " the President's directive has, in fact, only served to explicate my assurance further. The Home Minister has also given the same assurance in the Lok Sabha a day or two back."[9]

The DMK interpreting this as a promise that "Hindi will not be thrust upon us," called off its agitation and celebrated a "victory" by holding a large meeting on the Madras City Marina.[10] On that occasion Annadurai said,

It was a resounding success for the DMK to have received from the center in writing that Hindi will not be thrust upon us.

I will say with pride that the last true democrat in the Congress Circle is Mr. Nehru. It was because of this that Mr. Nehru was impelled to send the assurance sought by Mr. Sampath within four hours of its asking. Mr. Nehru though was poignantly aware that the representation of the DMK in the five hundred strong parliament is only two, he saw fit to send a reply to Mr. Sampath's letter without delay. Mr. Pant has also given an oral assurance in the Parliament. If the DMK is still adamant to stage a black flag demonstration, we will be branded as running from our duty and transcending our limits.[11]

The DMK felt they had accomplished as much as was reasona-

bly possible. They could claim victory. They also garnered
supportive publicity and projected themselves as the protectors
of Tamil. The DMK naturally hoped this could be parlayed into
additional election propaganda at the right time. Annadurai felt
this would bring a renewal of intraparty enthusiasm before the
elections. Instead, the unexpected occurred, and instead of unity
and party enthusiasm, 1961 brought the factional split discussed
in the last chapter, which weakened the party immediately before
the 1962 electoral campaign. Nevertheless, the DMK still attempted to capitalize on the 1959 and 1960 "successes" during
the 1962 campaign.

1962 ELECTIONS: CAMPAIGN AND BACKGROUND

During the 1962 campaign, the DMK claimed that as an egalitarian
party, they had brought about changes in the Corporation that
benefited the lower and middle classes. They cited the repeal
of the bicycle tax as an example. They also claimed that the
new administration had brought about desirable changes in the
provision of drinking water, and in education, health, road
maintenance, and a crackdown on tax evaders. The DMK's major
claim was that since they had administered the Corporation
efficiently, the Congress charge of lack of experience and ability
was refuted. The DMK used the 1960 agitation as "proof" to
substantiate its claim to be the true protector of Tamil, and
also promoted changing the state name to Tamil Nadu, and
changing the language of intrastate administration from English
to Tamil.

Apart from these issues, the DMK criticized the rise in prices,
reiterated their claim of gross disparity between northern and
southern economic development, and charged Congress with
corruption—all typical electoral issues. Although the DMK
leadership had not formally abandoned the Dravida Nadu goal
in 1962, given the inclination of the top leadership it was only
a matter of choosing the right time. In general, Dravida Nadu
was not emphasized in electoral propaganda. The exceptions
were Nedunchezhian's 1961 DMK history,[12] which emphasized
the commitment to a separate Dravida Nadu, as did "Murosoli"
Maran's[13] lengthy pamphlet, "Why Do We Want This Sweet
Dravidam?"[14]

Apart from language, successful administration of the

Corporation, and pragmatic, bread and butter issues, the DMK also criticized the Congress rule as despotic. They especially condemned the "unfairness" of the Congress 1962 electoral tactics. In that election, Kamaraj forged a daring strategy, concentrating disproportionate effort on the fifteen constituencies that had elected DMK candidates in 1957, apparently confident that the Congress would retain almost all its old seats. The strategy was based on a misconception of the 1957 DMK victories as flukes. Kamaraj also overestimated the potential benefits to the Congress of the 1961 DMK factional split.

In 1962, therefore, the DMK faced a critical challenge. In addition to the full weight of the Kamaraj electoral machine in those fifteen constituences, they faced the Tamil Nationalist Party, which had as its central goal exposing the DMK on the issue of Dravida Nadu and curbing the growing charismatic appeal and mobilizing power of Annadurai. The TNP attacked on a number of fronts, using public speeches, articles and pamphlets, wall posters, and so on. One of the most interesting series of articles appeared in Kannadasan's *Thenral*. They were collected and published by the TNP and entitled "A Glance at Anna's Politics" by "A Politician." In the preface, Kannadasan wrote,

> Mr. Annadurai is a man of good artistic taste. He is a good literary philosopher, a good orator. But it is doubtful how much he possesses the characteristic qualities and habits that a politician should have. Right persons though they undertake wrong responsibilities may succeed in their undertakings. Wrong persons taking reasonable and right responsibilities for lack of efficiency fail in their attempts. It is the sincere conclusion of those who lived and moved hand in hand with Mr. Annadurai that he is unfit to be a leader, he is a wrong leader.

Here the TNP sought to criticize the DMK, but at the same time, not to completely blame Annadurai. Annadurai was merely inefficient, perhaps timid and confused. Invectives were saved for the second-rank leaderhip, particularly Karunanidhi. Other TNP pamphlets argued that the Dravida Nadu demand was merely a pipe dream. One, entitled, "Dravida Nadu: an Onion," [16] argued that the demand resembled an onion: "as you peel off the layers, each layer leads you on expectantly until you reach the center layer and there is nothing." The TNP activity represented a kind of artistic political one-upmanship, since the DMK was famous for homey analogies and illustrations as the basis of complex political argumentation.

The sudden TNP exit, and the fact that both Karunanidhi and Kannadasan were crafty practitioners of political street fighting, meant that political violence in the 1962 election campaign was particularly high.[17]

If these had been the only factors in the 1962 electoral equation, DMK prospects would have been bleak. Between 1957 and the electoral campaign of 1962, however, a number of other significant political events had taken place. First, the Swatantra party was founded in 1959 as an all-India venture by C. Rajagopalacharia.[18] It opposed the "failures" of Congress socialism and represented the conservative pole in Indian politics. Rajagopalacharia's first goal was to oust Congress from power. Rajaji (as he was affectionately called) believed that party combinations and alliances against Congress could have the effect of consolidating the fragmented opposition, leading to the defeat of Congress on the state level. Rajaji sought to test his theories in the Madras 1962 elections. He sent numerous feelers to Annadurai about an alliance, and at certain points it seemed that an overall electoral agreement had been reached. Swatantra and the DMK finally agreed on an alliance in specific constituencies, but not on an overall alliance. The basic effect of Swatantra in 1962 was to provide a "respectable" alternative to Congress for some Brahmins and wealthier non-Brahmins.

Another factor was the revival of the Muslim League in 1960. A government order from the Public Department described the inaugural conference:

> The Muslim League which had been practically defunct since the partition of India is now showing signs of revival. It held a conference in Madras City on the 17th and 18th of September 1960. In his Presidential address Sri Mohammed Ismail endeavored to make out that the Muslim League is not a communal body and stated that certain Muslim institutions . . . and other properties of the Muslim community continued to be in the hands of non-Muslims to the detriment of their interest so that Muslim youths find it hard to get employment in establishments, official and private, and that, in the matter of defending

the country, they stood solidly with the government.

This conference, the first of its kind in the State, after Independence, indicates the growing influence of the Muslim League among the Muslim masses in Tamil Nad.

A noteworthy feature of the speeches made at the Conference was the stress laid on the services rendered by the League to the Congress to oust the Communists from power in the midterm elections in Kerala. There are persons who attribute the revival of the League in Tamil Nad and elsewhere in India to the electoral alliance with the Congress Party in Kerala. Such persons feel that by this action, the League had been given a quasi-official recognition which was all it needed to raise visions of holding a balance of power, if properly organized on an all-India basis.[19]

The Swatantra party was of more immediate importance than the Muslim League. The Swatantra party primarily hurt Congress by attracting Brahmins and wealthy non-Brahmins. Without that Swatantra alternative, these elements would reluctantly remain in the Congress or support independent candidates. In contrast, the Muslim League leaned toward alliance with the DMK. By 1967, both the Muslim League and the Swatantra party became part of the non-Congress electoral alliance organized and led by the DMK.

Despite the Congress electoral onslaught against the DMK, a significant result of the 1962 election was the spread of DMK influence and electoral support. During the 1962 election DMK film stars were used for propaganda purposes throughout Tamil Nadu. However, the relative importance of issues, heroic image, personalities, Tamil nationalism, linguistic politics, and radical ideology differed in various districts. In general, in the southern districts, which the DMK only effectively penetrated in the 1960s, the use of film stars, linguistic politics, Tamil nationalism, and the heroic image loomed large.

AFTERMATH OF THE 1962 ELECTION

The results of the 1962 elections were mixed for Congress and the DMK. Congress won a majority of seats in the Madras Legislative Assembly, and could thus form the government without alliances. However, Kamaraj's election strategy had gone awry, and instead of being destroyed, the DMK emerged stronger than ever. Furthermore, the fifty DMK MLAs elected in 1962 were enough to elect C. N. Annadurai to the Rajya Sabha.

The Congress strategy defeated all but one of the fifteen DMK sitting members of the 1957 Madras Legislative Assembly. Only Karunanidhi remained after the 1962 elections. (In 1967, however, the DMK regained most of these constituencies.) An additional party humiliation was the defeat of Annadurai by a little-known Congressman in his home constituency. Nevertheless, the 1962 elections left the Congress shaken and concerned about DMK potential.[20] Recall that in 1962 the DMK had not yet given up the demand for a separate Dravida Nadu. One might argue the extreme position that the DMK vote in 1962 was a vote for separation; or, that 27 percent of the voters favored separation! While this was clearly not so, nevertheless, this 27 percent was willing to vote for the DMK in spite of its separationist demand. Certainly the Congress party emphasized DMK adherence to separation in the 1962 elections. Kamaraj Nadar asked in every public meeting, "Can the DMK ever hope to succeed in their objective of Dravida Nadu?"[21] Whether or not this was a factor, it was only shortly after the 1962 elections that the central government passed the Sixteenth Amendment (discussed in the next section). At the conclusion of the Southern Zonal Council meeting on December 30, 1962, Home Minister Shastri announced that legislation amending Article 19 of the constitution and requiring oaths of candidates contesting for legislative seats would be introduced at the next Parliamentary session.

SEPARATION, THE SIXTEENTH AMENDMENT, AND THE DMK

Even before Independence, the Congress leadership had been critical of what they thought of as narrow, parochial loyalties to caste, linguistic group, and region. After Independence, this concern increased and was one reason for the reluctance of the central government to sanction linguistic states reorganization until 1956.[22] The completion of states reorganization into linguistic areas enhanced the fear of national disintegration. This concern led to a 1961 chief ministers' conference on national integration. One decision of this meeting was to prohibit secessionist demands by political parties. Then came the February election and the success of the DMK. In October the Chinese border war held nation-wide attention.[23] Both these events seemed to emphasize the necessity for firm action against organizations threatening integration.

A committee on national integration and regionalism grew out of a chief ministers conference, and recommended an amendment to the Indian constitution that had the effect of prohibiting secessionist activity by political parties. The amendment was passed in October 1963, and specified that the state assembly could make laws to penalize any individual who questioned the sovereignty or integrity of India, and amended freedom-of-speech clauses to allow a requirement that all candidates for the Lok Sabha or for any legislative assembly would have to take an oath to supporting the sovereignty of India.[24]

Lest any doubts remain, in commending the bill the central law minister, A. K. Sen, said that "this was the proper time to outlaw political activities of a secessionist nature."[25] Amendment Sixteen to the Indian constitution provided formidable justification for the DMK to abandon separation.[26] As we know, the DMK top leadership had already secretly decided that separation could not be achieved and should not be maintained in the face of government action. However, lower-level leadership was still committed to separation. The party's justification for officially abandoning the Dravida Nadu demand is contained in a pamphlet written by Annadurai, entitled "To My Friends," which was circulated within the party.

Annadurai began with a consideration of reactions to giving up Dravida Nadu. He felt it necessary to reassure his party men, and argued at length against the notion of DMK cowardice, stating that neither he nor the top leadership feared imprisonment or death for their ideals. Responding to unfavorable comparisons to the Congress independence movement, Annadurai said, "Once Gandhiji proclaimed that his body would float in the Arabian Sea if the ideal of Swarajya was not realized within the specified period. But Swarajya was achieved long after that and no one questioned why the corpse did not float in the Arabian Sea. Nobody has said that cowardice is the cause for this state of affairs."[27]

This analogy is interesting. It does not adequately answer the cowardice charge, because if Gandhi's body did not "float in the Arabian Sea," it was still true that he suffered deprivation.

If one carried the analogy through logically, then the DMK
abandonment of Dravida Nadu would be comparable to a tactical
reversal in an ultimately successful freedom movement.[28]

After disposing of the cowardice charge, Annadurai answered
the question: why continue if the central demand is abandoned?
This was the issue the party leadership feared would arise in
1961. He invoked core ideals other than Dravida Nadu:

> To make the Dravidian state a separate state was our funda-
> mental ideal. A situation has arisen where we can neither
> talk nor write about this ideal. Of course, we can destroy
> the party by undertaking to violate the prohibition. But once
> the party itself is destroyed, there will not be any scope for
> the ideal to exist or spread. That is why we had to give up
> the ideal. But still we have other ideals which assure people
> a good life and good government. I feel that the party can
> continue to serve for these principles.[29]

Next Annadurai considered why the prohibitory order had been
passed. He disagreed that the Sixteenth Amendment aimed at
preventing national disintegration, and argued rather that the
Delhi government feared DMK strength in Tamil Nadu.

Almost the entire middle section of the pamphlet was devoted
to a critique of Congress rule as a "dictatorship," since it (1)
used government funds for furthering party influence; (2) limited
benefits intended for all agriculturalists to Congress agriculturalists; (3) favored Congressmen in the industrial sector; (4)
retained loopholes in many Congress social welfare programs,
particularly the land reform legislation; (5) had enriched the
"capitalists" at the expense of the worker through industrial
expansion; (6) promoted inefficient planning; (7) subverted
democracy, which became a farce because Congress financial
backing gave some an undue advantage; (8) levied taxes that
primarily hurt the middle class, not the rich; (9) allowed prices
to go up and food to become scarce; and finally, (10) accepted
foreign aid and ran up a debt to foreign countries. Annadurai
then contrasted the Congress program with DMK ideals:

> It [DMK] has two ideals. One is to get freedom for the state
> and the other to set up a good government. The DMK should
> continue to function in order to achieve good government.

All the power at present rests with the center. Provinces like
Tamil Nad are not given enough powers. All the high tax
returns go to the center. The state has got to beg for its
needs. All the proposals for industrial development come from
the center. The states had to wait to get their orders sanctioned.
Language dictatorship has been introduced through Hindi in
the center. The state has to put up with the tragic treatment
given to its mother tongue.[30]

By 1964, Annadurai was putting forward a very moderate view
of DMK notions of political reform. It is interesting that the
language issue is mentioned last. Indeed, this intraparty document
seems remarkably restrained on the question of language as a
political issue.

Annadurai's arguments were evidently convincing, since the
party was not disrupted by the abandonment of Dravida Nadu
demands in the face of the Sixteenth Amendment. After officially
giving up Dravida Nadu, the DMK concentrated more than ever
on the issues listed by Annadurai and on the politics of language.

THE DMK AND THE POLITICS OF LANGUAGE[31]

The DMK had always been identified with the Tamil "renaissance," and rightly so, since many of its leaders were instrumental
in popularizing "pure" (that is, classical) Tamil and in stimulating
interest in Tamil literature. The DMK has among its adherents
many members of the Tamil literary and scholarly community.
Part of the widespread DMK appeal to youth is its identification
with the Tamil language. The process works both ways: the
DMK is involved with Tamil because of the high proportion
of young Tamil savants among its adherents, and it attracts
students because of this linguistic stance. That the DMK has
consistently been involved in, and has politically exploited, its
Tamil literary and artistic contributions, cannot be overemphasized.

But the language issue is more complex than DMK concern
for Tamil. The oppositions of Tamil to Hindi, Tamil to Sanskrit,
Hindi to English, and Tamil to English are all elements in the
problem. For the DMK there is the additional question of student
influence within the party. At times hesitation, vacillation, and
contradictions in party policy resulted from attempts by the top

leadership to maintain the very delicate internal balance of allegiance and support. Student involvement in the DMK has been crucial in building the party, and student leaders have been integrated into the middle levels of party leadership. Throughout his life, however, Annadurai remained a moderating force on their activities and tried to contain their influence. Many leaders, such as Nedunchezhian, Karunanidhi, and even Annadurai himself were, of course, student leaders at various points in their careers.

Another aspect, seldom adequately considered, is the relationship of language to regional power and national identity. As the language issue lingers unresolved, wider and wider audiences become aware of its subtle aspects. The choice of Hindi, not English, as the official language at the center was seen in terms of national pride and the development of national coherence and emotional identity. Also it was argued that having Hindi as the official language would democratize government by making it more accessible to the masses. But the question of identity is complex in a heterogeneous country of India's magnitude. The DMK argued that regional identity is the building block of the nation and is the basis for, and not incompatible with, national loyalty.

Furthermore, the DMK pointed out that the Hindi area is one region among many in India, and that it is equivalent to, not superior to, the others. In fact, Uttar Pradesh and the Hindi states do consider themselves the "heartland states,"[32] the "real" India. In this regard, some of the arguments used to promote Hindi are not only *ad hominem* but insulting to many southerners. For example, the argument that the majority speak Hindi, no matter how large that majority (or whether it is a majority and not merely a plurality), is meaningless if Hindi speakers are clustered in one area. Similarly, it is interpreted by southerners as insulting to argue that Hindi must be substituted for English to democratize the government. If the people in one's own region consider Hindi as foreign as English, and if the choice between Hindi and English is between a language with global scope and enhanced employment opportunities, and a language that only provides limited access to another region of the country, the mass argument seems superficial and self-serving.

In 1950 it was decided that English was to continue as the official language until 1965, when it would be superceded by

Hindi. In 1958 this was modified by Nehru's assurance that English would continue as long as the southern states desired it. For both northerners and southerners however, 1965 became a crucial date.

THE EVENTS OF 1965[33]

In accordance with the provisions of Article 313 of the Indian Constitution, Hindi replaced English as the official language of the Indian union on January 26, 1965 (Republic Day). The official language act, however, provided that English might continue for limited official purposes. When Hindi was adopted, the home minister. G. L. Nanda, assured the country that the changeover would keep pace with the spread of knowledge in non-Hindi areas. These assurances were unconvincing in Madras.

In protest, the DMK decided to observe January 26, 1965 as a day of mourning by flying black flags from party offices and homes of party leaders. As a precautionary measure leading members of the DMK were placed under preventive detention early that day. Nevertheless, clashes between DMK followers and the police occurred. On the same day a DMK adherent committed suicide by self-immolation, calling his action "a protest against the imposition of Hindi and a sacrifice at the altar of Tamil." Between January 27 and February 12, four other DMK supporters burned themselves to death, and two poisoned themselves to protest against Hindi.

Significantly, Annadurai condemned these political suicides. Nevertheless, the anti-Hindi "martyrs" became objects of widespread admiration among the student community. Annadurai's condemnation gives some indication of the DMK's dilemma. The DMK wanted to maintain legitimacy as a responsible parliamentary opposition party, but also to exploit the political advantage gained from opposition to Hindi. In previous agitations, DMK student organizations had consistently provided the leadership in the overall student community. In fact, most politically active Tamil Nadu students were DMK supporters because of the party position on language.

Within the party, student leadership passed into the orbit of Karunanidhi after the exit of Sampath in 1961 and the subsequent semi-retirement of former student leader T. K. Ponnuvelu. It was a symbiotic relationship: Karunanidhi could provide funds, strategy and organizational help to student leaders and student support enhanced his position within the party.

But in 1965 the Tamil Nad Students Anti-Hindi Agitation Council, initially inspired by the DMK, took an independent stand. During the course of the agitation, as the DMK sought to halt violence, support within the Anti-Hindi Agitation Council shifted to a more radical leadership. For the first time in almost thirty years, an issue involving cultural nationalism found organizations outside the Dravidian movement leading the militant vanguard. Thirty years of Dravidian movement activity had spawned a cultural sentiment and depth of emotional feeling that could sustain itself in the face of moderating DMK attempts to bring agitations within constitutional limits.

Clashes between students and police began January 25. By January 29, the situation was under temporary control after nine hundred people were arrested in Madras City and two hundred in Madurai. In Madras, all public assemblies, meetings, or processions were banned until February 15. Annadurai and other DMK leaders who were under preventive detention were released on February 1. At that time, Annadurai stated that the only solution was to postpone indefinitely the introduction of Hindi as the official language, and to amend the constitution to that effect. Annadurai also advocated writing Nehru's assurance into the constitution. Congress leaders responded similarly to the student demonstrations. In a speech at Bangalore, Kamaraj appealed to the Hindi-speaking areas to "go slow" in the introduction of Hindi. Kamaraj, like Annadurai, emphasized that Nehru had assured the non-Hindi areas in 1963 that English would continue as an associate language as long as the people of the non-Hindi areas wished. In other words, the public statements of Annadurai and Kamaraj differed little in their position on possible solutions to the language issue.

When colleges reopened on February 8, most students observed a strike called by the Tamil Nad Student Anti-Hindi Agitation Council. The Council demanded that the constitution be amended to allow the continued use of English. In Coimbatore, a successful hartal (cessation of activity—a form of general strike) was called. On February 9, lawyers refused to attend court. There was minor violence in Trichy: a bus was burned and two post offices attacked. Students were arrested and picketing was widespread. Annadurai made the first of many appeals for the students to suspend the agitation. Within the Student Council, DMK students pushed the same line, but by February 9, neither Annadurai nor the DMK students were in control. New militant student leadership had arisen that used Tamil cultural nationalist rhetoric, but whose actions were not controlled by the DMK.

From February 10 through 12, the most violent riots since the Quit India movement shook Tamil Nadu. Trains, post offices, police stations, factories, and public buildings were attacked. Student demonstrators were joined by chronically alienated people from the slums in often uncontrollable violence. Police and/or troops opened fire in twenty-one towns, killing over sixty people. Hartals were called in the larger cities and productive activities ground to a halt. More shocking incidents included the death of at least three children in a police firing and the murder of two constables beaten by mobs in Madurai district. Ten thousand people were arrested and ten million rupees damage assessed. Countless injuries were sustained, and about seventy people killed according to the government estimate, and one hundred fifty by DMK count.

Popular reaction in other parts of India to the riots was one of deep shock and surprise. The southern stereotype of passivity and acquiescence was shattered. This stereotype, like all others, is simplistic and may have led to dangerous miscalculations. Although most northern political leaders were sophisticated about the emotional potential of the language issue, the profound sense of injustice felt by Madrasis was not appreciated. Along with the emotional issues there were also material issues: choice of official language is linked to examinations for government jobs, and English was considered the language of opportunity. However, even on the leadership level, the possibilities of widespread riots were not anticipated.

Surprisingly, the behavior of the DMK was a factor in the violence. By 1965, the DMK had become "responsible" and predictable, and their activities could be calculated and anticipated. Had the DMK remained in control, the agitation would no doubt have remained nonviolent, limited, and largely symbolic. Both state and national government could have easily handled this through limited arrests, punitive measures, and increased propaganda to ease public suspicion. But while central and state politicians appreciated DMK political popularity, they did not realize the effectiveness with which DMK and Dravidian movement cultural and political ideas had been spread and internalized in Madras State. In fact, specific DMK identification often lagged behind the spread of Tamil as a focal point of cultural nationalism. The politicization of cultural identification through the language issue had preceded DMK victories at the polls. It was obvious by 1965 that the DMK was caught on the horns of a dilemma created by success. While they were no longer willing to risk their own existence through a sustained, radical challenge to the political system on the language issue, it was nevertheless true that the need to "protect" the Tamil language had become an accepted fact in Madras politics. This "fact" led otherwise law-abiding elements (for example, the lawyers in Coimbatore) to participate in, or at least sanction, radical measures taken to protect "the mother tongue." Although the DMK was largely responsible for creating this emotional attitude toward Tamil, it was unwilling to endanger its constitutional status through radical action. Into this vacuum stepped the Anti-Hindi Agitation Council.

If the extent of the riots was unanticipated and the initial reaction one of surprise, subsequent reactions were quick and effective. C. Subramaniam and O. V. Alegasan, Madras ministers of food and petroleum, respectively, resigned their central cabinet posts after their proposal for a constitutional amendment or legislation incorporating Nehru's assurances was rejected. These gestures had great symbolic import, and were politically necessary for the Madras Congress leadership to project concern. Subsequently both quietly withdrew their resignations.

On February 11, Prime Minister Shastri made a nationwide broadcast, reaffirming Nehru's 1958 statement that "for an indefinite period . . . I would have English an associate language . . . because I do not wish the people of the non-Hindi areas to feel that certain doors of advancement are closed to them. . . . I would have it as an alternative language as long as people require it, and the decision for that I would leave not to the Hindi-knowing people, but to the non-Hindi-knowing people." [34] He then stated certain policy decisions that purported to make Nehru's assurance operational: (1) every state could transact its business in the language of its choice, or English; (2) interstate communications could be in English or accompanied by an "authentic" translation; (3) non-Hindi states could correspond with the center in English; (4) transactions of business at the central level would be in English; (5) although recruitment exams for central service posts had been in English, in 1960 it was decided that Hindi was to be permitted as an alternate. Shastri assured the non-Hindi student community that even if Hindi were an alternative "every care would be taken to be sure that their employment prospects are not adversely affected."[35]

On February 22, the Anti-Hindi Agitation Council called off the agitation and stated regrets that their peaceful, nonviolent agitation had been taken over by "anti-social elements." But the end of the agitation and Shastri's assurances did not terminate the issue. Since the language issue, at least as perceived in Madras politics, was related to nationalism and cultural integrity, its roots could not be destroyed by pruning away troublesome branches.

What was the impact of the 1965 riots? It remains to be seen who won in the long run; but Congress lost a great deal in the short run. Despite the attempts of C. Subramaniam, O. V. Alegasan, and Kamaraj to defuse the situation, the Congress administration was inevitably blamed for the language crisis as well as for the destruction of life and property during the riots. Chief Minister M. Bhaktavatsalam was a particular target of censure. Public ire, rightly or wrongly, had been aroused against Bhaktavatsalam's regime. This hostility provided the backdrop for the 1967 elections. Although the 1965 riots were not the sole reason why Congress lost in Madras in 1967, they were a basic part of the total picture.

On the DMK side, losses from the 1965 riots were not immediately apparent. However, they too suffered. Students shifted toward more radical leadership during the agitations. For the first time in almost thirty years, the DMK did not have a monopoly on student support. Given the critical importance of this support, 1965 should have had a sobering effect on DMK leadership.

1967 ELECTIONS

As a result of the 1967 elections, the DMK moved from the major opposition party to the ruling party. In 1962, the Congress had 138 seats in the Madras Legislative Assembly, the DMK 50. In 1967, the DMK had 138 seats, Congress 47. The entire Congress cabinet was defeated, and perhaps the greatest humilia-

tion of all was the defeat of Kamaraj Nadar in a Nadar constituency by a 28-year-old DMK student leader.[36]

We begin our analysis of the 1967 elections with the two-day
Trichy-Tanjore regional conference of the Dravida Munnetra
Kazhagam on June 16, 1966. At this conference of over 50,000
participants, the formation of a united front to defeat the Congress
in the general elections was promoted in speeches by Annadurai
and Nedunchezhian.[37] At that time, an alliance of the Swatantra,
the DMK and the Muslim League was envisioned. Although
there was some opposition to a united front that would include
the right-wing Swatantra party, eventually nearly unanimous
accord was reached. In December 1966, the DMK announced
constituency-wide adjustments with *four* parties—the Swatantra,
the Muslim League, the Left-Communist and the Praja Socialists.
The united front agreement was based on the strategy of defeating
Congress by reducing the number of triangular contests. Since
1961, it had been accepted wisdom in Tamil Nadu politics that
Congress victories were often based on pluralities obtained against
a divided opposition, in which none of the other parties could
win a large proportion of the vote. However, as we shall see,
the DMK percentage of the vote went from 27 percent in 1962
to approximately 40 percent in 1967.

In many ways, the issues of the 1962 electoral campaign
reappeared in 1967, but with different priorities. The language
issue was foremost in the DMK campaign, since 1965 was a
recent memory. Although Congress had earlier attempted to make
the language issue nonpartisan and to emphasize their own
objections to Hindi, the Madras Congress inevitably had to bear
the burden of the unpopular national Congress position. In
addition, Bhaktavatsalam's actions during the 1965 riots were
a source of widespread criticism.

Another focal point of DMK propaganda was the issue of
reorganizing center–state relations to provide the states with more
power. The DMK (and United Front parties) also discussed
industrial development of Tamil Nadu in this context. There
had been a proposal to build a steel plant in Tamil Nadu's Salem
district, but it had not been incorporated in the fourth Five-Year
Plan. Failure to act on the Salem steel plant was an irritant,
especially for the middle class, and provided a reference point
for the DMK claim that the states should have more power
in decisions on industrial development.

Important also was the inflation immediately preceding the February 1967 contest. Prices were high, and there were serious rice shortages at the time of polling. Annadurai promised to sell rice for the low price of one rupee for three measures (later altered to one rupee for one measure) if the DMK was elected to power.

The DMK charged the Congress with bad management of state-owned industries, corruption, and "dictatorship." It maintained that the rich dominated Congress, and that promises to farmers and other groups had not been fulfilled.

On foreign policy issues, the DMK suggested setting up an Asian common market, and asked for a smaller foreign loan burden. It applauded the nonalignment policy of the center, but added that the policy gave the impression that it was formulated to get aid from both blocs.

As in other elections, the DMK freely used film stars, processions, held huge meetings, and so on, to further the cause. On December 29, 1966, for example, the DMK held an enornous procession. *Link* reported over 300 busses, over 12,000 cyclists, and 10,000 people on foot. The procession lasted for three miles and, according to *Link*, "The Thambis [younger brothers] shouted hoarse all their dreams and aspirations. They implored Anna [elder brother] to take over the 'crown' without any more delay. The educated should rule and not the illiterate. Arignar Anna [the learned brother] is certain to rule, they cried out in lusty slogans. That the DMK is the party of the educated pitted against the illiterate Kamaraj-led Congress is, of course, an old theme familiarized by Rajaji.[38]

An event many considered significant was the attempt on the life of M. G. Ramachandran, a popular movie star and DMK candidate for the Madras Legislative Assembly. M. R. Radha, another actor and adherent of the DK, allegedly shot at M. G. Ramachandran. This incident received enormous publicity, eagerly reaped by the DMK.

DETAILED ELECTORAL ANALYSIS OF DMK RISE TO POWER[39]

DMK opposition politics culminated in the 1967 DMK assumption of power in Tamil Nadu. Internal party problems arising out of the 1961 split were surmounted (at least temporarily), and the general strategy of elaborating and exploiting Tamil nationalist issues pursued successfully. The rise of the DMK transformed the Tamil Nadu electoral system from one-party dominance to a viable two-party system. The DMK was a key factor in the political mobilization of the state and in making Tamil nationalism a pervasive political force. A detailed analysis of electoral trends in Tamil Nadu between 1957 and 1971, shows the impact of the DMK rise to power on electoral politics.

Political participation in Tamil Nadu has been influenced over the years by social position, regional variation, and party mobilization. As we have observed, upper castes and upper-class individuals dominated pre-Independence politics until the 1940s. Along with social differences between mobilized and unmobilized segments of the pre-Independence political arena were regional and locational disjunctions that structured political participation. Both Congress and the Dravidian movement were better organized in the cities than in the countryside, and in the northeastern plains than in the western and southern mountainous areas of the state. Congress, however, had penetrated the entire state during the pre-Independence period. In addition, Congress was particularly strong in some districts where the Dravidian movement was weak (for example, Coimbatore, Tirunelveli, and parts of Madurai). Congress was also strong in some districts where the Dravidian movement was active and well supported (notably Chingleput, Salem, and Tiruchirapalli). Dravidian movement organizations concentrated their activities in the districts of Chingleput, North Arcot, and South Arcot, and in eastern Salem, northern Tiruchirapalli (Trichy), and parts of Thanjavur (Tanjore). Hence, certain regions and locations in Tamil Nadu experienced early competitive mobilization by the DMK and Congress, while others did not.

It is important to recall that both as a nationalist movement and as an electoral party, Congress tended to attract certain upper-caste groups and to use vertical means of mobilization. When the DMK entered electoral politics in 1957, therefore, its potential for mobilizing support (that is, "slack" in the electoral system) was considerable. The DMK attempted to win support by aiming appeals at castes and classes not already politicized by Congress; by trying direct rather than indirect methods of mobilization in order to erode that portion of the Congress vote based on social deference; and by penetrating new regions and rural areas that the Dravidian movement had not as yet thoroughly organized. In these attempts to expand support, the DMK articulated an ideological alternative (Tamil cultural nationalism) and linked it to important pragmatic and emotional issues, such as language.

There are two kinds of evidence for the existence of "slack" in the Tamil Nadu electoral system in 1957: low voter turnout (49.3 percent) and support for independent candidates. In 1957 a tenth of the assembly seats (22 out of 205) were won by independent candidates. Independents also secured a quarter (24.7 percent) of the total valid vote. The low turnout and high aggregate support for independent candidates in 1957 revealed to the DMK leadership both a vast reservoir of unmobilized votes and the depth of unorganized but clearly non-Congress support which the party might rally around its own banner. As Table 6-2 indicates, the dramatic expansion of voter participation after 1957, the sudden drop in votes secured and seats won by independents, and the steady decline of Congress' fortunes in the state, when combined with the spectacular improvement in the DMK's position, all suggest that the DMK's strategy succeeded.

More detailed examination of the election data confirm that the pattern of DMK spread and increased support was at least two-fold. The DMK both siphoned support away from Congress and mobilized support among previously apolitical segments. The first part of the pattern (expansion of DMK suport by coopting votes from Congress) was analyzed by examining DMK-Congress interaction in constituencies contested by the DMK from one to three times between 1957 and 1967, and in 1971 in constituencies contested by the DMK from one to four times.[40] Analysis was aimed at determining how varying degrees of DMK presence in a constituency, as measured by the number of times the party contested the constituency, and how DMK voter support affected Congress' share of the vote.[41]

Table 6-3 shows the result of this analysis and answers the question: for every 1 percent increase in the DMK vote between 1962 and 1967 and between 1967 and 1971, what is the predicted percentage of Congress increase or decline for any given constituency? (Since alliances did not play a strong part in DMK-Congress interaction, table 6-3 does not include alliance percent of the vote as a control. The question of DMK and Congress alliances will be taken up below.)

Table 6-3 shows a consistent pattern of decline in the Congress

vote as the DMK entered and continually contested a constituency. In 1967, when the DMK first contested a constituency,
each percent of vote it received was associated with approximately one-half percent decline in Congress vote (−.52460); in
constituencies contested twice, each percent of increase in DMK
vote was associated with approximately .21 percent decline
(−.20716) in Congress vote, and so on. In 1971, when the DMK
initially contested a constituency, each 1 percent of the vote
it received was associated with approximately a .4 percent
(−.40561) decline in Congress vote, while in constituencies
contested four times, each 1 percent of DMK increase in vote
was associated with approximately a half percent (−.52378)
decline in Congress vote.

The general pattern is that DMK cuts into Congress vote on
first entering a constituency, then is less effective (although
Congress vote continues to decline), but gradually increases its
impact as it continues to contest the constituency. However,
running once and twice in 1971 are not very reliable as predictors,
and 1967 and 1971 do differ in one crucial way. In 1967, this
analysis explains a great deal of the variation in Congress vote
change (as measured by R^2), but in 1971 there were other strong
factors operating. This analysis shows that DMK presence in
a constituency is associated with a decline in Congress' vote,
and it supports the hypothesis that the DMK increased its base
of support partially at the expense of Congress.

The second facet of the DMK strength during this period
involves the party's politicization and mobilization of new voters.
To examine this, changes in turnout from 1962 to 1967 and from
1967 to 1971 were analyzed for each category of DMK presence
in a constituency (that is, how many times the DMK ran).
Regressions of turnout were used to test for the character and
significance of the relationship between turnout and DMK presence over time.

Table 6–4 indicates the direction, magnitude, and significance
of this relationship. In general, the DMK increases total turnout
when it first enters a constituency, and significant increases
continue with its electoral presence. In 1967 the difference in
turnout was significant only when the party contested three times.
In 1971, however, the differences were significant for all categories of DMK presence. In 1971 there was increased turnout
in those constituencies initially contested by the DMK (from

TABLE 6-2
Electoral Change in Tamil Nadu, 1957–1971

Year	Total Voter Turnout (%)	Independents		Congress		DMK		Total Number of Seats
		% Vote	Seats	% Vote	Seats	% Vote	Seats	
1957	49.3	24.7[a]	22[a]	45.3	151	12.8	13[c]	205
1962	70.6	8.2	5	46.1	139	27.1	50	206
1967	76.6	5.1	4	41.4	50	40.6	138	234
1971	71.8	6.6	10	35.0[b]	17[b]	48.6	184	234

[a] Figures for independents do not include DMK candidates running as independents in 1957.

[b] Figures refer to the Organization Congress.

[c] The DMK won a total of 15 seats when DMK independents are included.

Note: Total Tamil Nadu population in 1971 was 41,163,125.

TABLE 6-3
Effect of DMK Presence on Vote for Congress
Regression Results, 1967 and 1971

Number of times DMK contested constituency	Change in Congress percent vote	Significance of individual coefficients	*1967* R² percent of variation explained	Significance of the R²	Number of constituencies[b]
All cases	−.14851	.01	.66	.01	134
Run once (1967 only)	−.52460	.01	.67	.01	19
Run twice (1962, 1967)	−.20716	.01	.53	.01	48
Run three times (1957, 1962, 1967)	−.23544	.01	.79	.01	69

1971

Number of times DMK contested constituency	Change in Congress percent vote	Significance of individual coefficients[a]	R^2 percent of variation explained	Significance of the R^2	Number of constituencies[b]
All cases	−.07406	.05	.24	.01	158
Run once (1971 only)	−.40561	.05	.33	n.s.	11
Run twice (1967, 1971)	−.03129	n.s.	.39	.01	42
Run three times (1962, 1967, 1971)	−.32661	.01	.44	.01	48
Run four times (1957, 1962, 1967, 1971)	−.52378	.01	.51	.01	62

[a]The figure .01 indicates significance at .01 or better; n.s. means not significant.
[b]Includes only constituencies with unbroken patterns. Constituencies where interruptions occurred (i.e., constituencies not contested in consecutive elections by the DMK) were excluded.

TABLE 6-4
Effect of DMK Presence on Turnout, Regression Results, 1967 and 1971

1967				1971			
Average turnout in constituencies where the DMK never ran = 75% (N = 134)				Average turnout in constituencies where the DMK never ran = 66% (N = 158)			
Number of times DMK ran in constituency	Impact on turnout (percent)	Significance of individual coefficients[a]	Number of constituencies.	Number of times DMK ran in constituency	Impact on turnout (percent)	Significance of individual coefficients[a]	Number of constituencies.
Once (1967 only)	(75%) + .890	n.s.	19	Once (1971 only)	(66%) + 6.096	.01	11
Twice (1962 and 1967)	(75%) + 1.989	n.s.	46	Twice (1967 and 1971)	(66%) + 5.873	.01	42
Three times (1957, 1962, 1967)	(75%) + 3.047	.01	69	Three times (1962, 1967 1971)	(66%) + 5.483	.01	43
				Four times (1957, 1962 1967, 1971)	(66%) + 8.079	.01	62

$R^2 = .04$
F = not significant

$R^2 = .07$
F = significant .01

[a]The figure .01 indicates significance at .01 or better; n.s. means not significant.

66 percent in 1967 to 73 percent in 1971), as in those contested twice, three times, and four times, with the greatest increase being in the latter ($66\% + 8.1\% = 74.1\%$).

Thus table 6-4 confirms the general picture of the DMK's increasing mobilization, reaching past Congress and other parties, and politicizing new groups. The table also shows that the longer the DMK is in a constituency, the greater is its mobilizing effect. Interviews with the party's leadership and attitudinal studies done in 1968 suggest the importance of cultural nationalism in enhancing the DMK's support and increasing political participation.

URBANIZATION AND THE DMK'S IMPACT ON CONGRESS

Although the DMK's initial successes were mostly in urban constituencies, urbanization as such seems to have had little long-term effect on DMK-Congress interaction, no doubt because of the DMK's substantial inroads in rural Tamil Nadu beginning in 1962. Indeed, in 1971 it was Congress that seemed to be marginally improving its position in urban constituencies. In 1967, in all urban contests except one where the DMK and Congress were in direct competition, the DMK won.[42] In 1971 Congress succeeded in winning two important Madras City constituencies against DMK candidates. One was Mylapore, where Thirumathi Ananthanayaki won over M. P. Sivagnanam.[43] The other was Thiagarayanagar, a largely upper-class section of Madras City, where Congress won an extremely close contest.

While urbanization failed to influence DMK-Congress interaction to any meaningful degree, it did have a strong effect on turnout in 1971. Although the urban variable does not change the effect of DMK constituency presence on turnout, urban constituencies had lower turnout in 1971. Table 6-5 shows 1971 turnout for urban constituencies according to DMK presence in a constituency. The results are derived from adding urbanization as a variable in the regression of DMK presence on turnout in 1967 and 1971.

In general, urban-rural distinctions have not conditioned the results of DMK-Congress competition. Even though urbanization was an important factor in the early twentieth-century development of a non-Brahmin elite with a nascent cultural nationalist orientation, and notwithstanding the DMK's early success in

TABLE 6-5
Urban Turnout in 1971 According to DMK
Constituency Presence (1957-1971)

Number of times constituency- contested by DMK	Urban turnout (percent)
1971 only	68.3
1967, 1971	66.7
1962, 1967, 1971	67.4
1957, 1962, 1967, 1971	69.7
Never	66.1

Note: Urban constituencies are identified as constituencies falling within or including cities of 100,000 or more people as of the 1961 census. Based on the 1966 delimitation, there were 25 such constituencies in nine cities: Madras, Madurai, Coimbatore, Salem, Tiruchirapalli, Vellore, Thanjavur, Tuticorin, and Nagercoil.

Madras City, cultural nationalism is not solely or even predominantly an urban phenomenon. As Table 6-5 shows, turnout in 1971 was higher in urban constituencies contested by the DMK than in constituencies it had never contested. For constituencies contested only once by the DMK, there was a 2.2 percent increase in turnout over constituencies not contested by the DMK. The second time the DMK contested an urban constituency the effect on turnout decreased. However, the third and fourth time that constituencies were contested by the DMK, turnout increased. In general, the relationship of the DMK's presence to urban electoral participation paralleled more general statewide trends. What is surprising is the lack of a distinctive urban pattern in light of the pervasive identification of the DMK with urban discontent, problems, and perspectives. In present-day Tamil Nadu, DMK cultural nationalist appeal is both rural and urban, and exists in all areas of the state, cutting across differences in literacy, location, and levels of economic development.

THE IMPACT OF ELECTORAL ALLIANCES

The general model of DMK mobilization seems to be confirmed. In broad contours, the pattern includes DMK capacity to diminish the Congress vote and to mobilize new voters. An additional factor influencing the scope and dimensions of Congress-DMK interaction is electoral alliances. The DMK headed multiparty

alliances in both 1967 and 1971. In 1967 Swatantra, the CPM
(Communist Party-Marxist) the Praja Socialist party, the Sa-
myukta Socialist party, and seven independents contested the
elections as part of the DMK's united front. In 1971 the DMK,
Congress (R),[44] the Praja Socialist party, the Muslim League,
Forward Bloc, and the CPI formed an alliance.

Regression analysis was again used to determine how much
assistance the DMK received from its allies in 1967 and 1971.
For both elections the independent variable measuring alliance
help was never significant. This held true in constituencies where
the DMK was contesting for the first time, as well as in
constituencies which the DMK had previously contested. Since
alliance strength was not transferred to the DMK in any clear-cut
way, the DMK's increasing support and electoral victories are
mainly attributable to other factors. However, the party's electoral alliances have helped to increase the number of two or
three-candidate contests. Reduction of a number of candidates
focuses the voter's attention on the two main parties, and provides
an opportunity for more clear-cut ideological and programmatic
choices.

ELECTORAL POLITICS AND POLITICAL DEVELOPMENT

We have already traced the dramatic emergence of the DMK
as an electoral party in Tamil Nadu. The map augments our
earlier discussion by showing the spatial spread of the DMK's
victories in 1967 and 1971. By 1971 even the broad base of
DMK support in 1967 was further expanded as the DMK moved
to consolidate its substantial support in all areas of the state.
While the extreme southern and western districts still had
relatively more constituencies not won by the DMK in either
1967 or 1971, the remarkable fact is the breadth of DMK electoral
appeal. The DMK expansion is observable not only in the number
of seats won and percentage of the vote received, but also in
territorial sweep. Whatever regional disjunctions existed in Tamil
Nadu, by 1967 virtually the entire state had been penetrated
by the DMK and was thus exposed to the party's cultural
nationalist propaganda and program. By 1971 the party program
had commanding electoral support from one end of the state
to the other.

While appreciating the depth, scope, and extent of DMK

The DMK's Victories in 1967 and 1971

■ DMK won in 1967 and 1971 (N=131)

▨ DMK won in 1971, not in 1967 (N=53)

▤ DMK won in 1967, not in 1971 (N=8)

□ DMK failed to win in either year (N=42)

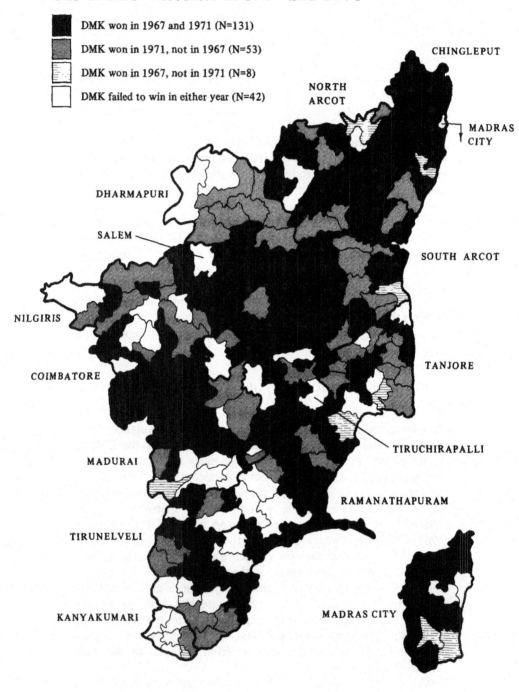

CHINGLEPUT

NORTH
ARCOT

MADRAS
CITY

DHARMAPURI

SALEM

SOUTH ARCOT

NILGIRIS

COIMBATORE

TANJORE

TIRUCHIRAPALLI

MADURAI

RAMANATHAPURAM

TIRUNELVELI

KANYAKUMARI

MADRAS CITY

Note: Constituency boundaries shown are based on the 1966 delimitation.

electoral support, it is important to realize that Congress received a higher percentage of the vote than the DMK in 1967, and even in 1971 Congress (O) received 34.9 percent of the vote and the Kamaraj-led Democratic Front 36.65 percent of the vote. Nevertheless, in terms of electoral effectiveness, the DMK has clearly been in the ascendancy, and Congress in decline. This is conveyed most succinctly by the "da Costa multiplier" (the percentage of seats won divided by the percentage vote received) shown in Table 6-6 for the two parties over the 1957-1971 period.[45] The table summarizes the increased effectiveness of the DMK in translating votes into victories, and the corresponding deterioration of the Congress' ability to do the same in Tamil Nadu. Of course, party effectiveness as gauged by the multiplier reflects a number of factors, including the capacity of a party to assess its overall electoral strength and to limit the number of constituencies contested accordingly. What makes the DMK's record all the more impressive is that its effectiveness has gone hand in hand with expanded electoral efforts.

Besides showing the change in DMK and Congress effec-

TABLE 6-6
Electoral Effectiveness of the DMK and Congress
in Tamil Nadu
(1957-1971)

		DMK	Congress
1957	Percent seats won	6.3	73.7
	Percent votes received	12.8	45.3
	Multiplier[a]	.492	1.6
1962	Percent seats won	24.2	67.5
	Percent votes received	27.1	46.1
	Multiplier	.892	1.45
1967	Percent seats won	59.0	21.4
	Percent votes received	40.6	41.4
	Multiplier	1.45	.517
1971	Percent seats won	78.6	6.5
	Percent votes received	48.6	35.0
	Multiplier	1.62	.186

[a] The multiplier is the percentage of seats won divided by the percentage of votes received. In 1971 Congress (O) data are used.

FIGURE 2

CHANGE IN NATURE OF CONTESTS OVER FIVE GENERAL ELECTIONS

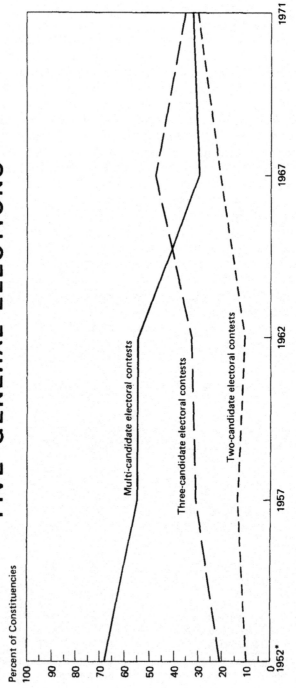

Percent of Constituencies

Multi-candidate electoral contests

Three-candidate electoral contests

Two-candidate electoral contests

100 90 80 70 60 50 40 30 20 10 0

1952* 1957 1962 1967 1971

*Before states reorganization

tiveness, table 6-6 draws our attention to the overall context
of electoral competition in Tamil Nadu. After 1957 two key
trends may be noted: increased electoral development and elaboration of two-party competition.[46] These are, in fact, interrelated
aspects of the electoral system's development in the state, since
the growth in participation has been both stimulated by and
contained within the scope of DMK-Congress competition. The
polarization of electoral competition in Tamil Nadu is reflected
in part by the trends shown in figure 2. Since 1952 the number
of multicandidate electoral contests has sharply declined, while
the number of two-candidate (that is, straight) contests and also
of three-candidate races has increased. Because the DMK and
Congress both contest so pervasively, the overwhelming majority
of electoral contests involve DMK and Congress candidates.
Indeed, the pattern in figure 2 is consistent in all regions of
the state, and holds despite varying caste majorities, class
composition, occupational, subregional and other differences.
The generality of the pattern indicates the extent to which
Congress and the DMK have increasingly come to dominate
Tamil Nadu politics, to the exclusion or impotence of other
parties and independents almost everywhere.

A related facet of the steady polarization of party competition
between 1957 and 1971 is the decline in support for other parties
and independents. In 1957 the DMK and Congress between them
won a modest 58.1 percent of the total valid vote, most of this
going to Congress. In 1971 the two parties amassed a formidable
83.6 percent of the vote, the majority now going to the DMK.
As Table 6-7 indicates, both independents and other parties have

TABLE 6-7

Polarization of Support in Tamil Nadu (1957-1971)

Year	Other parties[a] (percent)	+	Independents (percent)	=	Total (percent)
1957[b]	17.2		24.7		41.9
1962	18.6		8.2		26.8
1967	12.9		5.1		18.0
1971	9.8		6.6		16.4

[a] "Other parties" include all parties recognized by the Election Commission
excluding the DMK and Congress.

[b] Although DMK candidates ran as independents in 1957, they are not included
here.

suffered a loss of votes during this period, which reveals a linear if slowing decline in their capacity to attract support. To a degree that surpassed all other states in India between 1957 and 1971, politics in Tamil Nadu were increasingly bipolarized.

The declining success of independent candidates in Tamil Nadu is of particular interest because of its implications for assessing the continued viability of the factors that enable independents to garner electoral support. One source of independent candidates was caste groups which felt inadequately represented by the major political parties. For example, in southern Tamil Nadu during the 1950s many Maravars, Kallars, and Thevars supported independent candidates (as well as small parties such as the Forward Bloc) because of their discontent with Congress.[47] In later years the DMK was able to gain a foothold and mobilize some of the discontented caste groups in this area. Elsewhere in the state the same pattern of caste-backed independent candidates has existed, although lacking the drama of the circumstances that stimulated Muukoolathur independents.

Another source of independent candidates was local notables, usually high-caste landlords seeking to translate traditional relations with lower-caste economic dependents and allies into political power. As with caste-based independent candidates, this form of candidacy took many forms.

A third type of independent was the ideological independent whose views were not reflected by the platforms and orientation of the major parties. Prior to the DMK's entry into electoral politics, for example, some party members and sympathizers contested elections as independents. While the DMK was subsequently able to win the overwhelming support of Tamil nationalists, a number of radical Tamil nationalists remained outside the DMK, contesting elections as independents or on the We Tamils and Tamil Arasu Kazhagam tickets during the 1960s. A few radical social reformers and other ideological independents also continued to contest elections as independents.

The final important type of independent candidacy emerged from political party conflict and factionalism. This included disappointed candidates who became "spoilers," or perhaps members of alienated factions who sought to take their viewpoint to the electorate.

The decline in independent candidates and in voter support for independent candidates reflects the decreased political viability of some of the modes of protest, opposition, or mobilization represented by independents. It also reflects the impact of the DMK and DMK-Congress competition in establishing the "rules of the game"(that is, defining legitimacy), setting ideological priorities, mobilizing widespread support, and aggregating a wide variety of interests and groups within the two parties.

MODERNIZATION AND HEIGHTENED POLITICAL CONSCIOUSNESS

Thus far we have examined the spread of DMK popularity. But what are the underlying factors that account for the rapid and pervasive acceptance of the DMK?

It is ironic that growth and penetration of support for the DMK occurred in one of the best-administered states of India. Tamil Nadu was one of the five states that showed rates of growth higher than the all-India average (4.17 percent versus 3.01 percent for all states). In agricultural productivity and education the state had a particularly good record. In addition, there had been extensive irrigation, installation of village electric power, and a large-scale road building program. In fact, the picture is generally one of substantial and visible economic development in Tamil Nadu since the first Five Year Plan was inaugurated in 1952.

However, we must ask two questions about this economic development: who benefitted from it, and what was *believed* to be the state of development in Tamil Nadu? Even concrete economic improvements are not objective facts that speak for themselves, but must be put in the context of expectations—and expectations are structured by politicization and ideology. The interpretative framework can be as crucial in some cases as externally measurable facts.

While Congress policies were beneficial to the state as a whole, they benefitted some segments of the population more than others, thus becoming a source of discontent. Many whose lives were objectively improved because of Congress policies became critical of the Congress government because their horizons and expectations had been expanded and their political and social consciousness raised. In discussing the 1967 elections, C. Subramaniam placed great emphasis on this point.

People try to find simple reasons for the Congress defeat. More fundamental reasons are involved in the Congress defeat. It happened because of the success of the Congress administration. The implementation of the three Five-Year plans was the best in Madras State [out of all the Indian states]. There was economic development, provision of amenities and considerable educational progress. However, for many backward [class] families, that educated their children, after the children were educated if they are not able to get jobs, then education becomes a liability instead of an asset. In spite of economic development, it was not possible to provide [full or increased] employment. Education became a liability because then the person expected a higher standard of living. Thus, Congress could not reap the benefits of a good policy. [Recall that D.M.K. support came heavily from younger segments of the population]. With respect to economic development, in fifteen years large sections of the people had benefits of economic development. Even though the poor sections had disadvantages the gap between the richer sections and the poor sections had decreased. However, after fifteen years of having given support to Congress . . . poor sections found their lot looked more miserable . . . .

Rural electrification is an example. Initially it gave a thrill to the people [however] only the better placed sections were able to use electrification for irrigation and in their houses.

Roads are another example. Who gets the benefit of a village road? You must own a bullock cart to take advantage of that road. If you walk it makes no difference.[48]

C. Subramaniam then went on to say that because they could not take full advantage of improvements the way the rural elite could, eighty percent of the people thought they were worse off after fifteen years of Congress rule. This is important because growing discontent provided the fertile ground in which DMK ideology could expand and take hold, particularly among young people. These young people formed the cadres of DMK volunteers and filled lower-level leadership ranks. They also initially responded to Tamil nationalism and appeals to the present generation to emulate past greatness. Notions of Tamil nationalism and a national identity specifically Tamil in character spread as the DMK moved into every area of Tamil Nadu.

CONCLUSION

After entry into electoral politics in 1957, the DMK gradually began to modify earlier anti-Brahminism as well as its radical atheistic ideology. As the party gradually became more pragmatic, less ideological, more moderate, and less radical, it began to focus on specific issues, such as language, economic development, inflation, and corruption. All these were important in the 1967 elections. Their importance derived partially from events the DMK could not foresee or control (such as high levels of inflation and food shortages prior to the 1967 elections), and partially from the sustained emphasis given key issues over the years by the DMK.

DMK appeal is complex and multifaceted. Our discission has shown the pragmatic "bread and butter" context of cultural nationalism. It is important to note that discontent developed in a state where the Congress government was pursuing modernization policies. It should be emphasized, however, that although Tamil Nadu is relatively prosperous, it still contains many tragically poverty-stricken people whose truncated expectations reflect concrete exploitation and oppression.

In fact, relative deprivation, heightened expectations, and existence of exploitation and oppression are not mutually exclusive explanations. They may be linked features of a society characterized by social change and emergence of heightened political consciousness. Heightened political consciousness is a prerequisite to the ability to articulate criticism of exploitation and oppression. It is in the context of emerging political consciousness and competing ideologies that men with varying personal qualities judge and attach themselves to new parties, movements, and identities. Given appropriate ideological frameworks, Tamilians were able to formulate statements of their deprivation and link these statements to political activities.

[1] See Lloyd I Rudolph, "Urban Life and Populist Radicalism: Dravidian Politics in Madras," *Journal of Asian Studies* 20 (May 1961), 283-297, for further discussion of this election and the agreements between the various political parties in the Corporations of Madras and Coimbatore.

[2] In contrast to the 1959 Madras Corporation elections, the DMK performance in the 1964 municipal elections was not impressive. Since the DMK only started contesting elections in 1957, they were simply not well organized throughout the state.

[3] Partasārati, *Ti, Mu, Kalaka Varalāṛu (History of the DMK)*.

[4] *Ibid.*

[5] Approximately 100,000 attended this conference, held July 31, 1960.

[6] Paratasārati, *Ti, Mu, Kalaka Varalāṛu.*

[7] *Ibid.*

[8] *Ibid.*

[9] *Ibid.*

[10] *Ibid.* The Marina is the beach that runs the length of Madras City along the Bay of Bengal. Evening political meeting on the marina and colorful torchlight processions became a DMK trademark. Thousands would line the beach to hear Annadurai.

[11] *Ibid.*

[12] V. R. Neṭunseṛiyan, *Ti. Mu. Ka. (D.M.K.)*, (Madras: Tamilnad Puthaha Nilayam, 1961).

[13] "Murosoli" Maran is Karananidhi's nephew and a publisher of *Murosoli* newspaper.

[14] Murosoli Māran, *Ēn Vēṇṭum Inpatirāviṭam?* (Why Do We Want This Sweet Dravidam?), (Madras: Muthuval Pathipaham, 1962).

[15] "A Politician," *Aṇṇāvin Aracil Oru Kaṇṇēṭṭam (A Glance at Anna's Politics)*, (Madras: Tamil Dhesita Party, 1962).

[16] R. Sanmukam, *Tirāviṭa Nāṭu Oru Veṅkāyam (Dravida Nadu: an Onion)* (Madras: Madhura Nilayam, 1961).

[17] Tamil Nadu, Government Orders 4441 to 4443, December 19, 1961. Home 1961. Proceedings of the Law and Order Session of the Collector's Conference held on May 11, 1961.

[18] See Howard L. Erdman, *The Swatantra Party and Indian Conservatism* (London: Cambridge University Press, 1967), for a discussion of the founding of the Swatantra party, its policies, and strategy.

[19] Tamil Nadu, Government Order 53, January 10, 1961.

[20] Stanley A. Kochanek, in *The Congress Party of India: the Dynamics of One-Party Democracy* (Princeton: Princeton University Press, 1968) states that one reason Kamaraj was receptive to proposals to revitalize the Congress organization (the Kamaraj plan,) was his deep concern over DMK victories in the 1962 elections.

[21] V. K. Narasimhan, *Kamaraj, a Study.* (Bombay: Manaktalas, 1967).

[22] W. H. Morris-Jones, *The Government and Politics of India* (London: Hutchinson University Library, 1964), and Harrison, *India: the Most Dangerous Decades*, for a discussion of states reorganization.

[23] It is also interesting that the response of the DMK to the 1962 war was very patriotic in tone. Annadurai and other leaders took particular care to emphasize their support for the government in this emergency, and also their desire to contribute to the war effort.

[24] C. N. Annadurai, *To My Friends*, (Madras: n.p., 1963).

[25] *The Asian Recorder* (February 19-25, 1963), p. 5055 INI:D.

[26] *Ibid.*, 5055: INI:D; Specifically, the bill amended Articles 19, 84, and 173 of the third schedule of the constitution: "Amendments to Article 19 . . . enable the state to make any law imposing reasonable restrictions on the exercise of the rights of freedom of speech and expression, assembly and forming associations or unions, in the interests of the sovereignty and integrity of India." K. Manoharan, DMK spokesman, called the bill an attempt to curtail fundamental rights and inhibit democratic and constitutional processes.

[27] Annadurai, *To My Friends.*

[28] Later, diverse interpretation of Annadurai's actions emerged in the party. One was that he was not "really" abandoning the Dravida Nadu demand at

all. Manipulation of literary analogies and speeches replete with allusions to a separate Dravida Nadu furthered the hope of those who still denied that Dravida Nadu was a dead issue after 1963.

[29] Annadurai, *To My Friends.*

[30] *Ibid.*

[31] This discussion of the politics of language is limited to Tamil Nadu, with its peculiar perspective growing out of the total context of Dravidian movement politics. For a study of the evolution of language loyalty in India and the evaluation and political role of linguistic political association, see Fyotirindra Das Gupta, *Language Conflict and National Development* (Berkeley and Los Angeles: University of California Press, 1970).

[32] See Paul Brass, "Uttar Pradesh," in Myron Weiner, ed., *State Politics in India* (Princeton: Princeton University Press, 1968).

[33] The following account is based on *Keesings' Contemporary Archives* for April 17-24, 1965, pp. 20687-20690 newspaper reports, and interviews. Also see Robert L. Hardgrave, Jr., "The Riots in Tamil Nad: Problems and Prospects of India's Language Crisis," *Asian Survey* 5 (August 1965), 399-407. Duncan B. Forrester, "The Madras Anti-Hindi Agitation, 1965: Political Protest and Its Effects on Language Policy in India," *Pacific Affairs* (1966); and Hardgrave, "Politics of Tamil Nationalism," for more on the language riots and the events leading up to it.

[34] *Keesings' Contemporary Archives*, April 17-24, 1965.

[35] *Ibid.*

[36] Srinivasan was a key student leader in the 1965 anti-Hindi agitation. After 1967 he entered the labor field, organizing DMK labor unions.

[37] K. S. Ramanujam, *The Big Change* (Madras: Higginbothams, 1967).

[38] *Ibid.*

[39] These findings were previously reported in Marguerite Ross Barnett, "Cultural Nationalist Electoral Politics in Tamil Nadu," in Myron Weiner and John O. Field, eds., *Electoral Politics in the Indian States* (Delhi: Manohar Book Service, 1975). Constituency level statiscal data were supplied by the M.I.T. Indian Election Data Project.

[40] Tamil Nadu constituencies were the same in 1967 and 1971. Between 1957 and 1962, however, and between 1962 and 1967 constituencies were redrawn. In order to perform longitudinal analyses, constituency matches were made using census and delimitation volumes plus the 1967 and 1971 electoral issues oï *Madras Information* and *Tamil Arasu*, Tamil Nadu government publications.

[41] The dependent variable for 1967 is the change in Congress' vote from 1962 to 1967 for each constituency matching. For the 1971 data the dependent variable is the difference in the Congress' vote from 1967 to 1971. In each instance the independent variable is the change in the DMK's vote, e.g., the DMK's percent vote in 1967 minus the DMK's vote in 1962, and DMK's vote in 1971 minus its vote in 1967. Breakdown runs and regressions were performed to test the hypothesis. All regressions were down with Congress' vote in the prior election as a control. Another control was the influence (percentage vote) of the DMK's electoral allies when they were a factor.

[42] The one exception was a Tirunelveli constituency, Sattangulam (#225).

[43] "Ma Po Si," as Sivagnanam is popularly known, is leader of a small radical Tamil cultural nationalist party, the Tamil Arasu Kazhagam. The TAK has now virtually merged with the DMK Mrs. Ananthanayaki is now general secretary of Congress (R). She was at the time of this election a prominent Congress (O) member.

[44] Led by Kamaraj Nadar, Congress (O) inherited the organization, headquarters, and preponderance of mass support from the old Tamil Nadu Congress

party. Congress (R) did not contest any seats for the state legislative assembly in 1971. The "O" in Congress (O) stands for organization; the "R" in Congress (R) for ruling party. Congress (R) was also referred to as the new Congress and Congress (O) as the old Congress. On the national level the new Congress, Congress (R), consisted of Mrs. Gandhi and the majority faction of the Congress party, while the old Congress, Congress (O), consisted of the minority faction in the parliamentary party and party organizations.

[45] See Eric P. W. da Costa, *The Indian General Elections, 1967* (New Delhi: Indian Institute of Public Opinion, 1967), and for further discussion of the multiplier see Lloyd I. Rudolph, "Continuities and Change in Electoral Behavior: the 1971 Parliamentary Elections in India," *Asian Survey* 11 (December 1971), 1119.

[46] Over the past decade Tamil Nadu has consistently had one of the highest turnout rates in India, if not always the highest rate.

[47] Among the factors that alienated these castes was the Congress government's intervention in the Harijan-Muukoolathur clashes in the 1950s.

[48] At the time of the interview, Subramaniam was president of the Tamil Nadu Congress party. He had previously been state finance and education minister for a time, as well as Union minister for food and agriculture. In 1972 he became Deputy Chairman of the National Planning Commission and Minister for Planning, in 1973, Minister for Industrial Development. Since October 1974 Subramaniam has been Union Minister of Finance. After the Congress split in 1969, Subramaniam became a prominent member of Congress (R) and is currently one of Indira Gandhi's closest advisors.

PART THREE

Elites, Masses, and Cultural Nationalism

CHAPTER SEVEN

Tamil Nationalism and the Political Culture of the Tamil Nadu "Common Man"

APART from the impact of economic modernization in creating discontinuities and discontent, which we have already examined, another related transformation was occuring in Tamil Nadu. This involved a structural change from caste to ethnicity, and laid the groundwork for the emergence of individualism in modern South Indian politics.

POLITICAL IMPLICATIONS OF SOCIAL TRANSFORMATION

Louis Dumont has argued that hierarchy and collectivism are the central defining characteristics of Indian society.[1] Linking these notions to politics, Dumont has explained Muslim nationalism in terms of the complex cultural distinctions and interactions between colonial British and pre-Independence Indian society. These cultural distinctions center on the notions of Indian hierarchy and collectivism as against English egalitarianism and individualism. Dumont states:

What has been attempted here is to try and understand a particular but important political phenomenon as an aspect of the interaction on the one hand, of British domination and modern Western ideals and norms on the other. To spot the broad features of this interaction and the difficulties encountered in the emergence, to this day incomplete, of nations and nationalism, we have compared in their political aspect the two social universes thus confronted. It has been shown that elements such as people and territory, normatively stressed on one side, are found as *empirical and undifferentiated datum* on the other. The orientation to ultimate values shows a more drastic and complex difference. On the traditional side, the ultimate values are found in the conformity of each element to the role assigned to it in the whole of Being as such: in the modern society, they are found in the concrete human indivisible element, which is taken as an end in itself, and

161

as the source of all norms, rationality and order. In other words, the Individual.[2]

In the case of Tamil Nadu, however, recent ethnographic evidence[3] suggests that there is not so much a direct confrontation between cultural types (hierarchical-collectivism versus individualistic-egalitarianism) as there is a transformation in Tamil Nadu from caste to ethnicity, embodying a structural change in the society. The transformation to ethnicity also involves movement from a functionally interdependent society to one in which the separate units ("castes") are functionally independent.[4] Initially, this process can be understood in the breakdown of the traditional jajmani system.[5] In describing the impact of social change on the caste system and the change from caste to ethnicity, S. A. Barnett states:

The essential structural transformation is the removal of hierarchy from this system, or what may be called the transition from caste to ethnicity. The development of caste associations explicitly changing caste behavior and allowing, unlike traditional caste courts or panchayats, personal deviance in codes-for-conduct is but one aspect of this transition. Castes are now large regional blocs, incorporating (typically by widening the marriage network) many formerly discrete subcastes. These regional blocs reckon membership through ancestry alone, *not* through adherence to a particular code for conduct. Outcasting is thus impossible and individual caste members may behave toward other castes as they wish, without fear of losing caste standing. And so while different caste blocs may claim equivalence or superiority to each other, there is no transactional way to corroborate that claim. In this case, there is an ideological shift from an emphasis upon the whole to an emphasis upon the individual or groups conceived on the model of the individual. The person, with his freedom of choice, becomes the ultimate locus of value. There is no enjoined caste-wide code for conduct, rather theoretically a person may choose any behavioral stance since he embodies within himself the inviolable essence of his caste—his ancestral blood. Or, substance now inheres in the individual.
These caste blocs do not perceive themselves as interdependent, each performing a necessary function directed toward

the whole as in the traditional caste system, but as independent units having no direct need of other caste blocs.[6]

Robert Hardgrave also emphasizes the role of social mobilization in changing traditional clusters of social, economic, and psychological commitments. Following Karl Deutsch, Hardgrave suggests that as a result of social mobilization stimulated by modernization, "the individual becomes available for new patterns of socialization and behavior."[7]

Unlike Hardgrave, I do not believe that individualism can be assumed. If Dumont and S. Barnett are correct about the structural character of Indian society (Dumont) and its transformation as a result of modernization (Barnett), individualism is an emergent process. And it is necessary to situate this process in a discussion of the nature of holism and individualism. The breakdown of ideological holism in its classic hierarchical form (caste in India) is possible (thinkable by the participants), given some alternate concept of individualism. At the all-India level, as articulated most importantly by the Congress party, the idea of individualism took over Western ideas of abstract autonomous selves of whatever cultural configuration forming the Indian polity. But this abstract individualism is not the only form of individualism. Cultural nationalism is based—to use a seemingly contradictory phrase that emphasizes our lack of a genuine comparative vocabulary[8]—on "collective individualism." In a holistic universe, there are no selves; in Dumont's apt metaphor, persons and groups are to society as parts of the body are to the whole body: no part can represent the whole in miniature, no part can function alone. In an abstract individualistic universe, autonomous selves are the starting points, the building blocks of society; the initial equivalence of these selves is the first cause, uncaused, of social organization. In a collective individualistic universe, each self represents and embodies, not a set of abstract, ahistorical possibilities, but a particular cultural tradition bounded by the collectivity of similiar selves. In collective individualism, we see the ideological priority of the self as well as a recognition of a historical whole, a whole composed not of partial interdependent units, but of units each embodying the totality. (Annadurai emphasized both the common man and his individual "duty" to follow party policies, and the notion of Tamils jointly inheriting ancestral greatness.)

Using the distinction between abstract and collective individualism, we can distinguish ethnicity and cultural nationalism.
Ethnicity recognizes collective individualism at its own level,
but abstract individualism at the level of the nation; cultural
nationalism creates the polity on the basis of collective individualism.

Put this way, none of these ideological alternatives is internally
consistent; each contains contradictions, and analysis must account for their forms of coexistence and interaction. In contemporary Tamil Nadu, we find caste, ethnic-like, and cultural
nationalist sentiments, and the question of social mobilization
reflects this layered complexity. The symbols of caste society
are taken over and their meanings transformed in the ethnic-like
and cultural nationalist contexts. To understand present-day life,
then, we must explore its origins, and the ways in which holism
becomes both abstract and collective individualism. In part, it
is an encompassed-encompassing relation, exploring which perspectives have political efficacy and can be acted upon rather
than merely articulated. Here, we will develop this by looking
at the perspectives of actual Tamilians differing in caste, occupation, and political affiliation.

We can now understand the implications of the shift from
caste to ethnicity in laying the groundwork for new forms of
identity. Tamilians see themselves, however, not as an ethnic
group within a nationwide system of ethnic groups, but as a
nation with an intrinsic legitimacy of its own. This crucial
difference reflects the role of political leaders in articulating
the concept of nationhood as well as early belief in the qualitative
character of "racial" distinctions between Aryan and Dravidian,
Brahmin and non-Brahmin. Even after the notion of racial
differences between Brahmins and non-Brahmins was dropped,
the supposed Aryan/Dravidian racial distinction had been
mapped onto the north India-south India political cleavage.

At this point, it is useful to reiterate the differences between
Congress and DMK mobilization strategies and modes of political
communication during the 1950s and early 1960s. Congress often
relied primarily on the traditional but crumbling hierarchy typified
by the rural patron-client relationship. Thus, one prominent
Congress electoral strategy was to win votes by paying a headman,
landlord-patron, or household head to deliver a certain number
of votes. Consistent delivery of twenty votes could net an elder
as much as a transistor radio.

This political style emphasized winning elections and controling the government. Rooted in traditionalism, it often delivered greater power over to the hands of the already powerful. Kamaraj Nadar was successful in this context because he typified it. Like C. N. Annadurai, Kamaraj came from a "backward" caste—the low ranked Nadars. Kamaraj represented the lower castes and the lower class—the majority of Tamilians—in the sense that he saw himself acting on their behalf. His image was that of a father-figure, benevolent but strict with his children. Thus the popularity of his habit of responding "paarkaalaam" (we shall see) to any request rested on its aptness as a characterization of his political style. Kamaraj (also called "King-Maker") was an avowed power broker and pragmatic politician.

On the other hand, DMK political style and communication stressed direct appeal to the independent individual. Early DMK dramas and movies challenged traditional authority, even within the family, and emphasized individual integrity in embracing ideological (social reform) principles. Annadurai personified DMK style, as Kamaraj personified Congress style. Annadurai extolled the virtues of the "common man" and purported to "represent him in all his ruggedness." Annadurai did not project a benevolent father image, but that of elder brother ("Anna," Annadurai's nickname, means elder brother in Tamil). An elder brother represents what younger siblings can become—in time. Annadurai purported to mirror and express the desires of his "tambis" (younger brothers) or followers. He was the voice of the "true" Tamilian.

TAMIL NATIONALISM IN POLITICAL CULUTRE

Political culture is here defined as all aspects of a culture that have a political referent. Unlike ideological systems in which the need to rationalize produces a perhaps spurious logic and symmetry that includes and excludes certain values according to a set of normative criteria, political culture embodies all politically relevant symbols. Hence, political culture can include contradictory elements: racism and egalitarianism, territorial nationalism and cultural nationalism, fascism and communist ideological approaches, and so on. From an individual perspective, one could be a Jew in Nazi Germany and share and understand German political culture without supporting fascist ideology. Or one could be a Black African living in South Africa

and understand South African political culture without holding
the ideology of apartheid. However, an ideology may determine
which elements in a political culture are stressed. Therefore,
Nazi German political culture included more than fascism, but
fascism determined values that were stressed in that political
culture. Similarly, South African political culture includes (for
Africans) elements of traditional African political thought, but
apartheid determines which elements of the political culture are
stressed. In sum, political culture could be simply defined as
the politicization of (imputation of political meaning to) cultural
symbols.[9]

The paradigm for this chapter is based on Robert Lane's
Political Ideology.[10] In it he attempts to discover the "latent"
political ideology of the American urban common man: to explain
the sources of this ideology in the culture and experiences this
common man knows, and to examine the way in which the
American common man's ideology (or any ideology) supports
or weakens democratic institutions. His method involves conver-
sations with fifteen working-class men from one city. A critical
assumption of this study—that the individual embodies the main
elements of his own political culture with variations that reflect
his particular life circumstances—is complicated in India by caste
and caste political cultures.[11]

Lane's method results in biographies in which political themes
are integrated into personal social and cultural contexts. I used
this approach, combined with sampling that would allow for
caste variation. My hope was to capture the heterogeneity of
caste cultures by using in-depth, open-ended questionnaires, but
also to secure a sizable sample.

Almost two hundred interviews were conducted in 1968 with
a randomly selected sample of heads of households from one
neighborhood in Madras City. These interviews lasted from 2
to 2-1/2 hours and were completed in two visits. The advantages
of working in this one neighborhood were substantial—it had
been the subject of a year-long ethnographic analysis by an
anthropologist, and therefore I could design questions and inte-
grate responses into a known and broader cultural and cross-sec-
tional matrix.[12]

I shall use five case studies from this neighborhood to explore
Tamil Nadu political culture. Interviews of case study subjects
were supplemented by survey data and contextual analysis. Two

subjects were non-Brahmin caste Hindus, representing upper and low-income groups. Two were Adi-Dravidas, one a Congress supporter, the other a DMK supporter. The Congress supporter was a lower-class worker, while the DMK supporter was one of the poorest members of the sample, living in a dilapidated hut, but spending most of his time in the streets. There is also one Brahmin. The diversity of these case studies will help us identify elements in the political culture that are caste-specific and elements that cut across castes.

CASE STUDY A, CHINNASAMI NAICKER (A PSEUDONYM), DMK LABORER

Social Origins and Background. Our first case study subject is from a backward non-Brahmin caste, the Vanniya Kula Kshatriyas, commonly termed Naickers. He was a young (27-year-old) skilled laborer who had migrated to Madras City approximately nine years previously from the surrounding Chingleput district countryside, where his father worked as an agricultural laborer until his death. Chinnasami studied up to eighth standard in school, an educational level comparable to American grammar school. Living with Chinnasami was his 21-year-old wife, his 65-year-old mother, and a year-old son. Chinnasami's wife had studied up to seventh standard, but his mother was illiterate.

As a young low-caste laborer, Chinnasami is representative of a large and growing segment of Madras society. As a migrant of nine years' standing, he has managed to get a good job and a room in a pukka (brick) house. Chinnasami's counterparts fill many of the hut villages of Madras City. But still he has had to bridge rural-urban differences in recent memory.

Social, Religious, and Cultural Life. Chinnasami described himself as attempting to follow traditional community customs, but not as an "orthodox man." He attended temple every Friday night, and said that if he had more free time he would like to spend it "reading spiritual books." Despite Chinnasami's disclaimers, in the context of the constraints of his low caste position, he is quite committed to a religious orientation. Chinnasami wears viboothi, a religious marking on the forehead, as a manifestation of his traditional world view. When asked if he would accept cooked food from other castes, Chinnasami replied he would only accept cooked food from people of his own or a higher caste.[13] Surprisingly, although Chinnasami said he would not give his son or daughter in marriage to someone not a member of his subcaste of Naickers, he indicated he would arrange a Self-Respect marriage[14] for his children if they desired it. Chinnasami's unusual combination of orthodoxy and heterodoxy may be understood by the early death of his father. Chinnasami mentioned that when he was very young, he did not wear religious marks and did not pay attention to religion at all.

When asked to describe Tamilians in a phrase, Chinnasami said "Tamilians have good character and they welcome anybody and are hospitable and are always willing to give a feast." This characterization of Tamilians as generous to a fault is very common. It has also been a common theme in DMK movies, dramas, and literature. When asked about north Indians, Chinnasami responded that he did not know anything about north Indians and was unable to respond. This pattern is also typical. People described Tamilians in positive terms, but when asked about north Indians could not respond or were negative; for example: "north Indians are ambitious, greedy, go-getters while we are more cultured, warm hearted."

Political Perspective. Although Chinnasami supported the DMK, he had not voted in 1957, 1962 or 1967. He did say he followed political and government affairs daily in *Dinamani* and *Dina Thanthi* (both of which presented a generally Tamil nationalist viewpoint). Chinnasami said he often attended public meetings of all parties. Asked which meetings he attended most often, he said Congress meetings, because there were more Congress meetings held on his particular block. He also listened to public affairs on the radio and went to films about once a month.

When asked about the complexity of political and governmental affairs and whether the average man could really understand what was going on, Chinnasami said that "even youngsters speak politics." He did not feel that governmental affairs were too difficult for the average man to understand. He also felt that if he took a problem to a government office he would be treated fairly.

The above indicates this respondent felt a high degree of

political efficacy. There was also a series of questions to measure directly a sense of political efficacy: (1) The way people vote is the main thing to decide how things are run in this country. (2) If you don't watch it some people will take advantage of you. (3) A few strong leaders would do more for the country than all the laws and talk. (4) All candidates sound good in their speeches but you can never tell what they will do after they are elected. (5) Human nature is fundamentally cooperative. (6) People like me don't have any say about what the government does. (7) The individual owes his first duty to the state and only secondarily to his personal welfare. (8) No one is going to care much what happens to you when you get right down to it.

Chinnasami's responses show high political efficacy. He agreed with 1, 2, 3, 5, and 8, and disagreed with 4, 6, and 7. I have noted a "perfect" score and compared it to Chinnasami's responses (table 7-1). Less important than overall score are certain key responses: Chinnasami's belief that human nature is fundamentally cooperative, for example, and that the way things are decided is determined by the way people vote. Also significant in the context of the Congress upheaval of 1969-1970 was Chinnasami's belief (in 1968) that the country needed strong leaders rather than all the "laws and talk." Part of his pattern of political efficacy is a belief in the fundamental worth, honesty, and utility of politicians and politics. When asked to describe politicians in a phrase, Chinnasami said, "politicians are working for the people." This is in marked contrast to the cynicism about politics so often attributed to Indians.

TABLE 7-1
Political Efficacy, Chinnasami's Responses

Question	Efficacious response	Chinnasami's response	
1	yes	yes	+
2	no	yes	−
3	no	yes	−
4	no	no	+
5	yes	yes	+
6	no	no	+
7	no	no	+
8	no	yes	−

Definition of Political Problems. Chinnasami was asked a number of questions designed to determine his political concerns. He was asked which of the following six issues were most important: (1) spiritual and moral betterment; (2) making ends meet; (3) government control and regulation of business; (4) eliminating inequality and injustice; (5) foreign affairs and national defense; and (6) improving conditions for the family. He cited number 4, eliminating inequality and injustice, adding, "more important than anything the poor people must be helped."

Chinnasami defined the major problem of Madras State as "poverty," and suggested that "the ruling party in Tamil Nadu [the DMK] could do a lot to solve the poverty problem." When asked what he considered the most important problem facing India as a nation, he responded unhesitatingly, "unemployment." About Hindi, Chinnasami said he was "concerned about the Hindi question" and "Hindi was hated and it should not be imposed." Chinnasami did not think that the issue would lead to a separate Tamil Nadu. He was not in favor of a separate Tamil Nadu because "the unity of all states was good."

In general, Chinnasami seemed overwhelmingly concerned with the bread-and-butter issue of poverty and daily subsistence. Despite this, in the next section on attitudes toward political parties, Chinnasami indicated a more catholic political orientation.

Attitudes to Political Parties. In his response to questions on policies of various political parties, Chinnasami showed a broader and more encompassing perspective than was evident from his definition of immediate concerns. About the DMK, Chinnasami cited as good policies, "the DMK gives importance to Tamil," "the policy [of legalizing] Self-Respect marriages," "concern for the welfare of Harijans," and "[liberalized] loans to agriculturalists." When asked about bad policies, Chinnasami said that there were really no bad policies of the DMK.

I think it particularly notable that he departed from his overwhelming concern with the subsistence issues. When asked about the DMK, his first response had to do with Tamil and DMK linguistic policy. Another interesting departure was his perception of the DMK as working for the welfare of the Harijans. In general, Chinnasami's responses here indicated a surprisingly sophisticated knowledge of DMK policies. The DMK had passed a bill legalizing Self-Respect marriage, and had inaugurated a new loan policy for agriculturalists.

There are a number of thought-provoking aspects of the Chinnasami case study. First, although he was a DMK supporter, he remained a traditional man and within the context of his low caste position, highly orthodox. The DMK history of radical social reform did not prevent Chinnasami, as well as other orthodox non-Brahmins, from supporting the party. Another factor in Chinnasami's orthodoxy may have been his rural past and the presence of his orthodox mother in the household. Apart from orthodoxy, Chinnasami's political attitudes reflected the basic outlines of DMK ideological themes. The north-south dichotomy, Tamil greatness, and anti-Hindism, all emerge in his world view. Chinnasami was not, however, for Tamil Nadu separation. Finally, Chinnasami's responses reflected a sophisticated knowledge of public events, giving credence to his claim that he followed political and governmental affairs daily in newspapers.

Chinnasami showed high political efficacy and a noncynical attitude toward politics. Political cynicism is usually cited as a key characteristic of Indian political culture. But for Old Town, at least, political cynicism was not the most commonly expressed view of politicians. Our next subject, however, did provide a cynical contrast to Chinnasami.

CASE STUDY B, R. NATARAJAN PERIYARSWAMI (A PSEUDONYM), CONGRESS UPPER CLASS

Social Origins and Background. Natarajan is also a non-Brahmin member of a backward caste, the Agamudiar (part of the Muukoolathur). Natarajan, however, is wealthy and, unlike Chinnasami, his caste, although considered backward in the southern districts of the state, is not numerically significant in Chingleput or Madras City. Since Natarajan's exact position in the Chingleput and Madras City caste hierarchy is not determined by custom, his economic position plays an inordinately important role in determining the deference he receives in Old Town. This suggests an interesting consequence of urbanization in the context of disjunctive hierarchies determined by the caste makeup of specific districts. Geographical mobility within such a system may vitiate the consequences of a low position in the caste hierarchy. Geographical mobility does not establish a new position, because a position in the hierarchical system can only be occupied by a collective caste unit, not by an individual. However, it does mean that for an individual family, caste can assume a relatively less important position in determining deference patterns, and that other achievement attributes, such as economic class, can be relatively more determinative. This obviously does not mean that one could bridge the gulf between upper non-Brahmin and Brahmin, or even between backward non-Brahmin and forward non-Brahmin.

Natarajan was 55 years old and had studied up to SSLC (equivalent to an American high school diploma). He was a wealthy, well-known playwright, and owner of a drama company. He lived in a large bungalow, which he rented from a family in Old Town. Natarajan had always lived in Old Town, although his father's residence was in Tanjore. His father's occupation was cloth merchant. Living with Natarajan was his wife, who was 39 and had studied up to 2nd form (grammar school), an 18-year-old son studying for his bachelor's degree, a 14-year-old daughter, and a 12-year-old son.

Social, Religious, and Cultural Life. Natarajan reported that he spent his free time reading, and that if he had more free time he would like to write more. He was a member of a social club, and lived a sophisticated life consistent with his upper class status and urbane occupation. As an indicator of his urbanity, his five best friends were from other castes. They included a Kallar, a Christian, a Brahmin, and two Mudaliars.

However, Natarajan attended temples and characterized himself as a traditional man. He said he did not wear religious or caste marks, and that he would accept cooked food from all communities. He also indicated that he would use the polite form of address in Tamil when speaking to an elderly Paraiyan as well as to an elderly Naicker or elderly Brahmin. But Natarajan would not give his daughter or son in marriage to a boy or girl who was not a member of his own caste. He would arrange a Self-Respect marriage if the issue came up at the time the wedding was being planned. Natarajan reported that in his lifetime social customs in Old Town had changed. These were more liberal now, and this was connected with political policies.

In spite of Natarajan's support for the Congress party, the degree to which he had internalized the ideological perspective of the Dravidian movement is indicated by his support of Self-Respect marriage in principle, and his characterization of Tamilians. When asked to describe the Tamilians in a phrase, he said, "the language of the people of Tamil Nadu is one of the first to be born. Tamil has an unparalleled culture. If you go deep into Thirukkural, it surpassed human comprehension. Even day-to-day instances are described graphically. It is absolutely unique." His Congress support became evident when he said that "if we accept India as one, we should not distinguish between north and south." This is gratuitous, since he had already told us that the language and people of Tamil Nadu were the first to be born, and that Tamil culture is unparalleled.

Political Perspective. Natarajan reported no party membership, but supported the Congress and voted Congress in 1957, 1962, and 1967. He followed political and governmental affairs in *Dinamani* (a Tamil daily), the *Hindu,* and *Navasakthi* (a Tamil-language Congress daily); he attended public meetings regularly, particularly Congress and DMK public meetings, and often listened to public affairs on the radio.

When asked if political and governmental affairs were too complicated for the average person to understand, he felt that "any hungry man needs politics." By that rather literary phrase, he meant people could vote from their hunger even if they could not understand the intracacies of particular issues. He said that if he were to go to a government office, he would enjoy special privileges because he was an important man as owner of a drama company and former cinema director.

Natarajan's responses to the questions on efficacy indicate a developed sense of personal political efficacy, coupled with a profound distrust of politicians. Natarajan described politicians as "dishonest" and as "unfortunately not meeting [his] standards." Whatever the party, Natarajan felt there were a severe shortage of capable and honest men. He strongly believed the country needed to be run by some sort of benevolent dictator who would rule "with an iron hand." He saw little value in political parties. This viewpoint is common among many members of the educated upper class in India. Table 7-2 presents Natarajan's responses to the efficacy questions.

Definition of Political Problems. Among the six issues, Natarajan thought eliminating inequality and injustice, and improving

TABLE 7-2
Political Efficacy, Natarajan's Responses

Question	Efficacious response	Natarajan's response	
1	yes	yes	+
2	no	no	+
3	no	yes	−
4	no	yes	−
5	yes	yes	+
6	no	no	+
7	no	yes (qualified)	−
8	no	yes (qualified)	−

conditions for his family were the most important.

He was not concerned about the war in Viet Nam, closing the Coimbatore mills, or the devaluation of the English pound. He was concerned, however, about racism in South Africa, Chinese "aggression" against India's borders, Indian economic development, and the condition of Harijans. He felt the existence of the caste system should not be given any significance at all, that it was really not a major problem in the country, "this is simply the way things were and the way they should remain." However, when asked about the condition of the Suddhra caste as a problem, his response was emphatic and emotional: "the word Suddhra should not even be mentioned, because Suddhra means son of a prostitute." Even though the respondent was a Congress follower, he had internalized the Dravidian movement ideology on the Suddhras.

In Madras State, Natarajan said, "the major concern should be the suffering of the middle class people." Poverty must be wiped out. The gap between the rich and poor must be bridged somehow. But he did not believe that any party could do this, since there were fundamental difficulties with the party system. He said only "two parties should exist. Otherwise people are spoiled in the political paths. Now people are ruled only by selfish motives." About India as a nation, he felt that "generally the country is not prosperous. Some iron hand must rectify the confusion."

On the Hindi issue, Natarajan supported the three-language

formula: Hindi, English, and the regional language. He did not envisage a separate Tamil Nadu because "Tamil Nadu was too small to prosper." He said, "previously only because India was divided into so many small kingdoms, it fell to pieces." This reflects his Congress orientation and the emphasis that Gandhi and Nehru placed on England's "divide and rule" policy as the source of their success in colonizing India and maintaining control.

Natarajan felt that all policies of the Congress were good, but emphasized socialism. Neither capitalism nor communism could be the answer for India. He said about Congress: "Now we are self-sufficient in every aspect of the field. We have made tremendous progress. Under British domination, India was made only a market for British goods. In eighteen years, we have taken strides in economic development." Congress was responsible for this progress: "All policies of Congress are taken from the best aspects of every system of government." Finally, on Gandhi's approach: "We evicted the British using true nonviolence without a drop of blood. So, this is the greatest policy—Ahimsa."

Natarajan was so "uninterested" in other political parties that he refused to discuss them. In fact, Natarajan's support for Congress is an anomaly in an otherwise politically alienated man. This support and his feeling of political efficacy in the face of what he considers a corrupt political system may stem from his early association with the freedom struggle and from the real political influence his upper-class status confers. Although Natarajan refused to discuss other political parties, when the Swatantra party was mentioned he reacted strongly and negatively to Rajagopalacharia (the Swatantra party leader), as a "selfish, mean, and jealous person." About the DK he said, "Rajagopalacharia alone is the cause of the origin of the DK Favoritism for Brahmins by Rajaji created an antithesis which is the DK."

Natarajan illustrates an important point—the extent to which Dravidian movement themes cut across party lines, at least for many non-Brahmins. Natarajan's emotional reacton to the symbol "Suddhra" and the imputation of Suddhra status to non-Brahmins was an interesting throwback to currents of thought that dominated turn-of-the-century politics. He was articulate on the subject of Tamil cultural preeminence. His views on the north-south question reflected his Tamil cultural orientation, only slightly tempered by a long-time commitment to Congress. As a Congress supporter, he supported the three-language policy of the national government, but still emphasized the greatness of Tamil. In general, Natarajan's attitudes reflected Tamil nationalism as much as Congress ideology. This subject's attitudes reflected only a minimal attachment to the nationalist ideology of Congress leaders and to their ideological priorities. Although he did not like the DMK party, his attitudes reflected DMK ideology on Tamil culture, north-south differences, and Suddhras. Natarajan, perhaps more than any other case study subject, showed how thoroughly DMK ideology had been assimilated into the political culture.

CASE STUDY C, V. SIVA DORAI (A PSEUDONYM), CONGRESS ADI-DRAVIDA

Social Origins and Background. Dorai was a 50-year-old Adi-Dravida (Untouchable), a Congress supporter, and had lived in the Old Town cheri (the section occupied primarily by Untouchables) for nine years. His one-room flat was in a pukka house which also housed the landlord and about nine other families.

Dorai had studied up to 4th standard. Living with him was his 45-year-old wife and four children. She was illiterate, but all four children attended school. Dorai was a cook, and had held one position for thirty years. He was a relatively successful member of the Adi-Dravida lower middle class. Despite being relatively better off than his castemates, he could not identify three important people in Old Town. This lack of knowledge of the caste Hindu section of the neighborhood was characteristic of many Untouchable cheri residents.

Social, Religious, and Cultural Life. Dorai attended temples regularly, but did not characterize himself as "following traditional customs." He said he did not wear religious or caste marking, that he would marry a son or daughter to someone who was not a member of his community, and that he would arrange a Self-Respect marriage, all "Self-Respect" responses. However, Dorai also said that he would not accept cooked food from everyone, basically not from Untouchable castes below him. When asked if social customs had changed very much in his life, he replied "no." Dorai had little to say about his social, religious, or cultural life, but when asked to describe Tamilians, he stated they were "good people"; about north Indians, he "could not say."

Political Perspective. Dorai did not belong to a political party, but supported Congress and voted Congress in 1957, 1962, and 1967. He followed government affairs in the Tamil daily, *Navamani,* but had never attended a public meeting of the Congress, DMK, Communist party, Swatantra, or the DK. He did listen to political speeches on the radio. Almost every cheri has a radio attached to a loudspeaker. Usually they play film music. Many club houses (manrams) where radios are located have been erected by political parties or political film personalities. (Surprisingly, Dorai almost never attended the cinema. He did not have time.)

Although Dorai felt that political and governmental affairs were too complicated for the average man, he felt that he was able to understand both national and international affairs adequately. He believed that if he were to go to a government office he would receive equal treatment. He also felt that politicians "work for the country." Nevertheless, on the efficacy scale he scored low (table 7-3).

Definition of Political Problems. Of the six problems, Dorai said improving conditions for his family was the most important. However, he was very concerned and articulate about problems at the state level. He thought food was the most serious state problem, and defense the most serious for India as a whole.

On the Hindi issue, Dorai stated that "nobody likes Hindi"

TABLE 7-3
Political Efficacy, Dorai's Responses

Question	Efficacious response	Dorai's response	
1	yes	yes	+
2	no	yes	−
3	no	yes	−
4	no	yes	−
5	yes	no	−
6	no	yes	−
7	no	yes	−
8	no	yes	−

and that "Hindi should not be forced." He said he did feel
that the problem could lead to a separate Tamil Nadu, and that
people he knew were so emotionally concerned about the issue
they might demand separation. When asked if he favored a
separate Tamil Nadu he said yes, then "we can do what all
we want." Again we see an example of a Congressman articulating
a cultural nationalist DMK orientation.

Attitudes Toward Political Parties. Dorai believed the DMK
"was doing good for all the people," although he disapproved
of "the misunderstanding among leaders" (a reference to the
factional quarrel going on at the time). The Congress, he felt,
"had some good leaders to do good things." However, he said,
"now the members want to get money from the government."
So for him the Congress had been a good party in the past,
but has shown signs of corruption. He said, however, that all
people voted for and supported Congress, and that he himself
was a Congress voter. He also said the DK was a very good
party: "there are no parties as good as this one nowadays."
Here we note a respondent who had transferred his Dravidian
movement loyalties from the DK to the Congress party. Since
E. V. Ramasami supported the "Kamaraj" Congress until the
Bhaktavasalam period, there was no necessary inconsistency.

CASE STUDY D, A. MUNUSAMI (A PSEUDONYM), A DMK
ADI-DRAVIDA

Social Origins and Background. Munusami, like Siva Dorai,
is an Adi-Dravida (Paraiyan). He was sixty years old, and had
been a rickshaw puller for forty years. Munasami "rented" a
portion of an overcrowded hut, but spent most of his time
squatting at various places throughout the neighborhood. Three
years before, Munusami had moved from another Madras City
cheri to Old Town with his wife, a daughter (without her husband),
and five grandchildren.

Munusami and his wife had studied for two years. His daughter
had studied up to the ninth standard, but her five children were
perennial truants.

Munusami had migrated to Madras City as a young man from
Tanjore, where his father was a landless laborer. He was
extremely poor, barely scratching out a living at a back-breaking
job for which he was rapidly becoming physically unfit.

Social, Religious, and Cultural Life. When asked how he spent his free time, he sadly replied, "pulling my rickshaw." If he had more free time, he would also spend it pulling his rickshaw. The six problems elicited the emphatic statement that the most important problem was improving conditions for his family. Munusami emerged as a man whose working life consumed virtually all the time, thought, and energy of his waking life. He did attend temple every Friday, but did not belong to a club or organization.

Although Munusami attended temple weekly, he did not consider himself an orthodox or traditional man. He did not wear religious or caste markings, and would accept food from all people. He would allow his son or daughter to marry a spouse from another caste, and would arrange a Self-Respect marriage. Like Siva Dorai, Munusami did not feel that social customs had changed much in his lifetime.

In discussing Tamilians, Munusami emphasized the north-south dichotomy, saying in part that Tamilians were "good and active people" while north Indians were "bad people."

Political Perspective. Munusami followed political and governmental affairs in *Dina Thanthi* and *Malai Murasu,* both Tamil dailies with a DMK and Tamil nationalist orientation. He did not attend public meetings, listen to public affairs, or attend the cinema. He believed political and governmental affairs too complicated for the average man, and said that he himself did not understand important national and international issues fully.

Munusami did not feel that there were any people or groups that had influence on governmental processes. If he had to go to a government office, he believed he would be treated fairly. On the political efficacy questions, Munusami displayed a moderately low personal efficacy not correlated with cynicism about politicians or politics in general. "Politicians," Munusami declared, "are important because they work for their country." He added that he thought most worked hard and well.

Political Problems. Munusami could not say what the major problems in his neighborhood or state were, but he did respond about the nation: the most important problem was language, an indication of assimilation of a DMK set of priorities. Munusami had already indicated that his greatest concern was survival.

About Hindi he was decisive; he "didn't want Hindi" and

"the people should not be compelled to learn it," ending his statement with an emphatic "I don't like it." However, Munusami did not think that the Hindi issue could lead to a separate Tamil Nadu, and did not favor separation because Tamil Nadu "could not rule itself alone" (that is, economically and militarily).

Attitudes Toward Political Parties. Munusami was a DMK supporter who voted DMK in 1957, 1962, and 1967. When asked about the DMK, he enthusiastically characterized it as "a good party with good policies." But he could not single out particular policies. He added, however, that the DMK had just come to power and that it would take time to see how they ran the government. Munusami believed the DMK had no bad policies, and that the Adi-Dravidas were the ones who voted for and supported the DMK. He believed the Congress also had some good policies, but they did not follow them very well. He disliked the Communist party and the Swatantra party (Swatantra was "only a rich man's party").

CASE STUDY E, R. VENKATASWAMI AIYER (A PSEUDONYM), FROM THE CONGRESS BRAHMIN PERSPECTIVE

Social Origins and Background. Our last subject was a 38-year-old Brahmin who worked as a house inspector.[15] Venkataswami had lived in his present house for ten years. He had an SSLC education (high school diploma), his wife had studied up to the 10th standard. Living with him was a 24-year-old nephew, a bookkeeper; a 24-year-old brother-in-law, who was a clerk (both had studied up to SSLC); and Venkataswami's son, a student. His father lived in Tanjore district, where he was a clerk. Venkataswami was typical of middle-class Brahmin residents of Old Town.

Social, Religious, and Cultural Life. Venkataswami believed he was maintaining traditional social and religious customs. His orthodoxy is exemplified in the wearing of religious markings[16] and maintenance of orthodox eating habits. He said "I never mess [eat] anywhere [but home] except under forced circumstances." Venkataswami would only accept cooked food from people of his own subsect within the Iyer Brahmin community. However, he would use the polite form of address to an elderly

Brahmin, Naicker, and Paraiyan, and he encouraged the policy
of intercaste marriage. He said he would allow (and in fact
encourage) his son to marry a girl who was not a member of
his own community. He would not, however, arrange a Self-Respect marriage for his child. When asked if there had been any
change in his lifetime in social customs, he said "no." [17]

Venkataswami said he had no leisure time, depicted himself
as leading a very hectic life, and said he desired more time
for rest and relaxation. Although he belonged to no clubs or
organizations, he did attend temple regularly.

A Brahmin, and therefore a member of a group challenged
by the non-Brahmin movement and Dravidian ideology, Venkataswami nevertheless accepted the north-south dichotomy which
is so central to DMK thinking and at odds with the Congress
emphasis on all-Indian symbols. He took the position that while
Tamilians were good people, north Indians were aggressive.

Political Perspectives. Venkataswami was a Congress supporter who had voted Congress in 1957, 1962, and 1967. He followed
political affairs in the newspapers daily, usually reading the
Hindu. Although he did not attend public meetings, he listened
to political speeches on the radio. Even though he believed
political and governmental affairs too complex for the average
man to really understand, he felt he could understand national
and international issues adequately.

Despite the effect of the non-Brahmin movement, Venkataswami thought that if he were to go to a government office
he would be treated fairly. In the past he had gone to government
offices alone because he preferred "the direct approach."
However, if forced, he would "take a [letter of] recommendation
from a powerful person."

His answers to the political efficacy questions showed him
to be of middling efficacy.

Perception of Political Problems. Venkataswami believed eliminating inequality and injustice to be the most important problem
facing the country, and more important than spiritual and moral
betterment, making ends meet, government control and regulation
of business, foreign affairs and national defense, or improving
conditions for his family.

He was not interested in the war in Viet Nam, racism in
South Africa, the closing of the Coimbatore mills, Chinese

"aggression" against India's borders, or Indian economic development. Venkataswami did feel that the caste system should be removed, and said he was interested in that problem. He approached the caste problem from a Gandhian reformist perspective; the conditions of the Harijans, Venkataswami said, was a thousand times better than in the past. However, "the condition of the Suddhras was not at all improved." [18]

The major problems facing Madras State, he said, were food production, improving and expanding the water supply, and better medical facilities. For Venkataswami, the most important problem facing India was the labor problem, specifically "providing more employment" and dealing with labor unrest. He also mentioned improving health and medical facilities. He did not believe there were any problems peculiar to the Old Town neighborhood.

On the issue of Hindi he said that Hindi was necessary and "if it is passed as a national language everyone must learn it." When asked if he felt that this problem could lead to a separate Tamil Nadu, he responded, "yes." But Venkataswami did not personally favor separation: "You couldn't live and you couldn't provide employment even to one percent of the educated" if Tamil Nadu were to become separated.

Attitudes Towards Political Parties. In characterizing political parties, Venkataswami said he never appreciated the DMK party because it had supported separatism and "ruining the country." Even so, he said, "all sorts of people vote for and support the DMK."

The DK he characterized as the "DMK in another form." For this respondent, memories of the anti-Brahminism of the early radical Dravidian movement ideology were ever present. Venkataswami was naturally more enthusiastic about his own party. The best Congress policies were prohibition and "bringing up the scheduled castes." In spite of his enthusiasm for Congress, he worriedly whispered his concern about the existence of "a little corruption."

OVERVIEW OF THE CASE STUDIES

One of the most illuminating contrasts in our six case studies involves the responses on political efficacy. By Guttman scaling the five case subjects, the pattern in table 7-4 emerges: first,

TABLE 7-4
Political Efficacy, Five Case Subjects

	Questions								
	3	8	4	2	7	5	6	1	Total
Natarajan (Agamudiar drama company owner)	−	−+[a]	−	+	−+[a]	+	+	+	6
Chinnasami Naiker (Naicker laborer)	−	−	+	−	+	+	+	+	5
Venkataswami Aiyer (Brahmin)	−	−	−	−	+	+	+	+	4
Munusami (Adi-Dravida rickshaw puller)	−	−	−	−	−	+	+	+	3
Siva Dorai (Adi-Dravida cook)	−	−	−	−	−	−	−	+	1

[a]Natarajan's qualified responses.

the caste ordering. Although Natarajan belongs to a backward caste, he receives deference out of proportion to his caste status because his caste is not indigenous to Chingleput and Madras City. This caste ordering (assuming that Natajaran's wealth and ambiguous caste status make him more forward than backward) reflects a general consensus about the most politically influential caste groupings in Tamil Nadu. One is much more likely to hear grumbling about "Mudaliar" rule than Brahmin rule in contemporary Tamil Nadu.[19] Even backward caste Hindus are seen as politically powerful. For example, when I asked H. V. Hande, leader of the Swatantra party, what caste group he thought was most politically influential in Madras City, he said the Naickers (Vannia Kula Kshatriyas) because of their increasing numbers. True or not, it is an interesting perception of urban political arithmetic. In fact, the corporation councillor from Old Town was a Naicker.

Although the Indian government had made efforts to promote the welfare of Adi-Dravidas and to provide them with political representation, the two Adi-Dravidas still feel least efficacious. This is typical of the views of Adi-Dravida political leaders I knew. Many felt they could not change the condition of the Adi-Dravida community. I suspect low political efficacy is typical of Adi-Dravidas generally.

I do not overemphasize the significance of five case studies, but the "typicality" of each subject is supported by data from the 200 other interviews that were conducted.

Second, the pattern of efficacious responses is interesting. For the statement, "The way people vote is the main thing that decides how things are run in this country" ($Q1 = 8+$), to win general agreement seems particularly apropos in the state with the highest voting participation in India. On the other hand, the idea that "A few strong leaders would do more for this country than all the laws and talk" is also a salient and not inconsistent feature of Tamil Nadu political culture. All subjects heartily endorsed strong political leadership. Nehru was considered a strong leader, and so is his daughter Indira Gandhi. Her blunt purge of the Congress may have won her increased support for just that reason. Responses on this question also help us understand and situate the acceptance (at least initially) of the 1975 emergency imposed by Indira Gandhi. Later we shall see the importance of Karunanidhi's strong-man image.

This does not mean that other types of politicians cannot be admired. My survey data show Mahatna Gandhi (soft) was more popular than Nehru (strong), and Annadurai (soft) was more popular than Karunanidhi (strong). However, both Gandhi and Annadurai had special charismatic qualities.[20] People believe that strong leaders can be elected and work within the broad outlines of the rule of law (as a benevolent dictator, for instance). The answers to question one are consistent with the general disagreement (except for Siva Dorai) with the statement, "People like me do not have any say about what the government does" (Q 5).

The crucial similarity in the case studies centered on Tamil cultural nationalism. Some assortment of Tamil nationalist symbols was meaningful for all six, whether Congress or DMK. The Dravidian ideology in its cultural nationalist form (that is, attitudes on Hindi, Suddhras, north versus south, preeminence of Tamilians) has penetrated widely and cuts across caste and class lines. But the radical social reform aspect of Dravidian movement ideology (atheism, separation, anti-Hinduism) finds little expression (only Siva Dorai lauded the DK).

In contrast, Congress ideological priorities (socialism, emotional integration, the three-language formula, and so on) are not heavily emphasized. Even supporters of Congress articulate attitudes with roots in the Dravidian movement.

While internalization and articulation of the broad outlines of the Dravidian movement ideology cut across caste and class lines, there are caste-specific political styles that reflect caste culture. The qualitative social and cultural isolation of the Untouchables, I believe, is seen in their low political efficacy. Fifty years of Brahmin–non-Brahmin ideological conflict and the rise of political and administrative preference for backward non-Brahmins and Untouchables left its impact on both Brahmin and non-Brahmin political attitudes. The bitterness with which the Brahmin subject called the DMK the "DK in another form," and the emotion with which our upper-class non-Brahmin, Natarajan, reacted to the word "Suddhra" are examples.

In general, respondents in the survey and Old Town residents in general were surprisingly politically knowledgeable and sophisticated. They approached politics with wit and insight. There was a general feeling of being able to shape their own political destinies through voting, although this was accompanied by a desire for strong leadership.

[1] Dumont, *Homo Hierarchicus.*

[2] Louis Dumont, *Religion, Politics and History in India* (Paris: Mouton, 1970), pp. 109,110.

[3] See Stephen Alan Barnett, "The Structural Position of a South Indian Caste" (Ph.D. Dissertation, Chicago, 1970).

[4] Stephen Alan Barnett, "The Process of Withdrawal in a South Indian Caste," in M. Singer and B. Cohn, eds., *Entrepreneurship and the Modernization of Occupational Culture in South Asia* (Durham, N.C.: Duke University Press, 1973).

[5] See David C. Mandelbaum, *Society in India* (Berkeley and Los Angeles: University of California Press, 1970), pp. 161–180. The jajmani system involves performance of caste professional duties in villages, usually for payment of grain by landowners.

[6] See S. Barnett, "Urban Is as Urban Does," and S. Barnett, "The Process of Withdrawal in a South Indian Caste." The passage is taken from Marguerite Ross Barnett and Steve Barnett, "Contemporary Peasant and Post-Peasant Alternatives in South India: The Ideas of a Militant Untouchable," *Annals of the New York Academy of Sciences* 220, Art. 6, 385–410.

[7] Hardgrave, *The Nadars of Tamil Nad.* Also see Karl Deutsch, "Social Mobilization and Political Development," *American Political Science Review* 55 (September 1961), 494.

[8] L. Dumont, "On the Comparative Understanding of Modern Civilizations," *Daedalus* (Spring 1975), pp. 152–172.

[9] This definition of political culture was suggested by Leonard Binder of the University of Chicago.

[10] Robert E. Lane, *Political Ideology: Why the American Common Man Believes What He Does* (New York: Free Press, 1962). Lane's use of the term ideology corresponds closely to my definition of political culture.

[11] See, for example, Hardgrave's *The Nadars of Tamil Nad.* Hardgrave argues that Nadar caste political culture reflects the peculiar historical development of the Nadar caste, but also encapsulates the kind of mobility he feels is experienced by a wide variety of castes.

[12] See S. Barnett, "The Structural Position of a South Indian Caste." The

survey described in this chapter consisted of two parts: the first part was done jointly with Steve Barnett. See Appendix D for the questionnaire used in this survey.

[13] The distinction between cooked and raw food is crucial here. Everyone, including Brahmins, will accept raw food from anyone.

[14] Recall that this is a marriage without a Brahmin priest. First advocated by the Self-Respect movement, it is central to Dravidian movement notions of social reform.

[15] A position secured through the recommendation of a friend. Other case study subjects secured their positions themselves.

[16] A Vishnavite Brahmin wore vertically drawn marks of white (dried, specially prepared cow dung) ash across his forehead.

[17] That both Adi-Dravida subjects and the only Brahmin subject agreed there had been no changes in social customs in their lifetimes may reflect the fact that both represent polar positions in the caste hierarchy, separated from the rest by qualitative gaps in social behavior. The enormous change in the collective position of Brahmins and Untouchables does not rapidly effect individual social behavior.

[18] In ritual position, not political power. We already know he believes non-Brahmins "come forward," which in Indian English has the connotation of political and economic advancement.

[19] Annadurai was a Mudaliar, as well as top party leaders Nedunchezhian and Anbazhagan. In addition, many General Council leaders were Mudaliars. Chapter 8 explores caste composition of the party in detail.

[20] L. Rudolph and S. Rudolph, *The Modernity of Tradition;* and Erik Erikson, *Gandhi's Truth: on the Origins of Militant Non-Violence* (New York: Norton, 1969) for a discussion of Gandhi and charisma.

CHAPTER EIGHT

DMK Political Leadership: the Men behind Tamil Nationalism

THREE categories of leaders have been discussed in previous chapters. First, E. V. Ramasami and C. N. Annadurai, both exceptional men. They were political creators, commanded a special place in Tamil Nadu politics, and won a particularly intense response from their followers. Their decisions, strategies, and political perceptions have been key factors in shaping political events. The second category is the top leadership of the DMK: Karunanidhi, Nedunchezhian, Mathiazhagan, and so on: propagandists, organizers, and administrators. They have been important in mobilizing support, routinizing the movement, and administering party affairs.

This chapter will discuss a third category: local-level DMK leadership. These are branch, town, and circle leaders, nodes between the masses and ideologizing top-level leaders. This leadership constitutes the crucial link in the process of restructuring the world views of mass adherents. Furthermore, these cadres carry out agitations and campaign in local elections.

Analysis of these leaders is based on interviews; archival, journalistic, and other written material; and on a survey done in 1968 of DMK and Congress leaders. Two surveys were done of DMK leaders: branch, taluk, and circle leaders are included in the first sample; and members of the DMK General Council (the decision-making body of the party) in the second. Data on local-level leaders were collected by mailed, open-ended questionnaires (see Appendices). These were mailed to a random sample of 700 local-level leaders whose names were obtained through the membership files at the DMK general office. Of the 700 to whom questionnaires were sent, 459, or 65 percent, responded (see Appendix C). Not only is this remarkably high, but those who responded sent back very careful answers, often accompanied by letters, poems, and other indicative material.

Data on the DMK General Council were obtained in the same manner. Since the General Council contained many leaders I had previously interviewed, the actual sample was smaller than the total membership of 125. I sent questionnaires to 100 General Council members, of whom 38 responded.

For comparative purposes, data were also gathered from Congress leaders. The Tamil Nadu (Pradesh) Congress Committee has a membership of 350, of which 120 responded. The TNCC, like the DMK General Council, is the chief decision-making body for the state. Unlike the DMK, it is constrained by the national organization.

DEMOGRAPHIC PROFILE OF DMK LOCAL-LEVEL LEADERS[1]

Age. One of the most powerful stereotypes of the DMK during the 1950s and 1960s depicted the party as composed of lower-class youngsters. The frequently repeated characterization of Annadurai as "leading a ragtail band of urchins" in the 1950s and 1960s is a reflection of this image. Tables 8-1 through 8-10 broadly confirm distinctions between DMK and Congress leaders in age, income, and occupation. Table 8-1 shows that in 1968 almost 40 percent of DMK local-level leaders were 30 or under, and 83 percent were 40 or under! Almost 18 percent were 25 or younger.

Compare this with table 8-3, which shows the age of Congress leaders. No one was younger than 25 in the sample, and the modal age was 41 to 50. Among DMK local-level leaders, only 1.9 percent were over 50. While members of the DMK General Council are older than the local-level leaders, they are still younger

TABLE 8-1
Age, DMK Local-Level Leadership

Age distribution	Number	Percent	Cumulative frequency
Refused to say	5	1.1	
20 to 25	76	16.6	17.7
26 to 30	101	22.0	39.7
31 to 40	201	43.8	83.5
41 to 50	67	14.6	98.1
51 to 60	8	1.7	99.8
61 to 65	1	.2	100.0
Total	459	100.0	

Mode = 31 to 40

TABLE 8-2
Age, DMK General Council

Age distribution	Number	Percent	Cumulative frequency
20 to 25	1	2.6	2.6
26 to 30	2	5.3	7.9
31 to 40	17	44.7	52.6
41 to 50	15	39.5	92.1
51 to 60	2	5.3	97.4
61 to 65	1	2.6	100.0
Total	38	100.0	

Mode = 31 to 40

than Congress leaders (table 8-3). Over half of the General Council members are under 41; only 7.9 percent of DMK General Council are older than 50.

Comparison of the ages of DMK and Congress leaders will place the previous discussion on DMK growth in perspective. It suggests that many elements of generational conflict are involved in the growth of the DMK and in the emergence and spread of Tamil nationalism. And it also suggests that young people responded most decisively to the dislocations and inequities of modernization.

Year of Recruitment. Seventy-six percent of the DMK General Council were founders of the party. Sixty-six percent were members of the Dravida Kazhagam, and presumably left at

TABLE 8-3
Age, Congress Leadership

Age distribution	Number	Percent	Cumulative frequency
26 to 30	4	3.3	3.3
31 to 40	37	30.8	34.1
41 to 50	51	42.5	76.6
51 to 60	22	18.3	94.9
61 to 65	5	4.2	99.1
Over 65	1	.8	99.9
Total	120	99.9	

Mode = 41 to 50

FIGURE 3

DMK LOCAL–LEVEL LEADERSHIP
RECRUITMENT PATTERN

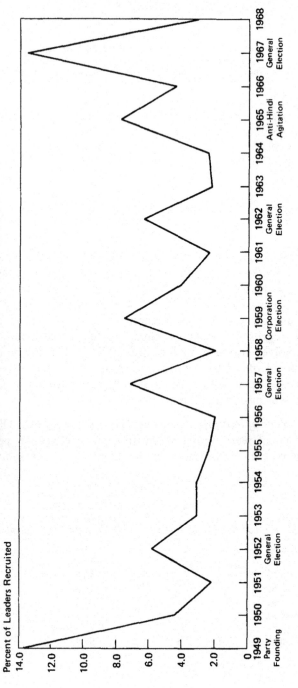

Annadurai's bidding. These 66 percent were in the Dravida Kazhagam when it was still radical and in the Dravida Munnetra Kazhagam in its most radical period. Presumably, during the early days at least, they accepted the most radical tenets of the Dravidian ideology, including atheism, anti-Brahmanism, socialism, anticasteism. The presence of these leaders, with their radical movement backgrounds, underscores the question: How was the DMK able to transform its ideology, yet maintain radical cadre loyalty and support? This is a question we will discuss later. Although the DMK continued to recruit into the General Council leaders who entered the party after 1949, the General Council was dominated by the perspective of founder-members.

Local-level DMK leaders were recruited throughout the 1950s and 1960s, and their distribution by year of recruitment is less skewed toward one mobilizing event than is that of the General Council. However, as figure 3 (based on table 8-4) shows,

TABLE 8-4
Year of Party Recruitment, DMK Local-Level Leadership

Year	Number	Percent
1949 (DMK founding)	63	13.7
1950	20	4.4
1951	9	2.0
1952 (general election)	27	5.8
1953	14	3.1
1954	14	3.1
1955	11	2.4
1956	9	2.0
1957 (general election)	33	7.2
1958	9	2.0
1959 (corporation election)	35	7.6
1960	19	4.1
1961	11	2.4
1962 (general election)	29	6.3
1963	10	2.2
1964	11	2.4
1965 (anti-Hindi agitation)	36	7.8
1966	20	4.4
1967 (general election)	62	13.5
1968	14	3.1
No response	3	.6
Total	459	100.1

TABLE 8-5
Year of Party Recruitment, DMK General Council

Year	Number	Percent
1949	29	76.3
1952	2	5.3
1954	1	2.6
1956	2	5.3
1957	1	2.6
1959	2	5.3
After 1959	1	2.6
Total	38	100.0

there is still a clear pattern of recruitment. Founding of the DMK; the State Assembly elections of 1952, 1957, 1962, and 1967; the 1959 Madras Corporation elections; and the 1965 anti-Hindi agitation were major "mobilizing moments" for these leaders. Figure 3 shows these seven periods of mobilization.

Like the DMK General Council, most members of the Tamil Nadu Congress Committee joined the party before the 1950s but Congress continued to recruit members who later became

TABLE 8-6
Year of Party Recruitment, Congress

Year	Number	Percent
1925–1941	37	30.8
1942 (Quit India campaign)	11	9.2
1943–1951	24	20.0
1952 (first election)	3	2.5
1953–1958	9	7.5
1957 (election)	3	2.5
1958–1961	10	8.3
1962 (election)	2	1.7
1963–1966	8	6.7
1967 (election)	2	1.7
1968	1	.8
No response	7	5.8
No recall	3	2.5
Total	120	100.0

Note: The years 1942, 1952, 1957, 1962, 1967 and 1968 are single years. While the largest percentage report joining during the years 1943–1951, the largest percentage in one year is in 1942.

TABLE 8-7
Income, DMK Local-Level Leaders, DMK General Council, and Congress

Yearly earning	DMK Local Level			DMK General Council			Congress		
	Number	Percent	Cumulative percent	Number	Percent	Cumulative percent	Number	Percent	Cumulative percent
RS 0 to 499	61	13.3		—	—		1	.8	
500 to 999	102	22.2	35.5	4	10.5	10.5	4	3.3	4.1
1,000 to 4,999	247	53.8	89.3	20	52.6	63.1	46	38.3	42.4
5,000 to 9,999	20	4.4	93.7	9	23.7	86.8	38	31.7	74.1
Over 10,000	7	1.5	95.2	4	10.5	97.3	18	15.0	89.1
No specific income	10	2.2	97.4	—	—		6	5.0	94.1
No income	1	.2	97.6	—	—		1	.8	94.9
No response	11	2.4	100.0	1	2.6	99.9	6	5.0	99.9
Total	459	100.0		38	99.9		120	99.9	

leaders throughout the 1950s and 1960s. In contrast to the DMK, there were no major mobilizing moments. Table 8-6 indicates that even elections were not significant points of recruitment of Congress members destined for leadership roles.

Income and Occupation. Not only were DMK leaders younger, but also of lower income and occupational status. Table 8-7 shows that 89 percent of DMK local-level leaders and 63 percent of DMK General Council leaders had incomes of less than 5,000 rupees per year. Only 42 percent of Congress leaders had incomes below 5,000 rupees. While 15 percent of Congress leaders and 11 percent of DMK General Council members earn over 10,000 rupees per year, only 1-1/2 percent of DMK local-level leaders reached that figure.

Since 25 rupees per capita per month defines the poverty line[2] in India, those leaders earning between 500 and 1,000 rupees a year and supporting a family were existing in dire economic circumstances. The deprivation attached to these incomes depends, however, on the number of dependents supported by the political leader. Since DMK local-level leaders include many young men who may be part of large joint families, their poverty may be less extreme.

While income differences between the DMK and Congress may partially reflect age differences, the occupational tables indicate important differences in the class and status of DMK and Congress leaders (tables 8-8 to 8-10). Most DMK local-level leaders by far are farmers—about 48 percent—almost half the local leadership structure. Shopowners, laborers, and service occupations are also well represented. Five percent of the DMK local-level leadership is unemployed, and only 7.2 percent have white-collar occupations.

In the DMK General Council, only about 5 percent are white-collar, but their occupations fall into the respectable lower middle-class spectrum; about 34 percent are farmers, 29 percent shopowners, and 16 percent hold political jobs.

Like DMK General Council leaders and local-level leaders, Congress has a large percentage of farmers—about 43 percent. However, the Congress TNCC has 20 percent white-collar job holders—more than double that of the DMK local leadership, and four times that of the DMK General Council. In both the DMK General Council and Congress TNCC, no one defined

TABLE 8-8
Occupation, DMK Local-Level Leadership

	Number	Percent
White collar		
Lawyer	3	.7
Manager	2	.4
Sales representative	3	.7
Superintendent	2	.4
Businessman, large business	9	2.0
Entertainment occupations	6	1.3
Clerk	2	.4
Teacher (and semiprofessionals)	6	1.3
		7.2
Traditional service occupations		
Goldsmith	1	.2
Barber	2	.4
Tailor	13	2.8
Dhobi (washerman)	2	.4
Weaver	24	5.2
		9.0
Small-scale proprietor		
Shop owner	68	14.8
Agriculture		
Farmer (landowners and renters)	220	47.9
Political jobs		
Political worker	5	1.1
Office holder	11	2.4
		3.5
Laborer		
Skilled laborer	22	4.8
Unskilled worker	6	1.3
Self-employed	16	3.5
Casual laborer	3	.7
		10.3
Miscellaneous		
Unclear occupation or no response	10	2.2
Unemployed	23	5.0
		7.2
Total	459	99.9

TABLE 8-9
Occupation, DMK General Council

	Number	Percent
White collar		
Lawyer	1	2.6
Clerk	1	2.6
		5.2
Traditional service occupations		
Tailor	1	2.6
Small-scale proprietor		
Shop owner	11	28.9
Agriculture		
Farmer	13	34.2
Political jobs		
Political worker	2	5.3
Office holder	4	10.5
		15.8
Government service		
Retired govt. post	1	2.6
Miscellaneous		
Refused to say	3	7.9
Unemployed	1	2.6
		10.5
Total	38	99.8

himself as a laborer, and the representation of service occupations is extremely small.

Education. For many years prior to 1967, the DMK characterized itself as the party of the educated, and demanded that the "uneducated let the educated rule." While seemingly in contradiction to the more prominent "common man" theme, it implied a not-too-subtle comparison between Annadurai and Kamaraj. Annadurai had a master's degree, and spoke and wrote English well. Kamaraj had no advanced degree, and spoke only Tamil. The claim that the DMK was "the party of the educated" finds little support in table 8-11. Seventy-nine percent of the

TABLE 8-10
Occupation, Congress

	Number	Percent
White collar		
Doctor	1	.8
Lawyer	9	7.5
Manager	1	.8
Editor	2	1.7
Businessman, large scale	9	7.5
Teacher	1	.8
Retired clerk	1	.8
		19.9
Traditional Service Occupations		
Weaver	2	1.7
Small-scale proprietor		
Shopkeeper	12	10.0
Agriculture		
Farmer	52	43.3
Political jobs		
Office holder	15	12.5
Government Service		
Government post	2	1.7
Miscellaneous		
Unemployed	6	5.0
Unclear occupation or no response	7	5.8
Total	120	99.9

DMK local-level leaders had only studied to the 8th standard or less. However, if we compare the DMK General Council with Congress TNCC, there is little difference. Congress had 21 percent BA/Postgraduates, compared to 11 percent in the General Council; but the DMK General Council had a substantial percentage of members with at least SSLC degrees.

Caste. Perhaps the most striking difference in the caste of DMK and Congress leaders is the presence of Brahmins (8.3 percent) among the Congress leaders. No Brahmins were in either DMK leadership sample. Tables 8-12 and 8-13 explode the

TABLE 8-11

Education, DMK Local-Level Leaders, DMK General Council, and Congress

	DMK local level		DMK General Council		Congress	
	Number	Percent	Number	Percent	Number	Percent
Illiterate	13	2.8	—	—	3	2.5
Primary to 5th std.	165	35.9	4	10.5	14	11.7
To 8th std.	185	40.3	9	23.7	29	24.2
To 11th std.	29	6.3	10	26.3	8	6.7
SSLC	52	11.3	10	26.3	26	21.7
Post-SSLC/trade	4	.9	—	—	1	.8
PUC	3	.7	—	—	14	11.7
BA post-grad.	4	.9	4	10.5	25	20.8
No response	4	.9	1	2.6	—	—
Total	459	100.0	38	99.9	120	100.1

stereotype that "the DMK is the party of low-caste fellows." Perhaps low-class, but not low-caste—at least not in the General Council. General Council members include a substantial representation of forward non-Brahmins: 10.5 percent Mudaliars, 10.5 percent Vellalas, 10.5 percent Chettiars.[3] Congress also has a substantial representation of elite non-Brahmins, (table 8-14). However, while the DMK General Council has 31.5 percent elite Tamil non-Brahmin castes, Congress has only 16.5 percent. Congress elite non-Brahmins include many non-Tamil-speaking castes[4] (Nair, Reddiar, Naidu).

Those who argue that the DMK is the party of lower castes can find support from local-level leadership data. Almost 43 percent of the local-level leadership comes from backward castes. The service castes supply 4.5 percent, and 8.1 percent are ex-Untouchables; thus approximately 55 percent of the DMK local-level leadership comes from either backward or scheduled castes.

OVERVIEW OF DMK AND CONGRESS SOCIAL ATTITUDES
AND POLITICAL BELIEFS

The notion of social reform has been central to DMK ideology. Earlier it connoted atheism, with a radical rejection of Hindu religion and practices. Even after the DMK gave up promulgating these ideas, party leaders portrayed themselves as "rational"

TABLE 8-12
Caste, DMK Local-Level Leadership

	Number	Percent
Forward non-Brahmins	81	17.6
Backward non-Brahmins	195	42.7
Service castes	21	4.5
Ex-Untouchable	37	8.1
Christian	2	.3
Atheist	10	2.2
Muslim	23	5.0
Hindu	54	11.8
No response	36	7.8
Total	459	100.0

Forward non-Brahmins

	Number	Percent
Mudaliar	16	3.5
Vellala	19	4.1
Chettiar	8	1.7
Yadava/Pillai	14	3.1
Naidu, Reddiar, Nair	24	5.2
Total	81	17.6

Backward non-Brahmins

	Number	Percent
Vanniya Kula Kshstriya	72	15.7
Muukoolathur	63	14.0
Nadar/Gramani	30	6.5
Misc. backward castes	30	6.5
Total	195	42.7

Service castes

	Number	Percent
Fisherman	3	.7
Udayar	9	2.0
Ochan (non-Brahmin priest)	1	.2
Vannan	2	.4
Others	6	1.2
Total	21	4.5

TABLE 8-13
Caste, DMK General Council

	Number	Percent
Forward non-Brahmins	16	42.1
Backward non-Brahmins	11	29.0
Muslims	2	5.3
Hindu	5	13.2
No response	4	10.5
Total	38	100.1

Forward non-Brahmins			Backward non-Brahmins		
	Number	Percent		Number	Percent
Mudaliar	4	10.5	Vanniya Kula Kshatriya	2	5.3
Vellala	4	10.5	Nadar	4	10.5
Chettiar	4	10.5	Muukoolathur	5	13.2
Pillai/Yadava	2	5.3			
Naidu, Reddiar, Nair	2	5.3			
Total	16	42.1	Total	11	29.0

and secular in thought and behavior. A survey question that asked leaders if they maintained traditional social and religious customs elicited different responses from DMK and Congress leaders. Table 8-15 shows one contrasting dimension of leadership political culture—attitudes toward traditional religious and social customs.

Negative responses do not imply that the respondent had totally abandoned traditional customs. My experience with DMK leaders indicates a complex cultural selection process. Social and religious customs include dress and household decorations, as well as such obvious things as marriage, eating habits, and temple attendance. Interviewing DMK leaders suggests that the response of no traditional social and religious customs masks a selective rejection. For example, leaders have no religious pictures on walls; interdine with all castes and do not wear caste marks; do not practice untouchability; and eat meat (but not beef and usually away from home). But such nontraditionalism would not entail "love" marriages. Even the rare cases of intercaste marriage are often arranged between the children of two radical parents with the consent of the participating families. While religious festivals might not be celebrated, holidays considered

TABLE 8-14
Caste, Congress

	Number	Percent
Brahmins	10	8.3
Forward non-Brahmins	36	30.0
Backward non-Brahmins	49	40.8
Untouchables	5	4.2
Muslims	2	1.7
Service castes	5	4.2
North Indians	2	1.7
Hindu	3	2.5
Christian	1	.8
No response	7	5.8
Total	120	100.0

Forward non-Brahmins	Number	Percent
Mudaliar	4	3.3
Vellala	14	11.7
Chettiar	3	2.5
Naidu	8	6.7
Nair	1	.8
Reddiar	3	2.5
Yadava	3	2.5
Total	36	30.0

Backward non-Brahmins	Number	Percent
Vanniya Kula Kshatriya	17	14.1
Nadar	13	10.8
Muukoolathur	11	9.2
Misc. other castes	8	6.7
Total	49	40.8

Service castes	Number	Percent
Vannan	2	1.7
Udayar	1	.83
Saliyar	1	.83
Goldsmith	1	.83
Total	5	4.2

TABLE 8-15

Social and Religious Customs, DMK Local-Level Leaders, DMK General Council, and Congress

	DMK Local Level			DMK General Council			Congress		
Response	Response	Number	Percent	Response	Number	Percent	Response	Number	Percent
Social Customs	*Social Customs*			*Social Customs*			*Social Customs*		
Yes, maintain traditional social customs	Yes, maintain traditional social customs	97	21.1	Yes, maintain traditional social customs	1	2.6	Yes, maintain traditional social customs	49	40.8
No	No	313	68.2	No	16	42.1	No	47	39.2
No response	No response	9	2.0	No response	2	5.3	No response	4	3.4
Some, Dravidian	Some, Dravidian	40	8.7	Some, Dravidian	19	50.0	Some, sometimes	20	16.6
Total	Total	459	100.0	Total	38	100.0	Total	120	100.0
Religious Customs	*Religious Customs*			*Religious Customs*			*Religious Customs*		
Yes, maintain traditional religious customs	Yes, maintain traditional religious customs	63	13.7	Yes, maintain traditional religious customs	0	0.0	Yes, maintain traditional religious customs	56	46.7
No	No	341	74.3	No	36	94.7	No	38	31.7
No response	No response	9	2.0	No response	2	5.3	No response	7	5.8
Some	Some	46	10.0				Some, sometimes	19	15.8
Total	Total	459	100.0	Total	38	100.0	Total	120	100.0

to be more indigenously Tamil, such as Pongal (a harvest celebration), are observed in grand style.

Turning from observation of traditional customs to politics, two questions from the survey indicate elite political perspectives: "What do you consider the major problems in your district?" and "What do you consider to be the major problems facing Madras State today?" Responses to these questions enable us to compare DMK and Congress leaders' definitions of key issues.

The General Council is the decision-making body of the DMK, and within the General Council the party leaders have a disproportionate influence. Between 1949 and 1961 the top leadership included C. N. Annadurai, E.V.K. Sampath, K. Anbazhagan, V. R. Nedunchezhian, Mathiazhagan, and Satyiavani Muthu. In 1968, when this study was done, there were many other members of the General Council with considerable influence, including Asaithambi, T. K. Ponnuvelu, and Era Sezhian; key district leaders such as Dharmalingam and Madurai Muthu, and movie star M. G. Ramachandran.

Questionnaires only provide a rough measure of the distinction between DMK and Congress elite political cultures. They are, however, a suggestive means of outlining relative emphases. Tables 8-16 to 8-18 show the first response of these three groups of political elites to the question "What do you consider the most important problem in your district?" (The assumption is that the answer written first by the respondent represents his own first priority.)

District Problems. As we might expect in a basically peasant society, agricultural problems stand out. A significant proportion of all three groups mentioned an agricultural issue first. For example, problems centering around the need for water facilities were mentioned by 21 percent of the DMK General Council, 25 percent of the Congress (Pradesh) Committee members, and 29.2 percent of the DMK district-level leaders. Other agricultural problems accounted for 15.7 percent of the DMK General Council response, 15.1 percent of the DMK local leadership response, and 23.1 percent of the Congress leadership response. Only among the DMK local leadership do we find land redistribution mentioned as a problem. Also only the DMK local-level leadership cited poor wages of agricultural workers. The lack of radicalism may reflect the conservatism of land ownership: recall the

TABLE 8-16
Perception of District Problems, DMK Local-Level Leadership
(N = 459)

First reason stated	Percent
Agricultural problems—water	
Water problems, irrigation	23.5
Drinking water necessary	4.4
Monsoon failure	1.3
Total	29.2
Agricultural problems—other	
Electrical facilities needed (for pump sets)	1.3
Coop societies needed	.2
Loans should be made more readily available	.7
Food processing factory necessary	.2
Land redistribution	.9
Crop diversity	.2
Modern farming implements difficult to acquire	.4
Materials necessary for agriculture difficult to acquire	.7
Production should be increased	6.8
Farmers not properly benefitted	1.1
Agriculture, DK which aspect	2.4
Low wages agricultural workers	.2
Total	15.1
Shortages/prices/facilities	
Food scarcity	5.9
High prices	2.8
Need more of everything	.7
Need improved medical facilities	.4
Need transport facilities	3.5
Need improved education	3.1
Poverty should be abolished	1.7
Total	18.1
Industrial problems	
Need industrialization	7.0
Specific industrial project mentioned	2.2
Tuticorin harbor project	2.2
New harbor should be built at Poombohur	.2
Need new dam	.7
Coimbatore Mills problems	2.6
Weavers should be helped	1.5
Industrial unemployment	5.7
Exploitation workers by capitalists	1.1
Laborers earn low wages	.7
Total	23.9

Moral problems

Bribery government officials, corruption	.4
Illicit toddy being made	.4
Equal opportunity	.9
Total	1.7

Caste problems

Casteism, social reformation	1.1
Harijans need advancement	.4
Vanniya Kula Kshatriyas need advancement	.2
Untouchability remains strong	.2
Nadars are exploitive	.2
Kallars and Pallars need improvement	.2
Total	2.3

Other problems

District headquarters should be changed	1.3
Name Dalmiapuram should be changed to Kallakudi	.2
Language problem	2.0
Cooum should be cleaned	.2
Poor need concessions	.9
Same as other districts	.9
Miscellaneous	1.3
DK	.4
No response	2.5
Total	9.7
TOTAL	100.0

substantial percentages of farmers in our sample. Even landless farmers often aspire to ownership.

Particularly significant here is the emphasis on industrial problems among the DMK General Council. Industrial issues were cited by 47.4 percent as the major district-level problem. The Congress and DMK district-level leadership figures are 26.6 percent and 23.9 percent, respectively.

Taken together, the political leadership cited a wide variety of issues as major district problems. Although agricultural and industrial concerns were central, concern was also expressed about casteism, fertilizer and food shortages, provision of public services, and so on.

State Problems. At the state level, we find greater divergence between DMK and Congress political leaders (see tables 8-19

TABLE 8-17
Perception of District Problems, DMK General Council
(N = 38)

First reason stated	Percent
Agricultural Problems—Water	
Irrigation	18.4
Drinking water	2.6
Total	21.0
Agricultural problems—other	
Modern farm implements needed	2.6
Food scarcity	2.6
Production should be increased	7.9
Agriculture in general	2.6
Total	15.7
Industrial problems	
Industrialization in general	13.2
Industrialization projects must be implemented	18.4
Tuticorin must be implemented	5.3
Laborers not paid decent wage	2.6
Unemployment	5.3
Unions not functioning well	2.6
Total	47.4
Caste problems	
Casteism, need social reformation	5.3
Other problems	
Poor education system	2.6
District headquarters must be changed	2.6
General backwardness	5.3
Total	10.5
TOTAL	99.9

to 8-21). The first distinguishing factor is the language problem. Among the DMK General Council, 31.6 percent gave "Hindi imposition" as the major state problem. The food problem was second, with 26.3 percent.[5] Among the DMK local-level leaders, 26.8 percent cited some aspect of the language problem (23.7 percent specifically mentioned "Hindi imposition" and 3.1 percent the need to improve Tamil). Equally important was the

TABLE 8-18
Perception of District Problems, Congress
(N = 120)

First reason stated	Percent
Agricultural problems—water	
Irrigation	20.0
Drinking water	1.7
Monsoon failure	3.3
Total	25.0
Agricultural problems—other	
Agricultural production should be increased	3.3
Agriculture should be improved	17.5
Rural unemployment	.8
Cultivator-landlord strife	.8
Funds community development panchayat reform	.8
Total	23.2
Shortages/prices/facilities	
Food scarcity	3.3
Need transport facilities	1.7
Improved education	.8
Need municipal amenities	.8
High prices	.8
General backwardness	.8
Housing needed	.8
Total	9.0
Industrial problems	
Need industrial development	10.8
Need small-scale industry	1.7
More trade	.8
Salem steel plant	2.5
Coimbatore mills	4.2
Unemployment	5.0
Low wages	.8
Improvement handloom weavers	.8
Total	26.6
Caste problems	
Harijan welfare	1.7
Vanniya backwardness	.8
Casteism	2.5
Total	5.0

Other problems

Extension rationing	.8
Communist trouble	.8
Language	.8
Deteriorating administration	.8
DMK harassment/Congress difficulties	2.4
Pudokottai should be separate district	.8
Miscellaneous	2.5
No response	2.5
Total	11.4
TOTAL	100.2

food problem, mentioned by 25.5 percent of DMK local-level leaders. Among Congress leaders, food was the most frequently given response, 25 percent, with language second, at 13.3 percent. Congress leaders, however, perceived the language problem differently. For them the issue was implementing the three-language formula or opposition to Tamil as the medium of instruction. Many Congress leaders simply responded "language" without amplification, while almost all DMK leaders wrote long explanations of the language problem and linked it to other aspects of DMK ideology.

Another aspect of these responses was the concern of Congress leaders with party problems. "DMK false propaganda," "Congress 1967 debacle," were some responses in this category. Of Congress leaders, 4.8 percent gave party problems as the most important state problem. Criticisms of the DMK government were also frequent. There were 6.7 percent who objected to alleged DMK "interference with the police," while 4.2 percent objected to poor DMK administration. A total of 10.9 percent gave DMK rule as a major problem. Combined with the 4.8 percent for party problems, this adds up to 15.7 percent—a larger percentage than for language-related issues.

Those attitudes and political perspectives that most often divide DMK and Congress leaders reflect the DMK cultural nationalist ideology. For example, Tamil cultural nationalism differentiates political elite views on traditional social and religious customs, and also accounts for the importance of the language issue to DMK leaders.

TABLE 8-19
Perception of State-Level Problems, DMK Local-Level Leadership
(N = 459)

First reason stated	Percent
Food	
Food problem in general	25.5
Labor	
Wages should be increased	.4
Unemployment	6.3
Equal employment	.2
Handloom weavers out of work	.7
Communist labor demands	1.1
Total	8.7
Language	
Improvement of Tamil	3.1
Hindi imposition	23.7
Total	26.8
Agricultural problems	
Irrigation	.2
Land redistribution	.2
Farmers must be helped	.7
Total	1.1
Economic development	
Industrial growth	8.5
Economic development	2.0
Tuticorin harbor project	.7
Socialism should be implemented	.2
Coimbatore mills in trouble	.9
Total	12.3
Caste	
Untouchability	.2
Casteism	.9
Total	1.1
Amenities	
Transportation	.2
Educational facilities	1.5
New housing	.2
Amenities in general	.2
Total	2.1

Other

Dravida Nadu separation	1.5
State government needs more power	5.9
Congress, unfair misrule	2.6
Bribery and corruption	1.1
Hut fires	.7
Loans needed	.4
Poor people must be helped	.9
Ceylonese and Burmese refugees	.4
Cinemas needed in village	.9
Family planning	.4
Rising prices	2.0
Must prepare for next election	.7
Total	17.5

Miscellaneous response

Miscellaneous	2.2
No problems (now that DMK is in power)	1.3
No response	1.5
Total	5.0
TOTAL	100.1

DMK RECRUITMENT

There are marked differences between the factors initially attracting DMK and Congress leaders. Tables 8-22 to 8-24 show that respondents were often initially attracted to their respective parties by prominent leaders. However, DMK and Congress "great" leaders projected radically different images and represented distinct ideologies.

Many Congressmen (half the Congressman in this sample) were attracted by the independence struggle, its leadership, and issues. Many others were attracted by patriotic or other all-India issues. A quote from a sixty-year-old Vellala Congressman from Coimbatore who joined in 1931 underscores the importance of the independence issue:

While I was a student in the Loyola College in 1930 I studied in detail the propaganda that Gandhiji made by going by walks to every village regarding the salt satyagraha. The thought of Gandhiji's suffering for the nation, after his vast education and at so old an age made me feel that keeping quiet looking

TABLE 8-20
Perception of State-Level Problems, DMK General Council
(N = 38)

First reason stated	Percent
Food	
Food problem in general	26.3
Labor	
Wages should be increased	2.6
Unemployment	2.6
Handloom weavers out of work	2.6
Coimbatore mill strike	5.3
Total	13.1
Language	
Hindi imposition	31.6
Economic development	
Industrial growth	2.6
Implementing socialism	2.6
Total	5.2
Caste	
Casteism	2.6
Amenities	
Educational facilities	2.6
Other	
State government lacks power	5.3
Student indiscipline	5.3
Party problems	2.6
Miscellaneous responses	2.6
North Indian domination	2.6
Total	18.4
TOTAL	99.8

at the developments will be cowardice and so I joined the Congress. Further, Gandhiji's policy on prohibition and his demonstration in front of the liquor shops attracted me very much, because I had personally seen how many families were ruined because of the poor people taking to drinking.

TABLE 8-21
Perception of State-Level Problems, Congress
(N = 120)

First reason stated	Percent
Food	
Food problem in general	25.0
Labor	
Rise capitalist power against labor	.8
Labor unrest	3.3
Unemployment	8.3
Total	12.4
Language	
Language issue (general)	11.7
Hindi and English should be official languages	.8
Tamil as medium instruction	.8
Total	13.3
Agricultural problems	
Monsoon failure	.8
Landlord-cultivator feuds	.8
Total	1.6
Economic development	
Economic development needed	6.7
Development village industries	.8
Coimbatore mills closed	.8
Slacking of planning under DMK	.8
Trade recession	1.7
Total	10.8
Caste	
Growth communalism	3.3
Party problems	
DMK false propaganda (about Congress)	.8
Congress 1967 debacle	.8
Congress factionalism/problems	1.6
Congress should regain popular support	.8
Party leaders' inability to understand problems	.8
Total	4.8
Amenities	
Standard of living ought to be raised	2.5
More electrification	1.7

Drinking water	.8
Child welfare should be looked after	.8
Total	5.8
DMK rule	
Interference with police	6.7
Poor DMK administration	4.2
Total	10.9
Other	
High prices	1.2
Threat to national integration	2.5
Student indiscipline	2.5
Better loan procedures needed	.8
Tamil Nad culture dying	.8
Prohibition	.8
Congress left no problems	.8
Many problems	.8
No response	1.9
Total	12.1
TOTAL	100.0

It should be remembered that while Tamil nationalism is a dominant, encompassing theme in Tamil Nadu politics, it is not the only theme. All-India, pro-Independence sentiment is also strong. Furthermore, for some Tamil Congressmen loyalty to Tamil Nadu was subsumed in an all-India perspective on every issue. However, if the factional split is any indication, these all-India nationalists were a minority within their own party. Periyar's (E. V. Ramasami) support of the Kamaraj faction and then the Tamil Nationalist party merger with Congress (more precisely with the Kamaraj faction) did much to isolate Congress all-India nationalists in a sea of non-Brahmin, often Tamil nationalist, sentiment. It should also be recalled that some supporters of the independence movement later became DMK adherents. Many wanted independence with the stipulation that India be divided and Dravida Nadu established.

Annadurai, either as a symbolic figure or associated with certain policies, was a direct source of attraction for 23.2 percent of DMK local-level leaders. The radical ideological policies of the party, separate Dravida Nadu, social reform, atheism, and socialism account for 22.3 percent of the responses. The party

TABLE 8-22
Initial Attraction to the DMK, DMK Local-Level Leadership
(N = 459)

First reason stated	Percent
Annadurai	
Annadurai's policies (general)	5.1
Annadurai's policy on social reform	.4
Annadurai's policy on attacks on Hinduism	.2
Annadurai's policy on religion (atheistic)	.2
Annadurai's affectionate nature	1.5
Annadurai's genius	1.1
Annadurai's evoked faith	.4
Annadurai's oratorical power	10.5
Annadurai's writings	1.5
Annadurai's service to Tamil	.4
Annadurai's service to the poor	.4
Annadurai's emphasis on poverty, duty, discipline	1.1
Annadurai's efforts to strengthen party	.4
Total	23.2
Radical policies	
Separate Dravida Nadu	8.7
Social reform	11.8
Atheism	.7
Socialism	1.1
Total	22.3
Language	
Anti-Hindi policy	10.5
General good policies	
Good policies, not specific	17.4
DMK works for Tamilians (Dravidians)	.7
DMK works for poor	1.5
DMK works for people	1.5
DMK supports fishermen	.2
DMK will accomplish good	.4
DMK working for country	.7
DMK brought about renaissance	1.1
DMK supports democracy	.7
DMK political acumen	.2
Total	24.4
Mentions leaders	
Nedunchezhian	.4
Anbazhagan	.2

M. G. Ramachandran	.2
Good leadership	4.6
Miscellaneous leaders	.2
Tamil speech of leaders	3.5
Persuasion of local DMK officials	.4
Total	9.5

Miscellaneous

Personal incident	.4
Persuasion relative	.2
Agitation	.9
Family atmosphere	.4
Against Congress	1.3
1-measure 1-rupee scheme	1.1
Self-respect marriage bill	1.7
Prohibition	.2
Economic development	.4
North exploiting south	.4
Party of poor people	.2
Nonviolence	.2
Rid government of bribery	.7
Nationalization	.2
Rich exploiting poor	.2
Egalitarian policies	.9
Total	9.4

No response	.7
TOTAL	100.0

policy on the language issue accounts for another 10.5 percent. Here we see the dual attraction of radical social reform policy and the personal appeal of Annadurai. In the DMK General Council 31.4 percent of the leaders mention Annadurai as a source of attraction, and 36.8 percent specific policies. There were 26.6 percent who said they went from the DK to the DMK because the policies were the same. Again we see the dual attraction of Annadurai and party policies.

Quotations from the local-level and General Council survey responses and accompanying material provides a better insight into the dynamics of DMK leadership. In their own words, they tell us why they became part of what is often termed the DMK family.

The first letter was written by a thirty-year-old Kallar (member

TABLE 8-23
Initial Attraction to the DMK, DMK General Council
(N = 38)

First reason stated	Percent
Annadurai	
Annadurai's policies	2.6
Annadurai's affectionate nature	2.6
Annadurai's genius	2.6
Annadurai's oratorical power	18.4
Annadurai's teachings	2.6
Annadurai's efforts to strengthen party	2.6
	31.4
x*Policies*	
Dravida Nadu separation	7.9
Radical social reform	15.8
Atheism	2.6
Language policy	7.9
DMK policy in general	2.6
	36.8
DK	
Went from DK to DMK, liked DK policies, DMK policies same	26.6
Miscellaneous	
Tamil speech of the leaders	2.6
Family atmosphere of the party	2.6
	5.2
TOTAL	100.0

TABLE 8-24
Initial Attraction to Congress
(N = 120)

First reason stated	Percent
Gandhi	
Gandhi's leadership freedom struggle	2.5
Gandhi's visit to south India	2.5
Gandhi's salt satyagraha	.8
Gandhi's speeches	1.7
Gandhi's writings	2.5
Gandhi's love of the country	.8

Gandhi's leadership, call	5.0
Gandhi's philosophy	5.8
	21.6

Policies

Wanted independence	29.2
Democratic socialism	4.2
Prohibition	1.7
Secularism	.8
Salt satyagraha	.8
Economic independence	1.7
Removal untouchability	.8
National integration	.8
Policies in general, all	7.5
	47.5

Other leader

Nehru	2.5
Kamaraj Nadar	3.3
Satyiamurthy	.8
District leader mentioned	3.3
	9.9

Miscellaneous

Internal party democracy	.8
Only Congress can run the country	1.7
Relative asked me to join	5.8
Long association DK	.8
Participation Kamaraj election campaign	.8
Sacrifice of leaders	2.5
(My) patriotism	5.0
(My) desire to work for the country	1.7
	19.1

No response	1.7
TOTAL	99.8

of the Muukoolathur) lawyer, who reported his earnings at about 6,000 rupees per year, a comfortable middle-class salary. He was general secretary of a town DMK branch in Trichy, and was attracted to the DMK "by the separation policy, Tamil Nadu, Dravida Nadu, a separate language, a separate quality, culture, and history. It should remain separate. We do not wish

to be under the north Indians.'' He appended this letter written
in English:

Dear Friend:
    When I received your letter I got astonishment and also
I felt pleasure in my mind to reply for you.
    In my school days, I happened to go to the meetings which
would be held by the followers of the great leader of South
who is called Periyar Ramaswamy. The principles of Periyar,
the speeches of Periyar and direction and methods of Periyar
attracted me. So I joined in the D.K. students organization
when I studied fifth form. During that period I was fully hostile
against the Brahmins and the Brahminism. I used to go to
the temple with my friends and I did there so many things.
I used to scold and ridicule the Brahmins without hesitation
and fear. Once Periyar conducted huge procession to contempt
the government for its atrocities and procession happened to
proceed in heavy rain and I also joined in that procession.
    After that I was ill for three days due to that heavy rain.
    I bought so many books which would teach the D.K.
principles and I used to go through it with all careful steps.
    After that I joined in the college beginning through the school
final examination. When I came to the college I began to
sensitize the principles and the difference between the D.K.
and the D.M.K. The principles, the paths and the democratic
method of the leader and revered Anna who is embodiment
of wisdom and the king maker [note the use of Kamaraj Nadar's
title to describe Annadurai], slowly attracted and enchanted
me. The idea of separation, and the formation of the Dravidian
Confederation by the democratic method showed light to my
mind, and I came to know the principles and preamble that
preaches about the history of the South and the culture of
the South. So I began to study in the library about the history
of the South which never surrendered to North but it conquered
the North many times. For example, I will cite about Kangaikondocholen who once conquered the North India and surrounding place of the Kongai River, so that he got the name
Kongai Kondo Cholen. I began to realize that we must get
liberty to our country. That Dravidam . . . so I joined in
the D.M.K. students organization. While I studied the B.A.
course in Annamalai University.

After I passed in B.A. Degree course, I went law college, Madras, where I joined in D.M.K. students organization and I gave so many ideas to the D.M.K. students organization. I went to election canvass on the Anna constituency. Kancheepuram, and so many constituency in Madras in 1964 [1962] general election.

There was break in my study due to my failure in getting pass in the B.L. examination. I got passed in the B.L. September exams. There was a six month gap to join in B.L. course so I planned to construct a small cottage in my village for spreading of D.M.K. principles and with help of my friends and my college I constructed a small cottage named after great saint Thiruvalluvar. The cottage is more or less a small reading room having four thousand five hundred books and daily newspaper.

I joined the B.L. courses during B. L. education career. We planned to conduct a strike against the imposition of Hindi. On that particular day we assembled in the college and we called out the students to run out of the classes. Most of them came out of the class rooms but handful of the students refused to come out.

I immediately planned and entered into the room and laid down before the professor and request the students to go out of the classroom. The strike was successful. And then I joined in the anti-Hindi agitation in the year 1965.

When the general election 1967 entered I planned to set up a [drama] . . . to give impetus to the election in the constituency of Thirubarappure, so I set up [drama] . . . about Chirumaswamy who had sacrificed his life for the cause of Tamil by the method of self-immolation and I began to perform it [the drama].

The [drama] . . . gave vivid picture about the imposition of Hindi and the corruption of the Congress people. I also went to deliver my lecture in some places in my constituency and I canvassed for D.M.K. candidates. But, D.M.K. candidate had been defeated in my constituency.

These are the days of democracy—the age of common man—days when the sparrow turns around and boldly faces the falcon. It is the commoner who now rules the country— these words are spoken by my reverent leader, Anna who has occupied all the hearts of the true Tamil people. His

words—his foretelling—rooted in the earth of Tamil Nadu
and youths captured the administration of the Tamil state.
But it is not the end of our travel. But there is something
to be done—what is it? The maturing time will tell you.

So I conclude my long letter to my friend, please do not
forget me. . . .

To provide more information on this Kallar lawyer: to the
question, "What is it about the DMK which attracts you now?"
he answered, "That policy [the separation policy] still attracts
me. Though Anna announced that we had given it up because
of the severe laws, we still have the hope in our heart that
we will achieve it. In this party we have the policy that the
poor people would rule the country. Also the policy that Hindi
should be abolished attracts people." To "What is the major
problem of Tamil Nadu now?" he answered, "(I do not tell
this out) I feel that separation is the biggest problem. Tamil
Nadu should become a separate country. Then only the language
problem and poverty can be solved."

These statements are revealing. This man joined the DMK
at age sixteen as a member of the Dravida Students Association,
and was in the party in that capacity between 1953 and 1957
(that is, during the movement years). He has now risen to the
position of the DMK secretary in his branch. He does not follow
traditional religious or social customs, and is very attached to
a separate Tamil Nadu. But note the relationship of cultural
materials to political propaganda. He tells us that history taught
him the south was never conquered by the north, but rather
the other way around. Kangaikondocholen is one of his heroes.
This story of the famous southern king who conquered the north
if often related by party adherents. Also note this attachment
to Annadurai, and his independent involvement in DMK and
Tamil-nationalist activities, such as setting up a "cottage" to
spread propaganda. All are characteristic of young people during
the early days of the development of the party.

In contrast to this fairly well-off middle-class Kallar lawyer
was a 31-year-old Kanyakumari district fisherman (meenpidi
Mukkevan) who was illiterate and had someone else complete
his questionnaire. He placed his thumb-print on the questionnaire
and the accompanying letter to show that his scribe spoke in
his name. This fisherman was general secretary of a local DMK

branch he joined in 1958. He reported his annual income as 250 rupees. The following tries to capture the spirit of the letter that accompanied the questionnaire, and is therefore a free translation from Tamil:

Dear Madame:

I have filled in all the answers to your questionnaire. I am a poor fisherman who doesn't know how to write. There are about 2,000 Christian fishermen who are DMK members in Vilaiangodu Taluk. It is surprising that you have found my name among all these names. One could get true facts only from poor people like me.

Under a heading "My Party History," he says,

I am an illiterate fisherman. I attend DMK meetings. I would go near people who read DMK papers and listen carefully. They will not go away from my mind. I would speak like the great speakers. I would sing the DMK songs, or the films by heart. I would make up my own songs. I am a poet! No, no, I am an illiterate poet. I am respected for my songs.

There are many people who learn from me. I would buy DMK papers and give it to those who can read and ask them to read them aloud. The DMK did not bother about the rules and regulations of the religious. They did not teach us to hate religion. They only told us to leave out the unimportant factors. I go to church regularly on Sundays. There is no good feeling between the religious pastor and myself. These pastors oppose even the good policies of the DMK. They feel that we, who have wisdom would get rid of the bad qualities of the pastors and they oppose us. They feel that if they respect us, we would become more popular and they would have to run away.

The DMK are backward in economy [poor]. DMK is our breath. Long live Arignar [genius] Anna. Long live the DMK government. For twenty-five to thirty years the Congress will not be able to shake the DMK government. Our strong enemies are the Communist parties. But we had political agreement in the elections. Nothing else. As far as Madras State is concerned they are a minority party. I cannot read or write. Our Vilaivangodu secretary is A.M.A. Kadar [a Muslim name] He wrote this.

This letter tells us something of the DMK viewed from the bottom. We see the impact of the DMK connection with the movie industry, its poetic propaganda, the DMK film song mystique. But this is accompanied by the penetration of the DMK stand on religion and on social and cultural affairs. Another letter from a 24-year-old Saliyan weaver who studied up to 8th standard and who earns 70 rupees a year provides another insight into the poorest strata of DMK local-level leaders. He is general secretary of his Ramnathapuram branch, and joined the party in 1962. In response to the question of why he joined, he wrote, "M.G.R.'s acting, Arignar Anna's speeches attracted me to the party. Also Arignar Anna's articles in *Dravida Nadu* attracted me." However, to the question, "What attracts you now to the party?" he said, "I am not attracted to the DMK now. I don't like its actions now." His answer to "What is the major problem in the district?" gives some insight into this loss of faith: "Before the elections, the DMK leaders said that if they came to power they would give one measure rice for one rupee. Immediately, they would help the farmers, and they they were the friends of the poor people. But they gave one measure rice to only Madras and Coimbatore. The people in our district asked them about this. This is our problem."

We have now looked at several types of leaders in the party: the student leader, now a lawyer; the poor fisherman; the poverty-stricken weaver. Another important element is the agriculturalist. A 34-year-old agriculturalist from Madurai district (earning 1,000 rupees a year) joined the party in 1949 and was secretary of his local DMK branch and an aspiring MLA. He writes:

At first I was in Dravida Students Association. Then I joined the DK. Then when the DMK was started I also became DMK . . . I had a great deal of interest in Tamil. I also had interest in art. Naturally the work of the revolutionary poet Bharati Dasan gave me the interest to join the DK. There is prose, music and drama in Tamil. It is not much to say the DMK improved these three. Arignar Anna in his radio speech "When Will this Bondage to Fate Be Over" said that the authors, speakers, musicians, and cine producers of our country should not deceive the people and not be enslaved by old customs, should take an interest in reformation and produce films on this basis and help the reformation to spread in the community. This is also one of the policies I liked. The letters to (Younger) Brother Anna wrote in Dravida Nadu still have a place in my heart.

There is a similarity in tone and structure among these diverse elements in the DMK district leadership. First, all refer at some point to Annadurai, and always with the prefix Arignar (genius). Second, all, illiterate or well educated, rich or poor, share a common interest in reading and a common curiosity about the world and life around them. No matter what their social or economic status, as individuals they stand out as leaders in their own limited arenas. They have clearly taken certain aspects of the DMK ideology and style seriously. That they live the DMK political style is evident from their forms of expression, the emotion and manner in which they refer to party leaders. Finally, it is interesting that all were attracted to the party as young men. Taking the questionnaires as a whole, it is clear that if it were possible to measure emotional commitment from the responses, young people (ages 14, 15, and 16) attracted to the Dravidian movement during the radical years constitute its present emotional backbone.

We see a similar pattern in the general council of the DMK. A Nadar General Council member from Ramnad wrote in response to the question on initial attraction to the DMK:

In 1942 the DK which was a social reformation movement attracted me. Then I was fifteen years old. Then the Congress "Quit India" agitation was taking place. Hence I was interested in politics [note here the unusual merging of Dravidian movement and independence sentiment]. The British people had made the people realize a little of their mistake in superstition and blind faith.

Just as there is trouble between whites and Negroes in America here also we have the trouble between the low caste and high caste. For some time this feeling has been encouraged by the members of political parties knowingly or unknowingly. Each political party should prevent the encouragement of this feeling. A full effort should be taken by the government to abolish the caste system.

Another General Council member, a 44-year-old Chettiar from Trichy district, was also attracted to Congress initially: "When I was young because the Congress was an independence movement and then later in 1957 when Hindi was forced on us, we felt that our mother tongue Tamil would be destroyed and the anti-Hindi movement which protected our mother tongue and taught everyone the fame of our language, literature and the culture of the Tamilians, I became interested in politics."

To supplement the questionnaire evidence on the nature of attachment to the DMK, there is an interesting book, *Life in a Forest*, written by a former DMK top leader, Kannadasan.[6]

Kannadasan, now a prominent member of the Congress party, but at one time an important DMK leader and a poet, describes in an autobiographical work (largely critical of the DMK) how he first reacted to Annadurai. Kannadasan first heard of the Dravidian movement in 1945 through a friend who talked to him "day and night of the DK movement." But Kannadasan states that he was a pious boy, and had been brought up in a religious home, so he showed no initial interest in the DK.

By 1945 he left his village to seek his fortune as a writer in the city. When he returned, he found his village friends sympathetic to DK policies. They argued with him for hours about "Brahmins, Puranas and the Aryans and Dravidians" and first presented him with Annadurai's *Dravida Nadu* and articles in *Kudi Arasu*.

He tells of first hearing Annadurai in a public meeting (the "he" in the quote refers to Kannadasan—he refers to himself in the third person throughout):

As soon as he got down in Egmore station he saw a worker from Mullaipadippaliam. He had come to receive a friend. He asked them to come to Gokale Hall that evening. He asked why. He said "Army Captain"[7] Anna would be speaking. The custom of that day was to call Anna "Army Captain." He said he would come. That evening was an important time in his life. He entered Gokale Hall exactly at six P.M. The hall was full. He sat in a corner. After a long time all the people applauded. They shouted "Long Live the Army Captain." He looked back. He was coming; exactly at 8 P.M. he started speaking. Words came out like a stream, beautiful examples in each line, new words [a new method of speaking].

Beyond the scope of Tamil grammar. He forgot himself. That
day Annadurai became one who could not be rubbed away
from his heart. His [Annadurai's] speech made . im [Kannada-
san] think that a wise man had come at the proper time.
When he returned to the lodge, his heart was full of strange
emotion. The simple devotee saw this thought being changed.
"Is God a lie?" Are the Puranas false? Are all the Itihasas
which have existed for thousands of years false? The Aryans
we learned in history, are in reality these Brahmins? Are all
the gods only false stories made up to deceive the Dravidians?
His mind was thinking about this the whole day. Annadurai's
speech was circulating in his head. Especially his attacks on
the Brahmins could not be forgotten. "The snake has poison
in his teeth, the Brahmin has poison all over his body." "The
Aryans who came from central Asia, came down and settled
in south India and have lowered the original dwellers." All
these facts are new to him. These opinions started getting
a hold on him. . . . He started thinking about these all the
time. He remembered incidents during his school days in his
village. The headmaster of his school was Sambasiva Iyer
[a Brahman]. He treated him very cruelly. He gave higher
marks to Brahmin boys in his exams. If any one was sent
to his house while he was eating, he would scold him harshly.
He completely accepted Annadurai's opinion that the Brahmins
are enemies of society. *The religious feelings of seventeen years
started vanishing in three hours* [my emphasis]. The words
self-respect attracted him. I am also a man, I will not spoil
my respect, and give respect to some other man. Whether
he is a king or a god. He became a new man. Even then
some of his old customs did not leave him. He put on vibhuti
and went to eat. After two days he went out and bought
a few books on the Self-Respect movement. He read every
one of them. He could not forget Annadurai . . . even then
he did not want to show himself as a Self-Respect man he
knew it would hinder him in the field he wished to enter.
In those days more people hated the Self-Respect movement
than liked it. Unless a man was well off, and had lots of
courage, he could not be a Self-Respect man. The people
around him, who could harm him were religious people. They
were enemies of the Self-Respect movement. So he kept
Self-Respect in his heart and religion on his forehead [Meaning

that he painted his forehead with sacred ash].

Annadurai's message penetrated Kannadasan's religious up-
bringing and started him questioning deep personal beliefs. Also
note the role of Annadurai's use of Tamil in positively mediating
this radical new message. The relation between Kannadasan's
experience with his Brahmin schoolmaster and his willingness
to accept the view of Aryan-Dravidian conflict is another aspect
of the complex process of internalization of a new radical
message. Annadurai was a charismatic leader for many people,
as Kannadasan puts it, he "could not forget Annadurai."

POLITICAL LEADERS VIEW THEIR PARTIES

For members or strong supporters of the DMK, Annadurai
remains a powerful attraction—an important reason for adherence
to the DMK. Of the DMK General Council members, 42.1 percent
specifically mentioned Annadurai as the motivating force for
their present adherence to the party (see table 8-26). In contrast,
however, DMK local-level leaders were more likely to talk about
government policies, particularly policies on language and poverty, as current attractions. Table 8-25 shows leaders citing
a multitude of different kinds of contemporary attractions to
the DMK.[8] Even among local-level leaders, however, 10.2 percent
mentioned Annadurai as the current attraction to the party. In
the General Council, by contrast, current attraction is more
heavily focused on Annadurai. Other points of attraction center
around nationalist issues—language, literary renaissance, changing the state's name, and so on. To move ahead a bit, the impact
of Annadurai's death on the party must be understood in terms
of these patterns. When Annadurai died the DMK lost a crucial
focal point, a source of initial attraction and emotional support
for many leaders. The consequences of this will be examined
in future chapters. At this point it is important to look at
Annadurai's relationship to other party leaders.

THE CENTRALITY OF ANNADURAI

Annadurai was the leader of the DMK from the inception of
the party to his death in 1969. After Sampath's exit, other top
leaders were clearly second to Annadurai. However, while

TABLE 8-25

Attraction to the DMK Now, DMK Local-Level Leadership

(N = 459)

First reason stated	Percent
Annadurai	
Annadurai's good rule	7.0
Annadurai's wisdom	2.6
Annadurai's speech and writing	.2
Annadurai's respect for opposition	.4
Total	10.2
DMK government policies	
Good administration policies	13.6
Food policy	12.6
Controlling inflation	9.2
Law and order, peaceful rule	2.9
Agricultural policies	1.7
Democratic orientation, good attitude toward opposition	5.0
Fulfilling promises	1.7
Miscellaneous (nationalization, buses, World Tamil Conference, World Trade Fair, Self-Respect Marriage Bill, industrial growth)	3.0
Total	49.7
Language, nationalism, radical policies	
Socialism	.4
Separation	2.6
Social reform	1.7
Two-language formula and improving Tamil	12.2
Total	16.9
Qualities of leaders (other than Annadurai)	
(includes austerity, honesty, humbleness, etc.)	5.4
Other favorable responses	
Helping poor	6.3
Helping others	6.3
Miscellaneous (good party, etc.)	2.9
	15.5
No response	2.0
Don't like	.2
TOTAL	99.9

TABLE 8-26
Attraction to the DMK Now, DMK General Council
(N = 38)

First reason stated	Percent
Annadurai	
Annadurai's good rule	15.8
Annadurai's wisdom/ability	13.2
Annadurai's speech/writing	2.6
Annadurai miscellaneous	10.5
Total	42.1
DMK government policies	
Two-language formula	10.5
Socialism	3.0
Improving Tamil language and culture, renaissance	7.8
Fulfilling promises	5.3
Agricultural policy	2.6
Law and order	2.6
Miscellaneous good policies	13.4
Total	45.2
DMK is good party	5.2
Leaders (other than Annadurai)	5.3
No response	2.0
Don't like	.2
TOTAL	100.0

Annadurai was always venerated within the party, only after 1963 was he fanatically referred to as "a God on earth."

In his biography, Annadurai is quoted as stating: "I am a simple man, I was born in a very ordinary family. . . . I also belong to a backward caste.[9] Although Annadurai has been listed in newspapers and elsewhere as "Annadurai Mudaliar" (a foreward caste suffix),[10] there have been strong innuendos that his background is only marginally respectable. In fact, during the movement period of DMK history, Congress politicians hinted that both Annadurai and Karunanidhi had disreputable mothers. The accuracy of these rumors is difficult to ascertain, but the important fact is that they are widely repeated. Of course, some

Tamilians also believed that Annadurai was from a high-caste background because of his Mudaliar name; but interviews seem to confirm Annadurai's own account of a simple background.

Annadurai was born in 1908 and entered politics during the late 1920s. He was poor and of low caste at a time when politics was dominated by wealthy and elite Brahmin and non-Brahmin castes. (Karunanidhi, in contrast, arrived on the political scene after a transition away from elite-dominated politics, and this may explain the differences in their style). Annadurai fought his way to political recognition in an arena where intelligence and low-caste origins were still considered anomalous. There is strong evidence that Annadurai's orientation to politics was significantly shaped by this experience, and may have provided the emotional ingredient in many of his early literary and political writings against casteism. It also gave him a direct interest in the success of radical social reform and a sense of commonality and identity with the "common man," the backward castes. Annadurai also had an engaging air of humility which was a decided political asset.

Annadurai's biographer cites one example of this humility during his college days. Annadurai attended Pachaiyappas College[11] in Madras on a scholarship for backward class students, and his biographer reports that without the scholarship he would not have been able to attend at all. The college principal asked Annadurai to join the BA Honors class. Annadurai initially refused because of his family background. The principal called him aside and said, "It is very rare for our people to study well, like you and get good marks, and get a first class. There are very few of such people, hence, isn't it necessary that people like you should come up?"[12]

Annadurai was recruited into the Justice party while still a student by T. V. Nathan and P. Balasubramaniam, the editor of the *Sunday Observer*. His first assignment involved translating the English speeches of some party leaders into Tamil so they could be understood by the masses. This ironic fact indicates some of the complexities of the language issue in Tamil Nadu. At that time, English was the language of the elite and of politics. Many elite non-Brahmins in the Justice party came from homes where English was the first language. To this day, many speak poor Tamil. (Annadurai also translated E. V. Ramasami's speeches from Tamil to English on certain occasions.)

TABLE 8-27
Attraction to Congress Now, Congress
(N = 120)

First reason stated	Percent
General government policies	
Democratic socialism	34.2
National integration	5.0
Democracy	4.2
Freedom	4.2
Equality	.8
Patriotism	.8
Total	49.2
Specific governmental policies	
Aiding poor	4.1
Preserving independence	2.5
Secularism	1.7
Economic development and independence	1.7
Helping Harijans	1.7
Helping cooperative movement	.8
Policies (nonspecific)	7.5
Total	20.0
Congress Party Characteristics	
Can save India	5.8
Expertise	1.7
Can govern	3.3
Youthful	.8
Congress majority in Parliament	.8
Disciplined	.8
No better party	.8
Total	14.0
Leadership	
Mahatma Gandhi and Gandhianism	4.2
Kamaraj	4.2
Indira Gandhi	.8
Leadership (nonspecific)	.8
Total	10.0
Miscellaneous	
Long-term attachment	1.7
Renewed enthusiasm after '67 defeat	.8
General attachment	.8
Total	3.3

Negative	1.7
No response	1.7
TOTAL	99.9

Annadurai's first contact with the Self-Respect movement occurred before his Justice party recruitment. In 1925, as a high school student, Annadurai first heard Periyar E. V. Ramasami speak at a conference in Kancheepuram, one of the conferences at which E. V. Ramasami changed his position from supporting the Congress and independence to advocating the non-Brahmin movement. But it was not until 1935 that Annadurai met E. V. Ramasami in person:

> only in 1935 I came into contact with Periyar. Then I wrote the BA examination. The results were not known. At Thirupur a Young Men's Conference was held. There for the first time I met Periyar. I had love and affection towards him. I liked his principles of reformation. Periyar asked me "What are you doing?" "I am studying, I wrote the examination." "Are you going to seek an employment?" "No. I have no desire for an employment. I desire to work for the masses." From that day he became my leader. I became his foster son from that day in social life.[13]

Up to 1935 he seems to have been a conformist in social attitudes. A pious child, he had an orthodox wedding in 1930 while still a college student. The bride was chosen by his family and the decision to have the wedding made by his mother's sister. Even about employment (about which he talked with E. V. Ramasami), Annadurai was influenced by his family's desire for status. In his biography, he humorously describes attempts to secure a high-status job.

In 1935, Annadurai stood for the Corporation elections, supported by prominent nonBrahmin leader Raja Sir Muthiah Chettiar, his "angel" in the Justice party. This election was the first time Annadurai used social reform propaganda for political purposes:

> M. Subramanyam, the Congress candidate, had assistance

from some of the major Congress leaders at that time including Satyiamurthy and Thiru Vi Ka (V. Kalyanasundaraman). Once in a meeting comprised of lower caste people, Annadurai said,

"My dear comrades I am the person who treats you all equally. Only for that reason will I sit with you and take my food. Do the Congress people treat you in the same way? No! please invite them to come and sit by your side and eat food. They will not eat your food. For that you can understand that they do not care for you."

Annadurai's biographer reports that after that meeting Annadurai ate with a "low-caste man" (probably an Untouchable). His biographer describes the sequel to Annadurai's action:

After a few days a Congress meeting was held there. In that meeting Srinivasa Rao [a Brahmin] spoke. When he was speaking one person from the audience went to him with fish soup and said that he would consider it treating him equally if he took it. This was an echo of the speech of Anna.

Srinivasa Rao was not a fish eater. They apprehended trouble in the meeting. "I am a vegetarian. If you give me that food [meaning vegetarian food] I am prepared to eat with you," he said. He was not left at that point. They prepared vegetarian food and invited him to come and eat it with them. Srinivasa Rao had no alternative to sit and eat with great difficulty. Anna had brought about a change among downtrodden men.[14]

Although Annadurai lost the election, he maintained his position as a rising star within the Justice party. Once in politics, Annadurai's ability propelled him into leadership. By 1944, when the Dravida Kazhagam was formed, Annadurai played a key role; this was partly because he realized the political potential of the students. While in the Justice party and the DK, Annadurai was recognized as a man of extraordinary talent. Within the DK, he was second to E. V. Ramasami, and when he left, many students followed him. As we know, 75 percent of the DK organization left with Annadurai to form the DMK. As early as the 1950s, men who heard Annadurai speak were deeply affected (for example, Kannadasan), and some joined the DMK because of him.

This short sketch of Annadurai's life is sufficient to indicate an interesting contrast between Annadurai and Periyar E. V. Ramasami. At age ten, E. V. Ramasami was challenging entrenched caste customs. His early village life is a record of rebellion against social structures, in contrast to Annadurai's early conformity. The combination of Annadurai's low-caste background, formidable intellectual talents, and the existence of a radical social reform movement provided the context in which he accepted the radical ideas of E. V. Ramasami and attached himself to the Dravidian movement.

Gradually, Annadurai began to be viewed as more than an important leader; he came to be considered a great leader, an "anna" or elder brother to his followers. By the 1960s the emotional response to Annadurai by many DMK members and supporters took on a charismatic aspect. Following Annadurai was considered a "duty." He was a "God on earth," always termed "arignar" (genius), and eventually "perarignar" (great genius). During this later period he certainly fits Weber's description of a charismatic leader: "a certain quality of an individual personality by virtue of which he is set apart from ordinary men and treated as endowed with supernatural, superhuman or at least specifically exceptional powers or quality. These are such as are not accessible to the ordinary person, but are regarded as of divine origin or as exemplary, and on the basis of them the individual is treated as a leader." [15] Although Weber states that charisma involves "a call," a "mission," or a "spiritual duty," it is also clear that "It is recognition on the part of those subject to authority which is decisive to the validity of charisma." [15] What is important, is how the individual is regarded by his followers or disciples. Weber's view of charisma represents a broadening and a secularization of its original meaning as a Christian concept: leadership based on a transcendental call by a divine being, believed in both by the person called and those with whom he had to deal in exercizing his calling.

Using recognition by followers as the decisive criterion, Weber discussed a number of charismatic types, including demagogues. The attitude of the follower toward the charismatic leader is characterized as "hero worship" or "absolute trust in the leader." This can take a number of forms. In the DMK, Annadurai was an inspiration for many; he motivated young people to try to realize the utopian vision he depicted for them; he expressed a sense of calling or mission, and has stated publicly a feeling

of mission to uplift the downtrodden Tamilians. His definition
of mission clarifies the duty felt by followers towards Annadurai:
only through following Annadurai could the goals of the Dravidian
ideology be achieved. Thus he constantly urged his followers
to obey the triple commandments of the party: "do your duty,
be disciplined, and be dignified."

Earlier the question was raised: "How did the DMK maintain
support from leaders (and followers) who believed in and wanted
radical social reform and/or separation while the party ideology
became transformed and deradicalized? One method suggested
was new attractions to the party—new reasons for adherence
and support. Another method centered around Annadurai. The
two, in fact, are interrelated: devotion to Annadurai generated
diffuse support for the party during and after the ideological
transformation. Interviews suggest that for some ideologically
committed leaders, faith in Annadurai's personal commitment
to radical principles was the basic factor in maintaining their
loyalty. For the party in general, difficult ideological issues were
papered over by reverent reference to the "Anna" (elder brother)
who would resolve all difficulties. For some, Annadurai became
an authoritative source of a new ideology. Devotion to him was
substituted for the radical DMK ideology, for the old social
reform and separationist goals. Others never abandoned their
radical beliefs. They, too, could maintain party adherence because
there was a myth among some lower-level party leaders that
the top leadership—especially Annadurai—still wanted separation; supposedly they were merely waiting for the right moment.

As long as Annadurai was the leader of the DMK, many
potential conflicts within the party were muted.

CONCLUSION

Chapter 7 probed the world view of the Tamil Nadu common
man. This chapter has focused on Tamil Nadu political leaders,
particularly local-level DMK leaders. These leaders, the backbone
of the DMK party and often the insistent purveyors of Tamil
nationalism, must be viewed against the backdrop of DMK and
Tamil Nadu development. Overall, they were young and were
recruited into the party during periods of enhanced party propaganda. Seven "mobilizing moments" were identified, which
included agitations, the party founding, and general elections.

Many leaders were attracted to the party by Annadurai and
retained a marked devotion to him in 1968, when these data
were gathered. Annadurai was shown to be a crucial focal point,
a factor in leadership recruitment, and a unifying force within
the party.

DMK local-level leaders were also younger, less well educated,
and of lower social status than Congress or DMK General Council
leaders. Both DMK General Council and DMK local-level leaders
articulated a secular perspective which contrasted with the
Congress outlook.

Perceptions of problems differentiated Congress and DMK
leaders more as the scope of the question expanded from the
district (where common concern with agricultural issues was
striking) to the state level (where DMK leaders emphasized
language and Tamil nationalist issues).

This examination of DMK leadership (particularly at the local
level) clarifies the process of rapid DMK growth and provides
perspective on the DMK government after 1967. Local-level
leaders, as has been emphasized, were central to DMK growth.
We can only understand the speed, determination, and dynamism
of the DMK during the 1950s and 1960s if we take into account
a leadership motivated by commitments beyond normal adherence
to a political party. Yet this commitment also had its price,
as we shall see in the next chapters. Those who were committed
to Annadurai had to find new sources of inspiration when he
died. Those committed to radical ideals had to rationalize their
involvement in the party when those ideals faded. Those who
believed the DMK was a "family" had to learn to cope with
mounting charges of corruption after 1970. Thus the test of DMK
mettle came with the assumption of power.

[1] This survey was done in 1968, prior to the split in both the DMK and Congress
party. There will be more on those splits in later chapters. Only DMK and
Congress leaders are included in this discussion. Tamil Nadu is basically a
two-party state, and certainly elite political culture is dominated by these two
parties.
[2] See Jagdish N. Bhagwati, "India in the International Economy: a Policy
Framework for a Progressive Society" (M.I.T. Lal Bahadur Memorial Lectures,
1973). That is 25 rupees per capita per month at 1960-1961 prices.
[3] Of course Mudaliar and Vellala have become titles that individuals may
take when moving out of traditional areas. A small number of Mudaliars, like
Annadurai, are from poor, low-ranked Mudaliar jatis, but by and large Mudaliar
are considered high-ranked.

[4] Castes originating from an area of south India where Tamil was not the principal language.

[5] 1966–1968 saw food shortages and monsoon failures.

[6] Kannatäsan, (*Vanavācam* Life in a Forest) (Madras: Valambiri Pathipaham, 1965).

[7] The title "Army Captain" was given to Annadurai during the 1946 anti-Hindi agitations.

[8] Congress is not discussed below, but table 8-27 shows many Congressmen attracted by Democratic socialism.

[9] A. Maraimalaiyam, *Pērarinar Aṇṇavin Peruvārvu* (The Biography of Anna) (Madras: Vanathy, 1967).

[10] There are an increasing number of castes (and sometimes individuals) "assuming" the suffix Mudaliar. Generally Mudaliars are landowners and a forward caste group. In other places where I have given caste breakdowns, only those Mudaliars who are forward caste (one knows from the entire jati name) have been put in that category. Annadurai belongs to one subcaste of a weaver community from Kancheepuram that also takes the suffix Mudaliar—the Sengunthars. The wide disparity in castes that could use the title Mudaliar produced two separate and interesting explanations of the meaning. "Mudali" (first) "yaar" (who) was interpreted by all Mudaliars as meaning "those who are first." Other castes would often jokingly refer to the subcaste of Sengunthars to which Annadurai belonged, and say Mudaliar meant "who is your first husband." This particular subcaste was allegedly composed of temple dancing girls.

[11] Pachaiyappas was founded in 1842 as a school from the proceeds of a bequest made in 1794 by Pachaiyappa Mudaliar. Its trustees were especially interested in enabling poor students from "respectable families to pursue higher studies. In the 1880's it became a college"(personal communication from Lloyd I. Rudolph). Since World War I it has been a major center of Dravidian movement ferment.

[12] A. Maraimalaiyam, *Pērarinar Aṇṇavin Peruvārvu.*

[13] *Ibid.*

[14] *Ibid.*

[15] Max Weber, *The theory of Social and Economic Organization,* trans. A.

PART FOUR

Cultural Nationalism and Public Policy

CHAPTER NINE

The DMK in Power: Contradictions of Cultural Nationalism in the Annadurai Era

By 1967, when the DMK took office, Tamil nationalist ideology had a ramified ideological structure developed through a complex transformational process. Tamil nationalism was shared, at some level, by a wide segment of the population, including some Congress adherents. A talented leadership cadre existed, and the party had deep roots in modern Tamil Nadu political history. All of these factors—political leadership, mass perceptions, and the ideological structure of Tamil nationalism—converged in shaping DMK government action and public policy priorities once the DMK gained power.

But there were also more immediate and compelling constraints within which policies and strategies had to be formulated. First were expectations from the masses that the DMK would visibly improve the economic position of the lower classes, and that the rise of the DMK to power meant the realization of Tamil cultural nationalism.

Second were expectations within the party. By 1967 the party embodied the entire DMK ideological history, with its contradictions, opposing tendencies, and emotional mode of appeal. The best way to think of this is a series of concentric circles. The outermost ring would be party members, whose ideological perspective encompassed all party positions from radical social reform to an anti-Hindi stance. The innermost circle would be those attracted only by opposition to Hindi (the least elaborated ideological position of the party), or by some other single goal. This ideological heterogeneity was rendered less divisive by charismatic attachment to Annadurai. Another important factor keeping ideological heterogeneity from becoming explosive was the DMK role as opposition party: there were few concrete actions for which the party could be held responsible. Ideological statements alone can always be interpreted in a rationalizing framework, whereas concrete decisions are not so easily rationalized.

Examination of the DMK in power, therefore, brings together crucial strands in DMK (and Tamil Nadu) political history, and

also enables analysis of the viability of cultural nationalism as
a ruling party ideology. Since cultural nationalism is often viewed
as a threat to stability, emphasis is usually placed on its global
implications: Is it a threat to territorial integrity and therefore
likely to have an impact on international relations? But the power
and importance of cultural nationalist movements and the impact
of their ideology and leadership cannot be measured solely
according to priorities, values, and standards external to the
ideology itself. In 1969 *Nam Nadu,* the DMK official organ,
referred to the DMK government as "the everyday life of the
Tamil people." That dramatic metaphor is compelling as political
rhetoric, and also underscores the need to begin analysis with
the DMK's goals and world view. How does the statement "the
DMK is the everyday life of the Tamil people" get translated
into government policy? What are the consequences for party
survival? When all politics are cultural nationalistic, what is the
role of a cultural nationalist ruling party? Once Tamil nationalism
has been legitimized through the DMK's assumption of office,
what is the further role of the party in power?

One final note. As we trace DMK public policy during the
Annadurai and Karunanidhi eras, there is a temptation to
juxtapose compromise positions necessitated by the realities of
power with the rhetoric of mobilization. But it is no surprise
that the DMK could not achieve its more radical goals through
assumption of power on the state level. Consequently, that is
not the most interesting approach to this historical period. Rather,
the pattern and dynamics of DMK governmental response illuminate the consequences of cultural nationalism to public policy.
In this chapter we shall take a detailed look at the issues, policies,
and strategies of the DMK government led by C. N. Annadurai.
As we shall see, on some issues the party showed expertise,
skill, and statesmanship, while other issues revealed ideological
contradictions, insufficient mobilization of key sectors of the
population, and unfocused leadership. This pattern of DMK
responses contains broader lessons on the public policy and
political implications of cultural nationalism.

THE DMK GOVERNMENT AND THE POLITICS OF LANGUAGE

The DMK assumed office in February 1967. In November the
new government faced its first severe test. Ironically, it involved

the language issue, and by implication DMK Tamil nationalism. In 1965, as a result of anti-Hindi agitations, Prime Minister Shastri agreed to give statutory recognition to Nehru's assurance on the continued use of English. On November 27, 1967, an amendment bill to the Official Languages Act of 1963, Section 3 was introduced into the Lok Sabha. Section 3 reads:

notwithstanding the expiration of fifteen years of the commencement of the Constitution, the English language, may as from the appointed day [i.e., January 26, 1965], continue to be used, in addition to Hindi (a) for all the official purposes of the Union for which it was being used immediately before that day, and (b) for the transaction of the business of Parliament.[1]

The southern states contended that Nehru wanted the "may" in the above section to have the force of "shall." Their desire was for a simple amendment to that effect. The 1967 bill stipulated, however, that English be used for *certain* purposes (such as communication between the Union government and non-Hindi states, or between states where either has not adopted Hindi as the official language), thus retaining part of the original "may."[2] In fact, this bill, originally designed to reassure the southern states, ended up embodying many provisions that would give Hindi states the option to dispense with English.[3] Although critical of the Union Official Languages Bill, the DMK decided to back it if "undiluted" (that is, if unamended), since it provided statutory sanction for continued use of English.[4] Kamaraj Nadar (Congress leader) agreed that the bill "must be passed as it is."[5]

Despite these strong sentiments from Kamaraj and other influential southern Congressmen, and the symbolic importance of DMK support, it was decided to amend the bill. A key amendment specified that "compulsory knowledge of either Hindi or English shall be required at the stage of selection of candidates for recruitment to the Union's services or posts, except in respect for special services or posts for which high standard of knowledge of English alone or Hindi alone, or both, as the case may be, is considered essential for satisfactory performance of the duties of any such service or post."[6] The original resolution stated, "A compulsory knowledge of Hindi shall not be required at

the stage of selection of candidates for recruitment to the Union
services or posts accepting any special service or post for which
a high standard of Hindi knowledge may be considered essential
for the satisfactory performance of the duties of the service
or post."[7] The resolutions were forced by the strong Hindi
contingent, led by Seth Govindas and Mrs. Kripalani, within
the Congress party.[8]

On December 16 the Official Languages Amendment Bill and
the resolution on the language policy were passed by the Lok
Sabha. DMK members walked out in protest before the vote.[9]
K. Manoharan (DMK member) declared, "while the DMK buried
deep long ago its demand for separation, government was sowing
seeds of disintegration."[10] K. Kamaraj declared himself "unhappy" over the language bill, characterizing it as a "threat
to unity."[11]

On December 19 anti-Hindi demonstrations began in Madras
and, significantly, in other southern states as well. Although
V. R. Nedunchezhian, Madras minister for education, and other
DMK party leaders "advised the student community to desist
from any agitation or demonstration on the language issue,"[12]
by December 21, demonstrations had spread throughout the state,
the largest being in Madurai and Coimbatore.[13]

The DMK attempted to handle the student demonstrations
by trading on the party's past anti-Hindi record. On December
22, Karunanidhi, minister of transport, went to the Central
Station, where students were conducting an anti-Hindi agitation.[14]
He told them that the DMK goverment, unlike its predecessor,
was against Hindi. He invoked the 1965 "martyrs," and said
the DMK would do everything in its power to achieve the purpose
for which the "martyrs" died. After repeated grumbling from
the students, he said he and the other DMK ministers were
ready to quit their offices and join the student campaign if there
was continued dissatisfaction. To that suggestion the students
shouted "no, no." Karunanidhi then promised that the chief
minister would meet with them, and asked the students to
constitute committees and convey resolutions to the government.

While ministers were trying to strike a pose of sympathetic
understanding and support for student aims, party workers were
quietly trying to undermine and end the agitations. It had become
evident to the DMK leadership that some of their own local-level
party activists and members were embroiled in the anti-Hindi

agitations.[15] A first strategic move, therefore, was to disengage their own "misguided party members and leaders." Then they hoped to vitiate the general agitational climate. Agitating party members and leaders believed they were opposing the all-India Congress government rather than the local DMK government, but DMK leaders emphasized that any agitations in Tamil Nadu were "willy-nilly" against the DMK government. To inhibit organization of agitations, Madras City colleges and many of the district colleges were closed down.

While the DMK attempted to quiet the situation, C. Rajagopalacharia, leader of the Swatantra party and DMK ally in the United Front that defeated the Congress in 1967, began angling for an all-party opposition to the center on the language issue. Rajagopalacharia, although in his nineties and in virtual retirement from public life, made public appearances articulating a strongly anti-Hindi position.[16] He had previously called Hindi foreign to Tamilians, but now he said it was necessary to form a militant anticenter front.[17] E. V. Ramasami of the DK, although he had not placed top priority on the language issue (see, for example, his later reference to Tamil as "barbaric"), was among the first to respond to Rajagopalacharia's call.[18] He said he was prepared to cooperate with C. Rajagopalacharia, the declared leader of the Brahmin community, against the north "and to achieve independent Tamil Nadu."[19]

Rajagopalacharia was certainly not an advocate of a separate Tamil Nadu. He considered this simply another avenue to create a strong all-India opposition capable of taking power from the Congress at the center. However, some students had raised separatist slogans (for example, "If Hindi comes, Tamil Nadu is out to live in separation,")[20] and it was in that context that E. V. Ramasami reiterated the DK's separation demand.

On January 6, 1968, Chief Minister Annadurai met in a heated four-hour meeting with student representatives from all over the state.[21] More than 120 representatives from colleges in Madras City and outlying districts were present. They demanded that Annadurai take steps to carve out a separate, sovereign Tamil Nadu, and as a first step, they suggested blocking all road, rail, air, and sea communications with the rest of India. Annadurai and the other DMK leaders impressed on the students the folly of their suggested path. They pictured the political scenario following such action as disastrous for the DMK government

and for the students' own interests. Annadurai said that the
Congress government at the center would be only too happy
to clamp President's rule on Madras (a provision under the Indian
constitution allows the president of India to declare an emergency
in a state and, as a result, the powers of the state government
are exercised by the president in conjunction with Parliament).
He asked the students for a year in which to "stem the tide
of Hindi imposition" by constitutional methods. These would
include representations to the center conveying the feelings of
Tamilians on the language issue; persistent efforts to get a
constitutional amendment providing the continued use of English;
and rebutting all moves by the Hindi-speaking states and the
center to use Hindi in communications to the Madras government.
The students were only satisfied when Annadurai said that if
the DMK government failed to achieve any tangible result through
constitutional methods, it would declare January 26, 1969 as
Mourning Day and would spearhead the agitation against Hindi.[22]

DMK leaders convinced these students to terminate their
agitation. Most were leaders of the Tamil Nadu Anti-Hindi
Agitation Council, and because of the DMK's strong interest
in and support among the students, many were DMK sympathizers. The full extent of the dilemma was revealed later, when
other students refused to accept the leadership of this group.
The immediate reaction of these dissident students was to recall
T. R. Janarthanam,[23] the leader of the Anti-Hindi Agitation
Council, a DMK sympathizer and protegee of Karunanidhi. R.
Ramasami, a militant Coimbatore Agricultural College student,
was elected in his place. Ramasami called on students to continue
their agitations after the World Tamil conference ended on
January 10. Other students denounced participants in the January
6 meeting as "a group of DMK flunkies and stooges."

Fortunately for the DMK government, there was a breathing
period of ten days during the World Tamil Conference, an
international gathering of scholars interested in Tamil Nadu as
an area of research. All student factions agreed not to agitate
for the ten days. During this conference, the DMK rejuvenated
its cultural nationalist image.

After the close of the World Tamil Conference, however,
agitations resumed, with the Coimbatore students in the lead.[24]
On January 23, when the Madras Legislative Assembly recon-
vened, it was evident to the DMK that decisive action had to

be taken. If the Coimbatore, Madurai, and Trichy student demonstrations continued and perhaps spread, the DMK would be in the unpleasant position of having forcefully to put down anti-Hindi (and one could read that pro-Tamil)[25] agitations. Accordingly, Annadurai placed this resolution before the Madras Legislative Assembly: "The activities of the National Cadet Corps in Madras State have been suspended, pending a reply from the Center to the state's plea for dispensing with the commands in Hindi. The Madras government has also passed orders abolishing with immediate effect the three-language formula in schools and replacing it with a two language formula."[26]

In statements to the press, Annadurai called for postponement of the language issue, and for fourteen official languages. Although fourteen languages seems far-fetched, it is a logical extension of the long-standing DMK demand for cultural recognition and regional equality. Specifically, Annadurai was asking that Hindi be treated only as a regional language. When schools and colleges reopened on February 5, the DMK was confident that it had stemmed the agitational tide. However, Salem, Madurai, and Trichy district students continued to agitate. During January and February they burned the national flag, designed and flew a Tamil flag in various places, boycotted classes, picketed, and continued to demand separation. This intransigence requires analysis of the student's understanding of Tamil cultural nationalism.

As early as the 1965 anti-Hindi agitations, students in the southern districts continued to demonstrate, even after Madras students had stopped. Although their militancy eventually ran its course, it was clear that these students were becoming difficult for any party to control. After the January 6 meeting with Annadurai, pressures were applied to the students from many sources. A Coimbatore informant[27] reported a meeting, called by the collector of Coimbatore (and attended by the principals of colleges and headmistresses and headmasters of schools), where the principal of Coimbatore Agricultural College (Ramasami's school) was upbraided for not controlling Ramasami. Not unexpectedly, this principal then promised to try to persuade Ramasami to cease agitational activities. Another approach was made by a "citizen's committee" of leaders of political parties, heads of educational institutions, parents, business men, and religious leaders, under the leadership of a prominent member of the Raja Sabha, K. Sundaram.[28]

Finally, Ramasami was directly persuaded by Annadurai (after having been summond to Madras City for a long interview with the chief minister) to call off the agitations. After that interview, he decided to leave the language issue in the hands of the "Tamil-loving DMK government." It is difficult to know exactly why Ramasami capitulated. He says he was reassured by Annadurai that the DMK would be firm on the language issue.[29] A more likely explanation would take into consideration his difficult position; criminal charges had been profferred because of his agitational activities,[30] and it was alleged that his diploma would be withheld. Ramasami might have continued with the hope of becoming a hero. But there was also a distinct possibility of becoming a martyr, or simply suffering the consequences of his actions without publicity. I interviewed Ramasami and a number of DMK, Congress, and "independent-minded" students during the last days of the agitation. Ramasami, who by then had agreed to curtail his leadership, claimed that he personally never wanted an independent Tamil Nadu, but that it was a tactic to emphasize language demands. Although Ramasami was anxious to talk about the language issue, he was decidedly circumspect about his withdrawal from further agitations. Unlike many students, Ramasami was thoroughly familiar with the facts of the language problem. Politically, he characterized himself as "independent-minded."[31]

The majority of student leaders in the agitations also saw themselves as politically "independent-minded." Most said they had inclined toward the DMK in the past, but were now unaffiliated. Generally, they saw the Congress as controlled by northerners on the language issue, and certainly not preferable to the DMK. Unlike R. Ramasami, they placed central importance on a separate Tamil Nadu. When asked how they would achieve separation, most said naively, "we will organize the students." Questioned about other segments of the population, such as laborers, one student responded, "No, we are not concerned with the laborers, we are only interested in the students." Most were ill informed about the legal and technical aspects of the language problem. They understood little about the specific bill they were agitating against. Rather, they had responded to the appeals of diffuse Tamil nationalism.[32]

DMK and Congress students had both remained fairly aloof

from the agitation. DMK students blamed Congress students
for precipitating the agitations, while Congress students believed
that the DMK and "some wealthy men" were instrumental in
organizing the agitations.

When the dust settled, it became clear that on the one hand
the DMK had been remarkably astute in handling the language
issue. They prevented the agitation from spreading and from
becoming too embarrassing. And the party had emerged from
a delicate situation with only a few specks of egg on its face.
In contrast to its short-run success, however, there were certain
disquieting long-run consequences. There was an overt split in
the student movement, and the emergence of a substantial faction
not controlled by or sympathetic to the DMK. Also, by eliminating
Hindi from the required curriculum, the DMK government played
its last card. If another anti-Hindi language crisis were to erupt,
there would not be many concessions left. I might be difficult
to prevent such an agitation from assuming the characteristics
of an independence movement, given the ideological connection
between anti-Hindi and Tamil Nadu separation. Even the small
1967–1968 language agitations were quickly broadened into an
independence demand.

This incident illustrates the paradoxical nature of Tamil cultural
nationalism as a basis of diffuse support. The DMK used cultural
nationalism as an alternate base of support in a time of crisis.
But when a competitive group arose that claimed to be more
protective or representative of that "culture," it easily became
a threat. In other words, cultural nationalism proved to be an
open ideological category usable by any party or group to serve
its own ends. Unlike an economic development ideology, where
achievement of the ideological goals require an institutional
structure and an organizational base, cultural nationalism can
be articulated freely by autonomous individuals and organizations. Thus, a party which depends primarily on cultural nationalism as a base of support must constantly protect and reinforce
its image. In 1968 Annadurai tried to argue that the language
crisis unnecessarily deflected concern from other more serious
issues. The argument was also made that the language issue
should be left to the "Tamil-loving DMK government." However
convincing this was to some supporters, it was nevertheless true
that students' intransigence posed a serious problem for the DMK.
Although Annadurai's attempts to defuse the language crisis by

reference to other issues and by reestablishment of the DMK position as the protector of Tamil was largely successful, it must be remembered that this success was at least partially due to his charismatic appeal, and could not easily be replicated.

Finally, looking at long-range effects of DMK government decisions concerning Hindi, one must take into consideration the fact that the government policy excluding Hindi from the Tamil Nadu curriculum is certain to limit job prospects for Tamil Nadu students in general, particularly for middle and lower-class students in the backward and scheduled castes. It will limit rather than expand mobility, and may even contribute to making class boundaries more rigid. Students from Brahmin and upper-caste families are more likely to have strong English backgrounds that could be substituted for Hindi, or to have access to private Hindi teachers. Hence more desirable jobs that require training in Hindi would go to these groups in the future, as they have in the past.

The Language Issue in Perspective. DMK problems with language are instructive because they reflect the party's own history of agitational politics and Tamil nationalist propaganda. Some contradictions of Tamil nationalism became clear as Annadurai tried to maintain a Tamil nationalist stance, while preventing his government from being undermined by agitations spearheaded by pro-Tamil, anti-Hindi students. If Tamil Nadu were a nation, the DMK could control cultural policy, but it is merely a state claiming national identity within a nation. Annadurai's broad-based appeal and political acumen prevented this issue from becoming a full-blown crisis. One result of the language agitations, however, with important consequences for Tamil Nadu's political future, was the creation of a large section of politically unaffiliated (and therefore uncontrollable) students. These students are responsive to the appeals of Tamil nationalism, but ideologically unsophisticated on substantive issues such as social reform and the achievement of economic equality. They are a potentially explosive force in Tamil Nadu politics.

Although the Karunanidhi government had a few other skirmishes with students during its first term in office, nothing approached the potential of the 1967–1968 language agitations. In 1970, as the DMK moved to create larger numbers of classes taught in Tamil, many students who wanted to study in the

English medium complained bitterly, and the language controversy increasingly took on an English versus Tamil character. Political pundits predicted a large-scale rebellion against the DMK in the next Assembly elections (1971) by middle-class parents who resented the curtailment of English studies. But this did not materialize.

THE DMK'S FIRST YEAR IN OFFICE

When the language agitations were grinding to a halt, in February 1968, a year of DMK rule had passed and the general consensus was positive. Before looking at the next issue area, economic policy and labor relations, I will outline some of the more salient events of that year. DMK strategy reflected a desire to satisfy the Tamil nationalist sentiment and to demonstrate a capacity to produce genuine and visible economic improvements. Economically, a crucial DMK policy was the "one-rupee-per-measure-of-rice plan."

In the election campaign, the DMK had promised three measures of rice for one rupee. Once in office, they reneged on this promise as fiscally impossible, but they did provide rice at the very low price of one rupee per measure in the cities of Madras and Coimbatore. The one-rupee-per-measure idea was extremely popular, particularly among the lower-class hut-dwelling population.[33] Beyond the one-rupee plan, the DMK government was instrumental in lowering prices on a number of other food commodities. And Mathiazhagan, DMK food minister, personally intervened to have restaurants lower their prices.[34]

Satisfying Tamil nationalism was easier for the DMK. They had quotations by Thiruvalluvar (an ancient Tamil sage) hung in the state-owned buses; ministers took every available opportunity to manipulate symbols of Tamil greatness; the World Tamil Conference and the activities surrounding it used Tamil nationalism to extend and solidify the DMK support base.[35]

At the end of a year, Congress tried to make law and order an issue, but it had not caught on by February 1968. Congress ministers in the Delhi government had been favorably impressed by the DMK government's handling of the language agitations specifically, and government activities generally.[36] An editorial in the Madras *Mail* expressed the general sentiment:

By and large the DMK ministry can look back with pride and satisfaction at its one-year rule of Madras Sate. There have been many alarms and excursions in many non-Congress states, at least three of which have come under President's rule. Generally speaking, the inherent weakness of Non-Congress coalitions have contributed to their downfall. Madras, on the other hand, has the remarkable phenomenon of a single party commanding a solid majority in the legislature and the DMK has the sense of discipline, restraint and responsibility in not misusing its power, at least deliberately. . . . All credit to the DMK government for its firm handling of the language controversy.[37]

Some opponents predicted that the DMK would run into fiscal difficulty because of its one-rupee rice plan. Annadurai's one-year budget avoided new taxation, however, and even contained a small surplus. And as an earlier symbolic gesture, DMK ministers had decided to take only half their allotted salary.

However, the DMK had just barely celebrated its first year of power when difficulties began. Madurai Muthu, one of Mu. Karunanidhi's lieutenants, started the Tamil Sena in response to Bombay's Shiv Sena.[38] By March it was attacked in the press as a threat to national integration. More damaging was a major breakdown of law and order in Madras City, as transport workers and students fought in the streets. A student was allegedly insulted by a young bus conductor, and the resulting riots caused thousands of rupees damage and chaos for three or four days in March. The DMK government was accused of preventing the police from taking action.[39] And in June, Madras City was hit by a rash of fires destroying thousands of huts in a matter of weeks.

But July saw a stunning DMK victory in Tenkasi (Tirunelveli), where the DMK captured a Congress stronghold. Congress was understandably shaken and surprised, and tried to recapture the initiative by holding a huge procession and demonstration in Madras City on August 1, 1968, over the law-and-order issue. The demonstration was a desperate move to mobilize support on what was largely a nonissue (by July the transport worker-student conflict was no longer a live issue). There was only limited mass participation in the demonstration; but during the course of the procession, the Madras police charged the marchers with lathis, claiming that they were becoming unruly. Three hundred people were hurt, fifteen seriously. The Congress press and the Congress high command rightly saw this as an opportunity to gain initiative. Kannadasan, a prominent Congressman and a leader in the Kamaraj faction of Congress, organized a silent procession of 50,000 on August 5 to protest the lathi charge. The demonstration attracted Congressmen who had not been involved in demonstrations since the independence movement. After the lathi charge and the Congress demonstration, the DMK lost political initiative. The charmed first year had run its course.

While language dominated the DMK's first year in office, economic and labor problems were major sources of unrest during the second year. In a year of intermittent industrial crisis and unrest,[40] a few disputes stand out: the Coimbatore textile mill strike, closure, and the general textile crisis in the south; the strike at the *Hindu* newspaper;[41] the strike and subsequent police firings at Tiruvottiyur match factory; and, most severe, the Tanjore landlord-laborer dispute, which resulted in the death by fire of forty-two Untouchable men, women, and children. I will examine two of these cases, the Coimbatore textile mills crisis and the Tanjore agricultural laborer-landlord conflict. Both illuminate DMK policy in the industrial and labor sphere.

ECONOMIC POLICY AND LABOR RELATIONS

The major ingredients of the Coimbatore mills crisis were succinctly described by an editorial in the March 14, 1968, *Hindu*, entitled "Sick Industry":

The cotton textile industry in the South, and indeed the whole country, is in the throes of a crisis. Both the Indian Cotton Mills Federation and Southern India Mill-Owners Association have been suggesting for some time past that there should be either regulation of production or closure of mills for a fortnight or so, in order to avoid a further accumulation of stock. The management of 15 "sick" mills in Coimbatore district have now given notice of their intention to close down from the beginning of next month and reopen only after there was a distinct improvement in trade conditions. Current production is not being freely absorbed and stocks of yarn with members of the South India Mill Owners Association have been increasing at a rate of 500 bales every month. . . .

Why should a major industry be in such a bad way and what are the reasons for the stagnant trend in the demand for cotton textiles? The truth of the matter is that the industry is having a capacity far in excess of present demand and in a period of depression, the outmoded units have proved extremely vulnerable. Even the new efficient units are reported to be not working on a reasonably profitable basis. The solution would, therefore, seem to lie in sealing off spinning capacity by 10 or 15 per cent for a limited period, so a block closure of mills can be avoided. But it will be necessary to go ahead with the modernization of mills in a methodical manner and also with rehabilitation of the worthwhile ones. The proposed Textile Corporation will have to help in cases where the cost of rehabilitation gets beyond the capacity of managements concerned. Mergers of uneconomic mills may also have to be considred. Many of textile industries' difficulties may disappear with another good harvest in 1968-69 and when the present abnormal phase is tided over, that the problems relating to the creation of new capacity later and modernization of sub-marginal units will still remain. A satisfactory answer will have to be found to these two major questions, if the industry to progress on sound lines.[42]

The *Hindu* editorial presents the management point of view, of course. The root of the crisis was the need for modernization and development of centralized procedures for regulating output according to market demand. At the same time, modernization and automation had to be achieved without undue hardship for textile workers. The immediate crisis in Madras State stemmed from the closure of those fifteen "sick" mills.

Annadurai's response was to call together representatives of the mill owners and workers. As a result of this tripartite conference, a scheme was devised that called for the reopening of some mills by inducing banks to extend financial aid. The chief minister emphasized that a glut of yarn on the market had caused the mill closing; that the textile crisis was the fault of the central government's economic policies toward the textile industry, and therefore the state government could not be blamed. Annadurai left for America soon after the mill closure was announced, but asked the fifteen mill owners not to close permanently before his return.

By April, the textile crisis assumed new proportions, when the Southern Mill Owners Association (SIMA) directed its 175 member mills in Tamil Nadu, Kerala, Mysore, Andhra, and Pondicherry to curtail their production by one-third, "until the position improves." The member mills agreed to suspend production for two days a week, but to pay lay-off wages, lower than regular wages, to their workers for the period of closure. K. Sundaram, chairman of the SIMA, told the press closure would keep the level of production at 60,000 bales a month, which was considered normal stocking. Of the 86 mills in Coimbatore District, 76 observed the hartal called by the SIMA the first week.[43] As a result of the SIMA decision, Nedunchezhian, state industries minister, arranged a meeting with Dinesh Singh, Union commerce minister.

Mill unions reacted negatively to the owners' suggestion, proposing a satyagraha as a response. Madhavan, labor minister, urged no action until Chief Minister Annadurai returned from the United States.[44] In the meanwhile, Nedunchezhian talked with Dinesh Singh, and on May 1 Singh enunciated a new government textile policy in the Rajya Sabha. The reaction of the mill owners was not enthusiastic. When this attempt to resolve the crisis failed, the threatened satyagraha by the unions became a reality on May 6.

Union politics surrounding the satyagraha are revealing. The May 6 satyagraha was originally proposed by the Communist-controlled AITUC (All India Trade Union Congress) and the Hind Mazdoor Sabha Unions (Socialist). The DMK-controlled Dravidar Panchalai Tholilelar Munnetra Kazagham asked their membership to hold off action until Annadurai's return from the United States. The INTUC (Indian National Trade Union Congress), the Congress-controlled union, originally supported the satyagraha, and claimed their leadership was among the first to suggest action if the state and central government did not move. However, the INTUC withdrew from the council coordinating the agitation after meeting with the Union commerce minister, Dinesh Singh. Their press statement reflected an attempt to balance the roles of labor representative, affiliate of the party in power at the center, and opposition to the party in power at the state level: "The satyagraha proposed by the Communists and HMS Unions from May 6 was a 'cheap attempt' to mislead labor, . . . and if the satyagraha was meant to focus the attention of the government to the need for immediate action, 'it has already been done.' Any moves to start the satyagraha would only mean that these unions want to take credit for what has already been done by the INTUC.''[45]

This lineup of unions shows clearly the importance of affiliation to a political party in power in determining union action. The Congress and DMK-controlled unions were out of the agitation, while the Communist unions (both left and right-affiliated Communist unions) (as well as the Non-Communist HMS) despite their support of the DMK government, were leading the satyagraha. Even the Swatantra-controlled trade unions supported the satyagraha.

The purposes of the agitation were to get effective government intervention in the mill crisis and to demand payment of three months' back wages that workers alleged had never been paid.[46] In six days, the hartal and satyagraha paralyzed life in Coimbatore.[47] Impressed with their success, the HMS and INTUC leadership called for an indefinite general strike of textile workers beginning May 20.[48] Meanwhile, on May 9, representatives from the southern Mill Owners Association met with Dinesh Singh to discuss ways of helping the textile industry.[49] It was not until later in May, however, that the textile mill crisis was partially resolved. After C. N. Annadurai returned from the United States, Dinesh Singh called a meeting of state ministers (chief-ministers and ministers of finance and industry from the states of Andhra Pradesh, Madras, Mysore, Madhya Pradesh, Gujarat, Maharastra, Assam, Pondicherry, and Uttar Pradesh)[50] to discuss the crisis.

A number of government actions were taken to assist the textile industry, including tax incentives and liberalized government controls on bank financial assistance to textile companies.[51] After this meeting, the SIMA agreed to cancel its two-day-a-week closure arrangements. When the mills cancelled the two-day closure, the textile unions postponed their general strike. Meetings were then arranged between the textile union, textile industry spokesmen, and DMK government representatives. As a result, the INTUC-affiliated National Textile Workers Union called off its participation. But the joint action committee of the HMS, Communist, and Swatantra trade unions went on an indefinite stay-in strike from May

25. Their demands were: (1) a date must be fixed for reopening of the closed mills; (2) steps must be taken for payment of wages for workers where they had been withheld, and satisfactory arrangements should be made to insure dispersement of wages regularly and on the stipulated dates; (3) criminal action should be taken against managements that fail to pay wages to workers on stipulated dates; and (4) irrespective of whether the managements contributed their share to the Providence Fund, etc., or not, the rights of workers to such statutory benefits should be protected.[52] The strike was effective in 52 of 82 textile mills. In 24 it was complete, while at 28 it was only partial.[53] Although the chief minister persuaded the textile unions to end their May strike, it was resumed in July, this time supported by Congress and DMK unions. The composite strike committee complained that "the assurance given by the government regarding the question of reopening the closed mills, payment of regular wages in running mills and remittances to ESI, Providence Fund had not been implemented."[54] Although this strike eventually ran its course, the textile crisis continued to plague the DMK government intermittently during its entire first term. The most serious crisis passed, however, by May 1968.

The Coimbatore mill strike and overall textile crisis has been discussed in detail because it is indicative of more general difficulties the DMK encountered in the labor and industrial arena. While members of the DMK cabinet had much prior experience with the language issue and knew its technical ins and outs, this was not so for labor and industrial issues. Although the DMK had been in the Assembly since 1957, there were no members who were leaders with financial and labor expertise comparable to that of C. Subramaniam or R. Ventakataraman. Annadurai spoke in general terms about "scientific socialism." But the DMK leadership seemed to have given only a modicum of serious thought toward development of innovative economic schemes.

Although leaders repeatedly affirmed that the DMK was a "laborer's government," actual policies were not especially pro-labor.[55] Given lack of a firm labor or industry policy or even a set of priorities, DMK leadership (at least during 1968) was open to suggestions from their ally, Rajagopalacharia of the Swatantra party, and he was reportedly an important force in DMK labor decisions.

During the first two years in office, DMK organizers rather frantically attempted to organize labor unions. Among students, the DMK had accumulated "capital" which they spent during the language crisis of December 1967, and January 1968. In the labor area, they had neither exceptional expertise, organization, nor "capital."

The movement of the DMK into the labor arena came at a time when trade unionism in Madras State was suffering from its own internal crisis.[56] The Madras trade union movement had developed originally on nonpartisan grounds with a largely Brahmin leadership. The Congress initiated the practice of union affiliation with a political party. In Madras State, the rise of the Dravidian movement and cultural nationalism slowly influenced the trade union movement, even though actual DMK and DK organizations were rare. Caste loyalties, particularly anti-Brahminism, became a factor. Also, widespread internalization of anti northern, pro-Tamil, pro-Dravidian sentiments added a new emotional element to trade unionism.

Because of leadership conflicts within the trade union movement, the disruption caused by the DMK and other political party attempts to infiltrate the movement, and the penetration of cultural nationalist issues into that arena, trade unionism in Madras was particularly diffuse in 1968 and 1969. After the DMK achieved stronger support in the trade union movement, things settled down. The party had greater opportunity to control worker activities, and trade union leaders gained access to decision-making councils of the ruling party.[57] After Annadurai's death in February 1969, Karunanidhi had to develop a support base, and he was open to influence by these union leaders.

Ideologically, the DMK attempted to manage its industrial labor difficulties by blaming Delhi for the economic ills of the state. This ideological approach was a temporary method of coping with the lack of an industrial and labor policy until an institutional and personnel infrastructure could be developed and a set of priorities worked out.

Although one must take with reservations the DMK characterization of itself as a laborer government, it is fair to say that the party attempted to be responsive to the needs of urban laborers by organizing them and providing an increasing role in party councils for labor leaders. Rural labor, however, is another story.

Tanjore Labor-Mirasdar Disputes. Agricultural trouble in Tanjore district has a long history. In the 1968 harvest period, open conflict developed, culminating in the December tragedy in which forty-two Untouchable laborers were burned alive. Before examining the DMK role in this disaster, it is necessary to explore the roots of the conflict and the party affiliations and social characteristics of the opposing forces.

East Tanjore, an area with a high proportion (29 percent) of Untouchables, has a twenty-five year history of acute laborer-mirasdar (landlord) tension, including periodic violence since the early 1950s.[58] The Pannayal Protection Act of 1952 destroyed the traditional pannayal system, under which landless laborers were attached to masters and given food, clothing, and a small daily or monthly wage or compensation in kind. Within four years of passage, many pannayals became casual laborers or coolies, not protected by any law. Through sporadic agitation and Kisan Sangams (peasant labor organizations), casual laborers fought for better wages. From one local measure of paddy plus one or two annas per day in 1943, wages rose to six local measures plus one rupee per day in 1968.

Early statutory arrangements growing out of kisan agitations included the Kalappai Accord of 1944, which gave a pannayal a daily wage of 2-1/2 measures of paddy and ended humiliating punitive measures, such as whipping or forcing offenders to drink cow dung mixed with water. Later in 1944, the Mannargudi Pact gave the pannayal three measures daily, plus a slight increase in harvest wages. The Sessions Judges Award of 1946 and the Mayuram Accord of 1948 also added to the harvest wages.

In the late 1950s a militant kisan movement emerged in Tanjore, accompanied by bitter strife, particularly in Mannargudi Taluk. Young Untouchable laborers were widely mobilized by the Communist Party of India in collaboration with the Tanjore wing of the Dravida Kazhagam. E. V. Ramasami tried to base his militant social reform party on the Untouchables.[59] Hence, through the 1950s, while the DK was formally supporting "Kamaraj Congress," it was also organizing Untouchables. Particularly active was the Tanjore wing of the party.

Tanjore was fertile ground for radical social reform and

Communist party development for many reasons. First, Tanjore is unusual in that many mirasdars are Brahmins.[60] Unlike most districts of Tamil Nadu, Brahmins form an important segment of the rural population. Using DK radical social reform ideology, it was, therefore, easy to identify Brahmins as the cause of the sad economic plight of the ex-pannayal Untouchable laborer. However, DK ideology lacked sufficient class analysis to come to grips with the realities of the Tanjore situation, where not only do the economic and caste hierarchy unite at the top in the person of the Brahmin mirasdar, but there are also situations in which the mirasdar is a wealthy elite non-Brahmin. Many elite non-Brahmin landlords had earlier opposed Tanjore Brahmins on social-reform issues.[61] In fact, many landlords or their children took the DMK route to cultural nationalism during the 1960s. According to informants from Tanjore, some of the younger, more militant members of these families were DMK supporters as early as the 1950s, although most supported Congress.

When the cultural oppression analysis failed in Tanjore, given non-Brahmin landlord economic exploitation, many Untouchables turned to the Communist party which, paradoxically, was primarily led by Brahmins. The Communist class analysis may have fallen on unresponsive ears elsewhere in Tamil Nadu, but in Tanjore it seemed particularly relevant.

By the 1960s, when many more non-Brahmin landlords were adherents of the DMK on cultural issues, but reactionary on the Tanjore economic home front, the gap between cultural oppression and economic oppression indicated the reactionary potential of a cultural nationalism grounded in a middle-class support structure. By the 1968 landlord-laborer conflicts, the DMK did not have the organizational basis among Tanjore laborers to control events on their terms. And in the one-dimensional world of moderate cultural nationalism, DMK leadership was ideologically incapable of dealing with the economic contradictions of the Tanjore situation.

The Kilavenmani arson was the end of a long period of these conflicts, in which the DMK role can only be described as confused and timid. The arson followed conflicts over wage increases. Tanjore landlords, not wanting to meet the increased wage demands of the laborers, tried to import laborers to break a union-imposed boycott. Union laborers retaliated by trying to prevent these "scabs" from entering the area. Most of the victims were women and children deliberately herded into one hut and then burned alive.[62] Most people interviewed at the time believed the arson to have been either instigated or carried out by the landlords. Immediately after the tragedy, thirty-nine members of the landlords' association were arrested.

Reactions to the arson were strangely subdued. For example, the *Hindu* seemed as subtly critical of the victims as of the culprits. In fact, the English-language news coverage was consistently prejudiced in favor of the landlords. A *Hindu* editorial, entitled "Arson Most Foul," read:

Every civilized person would share the Madras Chief Minister Mr. C. N. Annadurai's sense of shock and abhorrence over the gruesome incident in Kilavenmani hamlet (East Tanjavur) in which forty-two persons, mostly women and children, were burnt to death. The arson was a gory climax to a day of running clashes between the two groups of workers, one Marxist led in the village and the other (outside) labor which had been hired to harvest the crops. [Note the implication that the workers were responsible for the arson.] The Chief Minister has set the wheels of investigation moving and has promised that "whoever is responsible for this" which we presume will include the *agents provocateurs,* too "will be dealt with ruthlessly." The public will expect the laws course to run speedily and remorselessly. That will be essential to ally panic in the region and to the return of normalcy. The Kilavenmani tragedy is a grim reminder of what labor agitation can lead to if not kept within bounds. East Tanjavur has been the scene of agrarian unrest over wages for quite some time now and many violent clashes have occurred from the start of the current harvest season. As we had occasion to point out before, much of the violence has been Marxist-inspired. An agreement over wages, called the Mannargudi Agreement does not seem to have been honored by everybody. The local authorities have so far been dealing with trouble as and when it arose. But, obviously more than such sporadic effort is necessary if peaceful conditions are to prevail in the farms. The Madras government should take a hard, dispassionate look at the over all agrarian situation in Tanjavur and bear down firmly on the disrupters of peace.[63]

Following the arson at Kilavenmani, collectors' talks led to
a raise in wages for East Tanjore laborers of one-half measure,
unless the rate was already six measures, and one rupee for
each man per day.[64] However, the East Tanjore Mirasdars
Association rejected the award as financially unfeasible. The
Collectors Award reiterated the provisions in the Mannagudi
Accord of 1967 for imported labor, provided local labor was
used first.[65]

The conflict in East Tanjore district continued into the early
1970's. In 1970 Karunanidhi condemned "Naxalite violence"[66]
in the Tamil Nadu Legislative Assembly. Part of the problem
results from the "green revolution" in Tanjore.[67] The new
higher-yielding rice strain ADT-27 means that the number of
crops grown per year has increased, while the time available
for preparing land for transplanting the seedlings has decreased,
placing a premium on the efficiency of labor and on mirasdar-labor
cooperation.

Communist-organized labor in East Tanjore area made a
number of charges concerning the implications of the "green
revolution": (1) the land-owning class gets disproportionately
high returns for parasitism (nonlabor); (2) outside labor brought
in with the connivance of the police is a threat to the local
worker; (3) mechanization of farm operations without reforms
and the proper implementation of the Land Ceiling Act works
against the interests of farm labor;[68] (4) mechanization of farm
operations would create unemployment; (5) labor leaders claimed
that laborers lose between two and six months of work because
of tractors. Landowners contended that they could not afford
higher wages. They said that within one year of the Mannargudi
Accord, the cost of cultivation greatly increased, while the
procurement price of paddy remained the same. Hence, they
could ill afford any increase.

Paradoxically, the Kilavenmani case provoked little conflict
within the DMK. Given the ideology of social reform and the
ideological mix within the party, one might have thought this
incident would act as a catalyst to divide factions. A DK leader
stated that if forty-two Brahmin women and children had been
burned alive, the reaction would have shaken the entire country.
The moderate reactions in the DMK and in the general public
require separate explanations.

Within Tamil Nadu, there is much sympathy for the mirasdar. In order to understand this, it should be remembered a mirasdar is anyone who owns land. Many mirasdars own only small plots of land, as table 9-1 shows. As is indicated, there is a plethora of small landowners with miniscule plots. The large number of small landholders serves as a buffer against radical, rural movements winning public support. Some actions aimed at mirasdars alienate small landowners, who often identify their interests (at least on the question of agricultural labor) with those of large landowners. Also, landowning remains a high-status occupation, even among urban people without land. Similiarly, the ambition of rural landless laborers is to own their own land. The Communist-led kisan movement in Tanjore seemed an attack on one of the most sacred symbols of a predominantly peasant society—land ownership.

Apart from the small landowner acting as a buffer against radical agricultural labor movements, there is also caste prejudice against Untouchables. Finally, since the kisan leaders were Communists, it was easier for some to dismiss the entire movement in Tamil Nadu, where the CPI is not as popular as in many other states. This is particularly important in interpreting DMK party reactions. With the DMK, radical members who felt that some form of dramatic agitational action should be taken after the criminal arson in Tanjore were isolated and criticized for not realizing that the Communists "only wanted to embarass the DMK government."

But the analysis goes deeper than perception of conflict with the Communists. With the modification of the DMK radical social-reform ideology and the lack of class content in the cultural

TABLE 9-1
Estimated Land Holdings in East Tanjore

Percentage landlords	Acreage
12	Own 10 or more acres
9	5 to 10 acres
32	2.5 to 5 acres
47	Own under 2.5 acres
100	

Source: Information based on an article in Hindu, July 12, 1969.

nationalist ideological residue, sympathy for the landlords and lack of sympathy for the agricultural workers was quasi-legitimate, given some elite non-Brahmin landlord support for Tamil-Dravidian cultural goals. Even in its most radical days, the Dravidian movement did not come to grips with the reactionary potential of an analysis of cultural oppression without strong economic content. Although Periyar and Annadurai were sympathetic to Communist ideology, and although Annadurai declared the DMK "more Communist that the Communist party," neither was as interested in class issues as in cultural issues. Neither used Marxism in the Indian setting, integrating it with the cultural analysis already developed. In fact, when the subject of class oppression was broached with the editor of *Viduthalai*, Veeramani, he said that a strong class analysis would alienate many of the elite non-Brahmin supporters, and that the DK had a difficult enough job trying to attack cultural oppression without creating enemies on all sides. This response would have seemed more convincing in the 1930s than the late 1960s. Earlier it would have appeared a rational political adaption to the realities of the social and cultural context, while in the late 1960s it seemed to indicate lack of growth and failure to come to grips with a changing situation.

This is not to say that the DK and DMK never attacked elite non-Brahmins, especially over religious orthodoxy. The "villain" of Annadurai's famous play "Servant Maid" is a wealthy, orthodox Mudaliar. There are even a few speeches in which Annadurai and Periyar criticized non-Brahmin landholding interests, and both called for a classless as well as a casteless society. But analysis of the elite non-Brahmin class as an agent of exploitation was not emphasized. Throughout Tamil Nadu, on the other hand, the Communist party was incapable of making a profound impact because of its poor analysis of cultural oppression, its lack of focus on issues of Tamil-Dravidian identity, and a recruitment pattern that produced a heavily Brahmin leadership structure at the top. At best, DMK labor and economic policy could be termed ambivalent and a partial failure during its first term in office. Annadurai was more successful than Karunanidhi in influencing labor leaders and industrialists to end strikes. But, as the Tanjore incident suggests, even during the Annadurai era the DMK had difficulties with labor issues.

RADICAL SOCIAL REFORM: POWER IN THE SERVICE OF
SOCIAL CHANGE?

Social reform is another important issue area for analysis of
DMK public policy. While the language issue was largely unre-
solvable on the state level, and economic and labor questions
were not traditionally priority issues for the DMK, social reform
was both important to the party and a workable issue. Three
areas of the DMK's social-reform policy will be discussed here:
(1) untouchability and Adi-Dravida welfare; (2) religious reform,
anti-Hinduism, "anti-supersitition"; and (3) secularism.

Untouchability and Adi-Dravida Welfare. Although an important ex-Untouchable DMK leader, Dr. Satyiavani Muthu,[69] was
made minister for Harijan affairs, some Adi-Dravida leaders
felt untouchability[70] increased during the first year of DMK
rule. For example, in 1968 K.V.S. Mani of the Republican party
compared the DMK and Congress:

> In the Congress ministry there were two [Adi-Dravida]
> representatives Kakkan and Jothi Venkatachalem: one for
> Harijan affairs and one for health. The villagers were afraid
> of Kakkan. They thought if they did anything, Kakkan would
> come and so they were afraid. Now, Satyiavani Muthu has
> the affinity but not the intensity. [She wants to do something,
> but can not.] Her cabinet colleagues all look out for their
> own communities. What can she do?[71]

An Adi-Dravida student then interjected, "Even one (Adi-
Dravida) DMK M.P. was insulted by a peon and did not report
it. The peon told him to leave some place rudely. He simply
kept quiet." Mani continued: "Satyiavani Muthu talks, she makes
her policies on the platform instead of in the cabinet. The DMK
talks but they don't do anything."[72]

This is a serious indictment of the DMK government. I think
it true to say that initially the DMK cabinet was somewhat inept
and inexperienced. Insiders report that Annadurai was an energetic and effective administrator before his illness incapacitated
him, but the chaos during his absence indicates his central
importance. At one point a minister's brother alleged that many
senior civil servants were Brahmins hostile to the DMK.[73]

Satyiavani Muthu, like her colleagues, lacked the experience to handle civil servants under her.

My own interviews with Dr. Satyiavani Muthu confirmed that she was perplexed about how to make her desire for social reform operational. About religion and the DMK she said: "The DMK is purely against casteism and against Untouchability. It is even called atheist because if God created Untouchability why should we believe in God. Also, if there is a God, he should punish those who practice Untouchability. . . . He should punish those who oppress others even in the temples. . . ."[74] However, when I asked how she was working to eradicate untouchability, her answers came haltingly and were less convincing. She said the main DMK policy was "not to have disparity between the rich and the poor. So we take the side of the laborers and not the side of the capitalists." She then mentioned a number of specific schemes, such as providing land and housing (all, she admitted, initiated during the Congress government). Finally she said: "We preach *and* do [my emphasis], we don't plan to close temples or anything. We should not be rude—not force anybody to follow us. We ourselves set an example—by that others will follow our example."[75] Satyiavani Muthu's conclusion is weak compared with the intransigence of casteism.

There are a number of structural factors important in understanding the untouchability problem. First, for every decision made there is a multitude of caste, economic, and ideological pressures that must be resolved. In addition, it is widely believed that ministers have a certain responsibility to their own communities. As K.V.S. Mani said,

At least when the DMK came to power, we expected Annadurai to do something. But he has done nothing. He is simply Bhaktavasalam's representative in the chief ministership. All of those people, Nedunchezhian, Annadurai, all of them are working for their own communities. Kakkan had put Harijans in high places and had promoted them. This was Kamaraj's policy. Now, all Mudaliars are coming in high posts. The P.A.'s of all the Ministers are their relatives, or members of their own community. The DMK has been nothing but talk. Things have gotten worse since they came to power.[76]

His views reflect a widespread sentiment that the DMK government promoted Mudaliars into high political positions.

Second, in the late 1960s the politics of caste were changing. There was a vitiation of the conflict between Brahmins and elite non-Brahmins, and the emergence of a class alliance between them.

The attitudinal aspect of this change involved the increasing belief that Mudaliars form a coherent social unit and that "the Mudaliars and the Brahmins cooperate on certain issues." This belief about Brahmin and elite non-Brahmin (particularly Mudaliar) cooperation is spreading. Underlying it is a convergence of economic interest between elite Brahmins and non-Brahmins. With the mitigation of social reform propaganda (which fragmented Tamil Nadu elites with common economic interests into separate constituencies defined by communal identification), it is possible to unite these elites on class lines. The emerging pattern of Brahmin and elite non-Brahmin landlord cooperation in Tanjore is one example of this process. Another is cooperation among economic elites manifested in their common support for the Swatantra party.

Until the mid-nineteenth century, Brahmins were not an important economic and political force in Tamil Nadu; major landlords and entrepreneurs in Tamil Nadu belonged to elite non-Brahmin castes. At the turn of the century, mobilization of large numbers of Brahmins into the Congress party made them a power in politics during British rule. However, their economic potential was not exploited until the 1920s. Most Brahmins, when asked about this change in their economic position, call it a response to the non-Brahmin movement. One informant stated:

when the non-Brahmin movement was at its height, Brahmins thought that they were not to receive any posts [posts meaning positions in government administration] in the future. Many then migrated to other parts of India, joining the central services and gaining importance or else establishing businesses elsewhere in India and thereby accumulating capital. They became police and army class I officers and moved into the higher posts in the central government. They also sent money back home which because they are a frugal people was used to begin businesses and for investment purposes in general. For example, fifty years ago the Asofeotida [spice] business in Madras was dominated by the Nattakottai Chettiars, now the

Brahmins dominate it. Fifty years ago there were almost no
Brahmin engineers, now there are many of them. The Brahmins
formed large cooperatives and now dominate the provisions
and groceries business. T.V.S. auto distributors in Madras
and Andhra Pradesh is a Brahmin company. A man of my
own community, a relative, is the head of it. He says now
that our community has been "flung to the wall" we must
fight back and help each other. For even the lowest clerk,
mechanic or sweeper, a Brahmin will get priority.[77]

This respondent also noted that Brahmins were important in
all central government offices. He himself worked in the central
government for forty years and had many friends and relatives
among this elite group. He described the attitudes of Brahmins
who work in central government offices towards the present
Tamil Nadu government:

About 5 to 10 percent of our people there feel that we are
Tamilians, we should be sympathetic towards these people.
We might want to go home—that is our home. About another
40 to 60 per cent feel that these people must be taught a
lesson; that they chased us out of Tamil Nadu, now they
must come to us for help—but they still haven't learned their
lesson. Another 20 to 30 per cent feel that our ancestors
probably came from the north—what does it matter, north
or south, because we are educated, we can settle down here
and live comfortably. We no longer have any patriotic feelings
toward the south at all. We must do what is best for our
self-interests. About 20 per cent even advocate changing their
name to fit in in the north.
   When these people [DMK] go to Parliament and say they
get step-motherly treatment, that the South is victimized by
the North and all of these things, they are immediately hit
by a barrage of facts and figures to show that it is not true.
When they want to get more information or to plead their
case, they must go to see one of these secretaries who is
more likely than not hostile to them. Now they go with their
begging bowls to the center and find these people that they
have kicked out of here. The Salem project and the Neville
project [two proposals for steel plants in Tamil Nadu] are

both opposed by high government officials who are Tamil Brahmins.[78]

This interview is indicative of upper-class Brahmin attitudes inside and outside Tamil Nadu. Inside Tamil Nadu, many upper-class Brahmins are proud of their economic advances in the last fifty years. They feel that Brahmins are now a power to be reckoned with. With that increasing sense of security has come a willingness for extended cooperation with elite non-Brahmins.

While the radical Dravidian ideology separated Brahmins from all others, the deradicalized Dravidian ideology as propagated by the DMK in the 1960s ideologically united Brahmins and non-Brahmins as "Tamils." Under the new ideological dispensation, the opposition between Brahmin and non-Brahmin was replaced by the opposition between Tamils (Dravidians) and all others. Brahmins, too, can become protectors of Tamil. Although there were few important Brahmin student leaders in the 1967-1968 anti-Hindi agitations, many Brahmin students were supporters. Even the idea of "Dravidian" as a racial group that excludes Aryan Brahmins has changed in fifty years to include all castes. As one Brahmin informant told me, "what the non-Brahmin earlier failed to realize was that the Brahmins are as Dravidian as the Non-Brahmins." Tamil Brahmins outside Tamil Nadu are less sympathetic. They are not dependent on Tamil Nadu for their livelihood, and many still resent the non-Brahmin movement and its effect in curtailing Brahmin political influence.

Another aspect of this transformation is the breakdown of certain kinds of barriers among non-Brahmins as a result of urbanization and the ideology of the non-Brahmin movement.[79] Almost all informants report changes in intercaste relationships. These include, for the most radical, relaxations in restrictions on friendships, occupational choice, maintenance of rigid codes, orthodoxy, interdining, and meat-eating. Brahmins and Untouchables still share a qualitatively distinct ritual and theological isolation from other caste Hindus; however, as I have pointed out above, the Brahmin ritual isolation is being mitigated by new patterns of upper-class Brahmin and elite non-Brahmin economic cooperation. Not so with Untouchables. The intransigence of caste prejudice against Untouchables remains and seems worse, given the relaxation of caste bias.

After the death of Annadurai, four members were added to the Madras cabinet by the new chief minister, Mu. Karunanidhi, one of whom was an Untouchable.[80] This, plus the elevation of Karunanidhi as chief minister, portended an improvement in the position of Untouchables after 1969. That Karunanidhi became chief minister instead of Nedunchezhian is significant because a majority of the Untouchable members of the DMK General Council were members of the Karunanidhi faction.

By November 1970, however, some DMK leaders desired a separate organization within the DMK and under DMK aegis to promote the welfare of the backward classes and the scheduled castes. Dr. Satyiavani Muthu sponsored this proposal at a meeting of the Central Executive of the DMK General Council on November 3, 1970. Her proposal was debated in a heated session and finally voted down. The following resolution was adopted instead: "The DMK while functioning as an opposition party had always championed the cause of the Harijans, Backward Classes and the lower middle class and worked for a casteless common egalitarian society. After assuming power, the DMK government had taken energetic steps to protect their interests and redress their grievances."[81] The resolution continued by appealing to the government to continue its efforts to promote the welfare of those three groups.

If a structural realignment of caste alliances is taking place that will increasingly isolate Untouchables, then the Adi-Dravida issue will be raised again and again, not only in the DMK but in all parties. Thus far, the DMK has shown little creativity, committment, or special competence in handling so crucial an aspect of social reform.

Religious and Ritual Reform. A second aspect of social reform ideology involved opposition to Hinduism (see the discussion of *Arya Malai*), and the call for "rationalism." Rationalism, as expounded by different thinkers in the Dravidian movement at different times, meant atheism, agnosticism, and even monotheism (in contrast to polytheism). However, it always meant opposition to a ritualistic religion, including "clericalism" as a mode of thinking, and to caste and casteism.

In November 1967, Annadurai gave an important address at the convocation of Annamalai University. Focusing at first on the language issue, the chief minister declared the intentions of the government of Madras "not to be coerced into accepting Hindi as the official language."[82] Then, surprisingly, he moved on to the subject of rationalism, calling upon the graduates to "become torch bearers of rationalism."

> Rationalism does not mean repudiation of basic and fundamental truths—but the annihilation of dubious modes of thought and action.

> We have been for too long a period doting upon decayed forms of thought. Our religion has degenerated into rituals, our society which was once classless and casteless has degenerated into watertight compartments of caste and creed. And more than that, whenever a doughty warrior comes forth to fight against evils prevalent we denounce him.

> Periyar [E. V.] Ramasami represents and symbolizes the fury and frustration in a sizeable section of society at this state of affairs. To allow systems to degenerate and at the same time denounce those who champion the cause of rationalism is but to perpetrate superstition and orthodoxy.[83]

Although this speech contains some of the elements of radical social-reform ideology, it did not signal a return to radical social reform as a major party ideological theme. It does show that no matter how muted, the theme of radical social reform never completely disappeared from DMK discourse, even after the party assumed power.

One of the first actions of the DMK government was the Hindu Marriage (Madras Amendment) Bill, validating Self-Respect marriage.[84] A Self-Respect marriage is defined in the bill as one between any two Hindus solemnized in the presence of relatives, friends, or other persons (1) by each party to the marriage declaring that each takes the other to be his wife or her husband; or (2) each party garlanding the other or placing a ring upon any finger of the other; or (3) placing of the thali (wedding necklace).[85]

Another policy of the DMK encouraged intercaste marriages between members of scheduled castes and tribes and caste Hindus by awarding gold medals to partners in these marriages.[86] One member of the DMK General Council even proposed that people

contracting intercaste marriages be given preference in government jobs, but this was not implemented.[87] And as one newspaper
pointed out, "in the spate of Abbotsbury [an elegant site for
important ceremonies] weddings which they [the DMK] staged
in the last one year to signalize their social arrival on the heels
of their political, not one was advertized as 'mixed' [intercaste]."
The use of "mixed" in this context does not mean only marriages
between a caste Hindu and members of the scheduled castes
or tribes, but even marriages between Hindus of different castes.
Had there been intermarriages between caste Hindus, some
Adi-Dravida leaders would have considered it insignificant. For
example, K.V.S. Mani had nothing but scorn for considering
marriages between members of caste Hindu communities as
important advances toward social reform:

> You see, there are even different communities behind castes.
> Among the Mudaliars, there are many different communities.
> When they [Hindu reformers in general, DMK and DK
> reformers particularly] talk of intercaste marriage and the
> breaking down of casteism, they mean between a Vellala and
> a Pillai. What is that? They don't think about Harijans. Or
> the differences between a Gounder and a Padayachi. Nothing.
> They don't want anyone to be better than them, but they
> want all people below them to remain below them.[88]

In general, DMK policy on mixed marriages had a very limited
effect on the destruction of casteism.

Secularism. The third area of social reform is secularism. The
only significant policy involved a circular sent out by the chief
secretary requesting that pictures of gods and goddesses in
government offices be removed:

> The heads of departments, etc. are informed that in view
> of the secular nature of our state, the government considered
> that it is not proper, that pictures, idols, etc. of any Gods
> and Goddesses, including saints, messiahs, etc. be exhibited
> or installed in or on any government offices property . . .
> or where they are already exhibited they should be removed
> gradually and unostentaciously so as to avoid attracting any
> notice or creating any local incidents.[89]

Although approved during the rule of the DMK government, the circular was actually the outcome of a representation made by a radical social-reform oriented newspaper two years before. At that time, the editor drew the Congress government's attention to "indiscriminate display and installation of images and pictures of a variety of gods in government offices [causing] mental anguish to persons who were not devotees of these deities."[90] He urged the removal of religious pictures and idols displayed in public pathways and roads.[91] During the second year of DMK rule, a dispute arose concerning display of a particular deity in a government office. In light of this dispute and the previous representation, the DMK government issued the circular.[92]

Leakage of the circular to the press caused a furor. Indignant letters were written to newspapers, resolutions were sent to the government, critical editorials appeared, and everywhere one heard references to this action. In fact, it stirred more indignation that the Kilavenmani arson. Critics accused the government of being atheistic. An editorial in the August 1 edition of *Nava Sakti* speculated about the quandry in which the DMK found itself. The article was entitled "Rajaji or Periyar? Annadurai in Serious Dilemma."

Not a single Minister is prepared to voice an opinion about the government's order that all religious pictures should be taken down in government offices. It is as if they do not wish to touch a hot pot. Even Minister Karunanidhi who dared suggest that his colleagues Nedunchezhian, Mathiazhagan, Satyiavani Muthu step down from ministerial positions to help the party, hesitated to comment on this matter regarding God.

The ailing Annadurai also is said to be mentally perturbed over the matter. If this order is enforced, Rajaji will be put in a position where he can no longer support the DMK. If in his anger against the Congress Rajaji should close his eyes to this matter, taking satisfaction in the thought that God will look after him, his followers will make it difficult for him. He will be accused of double standards for he always speaks in favor of religious organizations. . . . They will ask if Rajaji will not practice what he preaches. Therefore, if Rajaji is not to be pushed into an embarrassing situation, the order will have to be rescinded.

However, such a course will displease Periyar, who has invited himself to give his support to the DMK. He will embark upon a program of holding meetings at every nook and cranny and will start talking.

Should the order be enforced, the government will be constrained to ask the Muslims to give up the room in the fort [Fort St. George] which has been converted into their prayer room for offering namas, failing which somebody is sure to take up the matter to the government on the grounds that the government is discriminating. Calling itself a secular state it would not be fair to grant facilities to one particular religion? Annadurai is struggling as between two wives.

In his anxiety to proceed to America, and in dreaming about the reception awaiting him, it seems as though Annadurai has ascribed his signature to the order as he would to an autograph hunter and this has changed into an arrow that pierces his heart. People say that he will somehow solve the matter. Both factions are anxiously waiting to see how he will proceed.[93]

Annadurai ducked the issue. On August 7 he told the press, "if a good number of government officers felt that the circular need not be operated upon, he was prepared to consider it. Since certain political parties expressed their feelings against the circular, I am having consultation with my officials whether to keep this inoperative, keep it in abeyance, or issue fresh clarification, or wait for still more solidified public opinion. A final decision will be arrived at in due course."[94] It is clear from this that if public opinion were sufficiently negative, Annadurai would contravene the order; after mid-August the controversy died down, so the government decided to let sleeping dogs lie. Although some pictures had been taken down, most were eventually replaced.

One incident used by the opposition Congress party to criticize the DMK on the issue of social reform concerned the events surrounding Annadurai's illness.

The news that Annadurai had cancer evoked a dramatic public response. When Annadurai left for the United States on September 11, 1968, for an operation, thousands lined the roads, weeping and shouting "Anna Vazhaga" (Long Live Anna) and "God will spare him to return and lead us."[95] While Annadurai was in America, M. G. Ramachandran, a prominent DMK legislator and movie star (now leader of the A-DMK) arranged for conduct of a special puja (ritual and prayers) in fifty temples on the morning of September 16, Annadurai's birthday.[96] DMK local-level leaders in many places also offered prayers for his recovery. Of course, the obvious letter appeared in the *Indian Express*, making a connection between this and the controversy over gods' pictures.

Dear Sir:

The DMK party in many places has offered prayers to God for the speedy recovery of Mr. C. N. Annadurai and proved that it is not an atheist party.

Secularism does not begin from the Legislative Assemblies or from the white paper on which the Constitution is written. Nor, can it be established by the removal of the portraits of God. Devotion comes within one's heart, however skeptical a person may be.

Those at the helm of affairs in the Madras government should take note of the tendency now and issue instructions not to remove the portraits of Gods, irrespective of any religion, from government offices.[97]

When Annadurai returned, *Navasakthi* printed an article on the preparations of Annadurai's family for his move to a new house. The article was entitled "Oh Rationalists Are You Lions?"

Rationalists' sun, atheist lion who wrote Arya Malai, Kanchi's [Annadurai's birthplace] Garibaldi, this country's Ingersoll [American atheist], next to England's Bradlaw [British free thinker]—Annadurai is the person burdened with titles a mile long. Yesterday he entered a new house. In the new luxurious house there is air conditioning, of that we have no complaints. But . . . awaiting the auspicious time, after the ragu kallam he went with his wife, heating milk and having drunk, he returned to his old house. We regret only that. Annadurai, who ordered the removal of Gods portraits, after learning he had cancer worshipped Murugan [a deity]! Rani [Annadurai's wife] worships Tirupati Veengadaalapthi [pilgrimages are often made to worship this deity during an illness]. When he enters the new house, he drinks warm milk for the sake of orthodoxy and observed the time and position of the planets.

Because of the auspicious day he looks over one or two files sitting in his air conditioned room. Even orthodox people, even the traditional devotee cannot approach him [in his orthodoxy] even they will not change houses in this kind of orthodox manner. How much they have fallen today. They who have become famous as orators [literally, acquired thick tongues] saying that Nataraja and Ranganada idols should be destroyed with a gun. How many principles are changing. How much are they practicing superstition. Only to Erode Periyar [E. V. Ramasami] all these things will be clear.[98]

The religious reaction of Annadurai's followers and even his family is typical of experiences of many radical social reformers. It is politically significant, because it constitutes another constraint on the potential for radical social reform. Within the Dravidian ideology there was no coherent alternative to religion or Hinduism. Therefore, when adherents and even family members of ardent social reformers faced life-cycle crises, they had no place to turn for answers. In a culture with overwhelming pressure to conform, it takes unusual courage to abandon standard cultural explanations and substitute nothing.

CONCLUSION

After the death of Annadurai, Tamilians saw the first two years of DMK government under his leadership as a halcyon period. But our analysis of the Annadurai era shows that from the very beginning and under the most favorable circumstances, including a popular, charismatic leader at the helm of government with a substantial electoral majority, the DMK government faced difficulties rooted in the contradictions of cultural nationalism and latent, internal pressures inside the DMK party. Most problems faced by the DMK government during their first two years in office reflected the major contradictions of cultural nationalism as an ideology of a ruling party.

In the DMK political regime, contradictions and conflicts centered around cultural policy and class. Central to the DMK nationalist stance was a cultural policy that reflected, supported, and gave priority to Tamil language and aesthetics. The national language policy, which contained economic incentives to learn

Hindi, was a direct challenge and threat to the DMK government. The party had reified a nationalistic universe and tried to portray its own rule as Tamil nationalism *realized*, yet as a state party in a larger territorial whole, the DMK could not completely control any policy, including cultural policy.

The class contradiction was more subtle. As a cultural nationalist party emphasizing unity of all Tamilians (horizontal unity), the party had difficulty handling concrete vertical cleavages that reflect economic fragmentation and conflicting class interests. And there is an additional problem: a diffuse cultural nationalist ideology does not require any policy other than achievement of an arena for realization of identity—that is, achievement of cultural self-determination, authenticity, and recognition. In the DMK case, radical social reform constituted the heart of the party ideology, but no radical reform policy of substance emerged from the first years of DMK rule.

What did emerge among some DMK leaders was a mounting sense of frustration and bewilderment. At this juncture, the DMK was unfortunate enough to lose its charismatic leader, C. N. Annadurai. As we turn to the Karunanidhi period in the next chapter, we will examine a cultural nationalist party without the benefit of a charismatic leader. As we shall see, not only are there governmental problems, but internal party conflicts and tensions, nascent in the party since the late 1950s, that come to the surface after Annadurai's death.

[1] *Hindu*, November 27, 1967.

[2] *Ibid.*, also see the *Indian Express*, November 4, 1967. Annadurai preferred a constitutional amendment to provide for the continuation of English along with Hindi as Union official languages for an indefinite period.

[3] *Indian Express*, November 4, 1970.

[4] *Hindu*, December 4, 1967.

[5] *Ibid.*, December 11, 1967.

[6] *Ibid.*, December 13, 1967.

[7] *Ibid.*

[8] *Ibid.*

[9] *Ibid.*, December 17, 1967.

[10] *Ibid.*

[11] *Ibid.*, December 18, 1967.

[12] *Ibid.*, December 20, 1967.

[13] *Mail* and *Hindu*, December 21, 1967.

[14] This account of Mu. Karunanidhi's dramatic confrontation is based on articles in the December 23, 1967, *Hindu*. My interviews with Madras students who were present corroborate the *Hindu* coverage.

[15] Interviews with Ponnuvelu (former DMK student leader, later an MLC still involved in the DMK student movement), Madras, 1968. Also corroborated by interviews with other DMK student leaders.

[16] I was present at one meeting before a largely Brahmin audience where "Rajaji" gave a rather rousing speech that was well received.

[17] *Link*, December 31, 1967.

[18] *Ibid.* Recall that this is an important difference between the DMK and the DK—while the DMK moved from radical social reform to cultural nationalism, the DK did not; hence the language issue never assumed the same porportions for them.

[19] E. V. Ramasami had earlier given up the Dravida Nadu demand, but never the demand for a separate Tamil Nadu. His *Viduthalai* newspaper proudly carried the old rallying cry, "Tamil Nadu tamizhrukee" (Tamil Nadu for Tamilians). On April 14, 1968, E. V. Ramasami arranged a Delhi Imperialism Condemnation Day at which the following resolution was passed:

"(1) That in the names of God, Religion and the puranas and creating precedents the Brahmins, though they form only 3 per cent of the population, have branded Tamilians as low caste people and just to keep up their supremacy have made Tamilnad, a vassal state of the Indian Union, which is unnatural, artificial and highly disadvantageous to the Tamils.

"Tamilnad, because of its subjugation to the Indian Union, is losing its individuality and is made an abode for perpetual Brahmin supremacy.

"To liberate it from the clutches of the Brahmin domination it is highly essential and important for all the Tamils to redeem Tamilnad from the tyrannical yoke of the Indian Union.

"(2) This social gathering for the Tamils do [sic] resolve, that so long as Tamilnad continues to remain as part of the Indian Union, it is impossible for the Tamils to enjoy any right, privilege, independence and even self-respect.

"(3) In view of the fact that Tamilnad is made like a vassal state under Indian Union, Judiciary in Madras, particular the Highcourt, has been monopolized by the Brahmins and other minority communities and the Tamilians are deprived of getting their legitimate due share and the progressive growth of the sons of the soil is hampered to a great extent.

"And on the executive side also, minorities like Brahmins, Muslims, Christians enjoying more than due share and have encroached very much upon our rights and this sad state of affairs is bound to be permament so long as Tamilnad remains a part of the Indian Union and the only remedy is to secede from the Indian Union.

"(4) This meeting resolves that Tamilnad's continuing to be a part in the Indian Union is injurious and detrimental to the interests of Tamils and profitable only to some other states and communities.

"Hence Tamilnad must be made an independent, sovereign state.

"(5) By [because of] Tamilnad's servitude in the Indian Union, industrial and other kinds of development are considerably affected and the larger interests of the Tamils. We do resolve that Tamilnad must be carved out of the Indian Union as an independent state. Secession is the only permanent remedy for the maladies constantly plaguing the Tamilians and the Tamilnad." The resolution was written in English.

On September 18, 1967, E. V. Ramasami had deprecated the language controversy, saying he preferred English to Tamil. This factor is a dramatic demonstration of the distinctions between the two organizations. The Dravida Kazhagam retained radical social reform goals and refused to support totally DMK cultural nationalism. However, the DK agreed with the basic theme of Tamil greatness.

[20] *Link*, December 31, 1967. In December, however, most of the slogans were of the insipid variety, "nasty Hindi, down, down." I did hear a number of students shout the old "Tamil Nadu is for Tamilians" slogan. Only later were more separationist slogans raised.

[21] This account of the January meeting is based on interviews with student and DMK leader-participants and on articles in *Hindu*, January 7, 1968.

[22] The sepation demand by students in 1967-1968 represents a repudiation of the argument that social mobilization leads to the extension of empathy and elimination of so-called primordial sentiment. Here we have the student community of Madras, a group one could argue was most subject to the impact of social-mobilization variables, demanding separation as late as 1967-1968.

[23] Interview with R. Ramasami (leader of the Tamil Nadu Anti-Hindi Agitation Council), Coimbatore, 1968; and interview with T. R. Janarthanam, Madras, 1968. Janarthanam's troubles only began in January. In March he was deposed as leader of the Madras Students Association by a coup organized by Congress students. This further indicates DMK problems among the student community. See *Navasakthi*, March 3, 1968, for a complete account.

[24] *Hindu*, January 14, 1968. Again Annadurai called a meeting of students in an attempt to quell the agitation.

[25] And to some extent pro-English.

[26] *Hindu*, February 27, 1968.

[27] In general what follows is based on interviews with R. Ramasami and other Coimbatore student leaders, and DMK leaders and Congress local-level leaders in Coimbatore. See also the *Hindu* series, "Background to Student Trouble in Coimbatore," February 27-28, 1968. The informant referred to here was connected with one of the Coimbatore educational institutions and was present at the meeting.

[28] *Hindu*, February 27, 1968.

[29] Interview with R. Ramasami.

[30] He was charged with offenses under Section 147 (unlawful assembly) and 124-A (sedition). See *Hindu*, February 23, 1968.

[31] Non-DMK and non-Congress. However, he and most "independent-minded students" I met were cultural nationalist in orientation.

[32] There were other reasons why students demonstrated. In my interviews and contact with college students, I found four general types of students with strong anti-Hindi sentiments on the language issue. First, strong DMK party supporters; second, strong Tamil nationalists, most of whom had been DMK-oriented at some point; third, students from backward classes and scheduled castes, who were often the first in their family to receive higher education. These students felt frustrated by their inability to learn English well, and exasperated at being forced to learn Hindi. Fourth were students from homes with a well-established tradition of learning, and often a strong English tradition. These students felt angry at having to learn Hindi, a language of less prestige and utility to them than English.

[33] Rice at one rupee per measure was the worst quality; middle-class housewives would only use it for dishes requiring ground rice. However, lower classes used one-rupee rice as a staple.

[34] Mathiazhagan acquired a reputation for concern about soaring food prices while still a member of the Legislative Assembly. As the DMK member specializing in that area he did things like walk into the Legislative Assembly with what he called a "paper thin idli" (steamed rice and lentil cake) from a Madras restaurant. The main impetus for lower prices came from the new food policy pursued by the DMK government. An article in *Hindu*, February 29, 1968, states: "The Chief Minister's strategy of development during the coming

year is centered on consolidating and extending the gains on the agricultural front, by increasing the area of cultivation of high-yielding varieties of food-grains, the enlargement of double-cropping and so on. The claim that the present year's increased output of 60 tons of food grains was achieved in spite of seasonal conditions and as such *is to be attributed largely to the new agricultural strategy is well made out*" [my emphasis].

[35] As part of the World Tamil Conference, there was an enormous procession with floats representing figures from Tamil literary and philosophical history. During the conference, continual entertainment was provided in an enclosed structure, bedecked with Tamil symbols. Poetry contests were held there daily, interspersed with political speeches and musical entertainment.

[36] See, for example, the March 10, 1968, edition of *Mail*, which carried a long article entitled "DMK Record in Office Impresses Delhi—Sound Democratic Alternative to Congress." In fact, Jagjivan Ram came to Madras and, to the embarrassment of the TNCC, praised the DMK government.

[37] *Mail*, March 5, 1968.

[38] The Tamil Sena or Tamil army was modeled after the Shiv Sena "sons of the soil" movement founded in Maharashtra. The Shiv Sena was extremely chauvanistic, and has a paramilitary appeal. Its purpose was protection of Maharashtrians against the encroachment of "foreigners," particularly south Indians.

[39] The initial conflict between one transport worker and one student expanded to mobs of each. Buses were burned and thousands of rupees damage caused when workers stoned hostels. One student was killed and many others injured. Particularly hard hit was the Madras Medical College, which precipitated a strike of doctors in the Madras City hospitals. Only the personal intervention of Annadurai persuaded them to return to work. After a long inquiry, it was found that the students were responsible for the conflict.

[40] To mention a few incidents: (1) the Aravankadu Condite factory police firing (5 deaths), March 2, 1968; (2) the Wimco strike, February 15, 1968; (3) continued unrest at the Ambattur industrial estate; (4) Madras City sweepers' strike, November 7, 1968. *Link* noted DMK ineffectiveness in a December 6, 1970, article entitled "Standard Motors Affair." It stated: "The pro-labour professions of the DMK government have always been held at a discount. Its ability to compromise the vital interests of industrial workers has earned it some notoriety in the last two years and more. The DMK government's record of dealing with its own employees and workers has been anything but shining. When the state-owned dairy-farm workers went on strike the State government used convicts to break the strike. When engineers of the Electricity Board went on a mass leave protest agitation, the Government refused to take them back except on the humiliating basis of individual apology letters. When the transport workers went on a day's token strike, the Government excluded the participants from its bonus scheme." The Standard Motors affair, *Link* argued, was an exception in which the DMK government had taken a prolabor stand.

[41] See the *Hindu*, August 19, 1968; August 21, 1968; August 23, 1968; and November 24, 1968 for the *Hindu's* version of the strike. See the *Indian Express* and *Mail* on August 31, 1968, and the *Indian Express* for a more balanced view, and the Tamil dailies *Navasakthi, Dinamani,* and *Malai Murosu,* for a slightly more prolabor position. Altogether, the *Hindu* suspended publication for thirty days. Rajagopalacharia was reportedly instrumental in shaping DMK policy in the *Hindu* strike.

[42] *Hindu*, April 25, 1968.

[43] *Hindu*, April 28, 1968.

[44] *Ibid.*, May 2, 1968.

[45] *Ibid.*, May 6, 1968.

[46] *Ibid.*, May 11, 1968.

[47] *Ibid.*, May 12, 1968.

[48] *Ibid.*

[49] It is an interesting reflection of the extent of the penetration of the north-south dichotomy and the sense of discrimination against the south that one newspaper reported about that meeting: "a feeling prevalent amongst the mill owners here that the Indian Cotton Mills Federation did not adopt a helpful attitude in regard to mills in the South and had not properly represented the case of the spinning industry to the government, but had only protected the interests of the composite units in the North. As is common, the complaint of Northern discrimination against the South led to the demand for a separate organization.

[50] *Hindu*, May 17, 1968.

[51] *Ibid.*, for the complete agreement.

[52] *Ibid.*, May 26, 1968.

[53] *Ibid.*, May 28, 1968.

[54] *Ibid.*

[55] The National Commission on Labor for the Southern Region reported that industrial relations in Madras State had worsened during 1968. They blamed government policy: "(1) Failure of the police effectively to put down acts of violence and harassment of managerial staff; (2) Constant and continuous interference at the ministerial level in labour disputes; (3) Refusal to pass orders promptly on conciliation reports; (4) Ministerial pressure on management to reinstate dismissed workers without even examining the merits of the case; (5) Suggestions that workers should not be dismissed even in cases of gross indiscipline and that the Government has no belief in the punishment of dismissal; (6) Reopening of closed cases on which orders were passed long ago and referring them to adjudication; and (7) Government's support to union leaders who had openly and flagrantly violated the code of discipline."

This report would seem to indicate a decided prolabor bias. However, all of the alleged DMK government failures reflected the DMK attempt to organize party trade unions. The DMK policy on the major strikes and incidents of industrial unrest was neutral, and even promanagement, as the DMK tried to respond to critics by opposing "labor violence."

[56] See *Mail*, November 20-24, 1968, for an excellent three-part series on the Tamil Nadu trade union movement. The following analysis is based on that series and on interviews with party leaders.

[57] On May 1, 1970, the DMK inaugurated their new umbrella labor organization, the Thozhelalar Munnetra Sanga Peravai. It is based on the AITUC (All India Trade Union Congress) and INTUC (Indian National Trade Union Congress) model, and is an indication of DMK "arrival" in the labor area.

[58] *Hindu*, July 13, 1969. The following account of the history of landlord-laborer conflicts in Tanjore is based on a series of articles in the *Hindu* of July 11, 12, 13, 1969.

[59] Interview with Mr. Veeramani (Madras, 1969), editor of *Viduthalai*. Despite a desire to avoid alienating elite non-Brahmins, a determined effort was made to organize Adi-Dravidas.

[60] See Andre Beteille, *Caste, Class and Power* (Berkeley and Los Angeles: University of California Press, 1966).

[61] Interviews during 1967, 1968, and 1969 with DK and later DMK leader A. P. Janarthanam, DMK MLC were most helpful in suggesting DK leaders

to interview and in illuminating DK history.

[62] See the *Hindu, Mail,* and *Indian Express* from the December 24 to December 31, 1968 for full details.

[63] *Hindu,* December 28, 1968. One of the most insightful comments came in this letter to the *Mail*:

"To brush off these incidents lightly as the consequence of misguided adventurism of the Left Communists is to be completely blind to the dynamics of socio-economic forces in the country-side. The much talked of agrarian revolution we are witnessing mostly in the irrigated tracts of the country has from all the accounts of informed observers, sharpened the relative inequalities in the countryside. The inequalities are more striking than ever due to conspicuous consumption of the upper strata, and the resentment of the lower strata is more bitter today. Landless labor, whose position has not improved, is seeking a share in the progress of agriculture through organized strength and the landlords are resisting it.

"It should be obvious that the laborers could exercise their pressure effectively only in a season when there is a relatively large seasonal demand for labor—during the harvesting and transplanting operations. The land-owners resist this pressure by importing cheap labor from the adjacent dry areas. This is the basic cause of tension.

"Today it is Tanjore delta, and tomorrow it will be Pennar, Krishna and Godavari deltas. This raises the broader issue whether a land saving, labor using technology could even be promoted on a large scale by big holders. Big holders should mechanize or they must lease out to tenant cultivators to avoid labor troubles. There is a likely danger that the agrarian revolution will come to a premature end under both the circumstances. Overcapitalization in a labor surplus economy is sure to deepen the social crisis in rural areas unless it is accompanied by a rapid rate of rural industrialization.

[64] *Hindu,* January 17, 1969.

[65] *Ibid.*

[66] The Naxalites are a radical wing of the Communist movement and have engaged in guerrilla activity.

[67] The following analysis is based on *Hindu,* July 11-13, 1968.

[68] For the first part of the DMK term of office, the ceiling on land was thirty acres per person. This was easily evaded, however, by parcelling out land to various members of the family. The land ceiling has now been reduced to fifteen acres.

[69] Dr. Satyiavani Muthu was a founder of the DMK. In 1944, she was a member of the Executive Council of the DK. She came from a staunch Self-Respect background. Her husband was Madras secretary of the Self-Respect movement until his death, and her father was a leader of the Self-Respect movement and propaganda secretary for seven or eight years. In addition, her father had been active in the Congress but, like E. V. Ramasami, left to help form the Self-Respect League. Dr. Satyiavani Muthu is a Buddhist, as are many of her relatives, converted in response to the leadership of Dr. Ambedkar. Information is based on interviews with Dr. Satyiavani Muthu.

[70] The word untouchability is used to mean caste Hindu treatment of Untouchables in general.

[71] Interview with K. V. S. Mani (of the Republican party), Madras, 1968.

[72] *Ibid.*

[73] This information comes from an interview with a professor at Madras University and a relative of one of the ministers.

[74] Interview with Dr. Satyiavani Muthu Madras, 1968.

[75] *Ibid.*

[76] Interview with K. V. S. Mani, Madras, 1968. Bhaktavasalam is an ex-chief minister and a member of the Tondaimondala Vellala Mudaliars; he is related to Nedunchezhian and Anbazhagan. A P.A. is a personal assistant to a governmental official.

[77] Interview with a Brahmin ex-army officer and a member of the Tamil Brahmin upper class.

[78] *Ibid.*

[79] It is crucial to realize that the ideology preceded the relaxation of barriers, not vice versa.

[80] Raising Untouchable representation in the cabinet to two members.

[81] *Hindu*, November 3, 1970 and November 4, 1970.

[82] *Sunday Standard*, November 19, 1967.

[83] Ibid.

[84] *Hindu*, November 29, 1967.

[85] *Ibid.*

[86] *Ibid.*, March 4, 1968.

[87] *Mail*, July 6, 1968.

[88] Interviews with K. V. S. Mani, Madras, 1968.

[89] *Mail*, July 19, 1968.

[90] *Hindu*, July 20, 1968.

[91] *Ibid.*

[92] *Ibid.*

[93] *Navasakthi*, August, 1968.

[94] *Hindu*, August 9, 1968.

[95] *Mail*, September 10, 1968.

[96] *Navamani*, September 16, 1968.

[97] *Indian Express*, September 25, 1968.

[98] *Navasakthi*, November 13, 1968.

CHAPTER TEN

The DMK in Power: Contradictions of Cultural Nationalism in the Karunanidhi Era

AFTER Annadurai's death in 1969, Karunanidhi became chief minister and leader of the DMK. His assumption of leadership was based on solid support from a majority of the DMK MLA's in the Tamil Nadu Legislative Assembly, and his influence in the party organization, particularly the General Council.

The Karunanidhi era marks the seeming decline of the DMK, but the continuance of the Dravidian movement in the form of the Annadurai DMK (A–DMK), started after a factional split in the DMK led M. G. Ramachandran to form his own party. Because of the importance of this split to future Tamil Nadu political development, this chapter will focus on internal party problems. Also, the parochialization of Tamil nationalism and Karunanidhi's major public policy efforts will be examined.

DMK FACTIONALISM

After E.V.K. Sampath's withdrawal in 1961, there was considerable emphasis on party unity. Annadurai, always a charismatic leader, was venerated as a "god on earth." Among second-level leaders, the struggle for supremacy was temporarily vitiated by the increased gap between all second-level leaders and Annadurai, and by Sampath's exit. However, factionalism was not eliminated. In fact, Mu. Karunanidhi's role in the Sampath affair put Annadurai in his debt—an advantage he used in the later leadership struggles.

Nedunchezhian was in competition with Karunanidhi for the number two spot. His claim was based on seniority within the party, as manifested by Annadurai's selection of him as general secretary in 1956.[1] Another source of Nedunchezhian's prestige was his master's degree and reputation as a Tamil scholar. Post-graduate degrees in the DMK carry more weight than usual because of opposition charges that only illiterates and "rowdy elements" of the population support the DK and DMK. To compensate, educated DMK leaders were given special deference and publicity, and the DMK even tried to characterize itself as the party of the educated.

Prior to the 1967 general elections, the situation was sufficiently unclear for Nedunchezhian to believe that if the DMK formed the state government, he would be chief minister.[2] This belief was reinforced when Annadurai did not contest a seat in the Tamil Nadu State Legislative Assembly in 1967, but ran instead from the South Madras Lok Sabha constituency. After the DMK won, Annadurai, much to Nedunchezhian's chagrin, gave up his seat in the Lok Sabha (later won in a by-election by "Murosoli" Maran, Karunanidhi's nephew) to become chief minister. Nedunchezhian then became number two in the cabinet; Karunanidhi, number three and Mathiazhagan (who emerges as an important figure in the 1968–1969 factional conflict, and again in the formation of the A–DMK), number four.

Severe intraparty factionalism did not arise until the beginning of the DMK's second year in power. A key factor was Annadurai's illness. As early as March 1968, Annadurai missed several sessions of the Legislative Assembly debate because of his "stomach ailment." In April, he went to the United States, ostensibly because of an invitation from Yale University to give a series of lectures as a Chubb Fellow, but also to see a cancer specialist. Whether Annadurai was told at the time that he had incurable throat cancer is a matter of speculation. However, even the prospect of a prolonged period of incapacity was enough to stimulate intraparty leadership conflicts. (In mid-1968 the public knew nothing of the serious nature of Annadurai's illness.)

The first skirmish was the humorous case of the Karunanidhi statue.[3] During the World Tamil Conference, a statue of Annadurai was erected in the center of Madras City. Although there was some criticism from the Congress about statues for living people, very little was to be gained from pursuing that tack, since statues of Kamaraj Nadar had already been erected during Congress rule.

In May a group of Karunanidhi's supporters proposed that a statue be erected of Karunanidhi for his birthday. This proposal was vigorously objected to by others, particularly by Mathiazhagan's followers. Annadurai maintained silence. After both the Congress and Mathiazhagan's followers within the DMK began to ridicule the idea, Karunanidhi vetoed it himself, maintaining that he had not known about it. Congress satirists, however, suggested that he had posed for the statue.[4] Although trivial, this incident brought the Karunanidhi-Mathiazhagan rivalry out into the open.

In June, intraparty leadership conflict dramatically came to the fore. During a speech in celebration of his forty-fifth birthday, Karunanidhi did some "loud thinking" about the future direction the DMK should take. He suggested that he, Nedunchezhian, Mathiazhagan, and Satyiavani Muthu give up their ministerships in order to concentrate on party work.[5] Although reminiscent of the Nehru-inspired Kamaraj plan,[6] the Karunanidhi plan was not sponsored by Annadurai. Furthermore, Karunanidhi had not discussed this bombshell with the ministers concerned or with Annadurai.[7] On June 12, Mathiazhagan called a press conference, and in an ill-tempered and ill-conceived series of statements, publicly answered Karunanidhi. The following article from the Madras Mail contains the substance of his statement:

DMK Differences to the Fore—
Mathialagan Opposes Resignation Plan—
Bona Fides of Karunanidhi Move Doubted—

Mr. K. Mathialagan, Food Minister, today disagreed with the suggestion of Mr. M. Karunanidhi, Public Works Minister, that senior ministers should quit office to devote time to party work. He questioned the bona fides of the move and objected to the manner in which Mr. Karunanidhi had expressed his view.

"With great respect to my beloved friend, the Public Works Minister," Mr. Mathialagan said: "if he has any reason to feel that our presence—myself and Mr. Nedunchezhian—is inconvenient and uncomfortable to him, let him straightway state things and come out with reasons."

He maintained that party work could not be completely isolated from government work and that the duties they were discharging as ministers was also party work. Mr. Mathialagan said: "To be in office or not to be in office is to be decided by the Chief Minister. Only at the pleasure of the Chief Minister, any minister, be it Mr. Karunanidhi, Mr. Mathialagan or Mr. Nedunchezhian. With great respect to Mr. Karunanidhi, I venture to say that no minister had the competence or right to decide by himself [whether he should be in office]. It is the contempt of the high office of the Chief Minister.

As far as I am concerned, I am not enamored of ministership, nor will I ever entertain any disrespect for such a responsible post in the democratic set-up. The office of Minister was only an opportunity and an instrument to serve the public. "So even now if my chief minister desires that I must quit, I will relinquish the post with pleasure."

But I regret that Mr. Karunanidhi has made such an incorrect and misleading statement that the DMK is deteriorating. His apprehensions are groundless and unfounded. It appears to me that he is under an illusion. Sooner he comes out of it, it is better for him and the party.

It may be true that the Congress is trying to set its house in order. But after the assumption of office, the DMK is growing stronger and stronger. This is most evident from the surging enthusiasm and the reception our ministers are accorded when they move about in the state and the DMK victories in the by-elections.

It is the considered opinion of millions of people in Tamil Nad that during the short tenure of office, the DMK government under the dynamic leadership and able guidance of the Chief Minister, Mr. Annadurai, has become more popular by the exemplary and spectacular achievements on many fronts.[8]

Later in the statement, Mathiazhagan said that many people "doubted the *bona fides* and genuineness of Mr. Karunanidhi's proposal. Caesar's wife must be above suspicion. It is for Mr. Karunanidhi to clear that doubt."[9]

When Annadurai heard about Mathiazhagan's action, he chastized him and insisted he withdraw the press statement. Mathiazhagan complied, saying:

The Chief Minister impressed upon me that such statements are bound to create controversy which could be exploited by interested people and parties, I, too realize that even a harmless and genuine controversy is apt to be misused by those who are out to disrupt the party. The Chief Minister pointed out the passage in my statement where I made a reference to "bona fides" and I explained that what I really meant was "bona fides" about the plan and not the motive behind the plan.

Two party men like me and Mr. Karunanidhi may hold diametrically opposite views with regard to the means to be adopted to strengthen the party, but the final decision rests with Mr. Annadurai.

I am only sorry that I had caused the statement to be published before consulting with the Chief Minister.

It was purely with a view to convincing my colleague, Mr. Karunanidhi that I presented certain arguments against his proposal. Our relationship is of the most cordial nature, the controversy may be treated as closed.[10]

Although Mathiazhagan's statement ended public aspects of that controversy, intraparty leadership rivalry remained. In fact, the controversey over Karunanidhi's statement, along with the statue incident, publicly defined two competing factions. Apart from bringing the rivalry into the open, the controversy also served other purposes. For instance, as Karunanidhi must have expected, it created an image of Mathiazhagan as impulsive and impetuous. This image hurt Mathiazhagan and made Karunanidhi appear stable by contrast.[11]

In 1968, the DMK held its first party elections since 1960 for the General Council and for a new general secretary. As soon as the decision was made, Karunanidhi began angling for the general secretaryship and for control of the general council. The only major faction opposing him was that of Mathiazhagan, since Nedunchezhian maintained his stance above the rough and tumble world of intraparty politics. As the organizational elections revealed the full extent of factional conflict, this stance became increasingly empty. It is rumored that Nedunchezhian believed that in a contest between Karunanidhi and Mathiazhagan for general secretary, either he or his relative, Anbazhagan, would emerge as a compromise candidate.

By September, when Annadurai left for America for a second operation, there were two factions in the party, more or less publicly at loggerheads. Before departing, Annadurai "appealed from his sick bed" for party unity.[12]

Of the two groups, the Karunanidhi faction was the stronger. However, as the organizational elections proceeded, two surprising factors emerged that prevented a quick Karunanidhi victory.

One was internal conflict within the Karunanidhi faction, and the other was a change in the role of the district secretary. Previously it was customary for the district secretary to prepare a list of people he wanted for the General Council. In 1968, in light of the factional struggle, the right of the district secretary to choose General Council members was challenged, and the elections were opened up. Karunanidhi's control of many district secretaries was less important than he had hoped. By 1968, therefore, although Karunanidhi had virtually consolidated his control of the party, pockets of strong opposition remained. It is fair to say that when the party elections were concluded, the results of intraparty machinations were indeterminate. Karunanidhi, Nedunchezhian, Mathiazhagan, even Anbazhagan—all could have emerged as general secretary and leader after Annadurai.

In the elections for the Madras Corporation in late October 1968, factional rivalry was not as significant as the emergence of indiscipline. The DMK's first difficulty was apportionment of tickets among the electoral alliance. That problem was surmounted largely because of the political astuteness of Karunanidhi. For example, against its claim for twenty-five tickets, the Swatantra party got only seven. Swatantra spokesmen hesitated to accept the allotment, but Karunanidhi moved in promptly to meet Swatantra leader Rajagopalacharia, and that settled the issue.[13] Other allies, such as the Tamil Arasu Kazhagam, CPI(M) CPI, DK, and Tamil Nad Toilers party, ran two candidates apiece. The Muslim League and Swatantra each contested seven seats. The DMK contested ninety-six seats.[14]

The success of the DMK in handling its alliance partners in the corporation elections was not matched in its handling of intraparty dissidents. Twenty-two DMK local-level leaders who had been denied the party ticket decided to contest against official DMK candidates. In October 15, they were issued "show cause" notices, and on October 18, thirty members of the party were suspended for five years for "acts of indiscipline and anti-party activities."[15] Those suspended included three DMK city councillors. The suspended members had either filed nominations for election to the city council as independent candidates, or were overtly working against official DMK candidates.[16]

As a result of the elections, the Congress received what it considered its first breakthrough on the Corporation level since

1959. The DMK failed to obtain an absolute majority in the civic elections, but retained control over the Corporation through leadership of the United Front. Of the 120 seats, the DMK won 54, the Congress 52, the Muslim League 7, Swatantra 3; and 1 each was won by the CPI, CPI(M), TAK, and Tamil Nad Toilers.[17] Together, the United Front parties had a majority of Corporation seats. Two DMK former mayors and three DMK former deputy mayors were defeated, and DMK administration of the Corporation was widely criticized as corrupt.[18] None of the rebel DMK candidates, won but they were believed to have swung the vote for Congress in a few places.[19] Karunanidhi attributed the DMK's comparative failure to "anti-party elements."[20] However, the situation seems more complex. Where the upper middle and upper classes (who by and large stayed away from the polls) did vote in large numbers, they tended to vote against the DMK. More significantly, DMK popularity in the slums seemed to have ebbed.[21] There seemed to be three causes: a spurt of slum fires,[22] the aggressive tactics used by many councillors to secure votes, and alleged corruption.[23]

In 1968, when it came time to choose a mayor, a number of factors entered into the decision. First, the DMK did relatively poorly in the Corporation elections, and perhaps results would have been worse had more middle and upper-class voters gone to the polls. Second, there were the allegedly corrupt activities of ex-DMK Mayor Munusami and Minor Moses, a member of the Munusami faction in the Corporation, both staunch supporters of the Karunanidhi faction. Karunanidhi worked hard for both, even canvassing door-to-door in some areas. The third factor was extensive newspaper criticism that the DMK had allowed Madras City to deteriorate. In the face of this, Annadurai announced that he would make the decision about the next mayor.

Annadurai picked Velur Narayan, a young lawyer relatively free from factional connections. Narayan surprised everyone after his election by drawing up a scheme to clean up Madras City, and pursued this with surprising vigor throughout his one-year term. This was Annadurai's last action opposing the Karunanidhi faction. It may have represented the beginnings of a campaign to revitalize the party and root out factionalism and indiscipline. But this was in November, and by January, Annadurai was physically incapacitated. On February 3, 1969, he died.

After Annadurai's death, the succession issue was clearly defined since there were only two strong factions in the party and the next chief minister would be elected by the D.M.K. M.L.A.s. Karunanidhi consolidated his faction and managed to secure support of the M. G. Ramachandran (M.G.R.) faction after Annadurai's death. The Mathiazhagan faction was clearly too weak for him to be chosen as chief minister. That left Nedunchezhian; the English press and many inside party sources thought he had a chance, since he was widely believed to be Annadurai's choice.[25] He also had no enemies within the party, and he enjoyed widespread support among the educated segments of the party and in the population in general.

However, there were decisive arguments against Nedunchezhian. He was pictured as too weak to be chief minister and leader of the party, in contrast to Karunanidhi, the "party strongman." Second, Nedunchezhian is a Mudaliar and a distant relative of M. Bhaktavatsalam. Bhaktavatsalam had been a minister in Congress governments for thirty years, chief minister at the time of the 1965 language riots, and it was believed by some that he controlled Nedunchezhian.

The alliance against Nedunchezhian was even more formidable than the arguments against him. E. V. Ramasami actively campaigned for Karunanidhi's election as chief minister, opposing Nedunchezhian because of his relationship to Bhaktavatsalam. (Recall that E. V. Ramasami had withdrawn his support from Congress when M. Bhaktavatsalam became chief minister.) E. V. Ramasami, along with S. B. Aditan, M.G.R., Siviji Ganesan, G. D. Naidu (a Coimbatore industrialist, educator, and inventor), Raja Sir Muthiah Chettiar (a wealthy business man), and Karunanidhi joined together to contribute strategy, and moral and financial support for Karunanidhi's election. Reportedly, a campaign chest was formed that allowed gifts of between Rs. 5,000 and Rs. 10,000 to be made to any DMK MLA who needed persuading on the question of the chief ministership. Karunanidhi already had enough support among the DMK MLA's to prevent Nedunchezhian from becoming acting chief minister during Annadurai's illness. Karunanidhi reportedly threatened to bring a no confidence motion if Nedunchezhian were chosen.

It only remained to convince a few stray leaders. Mathiazhagan was persuaded to go along with Karunanidhi after the strength of Karunanidhi's support became evident. One minister threatened to resign if Karunanidhi was made chief minister, but Mathiazhagan convinced him to remain in the cabinet. Finally, Karunanidhi was chosen, and Nedunchezhian resigned from the cabinet.

The succession from Annadurai to Karunanidhi was carried out with minimal public conflict. Karunanidhi publicly tried to persuade Nedunchezhian to remain in the cabinet, but without success.[26] Shortly after his election, Karunanidhi appointed four new ministers to the cabinet, S. B. Aditan; two prominent members of the party, P. U. Shanmugham and K. V. Subbiah; and an adi-Drauida, O. P. Raman.

After Karunanidhi's ascendancy to the chief ministership, the pattern of decision making within the DMK changed significantly. Unlike Annadurai, Karunanidhi was the leader of the most important faction, rather than a leader above factions. He therefore had to accommodate and control other factions; unlike Annadurai, he could not make important policy decisions and have them accepted without question.

THE 1971 ELECTIONS

Karunanidhi was successful during the remainder of the first DMK term in holding the party together, cutting down on indiscipline (although there were serious problems during the Panchayat elections of late 1969), and providing strong leadership. Nedunchezhian eventually returned to the cabinet. Mathiazhagan was purged from the cabinet, but later became speaker of the Madras Legislative Assembly. The conflict with Nedunchezhian over the party general secretaryship was adroitly handled by Karunanidhi: Nedunchezhian became the general secretary and Karunanidhi became the first president of the DMK.[27]

Although the English press was severely critical of DMK rule on a number of issues, Karunanidhi made no public policy blunders during his first term that would have alienated large segments of the electorate. His most serious problem was the student community. Even during the Annadurai regime, the DMK hold on college students had begun to slip, but Annadurai had maintained student respect and prevented wholesale disaffection.

Karunanidhi's problems with students resulted from the

proposed policy of progressively making Tamil the medium of instruction in government colleges. It would seem like a popular policy, given Tamil nationalism, and a recognition of the impracticality of achieving high-quality English-medium instruction for poorly prepared students. However, many students protested, demanding a free choice of medium of instruction. This caused colleges to close in late 1970 and early 1971. Many students were interested in high-quality English-medium instruction, believing it would improve their employment opportunities.[28] They did not see this as a Tamil nationalist issue, and resented the DMK's efforts to define it as such.

Karunanidhi responded by setting up a five-member panel[29] to make recommendations. Karunanidhi asserted he would follow their advice. When the committee made its "interim" report on January 15, 1971 (a month and a half prior to the 1971 elections), Karunanidhi moved to implement the recommendation that "the opportunity to choose the medium of instruction should be available to students."[30]

Thus a potentially troubling issue was resolved before the elections. But although student disquiet eased and colleges began to function again, there was resentment among students because Karunanidhi refused to talk to them as a sympathetic "elder in the manner of the late Mr. Annadurai."[31]

While the issue of the medium of instruction had serious potential, there were other concerns that some of the press felt would hurt the DMK. One was the controversy surrounding the renewed activities of E. V. Ramasami.

In February, E. V. Ramasami inaugurated a anti-Hinduism campaign consisting of a series of activities denigrating Hindu deities and attacking what he believed to be the reactionary character of Hinduism. In a press conference Periyar attacked Brahmin political leaders, and called for public support of the DMK. All this was consistent with his activities since the earliest days of the Self-Respect movement. However, he and the government received wide criticism in the English press. Eventually Karunanidhi issued a statement saying that the DMK government would not tolerate anti-God activities which would hurt the feelings of any section of the people."[32] This statement came after the elections. Before the elections, Karunanidhi disavowed Periyar's actions and disassociated the DMK from the anti-God campaign, but did not arrest or seriously alienate

E. V. Ramasami, since for many non-Brahmins, he was a highly respected elder statesman.[33]

Corruption also emerged as a political issue, but without the dramatic importance it later assumed. DMK opponents accused ministers and party leaders of acquiring mysterious wealth after coming to power. The lame explanation of one DMK tyro—that he had borrowed from his wife, who had recently acquired additional money—engendered the derisive slogan, "Don't Trust Ministers Who Borrow from Their Wives."[34]

Counterbalancing his problems, Karunanidhi had several electoral advantages. First, Tamil Nadu had had several good harvests, and food supplies were better than usual. Second, the DMK mounted its usual star-studded, emotion-laden campaign. Crucial in this effort was the work of M. G. Ramachandran. Third, since Karunanidhi was in alliance with Indira Gandhi during the 1971 elections (more on this shortly), he dissolved the Tamil Nadu legislature so that the State Assembly elections coincided with national elections. It is difficult to gauge the impact of the "Indira wave" in Tamil Nadu, but certainly Congress (R), Indira's party, had virtually no electoral support in the state. Karunanidhi's support of her was, therefore, more important than her support of him. Moreover, his alliance with Indira Gandhi probably neutralized some of the middle and upper-class disenchantment with the DMK.

Finally, a significant DMK advantage derived from the divided character of the opposition. Local repercussions from the 1969–1970 split in the national Congress party became the major concern of Tamil Nadu Congressmen. During 1968, the Subramaniam and Kamaraj factions in Congress engaged in acrimonious public debate, and on one occasion came to blows in front of the Congress headquarters.[35] With the split in the national Congress, local members of the C. Subramaniam faction supported the Indira Gandhi party, Congress (R). The Kamaraj faction supported the syndicate or Congress (O), of which Kamaraj was a leader. As the national picture became more complex, and as Indira Gandhi searched for additional support in the Lok Sabha, she won support from the DMK.

Although the DMK alliance with Indira Gandhi's Congress (R) seems paradoxical, given previous DMK separatist tendencies, it is in fact consistent with DMK priorities and cultural-nationalist orientation.[36] In analyzing DMK political activities and policies on the national level, it is essential to remember that the primary party priority was consolidation of their state-level base.[37]

After the November 1969 Congress party split, a unique opportunity was created for the DMK to enhance its national image, improve relations with the center, and most importantly, consolidate its state support base by linking itself to the left-leaning economic and social policies of Indira Gandhi. Since both Karunanidhi's DMK and Indira Gandhi's Congress were opposing Kamaraj Nadar's syndicate Congress (O), they had a common basis for joint effort. In addition, the alliance was almost a "natural," since the DMK's low priority on Lok Sabha issues and maintenance of an independent national posture meant its substantial bloc of votes (25) was available to Congress (R) on issues such as bank nationalization and the privy purses.

DMK priorities manifested themselves in the negotiations for seats during the 1971 elections. In working out an agreement, the DMK was willing to give the Tamil Nadu Congress (R) 10 seats of 39 for the Lok Sabha, but no Assembly seats. Congress (R), very weak in Tamil Nadu,[38] agreed to this arrangement.

The 1971 election result justified the DMK strategy. Contesting the elections in Tamil Nadu were two united fronts. The DMK-led "Progressive Front" consisted of Congress (R), the Communist Party of India, Praja Socialist party, Forward Bloc, Muslim League, Tamil Arasu Kazhagam, and was supported by the Dravida Kazhagam. In the Congress (O) "Democratic Front" were the following parties: the Swatantra, Samyukta Socialist party, Tamil Nad Toilers, Republican party, and the Coimbatore District Agriculturalists Association. The Communist party (Marxist) threw its weight to the Kamaraj-led Democratic Front in the midst of the electoral campaign. The DMK-led Progressive Front polled 52.78 percent of the vote, and won 209 of 234 Assembly seats. The Democratic Front polled 36.65 percent of the vote, and won 21 seats.[39] Alone, the DMK won 184 of the 234 seats.

After the 1971 elections, therefore all DMK ministers were reelected, and the DMK, with 184 seats in the Madras legislature, had the largest legislative majority in Tamil Nadu political history. The political opposition was scattered and soundly defeated, and there was "tremendous popular goodwill" for the DMK.[40] At the point it would have been difficult to predict the dramatic changes that would occur in two short years.

THE DMK SPLITS

Immediately after the DMK's dramatic success in the 1971 elections, Karunanidhi sought to strengthen the party through large-scale fund raising and membership drives.[41] While this seemed designed to strengthen the party as a whole, it also reflected growing concern over the popularity and strength of M. G. Ramachandran and his M.G.R. manrams.[42] Efforts to strengthen the party could counter the growing M.G.R. influence. As early as the 1960s, Karunanidhi, Nedunchezhian, Anbazhagan, and other top party leaders found it difficult to follow M.G.R. on a platform. Often audiences would simply not let anyone else speak, in showing their adulation for M.G.R. With a firm majority in the Legislative Assembly, it seemed appropriate to make cautious attempts to curb what was perceived as a growing menace.[43]

Although apparently unrelated to intraparty conflicts, prohibition (the first public policy issue tackled by the DMK after the elections) was linked to the competition between Karunanidhi and M. G. Ramachandran. Prohibition had existed in Tamil Nadu for thirty-three years when the DMK government decided to "scrap it." At the time, Tamil Nadu and Gujarat were the only Indian states with prohibition. Tamil Nadu wanted to end prohibition for the same reason it had been ended elsewhere—money. Since the DMK government promised to implement the recommendations of the Second State Pay Commission, which entailed providing pay raises to about 600,000 government servants, and which would cost about RS 21 crores,[44] additional funds were sorely needed.[45]

Abolishing prohibition was complicated by the adamant opposition of Congress (O) leader Kamaraj Nadar, by the repeated support the late C. N. Annadurai had given to prohibition, and by the opposition of two parties sympathetic to the DMK—the Muslim League and the Tamil Arasu Kazhagam. Inside the DMK General Council, M. G. Ramachandran and his faction also opposed lifting the dry law. It is widely believed that Ramachandran's opposition stemmed from his concern that the poor and lower middle class, who spent limited entertainment funds on movies (many starring M.G.R., shown in M.G.R. theatres, and made in studios partially owned by M.G.R.), might substitute liquor for films.

Nevertheless, Tamil Nadu's dry law was repealed. Karunanidhi had won a victory which he thought would weaken his opponent within the party. Not satisfied with this victory, it is alleged Karunanidhi later sought to weaken M.G.R.'s position within the cinema industry by trying to launch his son "Muthu" as a new star, and by trying to prevent M.G.R. from getting film contracts. Also Karunanidhi allegedly supported Shivaji Ganesan (Congress movie star) in certain cinema ventures. The details of Karunanidhi's anti-M.G.R. activities (and M.G.R.'s anti-Karunanidhi and anti-Muthu activities) in the cinema industry are not essential. What is significant is that again (as in 1961) a DMK factional split was linked to cinema industry quarrels. By fall 1972, when conflicts between Karunanidhi and M.G.R. came to a head, Muthu manrams had been organized in certain districts, M.G.R. manrams had expanded to a virtually parallel organization within the party,[46] and Karunanidhi, as well as other top leaders, were primed for a showdown.

The confrontation was initiated by M.G.R.'s thrust at what he rightly perceived to be the Karunanidhi faction's achilles heel—corruption. Since the stunning 1971 DMK victory, opposition charges of DMK corruption increased and were perceived by DMK leaders as undermining public confidence. Furthermore, inflation had increased, power shortages and cutbacks had affected employment, and there had been drought and a poor harvest. Popular discontent was diffuse, but M.G.R. focused on something concrete and visible. While addressing a meeting celebrating the late C. N. Annadurai's sixty-fourth anniversary of his birth, M.G.R. (then treasurer of the DMK) demanded that all DMK town, taluk and district secretaries disclose their financial assets. He wanted not only DMK ministers and members of the Legislative Assembly to disclose their assets, but also that of their relatives. "People were eager to know how bungalows and cars came to them after the DMK came to power," he said, adding that "I'm placing this view which was generally held by the public."[47] At that meeting, M.G.R. also criticized the DMK government for lifting prohibition, and said that if his views were not adopted at the upcoming meeting of the

DMK General Council, he would "go to the public and gain their support for his demand."[48]

M.G.R. probably picked this time to launch his attack because a meeting of the DMK General Council was approaching. He had been angling for a cabinet seat and for a change in the prohibition policy, and evidently thought he could bring enough pressure to bear on the corruption issue to get his other demands met. His statements were clearly a transgression of party discipline, a violation of the party's policy of democratic centralism, and a direct challenge to Karunanidhi.

If M. G. Ramachandran thought his speech would bring concessions from Karunanidhi, he was mistaken; rather it brought swift reprisal. M.G.R.'s speech was on October 8. On October 10 he was suspended from all party posts, and even from primary membership by the DMK president, Mu. Karunanidhi, and the general secretary, Nedunchezhian, following submission of a petition from twenty-six of thirty-one members of the executive committee of the DMK General Council.

If M.G.R. miscalculated the impact of his actions, Karunanidhi and Nedunchezhian miscalculated the impact of Ramachandran's suspension. When the public heard of it, crowds of M.G.R. fans ran through city streets attacking DMK flags and pictures of Karunanidhi. Reports of violent incidents, agitations, and protests flowed in from all over the state.

Unmoved by the mass emotional display over the party executive's action, when the full General Council met, 277 of 303 members in attendance approved the suspension and adopted a resolution prohibiting actions to secure a compromise and reconciliation.[49] Moving to eradicate "the manram menace," the General Council also passed a resolution stating that all manrams and reading rooms affiliated with the DMK should function through local party units. After registering with the DMK, organizers of these manrams and other associations should secure the approval of the local DMK units before arranging meetings for party propaganda.[50]

On October 18, rejecting DMK leadership demands for an apology as a condition for readmission, M.G.R. formed his own political party, the Annadurai Dravida Munnetra Kazhagam, using as a base the M.G.R. manrams and the M.G.R. rasikar manrams (fan clubs). Explaining the program of his party, he told reporters it would implement "Annadurai's policies and programmes including prohibition."[51]

Karunanidhi responded by asserting that M.G.R.'s intention all along was to form a new party and split the DMK. By the end of October a rudimentary party organization had been put together by the A-DMK and on October 30 M.G.R. boasted one million members.[52] While reliable estimates of party membership are not available, it is true there was a mass upsurge over the M.G.R. affair. However, very few DMK MLAs, MPs, or party leaders joined the A-DMK.

Once his new party was formed, M.G.R. attempted to discredit the DMK government and gain the resignation of the cabinet with corruption the central issue. In November, he submitted a list of charges of graft and corruption against the DMK government to the governor. Then he submitted the same list of charges to the president of India and organized hartals, demonstrations, and agitations to support his dual demand that the DMK government resign and a commission be set up to investigate all charges.[53] So confident was M.G.R. that on November 6, 1972, he stated he would not be surprised if the DMK government fell within a month.[54]

Had the center hastily organized a commission to investigate the A-DMK charges and/or imposed president's rule, perhaps M.G.R.'s prediction would have been realized. However, Indira Gandhi and the central government moved cautiously, adhering to constitutional restrictions and avoiding charges of trying to "bring down" the DMK government. On December 8, 1972, Karunanidhi ruled out a state-level commission of inquiry into the A-DMK charges and on December 15 released a detailed reply and placed it before the Madras Legislative Assembly. Furthermore, Karunanidhi made it clear to Mrs. Gandhi that he and his lawyers felt there was no constitutional provision for a commission of inquiry set up by the national government.[55]

Since the DMK cabinet remained intact and very few top leaders joined M.G.R.'s party, it would seem that the A-DMK could be dismissed as being of no more consequence than the now defunct Tamil Nationalist party. However, the A-DMK had a stunning electoral performance in the Dindigul Lok Sabha by-election in May 1973. The contest involved all four of Tamil Nadu's major political parties, the DMK, A-DMK, Congress

(O), and Congress (R). The DMK spent much time and money on this election. Practically every minister was involved, and two ministers were present at all times during the campaign in all the six Assembly divisions constituting the Parliamentary constituency.

The A–DMK had considerable advantages, however, their candidate, Maya Thevar, belonged to the Thevar subcaste of the Piramalar Kallar community which was the local majority. That southern area of the state was among the weakest areas of the DMK influence, and had never effectively been penetrated by the early Dravidian movement organizations. The DMK only achieved a foothold in the late 1960s. Finally, much party propaganda in this area had been done by M.G.R. (and others who like Mathiazhagan, had joined the A–DMK) and involved use and manipulation of his movie image.

While the Congress parties and the DMK were hard at work canvassing and trying to work up some enthusiasm among the electorate, M.G.R. was speaking to mammoth crowds between shooting scenes of his latest movie (Ulagam Sutrum Valibhan— The Youth Who Goes around the World).[56] Campaigning on a platform calling for resignation of the DMK cabinet, and claiming to represent true nationalism and socialism, the A–DMK polled 52 percent of the total vote in Dindigul. The Congress (O) was second, the DMK third, and Congress (R) a very poor fourth.

The A–DMK again showed its voter appeal in the March 1974 elections in Pondicherry. Although not part of Tamil Nadu, Pondicherry had been ruled by the DMK since 1969. In the 1974 elections the DMK lost every seat it held there. Nearly all its 26 candidates finished a poor third behind the A–DMK front (which included the CPI) and the Congress (O) front. The A–DMK formed a coalition ministry in Pondicherry on the basis of its victory in 12 of the 30 seats of the Legislative Assembly.

In the Coimbatore Assembly by-elections held at the same time, the A–DMK candidate won the Lok Sabha contest.[57]

While these victories are significant and suggest A–DMK strength, they do not conclusively portend the complete collapse of the DMK, as some allege. None of these electoral contests has been in traditional DMK strongholds. Pondicherry, like Dindigul, is an area of late DMK penetration. The Coimbatore constituences have always been areas of CPI strength. That the majority of old DMK strength there went to the A-DMK is important, but not decisive.

More significant for assessing the DMK future was the second split in the party.

THE DMK SPLITS AGAIN

Dr. Satyiavani Muthu, veteran of the Self-Respect movement and Dravida Kazhagam, founder-member of the DMK, and cabinet minister since 1967, began expressing public disenchantment with the DMK in May 1974. Reiterating early social reform themes, she charged that the "caste-Hindu" grip over politics and society can never be loosened, much less eliminated, by persuasive and passive methods."[58] She stated that although she was minister for Harijan Welfare, she was not able to promote Harijan welfare because the caste-Hindu officialdom summarily dismissed her proposals.[59] In a bitter commentary on her own political career she advised, "The Harijans should not take things for granted. They should not trust the governments of the day which are dominated by the upper classes and their interests. They should become militant and organize a powerful movement."[60] She urged Harijan mothers to have as many children as possible. Family planning, she asserted, would only perpetuate Harijan minority status.

At a number of public meetings Satyiavani Muthu said she would not resign from the cabinet and administered a verbal slap to Karunanidhi, stating that Dr. Ambedkar was her only leader. Karunanidhi responded by removing her from the cabinet. To his surprise, within hours of Satyiavani Muthu's ouster, ten MLAs, two MLCs, and an MP resigned from the DMK in solidarity with her. She had organized well among her Adi-Dravida (Harijan) colleagues.[61]

Although M.G.R. had tried to woo legislators away from the DMK to the A-DMK, his success had been minimal. Reportedly, Karunanidhi had put together a fund to keep DMK legislators in line (legislative loyalty was allegedly worth as much as Rs 15,000). Dr. Satyiavani Muthu's significant legislative following lent credence to her charges that Harijans were being ignored by the DMK leadership.

DMK FACTIONALISM: AN ASSESSMENT

Several questions arise: Why did the DMK split? What is the political significance of the split? What is the ideological significance of the split? And are there important differences between the DMK and the A–DMK?

Satyaviani Muthu's exit from the DMK and the smoldering "Harijan revolt" it revealed differs in important ways from the A–DMK split. Adi-Dravidas (Harijans) in Tamil Nadu have been steadily losing political ground since the mass mobilization of the backward castes in the 1940s and the subsequent decision of both major political parties to compete for backward-caste support. Recall that in contrast to elite non-Brahmins who felt challenged by Brahmins, backward castes feared improvement in social and economic position of the ex-Untouchables.

Thus, while Harijan leadership discontent may have been triggered by intraparty rivalries, its roots relate to the transformation of the political arena in the 1940s. Subsequent modification of DMK radical social reform ideology further undermined the DMK commitment to reform relevant to scheduled (ex-Untouchable) castes.

In many ways Satyiavani Muthu was correct when she said the Tamil Nadu Harijan community was losing ground. A 1971–1972 study found that community "lagging far behind any other."[62] She may also have been correct in arguing that the problems of the Harijan community are not amenable to easy political solution, given the support structure and leadership recruitment patterns of the major political parties. Certainly the A–DMK offers little more to Adi-Dravidas than the DMK.

This issue sheds further light on Tamil nationalism. Adi-Dravidas have been described as the first Dravidians, who should therefore be elevated in a Dravidian ideological scheme. Indeed, E. V. Ramasami attempted to do exactly that. The transformation to Tamil nationalism, however, accompanied by organizational grounding of the DMK in the backward community and modification of radical social reform ideas, has rendered the DMK and the A–DMK less capable of evaluating pressing Harijan problems. While the fissure between Brahmin and non-Brahmin is being healed at the top under the aegis of Tamil nationalism, the gap between Harijans and all others is widening at the bottom.[63]

Reasons given for the A–DMK split vary according to party.[64]

A-DMK members cite Karunanidhi's authoritarianism, and assert that they rebelled against his dictatorship. Some argue that Karunanidhi was so "paranoid" about controlling the party he alienated large sections of the leadership, even the Annadurai family. Invariably they mention the endorsement given by Rani Annadurai and the Annadurai family to the A-DMK. Supposedly Karunanidhi's failure to give M.G.R. a place in the cabinet and his "haste" in suspending M.G.R. from the party also resulted from his extreme insecurity.

Another reason offered by A-DMK leaders and members is widespread corruption in the DMK government. A-DMK members and leaders who were interviewed all asserted that the DMK government was more corrupt than the Congress regime.

More thoughtful A-DMK supporters point out that after Annadurai's death it was important to develop a stable leadership structure, but believe this should have been collective. In 1973 both A-DMK and DMK informants emphasized that the split was not ideological, and that there was no difference between the two parties.[65]

DMK adherents offer a radically different interpretation. They depict M. G. Ramachandran as an avaricious aging movie idol, anxious to shore up his flagging cinema image by attaining a prominent position in the DMK cabinet. After Karunanidhi refused M.G.R. a place in the cabinet, M.G.R. supposedly transformed his manrams and rasikar manrams into organizations for personal rather than party purposes. Allegedly, M.G.R. had been planning to start his own party for some time, and precipitated the conflict, which then legitimized this strategy. Indira Gandhi is also blamed. Allegedly, she used M.G.R.'s perennial tax problems as a lever to further his efforts to split the DMK. Supposedly she offered to ignore his delinquent taxes if he cooperated with her on the Congress (R) policies on the national level. Privately DMK members admit some graft, but assert that the corruption charges by the A-DMK are exaggerated. Some of the biggest rogues in the DMK went into the A-DMK, according to this interpretation.

These explanations are important because they reflect views held by important segments of the Tamil Nadu political elite. But the origins of current DMK factionalism go deep into DMK history. Three major results of the 1961 factional conflict are relevant to current problems. First, as we know, Annadurai became the unquestioned leader. The gap between him and the second-level leadership shaped his political style and the pattern of intraparty decision making. When Karunanidhi became chief minister, he tried to emulate Annadurai, working within the existing relationship between leader and followers. It is not necessary to assume paranoia or megalomania on the part of Karunanidhi to understand the problems of simply trying to work existing decision making mechanisms.

Given this, two phenomena become clearer: the nature of Satyiavani Muthu's exit, and party corruption. Annadurai was revered by party members as a "god on earth." DMK members reported that subtle pressures existed to revere Karunanidhi similarly. This might have been an attempt by Karunanidhi to unify the party by the same means used by Annadurai. Dr. Satyiavani Muthu's reference to Ambedkar as her only leader was, therefore, not simply a personal challenge to Karunanidhi, but a threat to his leadership.

Corruption and graft in the party existed before the Karunanidhi era. In fact, prior to becoming chief minister, Karunanidhi had used favors and material rewards as the means to obtain support within the party and within the Legislative Assembly. As ideological motivation was eclipsed, and as the need developed to secure his leadership position, Karunanidhi expanded this technique. Not all the alleged corruption can be explained this way, but much involves members of the Karunanidhi faction and seems to fall into this category. In contrast, the graft of some other top leaders seems almost purely personal or, at best, payment of caste debts.

After 1961 the DMK abandoned the last of the movement goals. While party leaders still talked of social reform and even of separation, the party was committed to pragmatic politics and Tamil cultural nationalism. This transformation enhanced two styles of leadership within the party: the organizer, as personified by Karunanidhi; and the charismatic (Annadurai) or glamor (M. G. Ramachandran) figure. As E. V. Sampath foresaw, the issue in 1961 was not simply whether or not to retain separation as a goal, but also what the role of glamor figures in the party should be. M.G.R.'s popular following in 1974 is linked to the direction chosen by the party in 1961.

Finally, the rapidity of the A-DMK's acquisition of support underscores a point made earlier—the openness of cultural nationalism to cooption as an ideology. When the A-DMK claimed it was as nationalist as the DMK, the DMK could only retort that M.G.R. was a "foreigner."[66] In light of M.G.R.'s long years of service in the Tamil nationalist DMK, it was a problematic response. As we shall see below, the DMK leadership was driven further and further into chauvinism and particularism to discredit A-DMK nationalist claims and reestablish themselves as the guardians of Tamilness.

This analysis of DMK factionalism, and the circumstances surrounding the major split which led to the founding of the A-DMK, suggest that, initially at least, there was little difference between the DMK and the A-DMK. However, political pressures soon produced some interesting differences. For one thing, the A-DMK was the first Dravidian movement or Tamil nationalist organization to have a prominent Brahmin politician as a key leader. H. V. Hande left the effete Swatantra party to join the A-DMK in 1973. Presumably Hande's example will encourage other Brahmins (particularly younger people sympathetic to the DMK nationalist line) to become active political leaders in the A-DMK. Recall that the leadership sample of the DMK showed no Brahmins in leadership positions. The A-DMK, therefore, has the opportunity to use the notion of Tamil identity defined by language to mobilize Brahmins.

The leader of the A-DMK, M. G. Ramachandran, has a Malayali family background, as does one of his key advisors, K. Manoharan. In trying to work out an anti-A-DMK propaganda strategy, the DMK has focused on that. First Ramachandran was called an alien, then Karunanidhi made the astounding statement that there could not be two Keralas in south India.[67] Presumably that meant that M. G. Ramachandran, because his family was from Kerala, could not be chief minister of Tamil Nadu.

Not satisfied with the "two Keralas" statement as a propaganda device, the DMK then began verbal attacks on Keralites resident in Tamil Nadu. By 1974 the notion of Tamil identity had so completely replaced Dravidian identity that one could be counterposed to the other. In place of the "racial" and linguistic unity emphasized earlier, antagonism and the separation of Tamils from all others is implied by the "sons-of-the-soil" theory. Thus the A-DMK came to stand for the older notion of Dravidian nationalism (including the unity of all Dravidian language speakers) and the DMK for Tamil Nationalism. Concretely, this means the A-DMK's own Tamil nationalism is linked to an encompassing Dravidian identity.

Finally, the A-DMK has repudiated the major public policy thrust of the DMK—state autonomy. While stressing the need for more powers for the states and expressing a desire for responsive federalism, the party's October 1973 manifesto did not support state autonomy. "We want neither dependence nor independence but inter-dependence," state A-DMK propagandists.[68]

A-DMK rejection of DMK views on state autonomy is crucial because that demand has been central to the entire DMK "theory" of Indian political integration. This is, in fact, the major public policy theme of the Karunanidhi era. While conceptions of political integration have always been important to Dravidian movement organizations, during this era the party moved to develop a concrete alternative to the existing constitutional framework.

THE DMK APPROACH TO POLITICAL INTEGRATION

In an interview in September 1967, Annadurai stressed the importance of an equitable solution to the language problem for "emotional integration" (this was before the language controversy of November-January), and the necessity for more state power.[69] Mu. Karunanidhi also emphasized the need for more power:

Q. What do you consider to be the major problem facing the DMK as a party?

A. There is no particular problem facing the DMK. When the party was started, we demanded separate Dravida Nadu. Then we have dropped that slogan. The reason for which we had demanded a separate Dravida Nadu exists still. Therefore we want to persuade the central government to solve these problems. For example, we wanted some powers for the states and we consider that the state should become more powerful and it should not be like a local self-government. The central government may retain to itself such fields as Railways, Finance, Transport, and Defense and Posts and

Telegraphs, and make the states more autonomous, and the other subjects may be transferred to the states to make them powerful. Only if the states are made powerful, will the center also become powerful.

For example, the state does not have even the power to name a railway station or change the name of an existing railway station. Even that power is vested with the government of India. When we approach the central government for more powers, they refuse to concede to our requests. We are very sorry to see this approach of the government.[70]

These statements by Karunanidhi and Annadurai are typical of the DMK position on political integration; regional equality and power are the cornerstones of political integration.

The DMK concept of equality also included the idea of cultural equality and recognition; hence the emphasis on language and the proposal to have fourteen official languages. *Nam Nadu*, January 20, 1968, reported a revealing statement made by Annadurai during the World Tamil Conference:

We have the good quality of praising fame [achievement] when we see it not only today, but for the past 2,000 years. People like Rabindranath Tagore, have all been praised by us. The people in the North do not know about our authors in this way. Once when I was speaking in Delhi I asked them "Don't you even remember one South Indian name to call one little place in your state?" If you came to our South, if you enter Rajaji Park, you will see Gandhiji's statue, and enter Lalapathi Roy Library and read books by Motilal Nehru. This is our condition but you do not have such a feeling.

This also they thought I was saying for separation. They do not realize that separation occurs because of such feelings. I told them that I was sorry for them.[71]

During the first DMK term in office, the DMK slogan that synthesized these dual aspects was "no domination under the guise of integration." This slogan was repeated frequently during the language crisis.[72]

After Annadurai's death, Karunanidhi escalated the demand for more autonomy and power for the states by appointing a high-powered three-man committee, the Rajamannar Committee, to explore the entire problem of center-state relations and to make a report to the government. The idea for such a committee had been voiced by Annadurai as early as 1967. While answering questions at the Press Club of India in New Delhi, Annadurai emphasized the need for a commission to examine the working of the constitution and the possibility of reallocation of powers between the center and the states.[73]

Annadurai's view that the state's powers were being slowly eroded by the center was expressed firmly during the two years of his chief ministership. In June 1967, presenting the budget to the Legislature, he observed:

There has been considerable change in the matrix of Centre-State financial relations since the provisions of the Constitution in this regard were settled. There have been a number of new trends and developments which could not have been visualized when the Indian Constitution was framed. The Constitution had already provided for considerable concentration of powers in the hands of the Central Government. Through a new institution which was beyond the ken of the architects of the Constitution, the Centre has acquired still larger powers causing concern about the position of the States. This new development relates to economic planning. The powers which the Central Government have assumed in regard to mobilisation, allocation and patterns of utilization of resources for the Plan have reduced the States to the state of supplicants for aid from Centre . . .

State governments cannot discharge their responsibilities in meeting the growing aspirations of the people for a new way of life unless the resource base of the State is considerably strengthened by giving them access to growing sources of revenue and by allocating the Plan resources on an agreed basis leaving the States with complete freedom to utilize them according to their judgement.[74]

And again on June 27, 1967, he noted:

I want the Centre to be strong enough to maintain the sovereignty and integrity of India as it is the fashion to call it.

I would put it another way. It is to safeguard the independence of the Country. I am prepared to say that anybody will accept without any remorse or without any renunciation that all these powers needed to make the Centre responsible for the safety of this country ought to be with the Centre. But that does not mean that the Centre in order to safeguard India from Pakistanis or the Chinese or the Baluchis, should think of having a health department here. In what way does that strengthen the sovereignty and independence of India? Should they have an education department here? In what ways does that improve the fighting capacity of the military personnel here?[75]

The Rajamannar Committee was established in August 1969 and charged with investigating measures necessary to augment the resources of the state and to secure the utmost autonomy of the state without prejudice to the integrity of the country.[76]

Composed of three distinguished non-Brahmins, Dr. P. V. Rajamannar, Dr. A. L. Mudaliar, and Thiru P. Chandra Reddy, the committee officially began work in September 1969 and published its report in May 1971.[77] The committee and its staff sent out numerous questionnaires, conducted interviews, and examined constitutional records. The far-reaching character of the final recommendations shocked many. Agreeing with the DMK government's thesis that there was an imbalance in the allocation of powers between the states and the center and concentration of power and resources in the hands of the central authorities, the committee characterized these "unitary trends" as unhealthy. Accounting for this constitutional development, the committee approvingly quoted a speech by Dr. K. Subha Rao (retired chief justice of India) in which he attributed concentration of power to one-party rule. In 1969 he stated:

till the recent elections the Constitution was worked practically as a unitary form of government. There was a tendency to whittle down the powers of the states which were already in attenuated form. The main reason for this was that the same party had been in power in the Centre as well as in the States for a long continuous stretch of time. . . . The result was that the Union Government had been able to control the State Governments both on the administrative as well as

on the organizational side. Some of the important members
of the High Command of the party in power were also important
members in the Cabinet. In fact the Prime Minister was
controlling not only the Central Cabinet but also the High
Command. Through the High Command he was controlling
the State political units and also the elections to the Pradesh
units and the selection of suitable candidates to the Legislature.
By calculated distribution of seats, the Central Government
through the High Command acquired the hold on the State
Legislatures and the State Ministers. *By this process the States
had practically become the administrative units of the Centre*
[my emphasis].[78]

To strengthen the states, the Rajamannar Committee made
a number of innovative and radical recommendations. For example, they suggested forming an Inter-State Council (consisting
of state chief ministers and the prime minister) to discuss and
make recommendations on every bill of national importance likely
to affect the interests of one or more states. Recommendations
of the Inter-State Council would "ordinarily be binding on the
Centre and the States"[79] and no decision of national importance,
except in regard to defense and foreign relations, could be taken
without prior consultation with the council.

The committee also suggested that the Planning Commission
should be placed on an independent footing, without being subject
to control by the executive or by political influences. They wanted
the Planning Commission to consist only of experts in economic,
scientific, technical, and agricultural matters. "No member of
the Government of India should be on it."[80] The duty of the
Planning Commission would be to give advice on development
programs formulated by the states.

While there were numerous other recommendations made by
the Rajamannar Committee, these two convey the dominant
themes of the report: decentralization of power and interstate
equality.

Outside Tamil Nadu, response to the Rajamannar report was
negative. The following comment is typical:

What Mr. Rajamannar has said in his report on Centre-State
relations is something extraordinary. The Committees recommendations seem to proceed on an of assumption that the

entire foundation and body of the Indian Constitution is basically wrong, unworkable, defective. In fact, if we accepted even half of the recommendations contained in the Rajamannar Report, it would be a qualitatively different Constitution and it would encourage a process of growth of separate sovereign States—and the country will again be pushed into the mire of anarchy which it witnessed for hundreds of years.[81]

Within Tamil Nadu, although the DMK made state autonomy a central issue, the government was very slow to approve the Rajamannar report. Party subcommittees were formed to review the report and make a recommendation to the General Council, but it was not until 1974 that the DMK adopted its key recommendations. On April 16, 1974, the DMK passed a resolution in the state assembly urging the center to accept the views of the Tamil Nadu government on state autonomy, and effect immediate changes in the nation's constitution.[82]

A separate Tamil Nadu flag, renaming Madras State "Tamil Nadu," and the demand for more autonomy and power are on one level attempts to satisfy and fulfill the emotional requirements of Tamil cultural nationalism. From this perspective, the demand for increased state autonomy is a significant counterpoint to the original DMK demand for separation. However, it would be misleading to see this demand or any other aspect of cultural nationalism as only emotional. There is a complex interweaving of emotional content with concern for the concrete realities of power politics. The concern for a balance of power among states and equality of influence for "non-Brahmins" inside Tamil Nadu, and for Tamilians at the all-India level, is a constant theme throughout the development of the Dravidian movement.

The shift from separatism to a redefinition of Indian federalism was not a sudden post-1967 phenomenon. While advocating separation, Annadurai had argued for more state power and greater regional cooperation among the four southern Dravidian-language states. As his tract, To My Friends, indicates, after the DMK formally rejected separation in 1965, they placed increased emphasis on decentralization and state autonomy. After assuming state control, a central explanation for economic and other difficulties was lack of state power. By appointing the prestigous Rajamannar Committee, Karunanidhi enhanced the legitimacy of demands for autonomy and decentralization.

Karunanidhi has repeatedly emphasized that the demand for autonomy is not a demand for secession: the demand for autonomy should not be misconstrued as a move for secession. But if the legitimate rights of the States to grow and develop on their own were denied, division of the country would become inevitable, if not immediately, at least in the distant future."[83] But there is an important paradox in the demand for autonomy. To achieve decentralization and greater state autonomy, the DMK would have to form alliances with parties and groups from other states and engage in the kind of all-India politics which the leadership has so far shunned.

CONCLUSION

Disintegration of the DMK party during the Karunanidhi era was not inevitable—but it was certainly a strong possibility, given the inherent ideological and organizational contradictions and strains that Karunanidhi inherited. Financial considerations, personality conflicts, and even draught and bad harvests contributed to DMK problems. However, of primary importance in explaining the split are the diachronic organizational ramifications of ideological change and DMK transformation from movement to political party. Rise of Tamil chauvinism after the split and the parochialization of Tamil nationalism grew out of the interaction of factionalism and cultural nationalism. As the DMK tried to dominate the cultural nationalist landscape, it moved further and further into an obscurantist, narrow nationalism, bereft of the earlier humanistic social-reform concerns. Hence Satyiavani Muthu's exit was related to the same factors that transformed Tamil nationalism into a reactionary force.

In this context, DMK views on political integration assume particular theoretical and pragmatic importance. The DMK and Tamil cultural nationalism have not been an inherent threat to Indian integration. State autonomy, as the thoughtful demand of a popular party struggling to govern well as one of only a few non-Congress governments, was an important idea. However, with the declining popularity of the DMK government, state autonomy became the empty slogan of a fearful ruling elite.

[1] In 1961, Nedunchezhian tried to stay above the factional conflict as much as possible, defining it as a struggle over who was to be number three and four in the party. He felt secure in the number two spot. However, Sampath and his followers saw Sampath as number two, and even briefly entertained visions of challenging Annadurai for the number one position. Sampath's selection as general secretary in 1960 would have made him the strongest contender for number two position in the party, while Karunanidhi's election to the general secretaryship would merely have solidified his right to contend for a number three spot, behind either Sampath or Nedunchezhian.

[2] One informant said he indicated as much in a preelection meeting in Madras City.

[3] The *Hindu*, May 20, 1968 had a short summary article on the events surrounding Karunanidhi's statue. However, the complete and humorous story was told in the Tamil press. See particularly *Navasakthi* during the first week of June.

[4] For a humorous account of this incident see the article "What Many People Wrote in their Diaries," *Navasakthi*, June 3, 1968.

[5] *Hindu*, June 11, 1968.

[6] See Kochanek, *The Congress Party of India* for a description of the Kamaraj plan.

[7] Interviews with party leaders.

[8] *Mail*, June 13, 1968.

[9] *Ibid.*

[10] *Ibid.*

[11] Another side issue in the Karunanidhi plan controversy was an article in a Tamil Paper, *Kumudam*. It stated that Karunanidhi was number two in the DMK next to Annadurai. K. *Krishnasami*, brother of Mathiazhagan, wrote a long letter to *Kumudam* stating that there was no one else in the party "just like Annadurai" and that after Annadurai there would be a collective leadership of Nedunchezhian, Anbazhagan, Satyiavani Muthu, Karunanidhi, and Mathiazhagan (*Kumudam*, June 1968). This incident contributed to the bitterness between Karunanidhi and Mathiazhagan.

[12] *Hindu*, September 11, 1968.

[13] *Mail*, October 5, 1968.

[14] See the *Indian Express*, October 2, 1968, and *Madras Mail*, October 5, 1968 for an account of negotiations.

[15] *Indian Express*, October 12, 1968.

[16] *Ibid.* and *Madras Mail*, October 24, 1968. In Congress there were about thirty members who could not get party tickets who contested the elections as independents.

[17] *Mail*, October 29, 1968. Tak-Tamil Arasu Kazhagam.

[18] *Ibid.*

[19] *Indian Express*, October 29, 1968.

[20] *Ibid.*, October 30, 1968.

[21] *Ibid.*

[22] Slum fires had broken out throughout Madras City. Each political party blamed the other, and termed the fires acts of revenge. Slum areas usually fly the flag of a political party and are identified with that party, although no slum is politically homogeneous. Despite a series of inquiries the perpetrators of the slum fires remain unknown.

[23] Many Madras City local level leaders said Munusami (ex-DMK mayor and the most powerful Kazhagamite in the corporation) had gone too far and blamed him for the electoral outcome.

[24] The information on the succession is based on informants. Most of the

machinations surrounding the succession were not discussed in the press.

[25] See, for example, the *Hindu*, February 8 and 9, 1967.

[26] *Hindu*, February 10, 1969.

[27] Supposedly as a mark of respect for E. V. Ramasami and a continuing statement of DMK commitment to DK principles, the DMK presidency had always been left vacant for him.

[28] Teachers, however, supported the government's proposal. *Times of India*, January 16, 1971.

[29] The chairman was Dr. A. L. Mudialiar, respected former vice chancellor of Madras University, whose preference for the English medium was well known.

[30] *Hindu*, January 16, 1971.

[31] *Times of India*, January 16, 1971. Karunanidhi had been accused of being antistudent early in the Annadurai regime.

[32] *Mail*, April 15, 1971.

[33] E. V. Ramasami died in 1973 at the age of 96.

[34] *Times of India*, February 19, 1971.

[35] *Hindu*, September 6, 1968.

[36] The following account is only a brief sketch of the complex events that culminated in the DMK-Congress (R) alliance. Also see *Link* for the period from November 1969, to the 1971 elections.

[37] Rajagopalacharia discovered this when he attempted (unsuccessfully) to get Annadurai and the DMK involved in a national Swatantra-DMK front against the Congress. Instead of following Rajagopalacharia, Annadurai tried to cultivate cordial relations with the center.

[38] They only had eight seats in the dissolved assembly. After the Congress split, the majority supported Kamaraj's Congress (O).

[39] *Times of India*, April 1, 1971.

[40] See *Mail*, March 15, 1971.

[41] *Mail*, March 25, 1971. At the time, total DMK membership was 960,000. The party designated the week of April 11, 1971 as "Thanksgiving Week" to celebrate their electoral victory. The first week in May was designated membership week, during which a state-wide membership drive was conducted. In 1971, the total population of Tamil Nadu was 41,163,125 (*Hindu*, April 14, 1971).

[42] Manrams are centers for political propaganda named after a popular leader. They can be as small as a stall or as large as a reading room. There are Annadurai manrams, Karunanidhi manrams, etc., as well as M. G. R. manrams.

[43] This interpretation is based on interviews conducted during July and August 1973. While the sources used were highly reliable, what Karunanidhi and the top leadership thought and discussed privately is still a matter of speculation. However, subsequent events support this interpretation.

[44] *Hindu*, January 3, 1971. Other estimates of the cost went as high as RS 30 crores. RS 1 crore = RS 10,000,000 = approximately $1,333,333.

[45] It was estimated that ending prohibition would yield enough virtually to cover this drain on the state exchequer.

[46] There were over 800 M. G. R. manrams within the DMK. *Hindu*, October 2, 1972.

[47] *Hindu*, October 9, 1972.

[48] *Ibid.*

[49] *Hindu*, October 15, 1972.

[50] *Hindu*, October 13, 1972.

[51] *Hindu*, October 19, 1972. In the press conference called to announce his new party, M. G. R. stated that there were 20,000 M. G. R. manrams and rasekar manrams.

[52] *Hindu*, October 30, 1972.

[53] See the *Hindu* for November 1-15th for discussion of these various events.

[54] *Hindu*, November 7, 1972.

[55] *Hindu*, January 3, 1973. Also see letters from M. G. Ramachandran to Mrs. Gandhi in *Hindu*, December 15, 1972.

[56] In this movie the 59-year-old movie idol plays a "youth" who fights his way around the world combatting evil—winning victories for good and, of course, getting the heroine in the end.

[57] *Link*, March 3, 1974.

[58] *Link*, May 5, 1974.

[59] *Ibid.*

[60] *Ibid.*

[61] *Link*, May 12, 1974.

[62] A. Vagiswari, *Income-Earning Trends and Social Status of the Harijan Community in Tamil Nadu.* (Madras: Sangam Publishers, 1972). There are methodological and statistical problems with this study, but the overall point is sustained.

[63] For further discussion see Marguerite Ross Barnett and Steve Barnett, "Contemporary Peasant and Post-Peasant Alternatives in South India."

[64] This and subsequent views were obtained from interviews conducted during July and August 1973.

[65] Shortly after the interviews both parties began to emphasize differences.

[66] M. G. Ramachandran's family had migrated to Tamil Nadu from Kerala.

[67] *Link*, March 24, 1974.

[68] *Link*, October 7, 1973.

[69] Interview with C. N. Annandurai, Madras, September 1967.

[70] Interview with Mu. Karunanidhi, Madras, July 1968.

[71] *Nam Nadu*, January 20, 1968.

[72] For a very interesting book, which also argues that there is a power conflict within India between heartland and rimland states and that this power conflict is the key to the language issue, see Mohan Ram, *Hindi against India* (Madras: n.p., 1968). Ram, a journalist for the *Mail*, believes the heartland-rimland power conflict to be a systemic aspect of Indian politics.

[73] *Report of the Centre-State Relations Inquiry Committee* (Madras: Government of Tamil Nadu, 1971), p. 7.

[74] *Ibid.*, p. 9.

[75] *Ibid.*, p. 19.

[76] *Ibid.*, p. 1, and also see GO Ms. No. 1741, Public (Political) September 22, 1969 and GO Ms. No. 2836, Public (Political) November 15, 1969.

[77] *Report of the Centre-State Relations Inquiry Committee.*

[78] *Ibid.*, p. 18.

[79] *Ibid.*, p. 215.

[80] *Ibid.*, p. 219.

[81] *Link*, January 26, 1974. Comment by Uma Shankar Dikshit.

[82] *Link*, April 28, 1974.

[83] *Hindu*, April 25, 1971.

CHAPTER ELEVEN

Conclusion

AT the outset, the notion that political identity was a direct translation of socio-cultural cleavage, a primordial "given" of social existence, was rejected. Rather the analytic focus was on the questions of what forces shape political identity? What factors lead to politicization of identity and can identities be "created," transformed, or redefined? Cultural nationalism (often pejoratively labeled tribalism, communalism, regionalism, and so on) is often openly condemned by politicians, subtly derogated and relegated to transitional limbo by social scientists.

But, false dichotomies between "civil" and "primordial" ties and blanket condemnations of cultural nationalism obscure and explain away rather than elucidate this increasingly important phenomenon. Hans Morgenthau has written of the A-B-C paradox of nationalism, in which nation B invokes the principles of nationalism and self-determination against nation A, and denies them to nation C—in each case for its own survival.[1]

If we substitute India for nation B, Great Britain for nation A, and the "Tamil people" for nation C, there are no inherent limits to the application of the principles of nationalism. Morgenthau asks:

> If the peoples of Bulgaria, Greece, and Serbia could invoke these principles against Turkey, why could not the people of Macedonia invoke them against Bulgaria, Greece, and Serbia? . . . Thus yesterday's oppressed cannot help becoming the oppressors of today because they are afraid lest they be again oppressed tomorrow. Hence, the process of national liberation must stop at some point, and that point is determined not by the logic of nationalism, but by the configuration of interest and power between the rulers and the ruled and between competing nations.[2]

False dichotomies between "civil" and "primordial" ties and condemnations of cultural nationalism wrongly slide past the Morgenthau A-B-C paradox. If there is no logical, philosophical, or sociological limit to nationalism, then the point at which one states the process of national liberation has proceeded far enough is a matter of political choice. While the politician is aware of the power component of this decision, the social scientist often shrouds the political dimensions of this issue in theories of political integration that reify existing state boundaries.

Once we reject the notion that "tribalism," "communalism," and various forms of cultural nationalism are atavistic, irrational retreats into tradition, but rather consider them to involve concrete configurations of power among groups within a nation and/or between nations, our perspective is broadened. Cultural nationalism should be seen as one of a number of ideologies available for purposes of mobilization to groups that seek greater power. The question, then, is under what circumstances cultural nationalist ideologies emerge, become progressive or reactionary, serve as effective mobilization tools, and so on.

The malleability of political identity has been shown in Tamil Nadu; it has been defined as non-Brahmin, Dravidian, and Tamilian at various historical moments. If Tamil Nadu were studied at only one historical point, this process of identity transformation would be lost since each identity seemed primordial during its era. Thus, in accounting for the emergence of the Tamil cultural nationalist movement, it would be misleading to assume a "basic group identity" that was merely politicized. Rather the first question must be, why did a certain form of political identity arise? How and why did it lead to a cultural nationalist movement?

WHY CULTURAL NATIONALISM?

A brief summary of the development of cultural nationalism is appropriate before answering these questions. In Tamil Nadu the first step was the emergence of the concept "non-Brahmin" as part of Justice party and Self-Respect League activities in the 1920s. These organizations were an ideological challenge to Brahmin orthodoxy, highest caste ranking, political prominence, and numerical domination of university seats and jobs in the British administration. Before the 1920s, "non-Brahmin" had no specific cultural, social, or political relevance. The "non-Brahmin community" is a cultural construct which united diverse castes within an encompassing political identity.

So the first change in identity was the addition of an inclusive "non-Brahmin" identity to the traditional discrete caste identities. Two factors in this process should be kept in mind. One is that "non-Brahmin" identity did not replace discrete caste identity at the local village or district level, but rather redefined the political implications of caste identity at the regional (that is, state) level in Dravidian ideological terms. A major factor linking the specific caste identity of "forward" non-Brahmin castes with a generalized "non-Brahmin" identity was the negative symbol "Suddhra." Second, only certain groups were affected by changes in identity during the 1920s. The relevant political community during this period consisted of Brahmins, elite (later "forward") non-Brahmins, and a smattering of wealthy, educated, or exceptional backward caste and Untouchable individuals. It was in this limited, elite-dominated arena that the Dravidian ideology emerged, and it was elite non-Brahmins (and particularly Tamil elite non-Brahmins) who first responded to that ideology.

The Justice party and Self-Respect League were composed of elite non-Brahmins who felt a loss of status and power as a result of both urbanization and the impact of the British administration in changing the relative position of Brahmins and elite non-Brahmins. It was this sense of loss that made "Suddhra" a poignant emotional symbol and instigated the demand for religious and social reform. The "downtrodden Dravidians" or "downtrodden non-Brahmins" metaphor became a powerful force for non-Brahmin political unity. It legitimated attempts to form new non-Brahmin political organizations and to redress Brahmin numerical superiority in the administration and universities. Although the symbolic elements of the Dravidian ideology were rather loosely integrated up to 1938 (the first demand for a separate Dravida Nadu), the conviction of past Dravidian greatness was a link between the status and power aspects of the ideology. Pre-Aryan (that is, non-Brahmin, Dravidian) civilization was supposedly casteless, classless, and the most advanced in the world. There was a messianic regression into the past, as well as a hopeful projection into a vague future. The projection into the future looked to the destruction of caste and ritual (and for many, of Hinduism itself), and the return of Dravidians (non-Brahmins or non-Aryans) to positions of power. Here was an explanation of present "oppression" and a nascent program for a "positive" future.

In the 1930s, Dravidian ideology was radicalized chiefly through the efforts of E. V. Ramasami. For the radicials, demands for religious reform became attacks against Hinduism itself. However, both radicals and moderates agreed on the necessity for uplift of "non-Brahmins" and the use of ancient Dravidian civilization (supposedly casteless and classless) as a social, cultural, and political model.

In 1938, the implicit cultural challenge of the introduction of mandatory Hindi in schools stimulated the transformation of Dravidian cultural identity into Dravidian political identity. The "Dravidian nation" demanded a homeland of its own—Dravida Nadu (literally, country of the Dravidians). At this point the "non-Brahmin" movement, a name used interchangeably with Dravidian and Self-Respect movement to describe individuals, organizations, and activities of the non-Brahmin elites during the 1920s and 1930s, became the Dravidian independence movement.

For those non-Brahmins who internalized the Dravidian political identity during the radical phase from the 1930s to the late 1950s, that identity was embedded in an elaborate radical ideology according to which separation and a free Dravidian nation would achieve radical social reform. A substantial articulate segment of the current Dravida Munnetra Kazhagam party leadership, as well as some A–DMK leadership, were recruited during this radical period.

A counterpoint to these circumstances (significant for leaders) was the development of Dravidian identity at the mass level. In the 1940s, universal manhood suffrage expanded the elite-dominated political arena of the 1920s and 1930s into a mass arena. In 1949, E. V. Ramasami and C. N. Annadurai chose separate paths to achieve Dravidian ideological goals. After 1949, E. V. Ramasami, who retained the radical ideology but eventually changed his goal to a separate Tamil Nadu, is less significant for our purposes. Annadurai and the DMK, after a brief period of frenetic radical movement activity, abandoned the goal of radical social reform and the DMK became a political party.

Crucial to the change in the political arena after the 1940s, was the widespread horizontal mobilization of the "backward castes." These were castes of low ritual rank and (generally congruently) low economic status. Unlike the forward non-Brahmins, who saw themselves in opposition to Brahmins and the caste system (especially *varnashrama dharma*, which relegated them to Suddhra status), the orientation of the backward castes stressed their economic and social position as they faced competition from Untouchables (and other backward caste groups) below. They perceived their status threatened by those below, particularly previously subservient Untouchables, rather than by orthodox Brahmins above.

Many symbols of "cultural oppression" (particularly the symbol of "Suddhra") so crucial for forward non-Brahmins were irrelevant for the backward castes. Furthermore, the forward and backward non-Brahmins were generally divided by economic position (large landowner versus small landowner, or landowner versus agricultural laborer), and by rank in the traditional ritual hierarchy. For Annadurai the strategic problem was how to achieve a mass following in this transformed political arena, while striving to achieve the goals of the Dravidian movement. Out of this dilemma, increased elaboration of and stress on cultural nationalism developed.

In trying to mobilize a mass following, the DMK forged an image of the party as the champion of the "common man," the "middleman." It was this "common man" whom Annadurai "claimed to represent in all his ruggedness." This appeal was directed at the rising urban lower middle class, the educated, unemployed youth, the middling farmer, and particularly the backward castes. As Annadurai and the DMK modified the radical social reform aspects of the Dravidian ideology, greater emphasis was placed on the language issue (pro-Tamil/anti-Hindi), the desirability of a Tamil literary and linguistic renaissance, and other aspects of Tamil cultural nationalism. The DMK promised material and spiritual "uplift" of the "common man." Social reform, which had meant destruction of the caste system, came to mean "uplift of downtrodden" Tamilians. Thus, while the outlines of the radical Dravidian ideology were maintained, the meaning of basic symbols and overall emphasis were changed.

The DMK was able to capitalize on discontents aroused by political and economic modernization initiated by the Congress government. Under that government, Tamil Nadu experienced significant economic growth and had the most rapid increase of political participation of any Indian state, as measured by comparisons of voting turnout for the three general elections of 1957, 1962, and 1967.

Although the lives of many who became critical of the Congress government were improved through Congress policies, their political and social consciousness also expanded. As a result, the DMK could claim that Tamil Nadu was woefully neglected by the center. What it termed "step-motherly" treatment became the basis for antinorthern agitations. The DMK remedy was increased autonomy for Tamil Nadu under a party truly representative of Tamilians.

The charge of "step-motherly" treatment was often related to the supposed Aryan (northern) vs. Dravidian (southern) opposition, and the demand for state autonomy and true Tamilian rule was a contemporary version of the early 1920s slogan, "Dravida Nad is for Dravidians." Thus cultural nationalism provided a continuously relevant framework for DMK organizational development and eventual assumption of power in 1967.

During the Karunanidhi era another significant identity change occurred. After the DMK split, the two parties, DMK and A–DMK, began defining Tamil nationalism in conflicting terms. While the A–DMK returned to the earlier notion of Tamil nationalism linked to a Dravidian identity, the DMK counterposed Dravidian identity to Tamil nationalism. As the DMK drifted further into chauvinism in 1973 and 1974, their version of Tamil nationalism increasingly lost humanistic content and even literary excellence. The narrow, defensive speeches of this period were not delivered in "chaste and pure" literary Tamil, but in the "harsh" tones of the urban street.

A number of themes run through the above synopsis of the emergence of Tamil nationalism in the wake of the Dravidian movement: (1) modernization and its impact on Tamil society, including shifts in status; (2) perceptions of relative deprivation on the part of the non-Brahmin elite; (3) economic and social oppression of ex-Untouchables and backward non-Brahmins; (4) enhanced expectations of large segments of the population, including ex-Untouchables and the backward castes; and (5) the role of political leaders in raising identity issues and translating discontent into a set of ideologically based political demands.

Underlying these themes is the fact that the caste system, a fundamental aspect of identity, is undergoing a structural transformation.

To recapitulate these themes: The advent of British rule was a major factor altering traditional relationships between south Indian Brahmin and non-Brahmin elites. New lucrative positions were created by the development of a large-scale British bureaucracy, and British educational institutions were established to fill these new positions. Urbanization also disrupted traditional life styles. Modernization, British rule, and urbanization initially enhanced the position of Brahmins vis-à-vis traditional non-Brahmin elites.

Karl Deutsch has noted the importance of the "leading social group" in nationalist development:

> At all times, however, it will be necessary for the "leading social group" to be "above" some of the main groups to be led, at least in terms of current prestige, and usually in the long run in terms of economic, political, and social opportunities, skills, wealth, organization, and the like. So that a member of another social group, on joining this "leading group" would have in some sense a real experience of "rising in the world," or . . . of "moving vertically in society."

> As an alignment with a center and a leading group, nationality offers to its members the possibility of vertical substitution unbroken from any one link to the next. In a competitive economy or culture, nationality is an implied claim to privilege. It emphasizes group preference and group peculiarities, and so tends to keep out all outside competitors.[3]

In the 1920s, elite non-Brahmins emerged as the "leading social group," the carriers of nationalism in Deutsch's sense. However, Dravidian ideology took the form it did not simply because elite non-Brahmins were the "leading social group" but because of the character of the pressures and constraints they faced at the time of initial ideological development. Nationalism, can be progressive or reactionary. At the outset, Dravidian ideology and Dravidian identity had a strongly progressive social-reform character because these elite non-Brahmins believed they had to attack the very structure of society to accomplish their ends.

As they achieved some goals and reestablished their position vis-à-vis Brahmins, their orientation changed.

After mass mobilization of the backward classes during the 1940s and their recruitment into positions of political leadership, the nature of the leading social group changed. While Brahmins and some elite non-Brahmins still occupy the top of the hierarchy and remain economically dominant, backward non-Brahmins, because of sheer numerical presence, have become assimilated into the leading social group. As the political arena has been increasingly impacted by backward non-Brahmin presence, and as they have come to constitute the new political elite—the leading social group—so, too, the character of nationalist ideology has changed. Emergence of Tamil nationalism as a diffuse idealization of the "common man" is rooted in backward non-Brahmin interests.

While the concept of relative deprivation provides a shorthand description of the underlying motivation for the transformation in political consciousness during the sixty years covered in this study, the nature of the perceived deprivation changes. When Brahmins were the leading political elite, many wealthy elite non-Brahmins believed themselves deprived because of a perceived decline in status in relation to Brahmins. They shook the entire society in their efforts to dislodge that tiny Brahmin minority from leadership. Once elite non-Brahmins became the leading political elite, backward non-Brahmins found both Brahmins and elite non-Brahmins above them blocking the road to enhanced political power. Most members of backward non-Brahmin castes are poverty-stricken victims of a caste system in which they are ranked low. Increased education, rapid advancements in communication, and a highly politicized environment increased the political awareness, consciousness, and expectations of backward castes. But their assimilation into the political elite was characterized by attempts to emulate elite non-Brahmins (hence the increase in individuals designating themselves "Mudaliars" or "Vellalas" in recent years) and efforts to maintain dominance over the poorest and lowest-ranked group, the Untouchables.

Crucial to the entire process has been political leadership, a leadership that decisively translated these social strains into a cultural nationalist framework. Rupert Emerson views nationalism as the psychological response of new nations to the West.[4]

While territorial nationalism was the response of the Congress-led independence movement to the West, Dravidian (and later Tamil) cultural nationalism responded to Congress territorial nationalism.

Whether or not cultural nationalism arises is not a function of the direct translation of "objective conditions," social cleavage, or primordial sentiments into political identity. The perception of "objective conditions" constitutes a necessary, but not a sufficient, condition for the rise of cultural nationalism. Someone must define (or create) the collectivity and relate it to a greater whole. Whether cultural nationalism arises, and the specific form it takes, is partially a function of leadership. Similarly, the relationship of a particular cultural unit to the whole is a matter of ideological definition—a definition made by political leaders. What is important is not only the heterogeneity of the social universe, but the perception and interpretation of that heterogeneity.

Leonard Binder has emphasized the crucial role political leaders play in the political development process: "the success of the process depends upon the almost chance creation of a strata which are, by virtue of the peculiarities of their socialization and education, both willing and capable of presenting a behavioral and ideological synthesis of historical values and values associated with modernity.[5]

Provision of such an ideological synthesis has been a crucial function of Tamil Nadu political leaders. To expand upon Binder's notion of the ideological synthesis: political leadership must develop an ideological world view that provides creative (or at least reasonable) answers to pressing issues. This ideological synthesis, like ideology in general, will "draw its power from its capacity to grasp, formulate, and communicate social realities."[6]

All the processes noted have occurred in a dynamic socio-cultural environment. Emergence of abstract and collective individualism and ethnic-like caste blocs has been briefly discussed; both forms of individualism emerge from the breakdown of caste, and both draw on, as well as transform, relevant symbols from caste society. Political identity in a cultural nationalist context is based on the concept of collective individualism, stressing the priority of a self with historical, cultural attributes. We have discussed the emergence of collective individualism in Tamil Nadu, and have followed Tamil political life in terms of the interplay of caste, ethnic-like, and cultural nationalist ideologies. Emergence of individualism concommitantly with the breakdown of traditional caste hierarchy did not produce cultural nationalism, but cultural nationalism could not have arisen in the traditional, hierarchical, holistic caste system.

CULTURAL NATIONALISM AND PUBLIC POLICY

Once cultural nationalism became the dominant ideological theme, and once the DMK came to power, what were the policy consequences of Tamil cultural nationalism? Once in power, some of the inherent contradictions in the DMK cultural nationalist perspective began to emerge. Of particular importance were the dilemmas created by the existence of groups within the DMK "family" with competing class interests but overlapping nationalist sentiments. While Tamil cultural nationalism united Tamilians in opposition to northerners, it could not bridge concrete economic differences within Tamil Nadu. This is related to the vapid economic perceptions of cultural nationalist ideologies in general and of the Dravidian ideology in particular. Although the DMK, or at least Annadurai, advocated "scientific socialism," its implications were never clearly drawn. It was certainly not distinctly different from Congress socialism except for frequent reference to the supposedly classless nature of ancient Dravidian society. Once in power, a number of the DMK government's dilemmas were exacerbated by lack of economic analysis and by the skeletal organization of certain key economic segments of the population. The fact that a host of economic and welfare issues are not given priority determined which social groups the DMK stressed in its organizational development. There was substantial effort to mobilize students, for example, and less attention paid, before 1967, to urban and rural laborers. After coming to power, the DMK belatedly attempted to remedy this situation.

Another set of problems resulted from excesses in cultural nationalist enthusiasm by groups, particularly students, attempting to outdistance the DMK and coopt cultural nationalism for their own purposes. The easy cooptability of cultural nationalism makes it a potentially unstable ideological basis for a party. During the Annadurai era, the DMK adroitly handled problems that could have been politically fatal. Karunanidhi was less successful.

Although issues coming directly under the aegis of Tamil cultural nationalist ideology are relatively limited, it must confront the issue of national integration. DMK views on this subject are important in relating cultural nationalism and Tamil political identity to the broader question of political development. The party insists that the key issue is not emotional integration but an ethnic and regional balance of power and cultural recognition. In other words, they desire a redistribution of power and regional equity as cornerstones of the integration of various cultural units within the all-India framework.[7]

There are several significant aspects to the DMK theory of Indian federalism and national integration. It specifically rejects the position (held by many politicians and social scientists) that political integration involves the creation of common values and the elimination of "primordial" attachments. Instead, the DMK supports attempts to resolve through institutional means what it poses as the two central issues of political integration: social and economic deprivation, and cultural recognition.[8] This view is seconded by a small but growing school of revisionist political scientists. Aristide Zolberg, for example, argues that

> social science tends to reflect two models of national integration only: a pluralist version derived from an idealisation of the American experience, which involves the creation of cross-cutting affiliations by superimposing non-coincidental cleavages over primordial ones, culminating in hyphenated identities; and an assimilationist version, derived from an idealization of French experience, which assumes that primordial and civil ties are virtually exclusive and that integration takes the form of a sort of zero-sum game culminating in the emergence of a homogeneous nation.[9]

Zolberg terms it "unfortunate from a theoretical point of view" that "models derived from the institutionalisation of arrangements which assume the persistence of distinct subnational identities tend to be dispersed as quaint sports if they are relatively stable and do not conflict with salient contemporary values . . . or as pathological cases if they appear to be a source of recurrent conflict."[10]

What is suggested by the revisionist conception of political integration is that value integration is not a goal per se, but should be viewed in the context of social change: so-called common values may center precisely around explicit recognition of communal identity.

More useful than pursuing value homogeneity might be a perspective that tries to understand how culturally pluralistic societies live with their pluralism: a perspective that emphasizes the conditions of political accommodation and mitigation of conflict. We begin by asking how diverse cultural nationalisms can be accommodated within one territorial (federal) unit. The example of Tamil Nadu is suggestive. Although separatism remains a strong underlying theme in Tamil Nadu political culture, this is not evidence of the incompatibility of cultural nationalism and territorial nationalism. The patriotic DMK response to the Indian-Chinese 1962 border incident shows clearly the compatibility of these two nationalisms. In fact, it may be that a strong commitment to either one could, under the correct historical circumstances, pave the way for the emergence of the other. The idea of nationalist commitment may be the important learned response, not the unit to which that commitment is made. Communal loyalties need not necessarily infringe on national integration, but can add a dimension to it. It would be incorrect to say that the burst of DMK patriotism in 1962 indicates that Tamil nationalist sentiment had been transformed; it was only a further demonstration that a zero-sum model of political identity is misleading.

Secondly, the Tamil Nadu example suggests the importance of federalism and decentralization in mitigating conflict between cultural and territorial nationalist perspectives or among competitive cultural nationalist perspectives. Control of Tamil Nadu provides the opportunity for at least partial Tamil cultural fulfillment, and the power base for tackling the equity question within the constitutional framework. This raises a third important point. Although cultural nationalism has an emotional component, it is a mistake to consider its appeal entirely nonrational. Besides the strong emotional element, there is also likely to be an issue of power and a concrete conflict of interest at stake: On whose terms is integration to be sought; and for what goals?

One must, of course, be cautious in extending these generalizations to other societies, and careful not to reify institutional arrangements and political accommodation as the final solution to problems of integration. As has been shown in this study, definition of political identity is neither automatic nor static, but a dynamic process shaped by leadership and government policy. The rise of cultural nationalism has been interpreted as a collective individualist response to territorial nationalism, which is historically and ideologically based on abstract individualism. If loyalty is assumed to be individualistic, a personal relationship between an historical self and the nation-state, other intervening communal solidarities are logically suspect. When collectivities that perceive themselves as communal seek to enhance their power in response to felt deprivation, the potential exists for politicizing the communal bond among historical selves with a shared culture. Since nationalism has come to be identified in world political culture as the locus of power, this politicization often takes the form of cultural nationalism. Whether the potential for cultural nationalism is exploited and the direction that nationalism takes depends on political leadership.

This interpretation of cultural nationalism sees it as coexisting with territorial nationalism in a dialectical relationship. Instead of viewing social cleavages as "givens" that create political identity, it has been shown that political leadership can emphasize and virtually "create" identities. When examined over time, the emotion surrounding seemingly primordial sentiments was found to have been shaped by political leaders. In analyzing nationalism, therfore, the effort has been to account for the factors that motivated top leaders (the leading social group of elites) and masses. Two kinds of issues have persistently lurked beneath the nationalist surface: status dislocations and perceived economic deprivation.

Over the past sixty years Tamil/Dravidian nationalism legitimized elite non-Brahmin rise to power during the 1920s and 1930s; rationalized backward non-Brahmin mass participation and assimilation into the political elite; and facilitated the political integration of Tamil Nadu society by providing an ideological basis for unity encompassing caste. While the continued relevance of a cultural nationalist ideological orientation to national (all-India) integration has been explored, continued internal (intra-Tamil Nadu) relevance is problematic.

Whether cultural nationalism can remain a viable ideology for future mass mobilization will depend on its perceived utility as a program, map, or guide; its legitimizing potential; and its capacity to arouse mass support. Since all major Tamil Nadu parties—the DMK, A-DMK, Congress (O), and Congress (R) are to some degree committed to Tamil Nationalism,[11] it might be increasingly difficult to use nationalism for mobilization on internal issues.

Two types of issues loom on the political horizon. The first involves adi-Dravida. Adi-Dravida caste social isolation is increasing, since rules of hierarchy are maintained for ex-Untouchables even while they are breaking down among other castes, and there is evidence that a belief that adi-Dravidas are phenotypically different is emerging.[12] Furthermore, the economic plight of adi-Dravidas has remained dismal. Ideologically, adi-Dravidas are integrated in the nationalist universe. They are the "Adi" or "first" Dravidians. In concrete social, cultural, and economic terms, this has meant little. Thus, like Blacks in the United States, adi-Dravidas will be faced with the difficult task of trying to use politics for social, cultural, and political purposes. This effort may well generate the next great status conflict in Tamil Nadu.

The second issue is the emergence of insistent class interests and the potential for class conflicts. This potential arises, given a growing urban industrial work force and a rising sense of deprivation and unrest among landless laborers and small landholders in the countryside. In a universe dominated by caste, class seemed more an abstraction than a template for action. But if class consciousness and conflicts develop, it will not necessarily mean the demise of Tamil nationalism. The argument has already been made that political identity is not a zero-sum concept. Class loyalties could be accommodated within a cultural nationalist political arena, and, indeed, success in mobilization around class issues may depend on the capacity to map caste, Tamil nationalism, and class onto the same outline.

Whatever the future of Tamil Nadu politics, Tamilians will confront it as a "people," with a sense of their past greatness and future destiny. It is this self-perception of peoplehood that is the outcome of a polity dominated by a search for identity for over half a century.

[1] Hans J. Morgenthau, "The Paradoxes of Nationalism," *Yale Review* 46 (June 1957), 481.

[2] *Ibid.*, p. 485.

[3] Karl Deutsch, *Nationalism and Social Communication* (Cambridge, Mass: M.I.T. Press, 1966) p. 102.

[4] See Rupert Emerson, *From Empire to Nation* (Cambridge, Mass: Harvard University Press, 1960).

[5] Leonard Binder, "National Integration and Political Development," *American Political Science Review* 58 (September 1964), 631.

[6] Geertz, "Ideology as a Cultural System," p. 58.

[7] For a similar view of Indian political integration see B. R. Ambedkar, *Thoughts on Linguistic States* (Delhi: B. R. Ambedkar, 1955).

[8] As Richard Sklar points out ("Political Science and National Integration," *Journal of Modern African Studies* 5, 1967, 1), political scientists have also tried "to comprehend the twin issues of social deprivation and parochial separatism together. The concept of national integration has been defined to satisy that need."

[9] Aristide Zolberg, "Patterns of National Integration," *Journal of Modern African Studies* 5 (December 1967), 451.

[10] *Ibid.*

[11] Congress (R) less so than the other parties. However, recently some Tamil nationalist members of Congress (O) have joined Congress (R).

[12] Barnett and Barnett, "Contemporary Peasant and Post-Peasant Alternatives in South India."

APPENDICES

Communal Representation of Gazetted and Non-Gazetted Officers in Province of Madras

(percent)

	1930	1931	1932	1933
Gazetted officers				
Brahmins	39.23	38.87	38.82	38.82
Non-Brahmins	20.71	21.28	20.84	21.68
Scheduled castes	—	.12	.12	.12
Muhammadans	4.40	4.65	4.79	5.27
Non-Asiatics and Anglo-Indians	27.20	25.76	26.21	25.02
Indian Christians	7.74	8.68	8.70	8.42
Others	.72	.64	.53	.67
Non-gazetted officers, RS 100 and over				
Brahmins	51.44	50.22	49.05	50.01
Non-Brahmins	29.35	29.64	30.11	29.87
Scheduled castes	.12	.09	.15	.20
Muhammadans	4.69	4.86	5.61	5.17
Non-Asiatics and Anglo-Indians	6.25	6.54	6.44	5.88
Indian Christians	8.05	8.56	8.50	9.01
Others	.10	.09	.14	.15

1934	1935	1936	1937	1938	1939	1940
			Gazetted officers			
39.07	39.35	38.47	38.78	38.25	37.52	36.39
21.86	21.66	23.25	23.56	25.00	25.14	26.11
.12	.36	.25	.25	.44	.56	.63
5.56	6.06	6.14	6.19	6.53	6.14	6.77
24.09	23.51	22.37	21.52	20.17	20.06	20.13
8.64	8.46	8.83	8.88	8.92	9.75	9.52
.66	.60	.69	.75	.69	.56	.45
		Non-gazetted officers, RS 100 and over				
49.21	48.49	47.76	47.23	46.44	45.53	45.07
30.38	30.88	30.71	31.45	31.56	32.53	33.27
.20	.33	.25	.21	.34	.36	.36
5.17	4.98	5.43	5.55	5.75	5.96	6.30
5.88	5.84	5.95	5.74	5.75	5.96	5.19
9.01	9.37	9.84	9.76	10.10	9.60	9.75
.15	.11	.06	.06	.06	.06	.06

Source: GO527 (Public Works), 1940.
Note: GO527 also provided the following information on population statistics: Brahmins, 1,351,814; non-Brahmins, 30,657,439; Muslims, 3,305,937; Christians, 1,774,276; others, 9,650,641. According to population in a twelve-unit allotment, Brahmins were entitled to .3 of all new vacancies, non-Brahmins, 8.5; Muslims, .8; Christians, .4; and all others, 2.

Method for Sampling Party Leaders

THE DMK was holding organizational elections in 1968 for the first time in eight years. In order to conduct these elections, the party had to reorganize its own files. A DMK branch consists of at least twenty-five members plus a general secretary, a treasurer, a chairmen, and six members of the executive committee. The universe from which the sample of DMK local-level leaders was drawn consisted of all village, taluk, and circle (city) secretaries, treasurers, and executive committee members in Tamil Nadu. Appendix C gives the number of branches, number of taluk committees, and size of the sample drawn from each district.

In taking the sample, I estimated from the information below that the total universe of DMK local-level leaders was somewhere around 60,000 leaders. (6,475 + 101 multiplied by 9, which is 59,175, rounded off to 60,000.) I originally wanted to get a sample of 600, so I went through the files and took every one-hundredth leader for the sample. This process yielded a sample of 700, indicating the original estimate was too low. The reason for this, I think, is clear. With the emergence of the DMK as the ruling party, there was a rush of new members. As the chairmen of the DMK head office, Mr. Veeraswami, indicated, the party was having difficulty handling all of the new members. Although new branches and members are cataloged in the file I used, it takes more time for the official tally to be reorganized.

The following questionnaires were sent to DMK leaders. The Congress questionnaire was modeled on this one, with appropriate modifications reflecting Congress organization and history.

DMK LOCAL-LEVEL QUESTIONNAIRE

1. Please indicate your branch:
   Please indicate your taluk:
   Please indicate your district:
2. Do you hold any office in the D.M.K. party?
   Yes____ No____

3. If you hold an office, which office do you hold? Party Office?
4. When did you first join the D.M.K.? Year:
5. Did you belong to the D.K.?
   Yes___ No___
6. Have you ever belonged to or supported another party?
   Yes___ No___
7. If you have belonged to or supported another party, which party?
8. What first attracted you to the D.M.K. party?
9. What is it about the D.M.K. party now (1968) which attracts?
10. Have you been active in any D.M.K. agitations?
    (a) 1938 Anti Hindi   Yes___ No___
    (b) 1950 Three corner   Yes___ No___
    (c) 1965 Anti Hindi   Yes___ No___
    (d) Others (Please give date and purpose of agitation below including non-D.M.K. agitations i.e., 1942 Civil disobedience movement).
11. What are the major problems facing your district?
12. What do you consider are the major problems facing Madras state today?
13. Do you try to maintain the traditional religious and social customs of your community?
    Religious   Yes___ No___
    Social   Yes___ No___
14. (a) Age
    (b) Occupation
    (c) Income per Year
    (d) Caste
    (e) Education
    (f) Father education
    (g) Father's income per Year

DMK GENERAL COUNCIL QUESTIONNAIRE

1. How long have you been a member of the General Council?
2. Do you hold any other offices in the D.M.K. Party?
3. Have you ever held any other offices in the D.M.K. Party?
4. How long have you been a member of the D.M.K. Party?

5. Did you belong to the D.K.?
6. Have you ever belonged to or supported another party?
   If yes, which party?
7. Have you ever held any elected public office?
   If so, when and which office?
8. Have you ever held any appointed public office?
9. When and how did you become interested in politics?
10. What first attracted you to the D.M.K. Party?
11. What do you personally find most attractive about the
    D.M.K. now (1968)?
12. When you first joined the D.M.K. what do you think
    attracted other new members and supporters?
13. Now (in 1968) what do you think attracts new members,
    supporters and/or voters?
14. Have you been active in any D.M.K. agitations?
    1938 Anti-Hindi?
    1953 3-Corner
    1965 Anti-Hindi
15. Have you ever been active in any non-D.M.K. agitations?
16. Are you now or were you in the past a member of the
    D.M.K. student federation?
17. Do you belong to any other organizations like Sabhas,
    Sanghams, labor unions, businessmen's associations, etc.
    Please list.
18. What do you feel are the major problems facing your
    district?
19. What do you feel are the major problems facing Madras
    State today?
20. What do you feel are the major national problems?
21. Are there any international problems that concern you?
22. What is the most important problem facing the D.M.K.
    as the ruling Party?
23. What would you consider to be the most important goal
    the D.M.K. can achieve as the ruling party in Tamil Nadu?
24. Do you try to maintain the traditional religious and social
    customs of your community?
25. Since 1949, the General Council has made many important
    decisions, what do you consider to be the three most
    important decisions made by the General Council?
26. In what way do you feel the decisions mentioned above
    have been important to the party. That is, why do you

feel they have been the -most important decisions made
by the General Council?

27. (a) Name
    (b) Birthplace
    (c) Date of birth
    (d) Age
    (e) Education
    (f) Father's education
    (g) Income per year
    (h) Father's income per Year
    (i) Occupation
    (j) Father's occupation
    (k) Caste

The following questionnaire was sent to the Tamil Nadu
Congress (Pradesh) Committee (TNCC).

CONGRESS QUESTIONNAIRE

1. Please indicate your branch:
   Please indicate your taluk:
   Please indicate your district:
2. What office do you hold in the Congress party?
3. When did you join the Congress? Year:
4. Have you ever belonged to or supported any other political
   party?
   Yes____ No____
5. Have you belonged to or supported any other political
   movement?
   Yes____ No____
6. What first attracted you to the Congress party?
7. In 1968, what attracts you to the Congress party?
8. Have you participated in any Congress agitations? Please
   list below.
9. Have you participated in any agitations of other political
   parties? Please list below.
10. What are the major problems facing your district?
11. What do you consider to be the major problems facing
    Madras State today?
12. Do you try to maintain the traditional religious and social
    customs of your community?

(a) Age
(b) Occupation
(c) Income per Year
(d) Father's income per Year
(e) Education
(f) Father's education
(g) Caste

DMK Organization

	Branches	Taluk committees	DMK local-level leadership sample by district
Chingleput	600	9	32
Coimbatore	600	10	35
Madras City	100	—	14
South Arcot	600	9	35
Tirunelveli	400	8	42
Salem	550	6	21
Tanjore	1,000	13	58
Madurai	500	8	49
Trichy	800	10	56
Ramnadapuram	500	9	46
Dharmapuram	175	4	13
North Arcot	450	11	48
Kanyakumari	200	4	10
Total	6,475	101	459

Other places not sampled:	Andhra Pradesh	28 branches
	Mysore	28 branches

Also some members in Delhi, Andamans, Bombay

Questionnaire for Neighborhood Survey

PART I

1. Address:
2. Name: Age
3. Caste (Specific):
4. Vegetarian or non-vegetarian:
5. Present occupation:
6. Held since:
7. Did anyone help get this job (who):
8. Previous occupation:
9. Educational level:
10. How long in present house?
11. Rented or own?
12. If rented, from whom?
13. Previous house location:
14. Father's occupation:
15. Father's residence:
16. Father's native place:
17. Other members of the house:
    Name   Age   Relation   Occupation   Education

18. Do you go to "Old Town" temples?
19. Which ones and how often (specific days)?
20. Are you a member of any club or organization?
21. Five best friends:
    Residence   Job   Caste
    (a)
    (b)
    (c)
    (d)
    (e)
22. Three most important people in "Old Town"
    (a)
    (b)
    (c)

23. Caste with most influence in "Old Town"
24. Three wealthiest castes in "Old Town"
25. Political party membership: Support:
26. Voting in 1957:   1962:   1967:
27. Do you follow community traditional customs?

Note: This survey was designed and administered together with Steve Barnett. This questionnaire was administered to every head of household in "old Town," approximately 1900 persons.

PART II: POLITICAL QUESTIONNAIRE

Name and Address of Respondent:
Interviewers Name:
Date:
Time:

1. We'd like to start out by talking about some of your more general interests. Now aside from your work and your family, what are the activities that interest you most, that you spend your free time on?
   (a) If you had more free time and opportunity, which activities would you like to engage in?
2. Here are some important problems facing the people in this country. Would you please listen to this list and tell me which one you feel is most important to you personally?
   (a) spiritual and moral betterment
   (b) making ends meet
   (c) government control and regulation of business
   (d) eliminating inequality and injustice
   (e) foreign affairs and national defence
   (f) improving conditions for your family
   Are there other problems not mentioned in this list that you feel are more important or as important as these?
3. What do you consider to be the major problems facing this neighbourhood?
   (a) Can any political party help solve the problems in this neighborhood? Which political party do you think is better able to help solve some of the problems in this neighborhood?
   (b) In September there will be an election for municipal council from this neighborhood. Besides the problems

which you mentioned above what other factors about the candidates or the parties will determine which candidate you support?

4. What about Madras State. What problems do you think are the most important problems facing Madras State? Which political party do you feel has the best program to solve these problems?

   (a) (If not previously mentioned) What about problems like the place of Hindi in Tamil Nadu. Are you concerned about that problem? What are your views on this issue?

   Some people feel that this problem could lead to a separate Tamil Nadu. Do you think so?

   Would you be in favour of a separate Tamil Nadu? Why?

5. What do you consider to be the most important problems facing India as a nation?

6. Do specific problems such as these interest you? That is, are you worried about them? (Pause after each problem)

   (a) The War in Vietnam
   (b) Racism in South Africa
   (c) Closing of the Coimbatore Mills
   (d) Chinese aggression on Indias borders
   (e) Indian Economic Development
   (f) Existence of the caste system
   (g) Condition of the Harijans
   (h) Condition of the Suddhra castes
   (i) Devaluation of the English pound.

   Do you feel that political parties should take a stand on any of the above problems? Which ones?

7. All of us have ideas about what people are like. If you had to describe Tamilians in one word or phrase, how would you describe them?

   (a) How about North Indians. If you had to describe them in one word or phrase, how would you describe them?

8. Within Tamil Nadu, there are many communities (jatis). Some are coming forward and others are not. Which communities would you describe as the *most* forward? Which would you say are the most backward? Why have some communities come forward while others have not?

9. Do you follow accounts of political and government affairs

in the newspapers? How often?

(a) Which newspapers do you read?

10. What about public meetings? Do you often attend public meetings at which political problems are discussed?

(a) Have you ever attended public meetings arranged by the: (pause after each organization)

Congress   Swatantra
Dravida Munnetra Kazhagam   Dravida Kazhagam
Communist parties

(If respondent attends more than one party meeting, ask: Which party meetings do you attend most often?)

11. What about the radio. Do you follow public affairs on the radio?

(a) regularly
(b) often
(c) never

12. Do you often attend the cinema?

(a) once a week
(b) twice a month
(c) once a month
(d) other

13. I would like to ask you about some of the social customs in this neighborhood.

(a) Do you wear any religious or caste marks?

(b) Will you accept cooked rice from all people? (If not) From which people would you *not* accept cooked rice from?

(c) Would you use the polite form to an elderly Brahman, an elderly Naicker, an elderly Paraiyan?

(d) Would you give your son or daughter in marriage to a boy or girl who was not a member of your community?

(e) Would you arrange a self-respect marriage for our son or daughter?

(f) Remembering back to when you were a child, say 10 or 11, do you feel that your attitudes toward any of the five social customs mentioned above (wearing of religious marks, accepting cooked rice, use of the polite form, marriage) have changed during your life time? (If yes) What would you say was the main reason for this change?

14. Some people say that political and governmental affairs

are so complicated that the average man cannot really understand what is going on. In general, do you agree or disagree with this?

(a) Thinking of the important national and international issues facing this country, how well do you think you can understand them?

15. I would now like to ask your opinion about the different political parties in Madras State.

(a) For example. What are some of the good policies of the Congress Party? What are some of the bad policies of the Congress Party? What kinds of people vote for and support the Congress party.

(b) What about the DMK. What are some of the good policies of the DMK? What are some of the bad policies of the DMK? What sorts of people vote for and support the DMK party?

(c) What about the communist parties. What are some of the good policies of the communist parties? What are some of their bad policies? What kinds of people vote for and support the communist parties?

(d) What about the Swatantra party. What are some of its good policies? What are some of its bad policies? What kinds of people vote for and support the Swatantra party.

(e) What about the Tamil Arasu Kazhagam. What are some of its good policies? What are some of its bad policies? What kinds of people support the Tamil Arasu Kazhagam?

(f) How about the Muslim League. What are some of its good policies? What are some of its bad policies? What kinds of people support the Muslim League?

Now I would like to ask you about a non-political organization, the Dravida Kazhagam. What does it stand for? What are some of its good qualities? What are some of its bad qualities? What kinds of people support the Dravida Kazhagam?

16. One sometimes hears that some people or groups have so much influence over the way the government is run that the interests of the majority are ignored? Do you agree or disagree that there are such groups?

(If respondent answers yes, ask)

(a) What are some of these groups? Why are they able to influence the government?

17. Here is a different kind of question. Suppose there was some problem that you had to take to a government office. Do you think you would be given equal treatment? I mean would you be treated as well as anyone else? (If respondent answers no, ask) Why not?

    (a) If you had to go to a government office for some important matter, would you take anyone with you to help you get a better bearing? Who would you take? Why would you take this person?

18. Suppose several men were trying to influence a government decision. Here are some things they might do. The first man works through personal and family connections with government officials. The second man writes to government officials explaining his point of view. The third tries to get people interested in the problem and to form a group. The fourth man works through his party. A fifth man organizes a protest demonstration. Which one of these methods do you think would be the least effective? I'll read the list again.

1. Working through personal and family connections
2. Writing to government officials
3. Getting people interested, forming a group
4. Working through a political party
5. Organizing a protest demonstration

    (a) Which one of these methods do you think would be the most effective?

19. How I'd like to ask you another kind of question. Here are some things that people say. We want to find out how other people feel about these things. I'll read them one at a time, and you tell me offhand whether you agree or disagree.

    (a) The way people vote is the main thing that decides how things are run in this country.

    (b) If you don't watch yourself, people will take advantage of you

    (c) A few strong leaders would do more for this country than all the laws and talk

    (d) All candidates sound good in their speeches, but you can never tell what they will do after they are elected

    (e) Human nature is fundamentally co-operative

    (f) People like me don't have any say about what the government does

(g) The individual owes his first duty to the state and only secondarily to his personal welfare

(h) No one is going to care much what happens to you, when you get right down to it.

20. I would now like to read to you a list of leading political personalities. If you have heard of the man, please indicate if you admire the man mentioned by responding either yes you admire him or no you don't. If you have not heard of him please say you don't know him.

1. C. N. Annadurai	14. Dr. Ambedkar
2. Mahatma Gandhi	15. Jayaprakash Narayain
3. Jawaharlal Nehru	16. Indira Gandhi
4. Lyndon Johnson	17. Ho Chi Min
5. Leonid Brezhnev	18. Dr. Martin Luther King
6. N. R. Nedunchezhian	19. M. P. Sivagnanam
7. C. Subramaniam	20. S. B. Adithan
8. E. M. S. Nambudiripad	21. M. Kalyanasundaram
9. Kamaraj Nadar	22. M. G. Ramachandran
10. Periyar E. V. Ramasami	23. Dr. Satyavani Muthu
11. Mao Tse Tung	24. Adolph Hitler
12. C. Rajaji	25. M. Karunanidhi
13. J. F. Kennedy	26. Dr. Zahir Hussein

21. Finally, if you had to describe politicians in one word, or phrase, which one word or phrase would you say best describes them?

Thank You

For the interviewer:

Rapport: 1 . . . (Excellent)   Economic Class
        2 . . . (V. Good)
        3 . . . (Fair)   upper
        4 . . . (Bad)   upper middle
                                    middle middle
Please list below any ques-   lower middle
tions which you feel the re-   lower class
spondents answered falsely   hut dweller
or hesitantly.

Other Comments:

Note: This questionnaire was administered to a sample of "Old Town" household heads. Over two hundred people were interviewed.

Bibliography

A NOTE ON SOURCES

NUMEROUS sources were used in this study, including Tamil and English newspaper articles; pamphlets, articles, and books in Tamil and English; unpublished manuscripts; and speeches and information from public events. Access to government documents at the Tamil Nadu Archives was of particular importance. I was allowed to consult government orders (GOs), files, and documents for the period 1920 to 1962. Some of the most helpful documents were collectors' reports and records of collectors' meetings; police reports (particularly reports on content and attendence of political meetings); and the Madras Presidency Native Newspaper Reports. These reports contain English translations of articles in the Madras Presidency vernacular press. I was specifically interested in articles on the ideology and activities of the Justice party and non-Brahmin movement during the 1920s and 1930s. In general, government records in the Tamil Nadu Archives provided an invaluable insight into government policy toward Dravidian movement organizations.

Private files and home libraries are the sole source of large collections of Dravidian movement propaganda material. Most DMK leaders have collections of their own published works. For the scholar interested in Dravidian ideology, a vast number of pamphlets, plays, poems, songs, etc., exist in Tamil. The most systematic way to collect these materials is through DMK mandrams and reading rooms.

I was fortunate enough to be given a virtually complete set of *Dravida Nadu* for the years 1956 through 1962. This enabled me to have a consistent record of DMK ideological statements and party activities during a crucial period. Other newspaper files were also consulted, including the *Mail, Hindu, Indian Express, Link, Times of India,* and *Hindustan Times* (these are major English newspapers). Major Tamil papers consulted included *Nam Nadu* (official organ of the DMK); *Viduthalai* (DK paper); *Murosoli* (published by DMK leader "Murosoli" Maran); and *Navasakthi* (Congress paper). *Homeland* (the DMK English weekly) files were also reviewed. Other newspapers, such as *Dinamani* and *Dina Thanthi*, were read as the occasion arose. The most complete historical use was made of three newspaper files: the *Indian Express*, 1949-1962; *Murosoli*, 1955 to 1969; and *Homeland*, 1957 to 1967. In general the Tamil press is a very useful source for political researchers. Also most newspapers keep good files, and are helpful in opening them to scholars.

The DMK headquarters staff was very helpful in securing material and in suggesting where to find particular kinds of information.

TAMIL PAMPHLETS AND BOOKS

Aṇṇaturai, C. N. "Molippōr" (War on Language). Trichy: Dravida Pannai, 1951.

———. "Aṇṇāvin Cor Celvam" (Wordly Wealth of Anna). Madras: Parry Nilayam, 1964.

———. "Apāya Arivippu" (Danger Signal). Madras: Anna Pathipaham, 1962.

———. *Āriyamāyai* (*Aryan Illusion*). Trichy: Dravida Pannai, 1954.

———. "Ellōrum Innāṭṭu Mannar" (All Are Kings in This Country). Kancheepuram: Sukamaran Pathipaham, 1961. Also appeared in November 1961 *Dravida Nadu*.

———. *Kānkiracin Kaṇmūtittarpār* (Blind Rule of Congress). Madras: Mackal Pathipaham, 1952.

———. "Kaṭcikaḷin Kataikal" (The Story of Political Parties). Madras: Anna Pathipaham, 1960.

———. "Makātmā Kānti" (Mahatma Gandhi). Trichy: Rajam Pathipaham, n.d.

———. "Maramalarcci" (Reawakening). N.p., 1945.

———. "Mēvirā" (May Day). Madras: Alamelu Nilayam, 1951.

———. "Nān Tanukin Rēn 1000 Kōṭi!" (I Gave 1000 Crores). Madras: Mackal Pathipaham, 1961.

———. "Nanparkal Kēṭpatalku" (For Friends to Hear). Kancheepuram: Parimalam Pathipaham, n.d.

———. "Pōnāṭṭam" (Agitation). Madras: Pathipaham Pannai, 1953.

———. *Tampikku Aṇṇāvin Kaṭitaṅkaḷ* (Brother's Letters to Brother). Madras: Parry Nilayam, 1963.

——. *Ti, Mu, Ka Virtu 68 Latsam* (68 Lakhs for the DMK). Madras: Mackal Mandram, 1962.

——. "Tirāviṭa Tecīyam" (Dravidian Nationality). Madras: Navalar Pathipaham, 1961.

——. *Varnāshramam (Varnashrama)*. Trichy: Dravida Pannai, 1952.

——. "Vitikku Aṭimaittamai" (Slavery to Fate). Velur: Dravidan Pathipaham, n.d.

Anparakam, K. "Toṇṭā Tuvēvimā?" (Service or Emnity?). Madras: Pudhu Vazhyoo Pathipaham, 1953.

Aramukkam, R. "Moṛi Enna Murunkkāyā?" (Is Language a Drumstick?) Pattukottai: Kumari Achamah, n.d.

Aṭaikkalam, S. "Mēṭaippāṭalkal" (DMK Stage Songs). Kancheepuram: n.p., 1956.

Iḷamāran, R. "Caṇtarppavāti Campaṭ" (Opportunist Sampath). Madras: Muthumani Pathipaham, 1961.

——. "Ti. Mu. Ka., Tēnicaippāṭalkaḷ" (Sweet Songs of the DMK). Madras: Muthumani Pathipaham, 1961.

Ilansilinkam, Vīram. "Moṛip Pōr" (Language War). Tanjore: n.p., 1949.

Iraimuṭimani, K. "Tirāviṭa Vācal" (Dravida Portacal). Madras: Thalapathi Pathipaham, 1955.

Kalaittōtan. *Tirāviṭk Kāmarācar, (Dravidian Kamaraj)*. Madurai: Seluyam Pathipaham, 1954.

Kannatāsan. *Vanavācam (Life in a Forest)*. Madras: Valambiri Pathipaham, 1965.

Karunaniti, Mu. "Orē Muttam" (Only One Kiss). Madras: Parry Nilayam, 1964.

——. "Palipēṭam Nōkki" (Towards the Goal). Madras: Munnetra Pannai, n.d.

——. "Tuṭikkum Iḷamai" (Eager Youth). Manuscript, 1951.

Kaunti. "Tērtalil Ti. Mu. Ka." (DMK in Election). Madras: Mackal Pathipaham, n.d.

Linkam, P. U. "Vaṛcakap Periyār (Scheming Periyar). N.p: K. Kannaiyan and Alagirisami Nool Nilayam, 1949.

Manokaran, K. "Urimaik Kural" (Sound of Right). Trichy: Tamil Mandram, 1952.

Maraimalaiyam, A. *Pērarinar Aṇṇavin Penavāṛvu (The Biography of Anna)*. Madras: Vanàthy, 1967.

Māran, Murosoli *Ēn Vēṇṭum Inpatirāviṭam?* (Why Do We Want This Sweet Dravidam?). Madras: Muthuval Pathipaham, 1962.

————. "Nāḷai Namatē!" (Tomorrow Is Ours). Madras: Muthuval Pathipaham, 1963.

Munisāmi, Tirukkural. "Tiruvaḷḷuvarum Tirāviṭa Koḷkaiyum" (Tiruvalluvar and Dravida Policy). Pudukottai: Senthamil Pathipaham, 1948.

Nākasanmukam. *Aṟinar Aṇṇaturai* (*Arignar Annadurai*). Madras: Vanathi Pathipaham, 1967.

Namasivāyam, M. "Ennai Kavarntavar" (One Who Attracted Me). Manuscript.

Neṭumāran. "Pōṭum Kanēcā Pulampatē" (Enough Ganesa— Lament Not). Madras: Anna Pathipaham, 1964.

Neṭunseṟiyan, V. R. *Tī. Mu. Ka.* (DMK). Madras: Tamilnad Puthaha Nilayam, 1961.

Ōṭuruvi. "Annavin Aṭukkuttoṭar" (Anna's Political Talk). Madras: Thuyamalar Pathipaham, 1961.

Paktavatsalam, Santirā. "Varalārril Tirāviṭam" (Dravidam in History). Madras: Chandrodayam, 1961.

Pālatatāyutam, K. *Jīvā Vārkkai Varalāru* (*Biography of Jeeva*). Madras: New Century Book House, 1966.

Pāratitāsan. "Aṟkin Cirippu" (A Beautiful Smile). Madras: Mullai, 1944.

————. "Tamiṟiyakkam" (Tamil Movement). Madras: Mullai, 1945.

Partasārati, T. M. *Tī. Mu. Kalaka Varalāṟu* (*History of the DMK*). Madras: Parry Nilayam, 1961.

Perunsittiran. "Ten Moṟi" (Southern Language). Cuddalore: Then Mozhi Min Pathipaham, 1967.

"Politician." *Aṇṇāvin Aracil Oru Kaṇṇēṭṭam* (*A Glance at Anna's Politics*). Madras: Tamil Dhesiya Party, 1962.

Rākavan, P. T. "Tī. Mu. Ka. Nāṉ Cūnyaṅkaḷ" (DMK Degenerates). Madras: Kanathara Veniyeedu, 1961.

Rāmasami, E. V. "Cāti Orippu" (Abolition of Castes). Erode: Kudi Arasu Pathipaham, 1961.

————. "Ciṇtani Tiraṭṭu" (Intellectual Collection). Tanjore: Sindanai Pannai, 1957.

————. "Ini Varum Ulakam" (The World To Come). Erode: Kudi Arasu Pathipaham, 1964.

————. "Inti Etirppuk Kiḷarcci" (Anti-Hindi Agitation). Madras: Unmai Vilakkam Pathipaham, 1965.

————. "Irāmayaṇa Kurippukal" (Points From the Ramayana). Madras: Kudi Arasu Veliyeedu, 1964.

————. "Tamiṟum Tamiṟ Ilkkiyalkaḷum" (Tamil and Tamil Literature). Madras: Pahutharim Veliyeedu, 1960.

———. "Tiravita Pōr Muraci" (Dravidians War Drum). N.p.: New Justice Publication, 1948.

———. "Tirukkuraḷum Manutarmamum" (Thirukkural and Manu's Dharma). Madras: Kalai Pathipaham, n.d.

Rāmasantiran, M. G. "Camanēti" (Equal Right). Madras: n.p., n.d.

———. "Ilatciyam Teevai" (Necessary Policy). Madras: Venkatesan, 1960.

Sanarttanam, A. P. "Tennattu Cākratēs" (South Indian Socrates). Madras: Arasu Nilayam, 1957.

Sanmukam, R. *Tirāvita Nātu Oru Veṅkāyam* (Dravida Nadu: an Onion). Madras: Madhura Nilayam, 1961.

Senkuttuvan, M. "Karakak Katirmaṇikal" (Important DMK People). Manuscript, 1967.

———. "Tamirc Col Kēḷir" (Listen to Tamil Words). Madras: Vanna, 1967.

Sinkāravēlu, M. "Camatarma Upanyācam (Lecture on Equality). Erode: Kudi Arasu Pathipaham, 1942.

Sitamparaṉār. "Suyārajyam Yārukku?" (Swaraj To Whom?). Erode: Kudi Arasu Pathipaham, 1947.

———. *Tamirar Talaivar (Tamilians' Leader)*. Erode: Kudi Arasu Press, 1939.

Tamirmani, S. "Ciraikkatavukal Tirakkattum" (Let The Prison Doors Open). Coimbatore: Subbu Pathipaham, 1964.

Tampi Turai. "Tirāvita Tōrakalē Kettu Pōkitarkaḷ" (Dravidian Friends, Don't Get Spoiled). Madras: Tamil Pannai, 1949.

"Ti Paravattum" (Let Fire Spread). Kancheepuram: Dravidanadu Achaham, 1943.

"Tirmañankaḷ" (Resolutions from Four-Day Provincial Conference at Madras in 1951). Manuscript from DMK headquarters.

Vēramani, K. "Tamira Nātā Tiravitanātā" (Tamil Country Or Dravidian Country). Erode: Kudi Arasu Pathipaham, 1961.

Villālan, Tillai. "Atikāra Pōtai" (Power Intoxication). Thiruvaiyar: Erimalai Pathipaham, 1948.

ARTICLES AND BOOKS IN EUROPEAN LANGUAGES

Almond, Gabriel. "Comparative Political Systems," *Journal of Politics* 18 (1956), 391–409.

Almond, Gabriel, and G. B. Powell, Jr. *Comparative Politics:*

A Developmental Approach. Boston and Toronto: Little, Brown and Co., 1966.

Ambedkar, B. R. *Thoughts on Linguistic States.* Delhi: B. R. Ambedkar, 1955.

Annadurai, C. N. "C.N.A. on Official Language" (text of the speech delivered by C. N. Annadurai in the Rajya Sabha April 3, 1965). Madras: Arivagam, 1965.

————. *To My Friends,* Madras: n.p., 1963.

Apter, David. "Nationalism, Government, and Economic Growth," *Economic Development and Cultural Change* 7 (January 1959), 117-136.

Barnett, Marguerite Ross. "Charisma and Politics in South India," in A. P. Janarthanam, ed., *C. N. Annadurai Commemoration Volume.* Madras: Janarthanam, 1969.

————. "Creating Political Identity: The Emergent South Indian Tamils," *Ethnicity* 1 (October 1974), 237-260.

————. "Competition, Control and Dependency: Urban Politics in Madras," in Donald Rosenthal, ed., *The City in Indian Politics.* Delhi: Thomson Press, 1976.

————. "Cultural Nationalist Electoral Politics in Tamil Nadu, South India," in Myron Weiner and John O. Field, eds., *Electoral Politics in the Indian States.* Delhi: Manohar, 1975.

————. "The Dravidian Movement and Political Development in Tamil Nadu," *Tamil Nadu Archives Diamond Jubilee Commemoration Volume.* Madras: Tamil Nadu Government, 1969.

————. "A Theoretical Perspective on Racial Public Policy," in Marguerite Ross Barnett and James A. Hefner, eds., *Blacks and Public Policy: Strategies and Perspectives.* Port Washington, N.Y.: Alfred Press, forthcoming.

Barnett, Marguerite Ross, and Steve Barnett, "Contemporary Peasant and Post-Peasant Alternatives in South India: The Ideas of a Militant Untouchable," *Annals of the New York Academy of Sciences* 220, (1974), Art. 6, 385-410.

Barnett, Stephen A. "The Process of Withdrawal in a South Indian Caste," in M. Singer and B. Cohn, eds., *Entrepreneurship and the Modernization of Occupational Culture in South Asia* (Durham, N.C.: Duke University Press, 1973).

————. *From Structure to Substance: The Past Fifty Years of a South Indian Caste* (forthcoming).

————. "The Structural Position of a South Indian Caste:

Kontaikkatti Vellalas of Tamil Nadu." Ph.D. dissertation, University of Chicago, 1970.

———. "Urban is as Urban Does: Two Incidents on One Street in Madras City South India," *Urban Anthropology* 2, (Fall 1973), 129-160.

Bay, Christian J.; Ingemund Gullvaeq; Harold Ofstad; and Herman Tonessen. *Nationalism: A Study of Identifications with People and Power;* I. *Problems and Theoretical Frameword.* Oslo: Institute for Social Research, June 1950.

Bayley, David. *Police and Political Development in India.* Princeton: Princeton University Press, 1969.

Beck, Brenda E. F. *Peasant Society in Koṅku; A Study of Right And Left Subcastes In South India.* Vancouver: University of British Columbia Press, 1972.

Beloff, Max. "Nationalism in the Western World," *Western World* 2 (January 1959), 15-18.

Beteille, André. *Class, Caste, and Power.* Berkeley and Los Angeles: University of California Press, 1965.

Bhagwati, Jagdish N. "India in the International Economy: a Policy Framework for a Progressive Society" (M.I.T. Lal Bahadur Memorial Lectures), 1973.

Binder, Leonard. "National Integration and Political Development," *American Political Science Review* 58 (September 1964), 622-631.

Binder, Leonard, et al. *Crises and Sequences in Political Development.* Princeton: Princeton University Press, 1972.

Brass, Paul. "Political Participation, Institutionalization and Stability in India," *Government and Opposition* 4 (Winter, 1969), 23-53.

———. "Uttar Pradesh," in Myron Weiner, ed., *State Politics in India.* Princeton: Princeton University Press, 1968.

Braunthal, Julius. *The Paradox of Nationalism.* London: St. Botolph, 1946.

Carr, Edward Hallett. *Nationalism and After.* New York: Macmillan, 1945.

Catton, William R., Jr., and Sung Chick Hong, "The Relation of Apparent Minority Ethnocentrism to Majority Antipathy," *American Sociological Review* 27 (April 1962), 178-191.

Conze, Werner. "Nationalism and Communism as Driving Political Forces in Historical Perspective," *Modern World* (1964-

1965), pp. 7-21.

da Costa, Eric P. W. *The Indian General Elections, 1967.* New Delhi: Indian Institute of Public Opinion, 1967.

Das Gupta, T. *Language Conflict and National Development.* Berkeley and Los Angeles: University of California Press, 1970.

deReuck, Anthony, and Julie Knight, eds. *Symposium on Caste and Race: Comparative Approaches.* Boston: Little, Brown and Co., 1967.

Deutsch, Karl. *Nationalism and Its Alternatives.* New York: Knopf, 1969.

————. *Nationalism and Social Communication.* Cambridge, Mass.: M.I.T. Press, 1953.

———— ed., *Nation-Building.* New York: Atherton Press, 1965.

————. "The Growth of Nations: Some Recurrent Patterns of Political and Social Integration," *World Politics* 5 (January 1953), 168-195.

————. "Social Mobilization and Political Development," *American Political Science Review* 55 (September 1961), 493-514.

Dumont, Louis. *Homo Hierarchicus: an Essay on the Caste System.* Chicago: University of Chicago Press, 1970.

————. *Religion, Politics and History in India.* Paris: Mouton, 1970.

————. "On the Comparative Understanding of Modern Civilizations," *Daedalus* (Spring 1975), pp. 152-172.

————. *Une Sous-Caste de l'Inde du sud: organisation sociale et religieuse des Pramalai Kallar.* Paris: Gallimard, 1957.

Duncan, Otis Dudley, and Stanley Lieberson. "Ethnic Segregation and Assimilation," *American Journal of Sociology* 64 (January 1959), 364-374.

Elliott, Carolyn Margaret. "Participation in an Expanding Polity: a Study of Andhra Pradesh." Ph.D. dissertation, Harvard University, 1968.

Emerson, Rupert. *From Empire to Nation* (Cambridge, Mass.: Harvard University Press, 1960).

————. "Nationalism and Political Development," *Journal of Politics* 2 (February 1960), 3-28.

Erdmann, Howard L. *The Swatantra Party and Indian Conservatism.* London: Cambridge University Press, 1967.

Erikson, Erik H. *Gandhi's Truth: on the Origins of Militant Non-Violence.* New York: Norton, 1969.

————. "Identity," *International Encyclopedia of the Social Sciences*, Vol. VII (New York: Free Press, 1968), 61-65.

Forrester, Duncan B. "The Madras Anti-Hindi Agitation, 1965: Political Protest and Its Effects on Language Policy in India," *Pacific Affairs* 39 (1966), 19-36.

Galanter, Marc. "Changing Legal Conceptions of Caste," in M. Singer and B. Cohn, eds. *Structure and Change in Indian Society*. Chicago: Aldine, 1968.

Geertz, Clifford. "Ideology as a Cultural System," in David Apter, ed., *Ideology and Discontent*. New York: Free Press, 1964, pp. 47-76.

————. "The Integrative Revolution: Primordial Sentiments and Civil Politics in the New States," in Clifford Geertz, ed., *Old Societies and New States: the Quest for Modernity in Asia and Africa*. New York: Free Press, 1963.

Ghazi, H. K. *Report on the Fourth General Elections in Madras, 1967*. Madras: Government of Madras, 1968. Vols. I, II, III.

Gough, Kathleen E. "The Social Structure of a Tanjore Village," in McKim Marriott, ed., *Village India: Studies in the Little Community*. Chicago: University of Chicago Press, 1955.

Gurr, T. R. *Why Men Rebel*. Princeton: Princeton University Press, 1970.

Hardgrave, Robert, Jr. *The Dravidian Movement*. Bombay: Popular Prakashan, 1965.

————. *The Nadars of Tamil Nad: Political Culture of a Community in Change*. Berkeley and Los Angeles: University of California Press, 1969.

————. "The DMK and the Politics of Tamil Nationalism," *Pacific Affairs* 37 (Winter 1964-1965). 396-411.

————. "Politics and the Film in Tamil Nadu: the Stars and the D.M.K.," *Asian Survey* 13 (March 1973), 288-305.

————. "The Riots in Tamil Nad: Problems and Prospects of India's Language Crisis," *Asian Survey* 5 (August 1965), 399-407.

Harrison, Selig. *India: the Most Dangerous Decades*. Princeton: Princeton University Press, 1960.

Herman, Simon N., and Erling Schild. "Ethnic Role Conflict in a Cross-Cultural Situation," *Human Relations* 13 (August 1960), 215-228.

Hertz, Frederick O. *Nationality in History and Politics: a Study of the Sociology and Psychology of National Sentiment and*

Character. London: K. Paul, Trench, Truber, 1944.
———. "Nature of Nationalism," *Social Forces* 19 (March 1941), 409–415.
Hirabayashi v. United States. 320 US 81 (1943).
Hopkins, Vincent C. "Nationalism Re-examined," *Thought* 30 (Autumn 1955), 389–401.
Irschick, Eugene. *Politics and Social Conflict in South India: The Non-Brahman Movement and Tamil Separatism, 1916–1929*. Berkeley and Los Angeles: University of California Press, 1969.
Justice Mirror of the Year 1927. Madras: n.p., 1928.
Justice Party Golden Jubilee Celebration Volume. Madras: n.p., 1968.
Keesings Contemporary Archives (April 17–24, 1965).
Kochanek, Stanley. *The Congress Party of India: the Dynamics of One-Party Democracy*. Princeton: Princeton University Press, 1968.
Kohn, Hans. *The Age of Nationalism*. New York: Harper and Row, 1962.
———. *American Nationalism, an Interpretive Essay*. New York: Macmillan, 1957.
———. *The Idea of Nationalism: a Study in its Origins and Background*. New York: Macmillan, 1944.
———. "Nationalism," *Current History* 30 (April 1956), 213–216.
———. *Nationalism: Its Meaning and History*. Princeton: D. Van Nostrand, 1955.
———. "The Nature of Nationalism," *American Political Science Review* 33 (December 1939), 1001–1021.
Kothari, Rajni. *Politics in India* (Boston: Little, Brown and Co., 1970).
Lane, Robert E. *Political Ideology: Why the American Common Man Believes What He Does*. New York: Free Press, 1962.
MacPherson, C. B. *The Real World of Democracy*. Oxford: Clarendon Press, 1965.
Madras Information, 1967. Madras: Tamil Nadu Government, 1968.
Madras Legislative Assembly. *Who's Who*, 1962, 1967, 1971. Madras: Tamil Nadu Government, 1962, 1967, 1971.
Mandelbaum, David C. *Society in India*. Berkeley and Los Angeles: University of California Press, 1970.
Marriott, McKim, ed. *Village India: Studies in the Little Commu-*

nity. Chicago: University of Chicago Press, 1955.

Melson, Robert, and Howard Wolpe. "Modernization and the Politics of Communalism: a Theoretical Perspective," *American Political Science Review,* 64 (December 1970), 1112-1130.

Merton, Robert K. *Social Theory and Social Structure.* New York: Free Press, 1963.

Mohan Ram. *Hindi against India.* Madras: n.p., 1968.

Morris-Jones, W. H. *The Government and Politics of India.* London: Hutchinson University Library, 1964.

Morgenthau, Hans J. "The Parodoxes of Nationalism," *Yale Review* 46 (June 1957), 481.

Narasimhan, V. K. *Kamaraj, a Study.* Bombay: Manaktalas, 1967.

Owen, Hugh F. "Mrs. Annie Besant and the Rise of Political Activity in South India, 1914-1919, "Paper presented to the Second International Conference Seminar of Tamil Studies, Madras, 1968.

Paranjoti, V. *Saiva Siddhanta.* London: Luzac, 1954.

Parsons, Talcott, and Edward Shils, eds. *Toward a General Theory of Action.* Cambridge: Harvard University Press, 1951.

Pears, Gordon. "A Question of National Identity," *Crossbow* (January-March 1963), pp. 37-39.

Ramanujam, K. S. *The Big Change.* Madras: Higginbothams, 1967.

Ramasami, E. V. *The Ramayana; a True Reading.* Madras: Rationalist Publications, 1959.

Report of the Centre-State Relations Inquiry Committee. Madras: Government of Tamil Nadu, 1971.

Report of the National Council of Applied Economic Research. Techno-Economic Survey of Madras. Madras: Tamil Nadu Government, 1961.

Revolt 1, 16 (February 20, 1929).

Rosenblatt, Paul C. "Origins and Effects of Group Ethnocentrism and Nationalism," *Journal of Conflict Resolution* 8 (June 1964), 131-146.

Rudolph, Lloyd I. "Continuities and Change in Electoral Behavior: the 1971 Parliamentary Elections in India," *Asian Survey* 11 (December 1971). 1119-1132.

————. "Urban Life and Populist Radicalism: Dravidian Politics in Madras, *Journal of Asian Studies* 20 (May 1961), 283-297.

Rudolph, Lloyd I., and Susanne Hoeber Rudolph. *The Modernity of Tradition.* Chicago: University of Chicago Press, 1967.

————. "Survey in India: Field Experience in Madras State," *Public Opinion Quarterly* 22 (1958), 235-244.

Rudolph, Susanne Hoeber. "From Madras, View of the Southern Film," *Yale Review* 60 (Spring 1971), 468-480.

Saveth, Edward Norman. "Race and Nationalism in American Historiography: the Late Nineteenth Century," *Political Science Quarterly* 54 (September 1939), 421-441.

Seal, Anil. *The Emergence of Indian Nationalism: Competition and Collaboration in the Later Nineteenth Century.* Cambridge: Cambridge University Press, 1968.

Shafer, Boyd C. *Nationalism: Myth and Reality.* New York: Harcourt, Brace, 1955.

Singer, Milton. "Beyond Tradition and Modernity in Madras," *Comparative Studies on Society and History* 13 (April 1971), 160-195.

Singer, Milton, and Bernard Cohn, eds. *Entrepreneurship and the Modernization of Occupational Culture in South Asia.* Durham, N.C.: Duke University Press, 1973.

————, eds. *Structure and Change in Indian Society.* Chicago: Aldine, 1968.

Sklar, Richard. "Political Science and National Integration," *Journal of Modern African Studies* 5 (1967), 1-11.

Smelser, Neil. *A Theory of Collective Behavior.* New York: Free Press, 1962.

Snyder, Louis, ed. *The Dynamics of Nationalism: Readings in Its Meaning and Development.* Princeton: D. Van Nostrand, 1964.

————. *The Meaning of Nationalism.* New Brunswick, N.J.: Rutgers University Press, 1964.

————. *The New Nationalism.* New Brunswick, N.J.: Rutgers University Press, 1968.

————. *Race: a History of Modern Ethnic Theories.* New York: Longmans Green, 1919.

Somjee, A. H. "Caste and the Decline of Political Homogeneity," *American Political Science Review* 67 (Summer 1973), 799-816.

Spratt, Phillip. *Dravida Munnetra Kazhagam in Power.* Mystic, Conn.: Lawrence Verry, 1970.

Srila-Sri Arulnandi Sivacharya Swamigal Sivagnana Siddhiya Endowment Collected Lecturers on Saiva Siddhanta 1946-1954. Annamalai Nagar: Annamalai University, 1965.

Stein, Burton. "Brahman and Peasant in Early South Indian History," *Dr. V. Raghavan Felicitation Volume of the Adyar Library Bulletin* 31-32 (1967-1968), 244.

Stouffer, Samuel. *The American Soldier.* Princeton: Princeton University Press, 1949.

Subramaniam, T. V. "The Tamil Brahmins: Some Guidelines to Research on Their Emergence and Eclipse," *Economic and Political Weekly* 4 (July 1969), 1133-1136.

Sulzbach, Walter. *National Consciousness.* Washington, D.C.: American Council on Public Affairs, 1943.

Suntharalingam, R. *Politics and Nationalist Awakening in South India 1852-91.* Tucson: University of Arizona Press, 1974.

Tamil Arasu, 1971. Madras: Tamil Nadu Government, 1971.

Thillaivillalan, R. *Gone with the Wind.* Madras: n.p., 1968.

Toch, Hans H.: Albert J. Rabin; and David M. Wilkens. "Factors Entering into Ethnic Identifications; an Experimental Study," *Sociometry* 2 (September 1962) 297-312.

Uyeki, Eugene S. "Correlatives of Ethnic Identifications," *American Journal of Sociology* 65 (March 1960), 468-474.

Vagiswari, A. *Income-Earning Trends and Social Status of the Harijan Community in Tamil Nadu.* Madras: Sangam Publishers, 1972.

Ward, Barbara. *Nationalism and Ideology.* New York: Norton, 1966.

Ware, Caroline F. "Ethnic Communities,"*Encyclopedia of the Social Sciences.* New York: Macmillan, 1937, pp. 607-613.

Weiner, Myron, ed. *State Politics in India.* Princeton: Princeton University Press, 1968.

Weiner, Myron, and John O. Field, eds. *Electoral Politics in the Indian States.* Delhi: Manohar, 1975.

Wiggin, Gladys Anna. *Education and Nationalism: an Historical Interpretation of American Education.* New York: McGraw-Hill, 1962.

Willis, Richard H. "Ethnics and National Images: People versus Nations," *Public Opinion Quarterly* 32 (Summer 1968), 186-201.

Wirth, Louis. "Types of Nationalism," *American Journal of Sociology,* 41 (May 1936), 723-737.

Zald, Mayer N., and Roberta Ash. "Social Movement Organizations: Growth, Decay and Change," *Social Forces* 44 (1966), 327-341.

Znaniecki, Florian. *Modern Nationalities: a Sociological Study*

Urbana: University of Illinois Press, 1952.
Zolberg, Aristide. "Patterns of National Integration," *Journal of Modern African Studies* 5 (December 1967), 449-467.

Index

364   INDEX

Mudaliar, C. Natesa, 53, 55n
Munusami, V., 111, 112, 288, 311n
Murosoli newspaper, 82, 93, 97, 107,
  116n
Muslim nationalism, 161
Muslim League, 124, 125, 136, 147,
  228, 293, 294
Muslims, 21, 34, 40, 41, 46, 49, 50,
  124, 125, 199, 200, 201, 221, 272,
  329
Muthu, M. (Karunanidhi's son), 295
Muthu, Madurai, 110, 203, 250
Muthu, Dr. Satyiavani, 115n, 203,
  263, 264, 268, 271, 280n, 284, 299,
  300, 302
Muukoolathur castes (also see
  Maravar, Thevar, Agamudiar,
  Kallar castes), 56, 61, 62, 63, 64,
  84n, 85n, 91, 171, 199, 200, 201,
  217
Mylapore constituency, Madras City,
  145
Mysore, 109, 113, 253

Nadar caste, 49, 56, 61, 63, 64, 136,
  165, 199-201
Nadar, K. Kamaraj, 77, 78, 80, 81,
  91-93, 97, 98, 102, 112, 114, 123,
  125, 126, 132, 135-137, 149, 156n,
  157n, 165, 196, 213, 217, 218, 223,
  230, 241, 242, 251, 264, 283, 284,
  292-294, 312n
Nadar Mahajana Sangam, 85n
Naicker caste (Vanniya Kula
  Kshatriya), 49, 56, 61, 62, 167, 168,
  172, 181, 183
Naidu caste, 34, 49, 59, 62, 198-201
Naidu, G. D., 289
Nair caste, 17, 49, 64, 198-201
Nair (also Nayar), Dr. T. M., 39, 60
Nam Nadu newspaper, 82, 240, 305
Nanda, G. L., 131
Narasimhan, V. K., 86n, 156n
Narayan, Vellore, 288
Natarajan, N. V., 107, 111
Nathan, T. V., 229
nation, 47, 161, 315; nation-state, 4,
  7, 8, 326
national integration, 4, 126-128, 217,
  230, 250, 304, 310, 315, 324-326
nationalism, 3, 4, 6, 7, 8, 135, 161,
  312, 314, 315, 325-327; class and,
  3, 84, 97, 115, 262, 275, 323, 327;
  territorial nationalism, 4, 10, 45,

322, 325, 326; territorial nationalism
  defined, 8, 9; cultural nationalism,
  3, 10, 45, 57, 84, 89, 114, 132, 134,
  135, 155, 208, 240, 244, 256, 258,
  262, 274, 275, 292, 293, 310, 314,
  318, 322, 323, 325-327; cultural
  nationalism defined, 8, 9, 10, 163,
  164; Tamil cultural nationalism, 3,
  8, 10, 120, 125, 133, 134, 138,
  145-147, 152, 154, 165, 168, 176,
  178, 179, 184, 208, 213, 220, 226,
  234-236, 239-241, 245-249, 256,
  275, 282, 291, 298, 300, 302-304,
  309, 310, 315, 319, 321-324, 326,
  327; the politics of emergent
  nationalism, 89-158, elites, masses,
  and cultural nationalism, 161-236;
  contradictions of cultural
  nationalism, 239-313
Navamani newspaper, 177, 281n
Navasakthi newspaper, 173, 271, 273,
  277n, 278n, 281n
Naxalites, 260
Nedunchezhian, V. R., 106, 107, 110,
  111, 122, 130, 136, 156n, 186n, 187,
  203, 214, 242, 253, 264, 268, 271,
  281n, 282-284, 286, 287, 289, 294,
  296, 311n
Nehru, Jawaharlal, 4, 10n, 71, 80, 99,
  121, 131, 132, 134, 175, 184, 217,
  241, 284
Nehru, Motilal, 305
Nelson, J. H., 18, 30n, 18, 30n
New India newspaper, 45
Nilgiris district, 95
non-Brahmin: backward
  non-Brahmins, 17, 21, 28, 35, 49,
  50, 56-58, 60, 64, 65, 78, 90, 114,
  115, 167, 199-201, 321, 326;
  forward non-Brahmins, 16, 17, 21,
  23, 24, 26, 28, 29, 33-35, 42, 48-50,
  56, 57, 59, 60, 62, 64, 78, 83, 84,
  98, 99, 115, 124, 125, 145, 198-201,
  258, 262, 265, 316-318, 320, 321,
  326; dichotomization of
  non-Brahmin category into
  "forward" and "backward"
  categories, 57; movement, 19, 29,
  32, 181, 265, 267, 317;
  non-Brahmins, 15-19, 21-23, 25,
  26, 28, 29, 32-34, 37-49, 52, 54n,
  56, 57, 64, 66, 67, 78, 80, 82, 97-99,
  102, 115, 124, 125, 164, 167, 171,
  172, 175, 181, 185, 198, 199, 201,

Library of Congress Cataloging in Publication Data

Barnett, Marguerite Ross.
　The politics of cultural nationalism in south India.

　Bibliography: p.
　Includes index.
　1.　Tamil Nadu—Politics and government.　2.　Nation-
alism—Tamil Nadu.　3.　Dravida Munnetra Kazhagam.
I. Title.
DS485.M28B37　　　　320.9'54'82　　　　76-2457
ISBN 0-691-07577-8

CPSIA information can be obtained at www.ICGtesting.com
Printed in the USA
BVOW06*1757250416

445335BV00011B/554/P